Ethical Dilemmas in Educational Research

ALSO AVAILABLE FROM BLOOMSBURY

Educational Research, *Gert Biesta*

Building Research Design in Education, *edited by Lorna Hamilton and John Ravenscroft*

Philosophy of Educational Research, *Richard Pring*

Narrative Inquiry, *Vera Caine, D. Jean Clandinin and Sean Lessard*

Research Methods for Early Childhood Education, *Rosie Flewitt and Lynn Ang*

Research Methods for Educational Dialogue, *Ruth Kershner, Sara Hennessy, Rupert Wegerif and Ayesha Ahmed*

Research Methods for Classroom Discourse, *Jenni Ingram and Victoria Elliott*

Research Methods for Social Justice and Equity in Education, *Liz Atkins and Vicky Duckworth*

Higher Education Research, *Malcolm Tight*

Educational Research, *Jerry Wellington*

Ethical Dilemmas in Educational Research

BERA Case Studies for Researchers by Researchers

Edited by
Alison Fox, with Sally Baker,
Nicole Brown, Matthew Courtney,
Aimee Quickfall, Natalie Tegama
and Sin-Wang Chong

BLOOMSBURY ACADEMIC
LONDON · NEW YORK · OXFORD · NEW DELHI · SYDNEY

BLOOMSBURY ACADEMIC

Bloomsbury Publishing Plc, 50 Bedford Square, London, WC1B 3DP, UK
Bloomsbury Publishing Inc, 1359 Broadway, New York, NY 10018, USA
Bloomsbury Publishing Ireland, 29 Earlsfort Terrace, Dublin 2, D02 AY28, Ireland

BLOOMSBURY, BLOOMSBURY ACADEMIC and the Diana logo are
trademarks of Bloomsbury Publishing Plc

First published in Great Britain 2026

Copyright © Alison Fox, with Sally Baker, Nicole Brown, Matthew Courtney, Aimee
Quickfall, Natalie Tegama and Sin-Wang Chong, 2026

Alison Fox, with Sally Baker, Nicole Brown, Matthew Courtney, Aimee Quickfall, Natalie
Tegama and Sin-Wang Chong have asserted their right under the Copyright, Designs and
Patents Act, 1988, to be identified as Editors of this work.

Cover design by Aneeka Makwana
Cover illustration © andipantz via iStock

All rights reserved. No part of this publication may be: i) reproduced or transmitted in
any form, electronic or mechanical, including photocopying, recording or by means of
any information storage or retrieval system without prior permission in writing from
the publishers; or ii) used or reproduced in any way for the training, development or
operation of artificial intelligence (AI) technologies, including generative AI technologies.
The rights holders expressly reserve this publication from the text and data mining
exception as per Article 4(3) of the Digital Single Market Directive (EU) 2019/790.

Bloomsbury Publishing Plc does not have any control over, or responsibility for, any
third-party websites referred to or in this book. All internet addresses given in this
book were correct at the time of going to press. The author and publisher regret
any inconvenience caused if addresses have changed or sites have ceased
to exist, but can accept no responsibility for any such changes.

A catalogue record for this book is available from the British Library.

A catalog record for this book is available from the Library of Congress.

ISBN: HB: 978-1-3504-5081-3
PB: 978-1-3504-5082-0
ePDF: 978-1-3504-5084-4
eBook: 978-1-3504-5085-1

Typeset by Integra Software Services Pvt. Ltd.
Printed and bound in Great Britain

For product safety related questions contact productsafety@bloomsbury.com.

To find out more about our authors and books visit www.bloomsbury.com
and sign up for our newsletters.

Contents

List of Figures xi
List of Tables xii
List of Contributors xiii

Section 1: Scene Setting

a. Section 1 and Book Foreword 1

1 Virtue Ethics and Being a Researcher: Introduction to Ethical Decision-Making
(Alison Fox, The Open University) 5

2 Ethical Guidelines in Educational Research: The State of Play
(Sin-Wang Chong, University of St Andrews and Qi Liu, University of Leicester) 23

Section 2: Case Studies

2-1 Subsection – Responsibilities to Participants (Subsection lead: Aimee Quickfall)

b. Subsection Foreword 41

3 Applying BERA Principles to International and Intercultural Research *(Una Connor-Bones and Felicity Hasson, University of Ulster)* 45

4 **Decolonising Research Ethics, Exemplifying Definition and Principles** (Carol Azumah Dennis, The Open University) 71

5 **International Research and the Ethics of Language** (Phil Wood, Nottingham Trent University, Aimee Quickfall, Leeds Trinity University and Kaisa Pihlainen, University of Eastern Finland) 95

6 **Placing Children's Rights at the Centre of Ethical Researcher Decision-Making** (Carmel Capewell, Oxford Brookes University; Helen Hanna, University of Manchester and Chawin Pongpajon, University College London and Chulalongkorn University, Thailand) 113

7 **Dilemmas of Care in Online Interviewing** (Aimee Quickfall, Leeds Trinity University and Phil Wood, Nottingham Trent University) 143

2-2 Subsection – Responsibilities to Sponsors, Clients, stakeholders and the Environment (Subsection lead: Matthew Courtney)

c. Subsection Foreword 165

8 **Working with Large-Scale Quantitative Data: Two Ethical Dilemmas around Anonymity** (Sonia Ilie and Michelle R Ellefson, University of Cambridge) 167

9 **Thinking It through or Thinking through 'It'? The Ethics of Research Involving Artificial Intelligence and Education** *(Robert Farrow, The Open University and Wayne Holmes, UCL Knowledge Lab)* 191

10 **Ethical Dilemmas in Observational Research** *(Daniel Muijs, Queens University Belfast and Matthew Courtney, Wandle English Hub, Wandle Learning Partnership, South West London)* 221

11 **Environmental Sustainability in Education Research Ethics** *(Lynda Dunlop, University College London, and Lizzie Rushton, University of Stirling)* 243

2-3 Subsection – Responsibilities to the Community of Educational Researchers and for Researchers' Wellbeing and Development (Subsection lead: Sally Baker)

d. Subsection Foreword 269

12 **Tackling Undercare: Towards Wellbeing and Care in Academia through Collaborative Writing** *(Emily Dowdeswell, Cambridge Curiosity and Imagination, Carolyn Cooke, The Open University, Petra Vackova, Aarhus University, Donata Puntil, King's College, London and Lucy Caton, University of Bolton)* 271

13 **Power Inequalities and Quality of Supervised Evidence Syntheses: Ethical Use of Reflexive Practices** (Sin-Wang Chong, University of St Andrews, Qi Liu, University of Leicester, Natalie Tegama, Oxford University and Grace Anna Baby, University Hospitals Leicester) 297

14 **The Ethics of Doctoral Researcher Care: Learning to Research in Fragile Contexts** (Anna Xavier, Deakin University; Carly Hawkins, University of New South Wales and Sally Baker, Australian National University) 323

2-4 Subsection – Responsibilities for Publication and Dissemination (Subsection leads: Alison Fox and Nicole Brown)

e. Subsection Foreword 347

15 **Publish, Perish, or Build Community? Towards Alternative Ethical Publication and Dissemination Practices** (Amber Fensham-Smith, The Open University; Alison Twiner, University of Cambridge and Fadoua Govaerts, University of Bath) 349

16 **Openness, Inclusivity and Diversity: Supporting Early Career Researchers as Ethical Practice of Journal Peer Review** (Sin-Wang Chong, University of St Andrews and Natalie Tegama, Oxford University) 375

Section 3: Situating Ethical Guidance
(Section lead: Nicole Brown)

f. Section Foreword 395

17 **'I'm Going to Be in a Book': Negotiating Research with Adolescents in Accordance with Ethical Guidelines** *(Sara Young, University College London)* 397

18 **The Chartered College of Teaching Research Ethics Panel: Exploring Practical Relevance, Workload Implications and Representativeness of Research** *(Lisa-Maria Müller and Victoria Cook, Chartered College of Teaching)* 409

19 **Research Ethics: Issues and Solutions in Education Research in Ukrainian Universities** *(Oksana Zabolotna, Pavlo Tychyna Uman State Pedagogical University as members of the Ukrainian Educational Research Association; Iryna Kushnir, Nottingham Trent University)* 423

20 **Ethical Research in Multilingual Education Contexts: Working with Non-Professional Interpreters** *(Barbara Skinner, Ulster University; Ronan Kelly, Queensland University of Technology, Australia and Maria Stewart, Education Authority, Northern Ireland)* 437

Section 4: Takeaways 449

21 Conclusions for the Ecological Web of Educational Research *(Alison Fox, The Open University and Nicole Brown, University College London)* 451

Index 467

Figures

1.1   A representation of avoiding non-virtuous forks in the path – of excess or of deficit 16
7.1   Email from Jo (researcher) to Ali (research participant) 151
11.1 Representation of relationships of responsibilities of and to educational researchers, underpinned by responsibilities of all for society and the environment 245
11.2 An important consideration in educational research is who speaks for nature? 246
13.1 Excluded articles with reasons 304
13.2 Questions for the next supervision meeting 305
13.3 Initial researcher logbook 306
13.4 The revised researcher logbook 307

Tables

1.1	A summary of Kitchener and Kitchener's levels of ethical thinking 6
1.2	An overview of virtues held by different cultural traditions 9
1.3	The Virtues and Vices of Research according to Macfarlane 17
1.4	Virtues and Vices interpolated from the TRUST code 17
2.1	A summary of the 20 ethical guidelines reviewed 24
3.1	Original overview of stakeholders and methods 48
3.2	Overview of stakeholders and methods 57
15.1	Camtree Quality Criteria 355
19.1	Contradictions between local practices and BERA Guidelines – issue 1 425
19.2	Contradictions between local practices and BERA Guidelines – issue 2 428
19.3	Contradictions between local practices and BERA guidelines – issue 3 430
21.1	A Think-Listen-Act framework for supporting ethical reflexivity 462

Contributors

Alison Fox is Professor of Collaborative Ethical Research and Practice and chairs the Human Research Ethics Committee and Education Research Excellence Framework submission for The Open University, UK. She has been involved in the latest two editions of the BERA *Ethical Guidelines for Educational Research* and acts as a research ethics consultant. Alison supports researcher capacity building in early career researchers, in particular supporting practitioner research. Her research supports practitioner development and also champions environmental sustainable research at The University. She currently leads the intergenerational, international, multilingual and multimedia Connecting Communities and Heritages against Climate Change (CCHCC) project using artivism.

Sin-Wang Chong is a Director at the University of St Andrews, UK and a visiting full Professor at King's College London, UK. His research interests are in evidence synthesis methodologies, research-practice integration, and language education. Sin Wang has over 70 publications and has been involved in research projects worth over £3 million on these topics. He is also the lead of a research contract with the Department for Education in England that is worth £2 million, conducting high-impact evidence syntheses on teacher education. Sin-Wang is named a Top 2% Scientist in Education in 2023 and 2024, according to the "Elsevier-Stanford List".

Qi Liu was a fully-funded PhD student at the University of Leicester, at the time of writing this book. Her research interests focus on language assessment and feedback literacy. She is a Committee Member of the Research Synthesis in Applied Linguistics Special Interest Group of the British Association for Applied Linguistics (BAAL). She is a Research Assistant at the National Institute of Teaching in England and an Honorary Research Assistant at the University of St Andrews in Scotland.

Dr. Felicity Hassan is a Senior Lecturer in the Institute of Nursing Research at Ulster University, Northern Ireland, with twenty-five years' experience in research. A social researcher by background, she has extensive experience and knowledge of palliative and end of life care research. For more information visit https://www.ulster.ac.uk/staff/f-hasson.

Una O'Connor Bones is Professor of Educational Inclusion and Research Director in the School of Education at Ulster University. Her teaching and research experience is informed by the social, cultural, economic and political influences on where and how education takes place, and the impact of these on access to learning. Her work includes extensive stakeholder engagement on issues relating to school sustainability, curriculum development and reform, special educational needs and inclusion, and the role of classroom assistants. Research activity includes empirical and secondary research; this includes development and implementation of the Community Conversation methodology as part of sustainable school provision in NI; large scale survey of the Classroom Assistant workforce; and longitudinal analysis of pupils with SEN using education and social data. She is a Senior Fellow of the Higher Education Academy and recipient of the British Educational Research Association (BERA) Team Award for Public Engagement. Her most recent research can be found in Educational Review, the European Journal of Special Educational Needs and the Curriculum Journal.

Carol Azumah Dennis Carol Azumah Dennis is Professor of Education, Policy and Practice in the Faculty of Wellbeing, Education and Language Studies at The Open University, UK. Her research interests include decolonisation, ethics, equity and post-16 education. She is a lead editor of the BERA Curriculum Journal and co-author of EDI in Research, an Open Learn collection. Her 2024 paper Dennis et al (2024) Professional doctorates reconciling academic and professional knowledge: towards a diffractive re-reading, was awarded paper of the year by the journal Higher Education Research & Development.

Phil Wood is Professor of Education in the Nottingham Institute of Education, School of Social Sciences at Nottingham Trent University, UK. He is a Senior Fellow of Advance HE. His research focuses on the nature of change, particularly organisational change in educational settings, using process philosophy and complexity theory as ways to explore this area of research.

Dr. Aimee Quickfall is Head of the School of Education at Leeds Trinity University, UK, a member of the British Educational Research Association

(BERA) council, one of the BERA SIG leads for Mental Health and Wellbeing, and a member of the BERA Conference and Events Committee. She was involved in the design of the BERA 2024 ethical guidelines and is part of the research ethics committee at Leeds Trinity. Her research interests are well-being and workload in education, ITE policy and experiences of academics, mentors and teacher trainees, feminist methodologies and approaches; and research ethics. Aimee is interested in collaborative projects and supporting research across education.

Dr. Kaisa Pihlainen works as an Assistant Professor (tenure track) at the Faculty of Philosophy at the University of Eastern Finland. In her PhD thesis she investigated the activities and participation of children with special needs and their parents in free-time technology clubs. Currently her research interests include inclusion, participation and learning environments of children in early childhood education, qualitative research methods as well as lifelong learning. https://orcid.org/0000-0001-9437-4481

Dr. Carmel Capewell was a Lecturer in Early Years and Child Development at Oxford Brookes University, UK, at the time of writing this book. She has a strong interest in developing innovative research methods, particularly to encouraging the participation of young people in expressing and sharing their perspective on their experiences. While completing her PhD into the Lived Experience of Glue Ear: Voices of mothers and young people, she became interested in using visual methods and adapted the Photovoice methodology for data capture. Carmel has a range of experience in using both qualitative and quantitative research methods with a focus on identifying the best tool to answer the research question. She has worked collaboratively with colleagues from a range of countries and is keen to further explore such opportunities. Her main research interest is in supporting students with auditory processing issues so that they can better access the spoken word in classroom environments – this is from early years through to higher education. In addition, she is interested in developing involved learners and is active in reviewing and improving her practice. She is a Senior Fellow of the HEA and a Chartered Psychologist, with teaching experience at secondary and tertiary level.

Dr. Helen Hanna is a Lecturer in International and Comparative Education at the University of Manchester, UK. She is a Co-convenor of the BERA Special Interest Group for Comparative and International Education. She is passionate about citizenship education, education rights, and educational inclusion, particularly of migrant learners and those from racial, ethnic and cultural minorities, as well as using creative visual methods. Helen has completed funded research in England, South Africa, Northern Northern Ireland, Israel, Canada, Kenya, Hong Kong and Thailand. She is Editor of Human Rights Education Review.

Chawin Pongpajon is a Lecturer, training Thai language arts pre-services teachers at the Faculty of Education, Chulalongkorn University, Thailand. He is also a guest researcher at the Multicultural and Social Innovation centre, passionately working on peacebuilding education and educational for social justices. His interests are interwoven by three focused areas: curriculum, pedagogy and assessment for literacy and Thai language arts; education, conflict and peace; and critical education with decolonial thinking. Chawin has completed work and research with educational institutions at all levels across Thailand and internationally collaborated with professionals from many countries to promote partnerships for teaching and research in Thailand. Chawin is now doing his PhD at IOE, UCL's Faculty of Education and Society, University College London. His thesis explores education for peace in the conflict-affected southern Thailand, where education has been politicised both by the Thai state and by the Malay-Muslim insurgents to promote their own political ideologies inextricably intertwined by nationalities, ethnicities, religions, historical narratives and languages.

Sonia Ilie is Professor of Education at the Faculty of Education, University of Cambridge, UK. Her research explores inequalities in access and outcomes from education and builds evidence around effective ways to address these inequalities. She has published on barriers to access to higher education and the impact of higher education widening participation, fair access, and student support programmes.

Michelle R Ellefson is Professor of Cognitive Science at the University of Cambridge Faculty of Education, Cambridge, UK. Initially trained in developmental cognitive neuroscience, her interests in improving cognitive outcomes for all children have inspired her to reach beyond this foundational training to develop her integrative, multi-disciplinary approach that informs both school practice and theoretical accounts of cognitive development. Her current research projects focus on the role of executive functions in school achievement and how children's reasoning about causes and effects impacts how they think about scientific phenomena.

Dr. Robert Farrow is Senior Research Fellow in the Institute of Educational Technology at The Open University, UK, where he leads the research programme Learning in an Open World. He is the Co-Director of the Global OER Graduate Network, Co-Lead for the International Council for Distance Education's Open Education Network and the Co-Editor of the Journal of Interactive Media in Education. His research focuses on technology enhanced learning and the design, implementation and evaluation of socio-technical learning systems.

Wayne Holmes is Professor of Critical Studies of Artificial Intelligence and Education, University College London, UK. His research explores the ethical, human rights, and social justice implications of teaching and learning with and about Artificial Intelligence (AI&ED). Wayne holds a UNESCO Chair in the Ethics of AI&ED (International Research Centre of Artificial Intelligence, Slovenia), is co-leading the Council of Europe's AI&ED expert group, and is an AI&ED consultant for UNESCO and the UN. His recent publications include 'The Handbook of Critical Studies of Artificial Intelligence and Education' (2025). He has given keynotes on AI&ED in more than 20 countries.

Daniel Muijs is Head of the School of Social Sciences, Education and Social Work and Professor of Education at Queen's University Belfast, Northern Ireland. He has held key advisory posts in a range of academic and professional organisations. He previously held professorial and leadership positions at Academica University of Applied Sciences and the universities of Southampton, Manchester and Newcastle, and was Head of Research and Evaluation at Ofsted.

Matthew Courtney is the Director of Wandle Learning Partnership. He has previously worked as a primary teacher, school leader and English Hub Lead, specialising in early reading and reading for pleasure. He holds an MSc in Education Research Design and Methodology from the University of Oxford. Matthew has been awarded a Churchill Fellowship to research the use of EdTech and AI to teach reading and support reading for pleasure in Germany, Belgium and Denmark.

Dr. Lynda Dunlop is Senior Lecturer in Science Education and Director of Education for Environmental Sustainability at York, University of York, UK. Her research interests are in climate change and environmental education, environmental activism, environmental games and youth participation in environmental decision making. She enjoys collaborating with artists, teachers, game designers and writers on environmental communication.

Lizzie Rushton is Professor of Education and Head of the Education Division, University of Stirling, Scotland, UK and Deputy Chair of the Scottish Council of Deans of Education. A former geography teacher and geography teacher educator, her research interests are in climate change and sustainability education, with a focus on curriculum making, teacher agency and youth participation in environmental decision making.

Dr. Emily Dowdeswell is Director of the Arts and Wellbeing charity, Cambridge Curiosity and Imagination. Her research interests include education, children and young people, and arts-based research methodologies. She has recently completed doctoral research focused on the relationship between fun and learning, applying the scholarship of Sylvia Wynter and Rosi Braidotti.

Dr. Carolyn Cooke is a Senior Lecturer in Education at the Open University, UK. Her research focuses on professional learning (particularly teacher education and higher education Scholarship of Teaching and Learning), the arts as part of transdisciplinary education, creative methodologies and posthumanist theories. She is a co-editor of Routledge's *'Learning to Teach Music in the Secondary School'* series, as well as publishing articles on *Sensing bodies: Transdisciplinary enactments of 'thing-power' and 'making-with' for educational future-making (2023)*, the importance of *'Storying otherwise towards care-full writing practices in higher education' (2025)* and imagining professional learning differently using Appreciative Inquiry (2025).

Dr. Petra Vackova is a postdoctoral research fellow at the Aarhus University in Denmark in the Department of Museology. She researches and publishes work that focuses on educational justice in primary and pre-primary education, cultural sustainability and children's rights with a particular interest in the potentialities of the arts and arts education for building more creative, response-able and care-full learning environments.

Donata Puntil is a Lecturer in Psychotherapy within the Department of Psychological Medicine at the Institute of Psychiatry, Psychology and Neuroscience at King's College London, UK. Donata is a qualified Psychodynamic Psychotherapist and a member of the British Psychoanalytical Council (BPC) and of the Tavistock Society of Psychotherapists (TSP). Donata is also a Senior Fellow of the Higher Education Academy (SFHEA) and is very passionate about supporting learning and teaching and collaborating with students throughout their transformative journeys in HE. Donata's academic background is multidisciplinary, with a strong interest in posthumanism and new materialism; her main research interests are grounded on narrative inquiry and art-based methodologies to explore lived experiences and professional identity, with a focus on collaborative writing and 'doing academia differently'.

Dr. Lucy Caton is Lead for the Centre of AI in Education and Senior Lecturer at the University of Greater Manchester, UK. Her research explores the application of artificial intelligence to support neurodivergent learners, with a particular focus on formative feedback, digital equity, and the broader implications of AI for equality and society.

Dr. Natalie Tegama is a postdoctoral researcher in Global Health Ethics at the University of Oxford, where she works on the demarginalisation of philosophies of the global south. She uses decolonial concepts and ideas around pluriversality to explore how philosophies of the global south can inform bioethics and the broader research ethics landscape. This work is with a view to develop ethical frameworks that are reflective of multiplicity in value systems.

Dr. Grace Baby is a Foundation Year 2 doctor currently on the Leadership and Management Academic Program at University Hospitals Leicester (UHL). She studied medicine at Keele University and completed an MSc in Global Public Health and Policy at Queen Mary University of London. Her dissertation explored the barriers and facilitators to implementing mHealth tools for cancer diagnosis in sub-Saharan Africa. With strong interests in research, education, and leadership, Dr Baby is now beginning a Postgraduate Certificate at the University of Cambridge, focusing on Clinical Research, Education, and Leadership.

Anna Xavier is a Postdoctoral Research Fellow at the Centre for Refugee Employment, Advocacy, Training and Education (CREATE) at Deakin University, Australia. Her research interests centre on advancing socially just education and employment, with a particular focus on fragile and forced migration contexts. Anna's current work explores equitable access to employment for individuals from refugee and asylum-seeking backgrounds. She has published across several areas, including inclusive education and culturally and linguistically marginalised (CALM) students' education and employment experiences in Australia.

Carly Hawkins teaches in the School of Social Sciences at the University of New South Wales, Sydney, Australia. Her research focuses on Australian migration policy and its impact on child asylum seekers and refugees. She has particular expertise on the way refugee policy intersects with children's education, having been a specialist teacher for over 20 years.

Dr. Sally Baker is an Adjunct Associate Professor (Migration and Education) at the University of New South Wales and is founding CEO of Refugee Education Australia. Sally is a co-lead of the new Refugee Student Settlement Pathway to Australia. Sally's academic work centres on policy and practice related to equitable participation in higher education, particularly with students with forced migration backgrounds, focusing on issues of language and literacies, transitions, care, and ethics in practice.

Dr. Amber Fensham-Smith is a Senior Lecturer, Programme Leader in Childhood and Youth and a Co-director of Children's Research Centre, School of Education, Childhood, Youth and Sport, Open University, UK. As a Sociologist, her research inquiries seek to represent alternative education and social justice with participatory and inclusive methodologies. She is an advocate for brokering and extending collaborative opportunities to bridge academic research with research into practice and supporting authentic knowledge exchange within communities.

Dr. Alison Twiner is a Senior Research Associate with Camtree (Cambridge Teacher Research Exchange), Hughes Hall, University of Cambridge, UK; and a Research Associate and co-lead of the multimodal dialogue strand of the CEDiR group (Cambridge Educational Dialogue Research) in the Faculty of Education, University of Cambridge. Her research interests, practices and publications reflect these two areas. Particularly, she seeks to encourage and understand multimodal participation and communication to support meaning making and learning; alongside facilitating educators to explore and adapt their practices in ethical and locally-meaningful ways, and to share their practitioner-authored insights to benefit the wider education community.

Fadoua Govaerts is a researcher at the University of Bath whose work centres on participatory research methods, ethics, and home education. With over 16 years of experience in the home education community, she explores how young people engage with research, ensuring ethical inclusion and meaningful participation. She is Convenor for Alternative Education at the British Educational Research Association (BERA) and founder of RE-KnoX, an initiative dedicated to decolonising educational research and knowledge exchange between the Global North and South. Her research critically examines power, voice, and access in educational and policy contexts.

Dr. Sara Young is Lecturer in Education at Institute of Education, University College London's Faculty of Education and Society, University College London. She specialises in multilingual studies and migration, and the intersection with language education. Her research focuses primarily on the experiences of children and adolescents, with particular expertise in the area of Polish migration, on which she has published extensively. Her most recent publication explores the ethical challenges of dissertation supervision: Young, S., Buchanan, D., & Girling, A. (2025), 'Supervising sensitive Masters dissertation research: challenges and mitigation strategies'. Her current project explores the multilingual practices of migrant adolescents from the Turkish community in London.

Lisa-Maria Müller is Head of Research and Policy at the Chartered College of Teaching, UK, where she leads on linking education research, policy and practice. Prior to joining the Chartered College of Teaching, she worked as a postdoctoral researcher at the Universities of Cambridge and York and as a secondary school teacher. Her research interests focus on teacher professionalism, effective approaches to teacher professional development, evidence-informed practice and curriculum development. Her most recent publications include the following co-authored reports; Revisiting the notion of teacher professionalism (2024) and Cognitive science in education – teachers' priorities for research (2023).

Victoria Cook is Lead Researcher at the Chartered College of Teaching, UK. Prior to joining the College, Victoria worked as a Research Associate at the Faculty of Education, University of Cambridge and as a secondary geography teacher. Her research interests focus on teacher professionalism, teacher retention, dialogue and cultural literacy. She has published on building cultural literacy through dialogue and technology-mediated dialogue. Her most recent publications include the co-authored report *Revisiting the notion of teacher professionalism* (2024) and *Adapting research evidence for students with SEND* (2025).

Oksana Zabolotna is a Professor at Uman National University, Ukraine, and serves as a Research Coordinator in the War Child Alliance. Her research interests focus on language education, teacher professional development, and education in crisis contexts and forced migration. She is the President of the Ukrainian Educational Research Association. Her most recent work (co-authored with Iryna Kushnir) is "Pursuit of ethical research in a war zone: a quest for freedom" (2025).

Dr. Iryna Kushnir is an Associate Professor at Nottingham Trent University UK, in the Nottingham Institute of Education. Her research interests focus on higher education policy, politics and internationalisation; education and sustainable development; and higher education in crisis contexts and forced migration. She has published widely, particularly in the area of higher education policy and politics in the European region. Her most recent book is "European cooperation in higher education: shaping the future of Europe" (2025).

Barbara Skinner is Professor of Education and TESOL at Ulster University in the School of Education. Her research addresses real, current education issues and impacts locally, nationally and internationally with a focus on minority ethnic pupils, pedagogies of overseas students, and second language education and teacher education. Her most recent publication is on 'Home-School Partnerships: values and expectations of rural teachers and parents' (2025).

Ronan Kelly is a Lecturer and the TESOL Study Area Coordinator in the School of Education, Queensland University of Technology, Australia. Ronan's research focuses on translanguaging, technology enhanced learning and students' sense of belonging in multilingual education contexts.

Maria Stewart is a School Improvement Professional in the Education Authority Northern Ireland and an Associate Lecturer in Education at St Mary's University College Belfast, Northern Ireland. Maria's research focuses on learners who use English as an Additional Language, home-school partnership and teacher wellbeing.

Nicole Brown is Associate Professor at University College London in the department of Culture, Communication, and Media of the Institute of Education, UK. Nicole's work sits on the cusp of practice/teaching/research, thereby emphasising that through thinking-doing-being each area of expertise intersects with and impacts on another. She is a leading voice in embodied research practice, often drawing on creative and arts-based methods to challenge conventional academic approaches to researching ableism and disability, chronic illness, and neurodivergence in higher education. Her research foregrounds lived experience and advocates for structural change. Nicole's latest book is *Photovoice Reimagined*.

Section 1

Scene Setting

Section 1 and Book Foreword
by *Alison Fox*

This book complements and illustrates the Ethical Guidelines for Educational Research published by the British Educational Research Association (BERA, 2024). In crafting its fifth edition (BERA, 2024), BERA aimed to cover what was relevant and topical as ethical guidance for educational researchers. The guidelines are written principally for BERA's members, who are a broad church of educational researchers and practitioners, but have broader applicability across the Social Sciences. By publicly making the guidelines open access on their website, BERA's advice can reach beyond its membership to this wider, international audience.

This book therefore has been designed for its relevance to educational researchers based in and covering research of a wide range of educational settings – whether practitioners in early years, primary, secondary, tertiary or higher education practitioners or those in training settings in other workplaces. It offers the chance to explore in depth some of the issues identified by researchers commissioned to review the previous, fourth, edition of the guidelines (BERA, 2018) who came together to determine what was prescient and important going forward. The book centres around a series of case studies written by a wide range of educational researchers based on real and imagined scenarios to allow researchers' ethical thinking to be made explicit. The authors reveal the tensions researchers might experience and the options and decisions they then consider and make when applying the BERA (BERA, 2024) guidelines. Many of the chapters use fictionalisations for authors to draw on their experiences to illustrate how ethical tensions can be identified and navigated in educational research. Their learning is offered to benefit future research. As a reader, you are invited into the conversations the chapter authors have with themselves and one another to gain a sense of belonging to a wider community of educational researchers when planning and conducting your own research.

Before setting off on these thought-adventures, Section 1 offers scene setting to think about what could, or arguably should, underpin any such ethical guidelines. Chapter 1 explores the notion of virtuous living to extrapolate which virtues we should expect researchers to aspire to in their behaviours. This takes a reader on a journey both in time and place to recognise how questions of what we should aspire to are culturally situated. Chapter 1 challenges us to consider our place as researchers as we increasingly live in a globalised world, whether we study locally or through international research.

To complete Section 1, Chapter 2 covers a review of guidelines which was conducted in 2022 at the time of the review of the fourth edition of the BERA ethical guidelines (BERA, 2018). Guidance was selected as relevant to educational research, aiming to learn from other learned associations to offer sound and up-to-date guidance. This offers an overview of where there are common principles and where some associations highlight particular aspects of ethical research. This was the backdrop to the BERA fifth edition guidance for educational research.

What to expect from the rest of the book

Following the two scene setting chapters in Section 1, Section 2 presents the book's set of ethical dilemmas case studies organised according to the main subsections of the BERA ethical guidelines: responsibility to participants (Section 2A), responsibility to sponsors, clients, stakeholders and the environment (Section 2B), responsibilities to the community of educational researchers and for researchers' wellbeing and development (Section 2C), responsibilities for publication and dissemination (Section 2D). In the case studies, authors will be illustrating how education researchers have navigated ethical dilemmas in their research to care for all of those involved, including themselves, analysed against national guidelines for educational research. Each case study will follow researchers in their decision-making through possible research projects in a range of settings to consider alternative ways to deal with ethical dilemmas raised. The application of particular BERA (2024) guidelines will be cross-referenced as points are made and, whilst focused on those relating to the relevant section of the guidelines to the section of the book, will draw on whichever paragraphs of the guidance are pertinent. The authors draw on their experiences to explain researcher thinking and how interpreting guidelines relates to enacting values. They will also explore choices not taken, considering the possible knock-on implications from such decisions and how other researchers might have made different decisions based on different positionality.

Following these case studies, Section 3 chapters situate the ethical guidelines through exploration of key topics relevant to educational research: ethical review for practice as research; setting up an ethics review panel; issues specific to the Ukrainian context for which the BERA ethical guidelines have been translated; multilingualism and multiculturalism as ethical lenses for educational research.

As foregrounded in Chapter 1, the book confronts rather than avoids the application of Global North-derived guidance for research in settings other than the UK, and also illustrates how inclusion needs to be considered in all educational research. Within each chapter, authors will set questions for readers to relate to their own research contexts and offer recommended reading for further thinking about the issues raised.

1

Virtue Ethics and Being a Researcher: Introduction to Ethical Decision-Making

by *Alison Fox*

Introduction

Researchers as members of societies, as individuals and groups, represent cultural backgrounds and values. They become aware of how they view the world (ontologically) and how it can become known (epistemologically) as they navigate their own life experience but, as researchers, they will come to interact with others holding different value systems, cultural heritages and worldviews. Ethical guidelines seek to advise how to navigate research with others. Ethical traditions have handed down sets of principles outlining what researchers should hope to achieve in the conduct of their research – such as avoidance of harm (maleficence), maximisation of benefits (beneficence), respect for the rights of participants (e.g. privacy, confidentiality, autonomy) and taking just approaches. However, these are not straightforward to navigate. Researchers also therefore need guidance about how to enact principles; how to behave as a researcher. Again, there are choices and different researchers, or even the same researcher in different contexts, will make different choices. Virtue ethics are used to underpin ways of living and being across the globe. This chapter explores how virtuous behaviours might be defined and enacted in different research contexts. This seeks to set the scene for the case studies in this book which are organised for the main body of the book according to the responsibilities for researchers set out to guide their conduct in the BERA *Ethical Guidelines for Educational Research* (BERA, 2024): to participants; to sponsors, clients, stakeholders and the environment; to the community of researchers; for publication and dissemination and for researchers' wellbeing and development.

In search of guidance

The chapter takes a meta-ethical (Kitchener and Kitchener, 2009) approach. This is one analysis that explores the status, foundations and scope of moral values, properties and ideas. Table 1.1 captures Kitchener and Kitchener's five levels of ethical guidance to act as a framing for this book.

Chapter 1 takes the reader on a global journey around a theoretical field at level four. Chapter 2 explores the landscape of level two (codes and guidance) for the UK sector at the time preceding the writing of the book. Chapters in Sections 2 and 3 focus on principles (level three) being put into action to reveal researcher decision-making (level one) with reference to codes and guidance (level two), specifically the BERA *Ethical Guidelines for Educational Research* (BERA, 2024), with reference as the authors see relevant to theoretical justifications (level four).

A meta-ethical stance (at level five) helped identify how an ethical theoretical framework – that of virtue ethics (at level four) – could be useful to readers, as researchers, in their decision-making (at level one). The case

Table 1.1 A summary of Kitchener and Kitchener's levels of ethical thinking.

Level	Type	Purpose
Five	Meta-ethics	This problematises which…
Four	Ethical theories	To use as a framework to identify…
Three	Ethical principles	As justifications for…
Two	Professional codes, ethical guidance and regulatory requirements	To act as reference points as …
One	Researcher decision-making	…In response to their research setting and awareness of the above levels.

Source: Author.

studies in Section 2 and the situated reflection chapters in Section 3 illustrate how a researcher can navigate the levels in between. This chapter makes the case for virtue ethics as an inclusive, adaptable and negotiable theoretical basis for guiding researcher actions.

Whose guidance should we follow for a virtuous life?

Greek philosophers such as Aristotle (384–322 BCE[1]), if indeed it was Aristotle who authored 'On Virtues and Vices' from which the following translated quotation is taken, explored how to live well and hence be happy. Aristotle took a particular philosophical stance which examined the role of human agency in recognising virtues which should guide desirable human actions.

> 'Praise is due to things noble; blame to things disgraceful. Among things noble the virtues lead the way; among things disgraceful the vices. Praise too is due to the causes of the virtues, to what comes along with the virtues, to what results from them, and to their deeds; blame to the contraries'. (Simpson, 2013: 189 – translation of Aristotle)

Finding guidance about virtuous behaviours to inform decision-making could be a moral philosophical approach all researchers could seek, assuming research is considered an activity within society which affects the lives of the researcher, participants and other stakeholders invested in, involved in or affected by the research.

Aristotle and other Greek philosophers presented a series of texts termed a tradition of Eudaemian ethics which sought to examine how we should live and capture what makes for a good life. Plato too debated virtuous behaviour, for example, through acts of justice in his text 'Republic' (White, 2015). The 'Republic' examined which acts and effects of actions were considered virtuous. This is a different approach to focusing on the drivers for virtuous behaviour, and more akin to consequential ethical traditions, which pay attention to likely consequences of actions.

During the review of the five Academy of Social Sciences (AoSS) Ethical Principles adopted in 2015 (AoSS, 2015), the AoSS held a 'back-to-basics' discussion series. David Carpenter began with the proposition that 'A principle requiring researchers to act virtuously (which would also mean selflessly) in recognising their social responsibilities and contribution to the common good by undertaking scientifically worthwhile and valuable research would appear to be worthy of further consideration' (Carpenter, 2013: 5). He pointed to the work of Bruce Macfarlane (2009), who developed this perspective into a formalised approach to virtuous research. Macfarlane inferred key virtues from Aristotelian thinking relevant to contemporary times and applied them to six identified phases of research enquiry.

Whilst we find ourselves in the West turning to the Ancient Greeks to find the origins of thinking about how to behave virtuously, we are neglectful and even disrespectful if we assume this to be the only, the "main" or the "best" starting point. This would not recognise earlier philosophical traditions which have been guiding moral behaviours even before the Greeks were articulating views as texts. See Table 1.2 for an incomplete overview of moral and cultural global traditions.

If we turn our heads to Asia, for example, Angle and Slote (2013) report a recent extended dialogue between American and Chinese philosophers about how virtue might be mutually understood between those brought up with the teachings of Confucius and Greek traditions. After a seminar in 2018, the book *Virtue Ethics and Confucianism* was published. It concluded that alignment can be found if a broad view of virtue ethics is taken which focuses on the role of individual's seeking and demonstrating 'exemplary excellence' (Sim, 2015: 63). Centuries-old Hindu traditions can similarly be seen to promote virtues, although not associating these directly with individuals as agents (Perrett and Pettigrove, 2015). Sanskrit and Tibetan, associated with Buddhist traditions, contain terms which refer to a person's 'good qualities' or 'abilities' – *guna* and *yon tan*, respectively. *Dge ba* more explicitly refers to 'virtue' or 'virtuous' in Tibetan and Buddhist lists of recognised virtues (see Table 1.1). Common threads of truthfulness and attitudes towards others, such as benevolence and generosity, run through Buddhism, Confucianism and Hinduism. Truthfulness as a universal principle will be returned to in the light of a global code of conduct later in this chapter and, more fully, in Chapter 21. Benevolence relates to the attitude or disposition of goodwill towards others, while generosity involves the concrete action of giving or sharing resources with others. All these virtues are relevant for a researcher to aspire to.

Turning to the African diaspora, in particular of Bantu-speaking peoples, we find virtue ethics captured in the notion of ubuntu. This not only embraces the virtues of living with other humans but also points us to recognise our responsibilities and relationships as part of the natural environment.

Table 1.2 An overview of virtues held by different cultural traditions.

Moral philosophical traditions	Ubuntu (Matolino, 2020)	Hinduism (Perrett & Pettigrove, 2015)	Buddhism (Goodman, 2015)	Confucianism (Sim, 2015)	Plato (White, 2015)	Aristotle (Simpson, 2013)	Christian traditions developed by particularly influenced by St. Ambrose, St. Augustine and Aquinas (Pinsent, 2015)	Care ethics (Noddings, 2015) linked to sentimentalist virtue ethics
Virtues articulated within the tradition	**Compassion & Empathy towards others** – recognising the humanity and dignity of all individuals **Hospitality** – involving openness, generosity, and a willingness to share resources and support with others **Harmony** – highlighting cooperation, collaboration, and conflict resolution	Obligatory versus Optional versus Forbidden deeds with dharma relating to how complete or avoid these, involving virtues of: **Benevolence** – virtue of the mind *daya*	**Generosity** -उदारता (Udaarta) **Moral discipline** – नैतिक अनुशासन (Naitik Anushasan) **Patient endurance** – धैर्य (Dhairya) **Perseverance** – सततता (Satatata)	**Appropriateness** – *yi* **Doing one's best** – *zhong* **Filial and fraternal piety** – *xiaodi* **Knowledgeable** – *zhi* **Love of learning** – *haoxue* **Observing ritual propriety** – *li* **Reciprocity** – *shu* **Truthfulness** – *xin*	**Courage** – obedience of spirit **Justice** – overall condition which should not encroach on other parts **Moderation** – obedience of the appetites	**Courage** – hard to panic in face of fears of life **Justice** – metes out what is deserved **Liberality** – virtue of soul which values fine things **Magnanimity** – bear either good or bad luck, honour or dishonour **Mildness** – slow to get angry	**Charity** (or Divine Love) – Selfless, unconditional love for God and others. **Courage** (or Fortitude) – Strength and endurance in facing difficulties or danger. **Faith** – Trust and belief in God's promises and teachings. **Hope** – Confident expectation of divine fulfilment and eternal life.	This relational ethic covers individual relationships to global politics; Involves establishing and maintaining caring relationships involving all parties; Involves attention to others – **Ethical caring** requires moral effort but can also be exhibited naturally, which is no less virtuous **Feeling-with** (linked to empathy)

Moral philosophical traditions	Ubuntu (Matolino, 2020)	Hinduism (Perrett & Pettigrove, 2015)	Buddhism (Goodman, 2015)	Confucianism (Sim, 2015)	Plato (White, 2015)	Aristotle (Simpson, 2013)	Christian traditions developed by particularly influenced by St. Ambrose, St. Augustine and Aquinas (Pinsent, 2015)	Care ethics (Noddings, 2015) linked to sentimentalist virtue ethics
	Respect – involves treating others with dignity, fairness, and consideration, regardless of their differences or social status. **Solidarity** – emphasising the idea of 'I am because we are', hence solidarity and collective responsibility for the well-being of others.	**Charity** – virtue of the body *dana* or **Non-violence** – *ahimsa* which includes truthfulness, non-stealing, continence and greedlessness associated with non-injury.	**Meditative stability** – ध्यानिक स्थिरता (Dhyaanik Sthirta) **Wisdom** – ज्ञान (Gyaan) **Skilful means** – कुशल साधना (Kushal Saadhana) **Vow** – व्रत (Vrat) **Power**: शक्ति (Shakti)		**Wisdom** – rule of the person	**Prudence** – puts together what will bring happiness **Temperance** – lack of appetite for base pleasures	**Humility** – freedom from arrogance and pride, acceptance of one's place in divine order **Justice** – Fairness and righteousness in dealings with others.	Is **'Other-oriented' Extends to relationships with the environment.**

Moral philosophical traditions	Ubuntu (Matolino, 2020)	Hinduism (Perrett & Pettigrove, 2015)	Buddhism (Goodman, 2015)	Confucianism (Sim, 2015)	Plato (White, 2015)	Aristotle (Simpson, 2013)	Christian traditions developed by particularly influenced by St. Ambrose, St. Augustine and Aquinas (Pinsent, 2015)	Care ethics (Noddings, 2015) linked to sentimentalist virtue ethics
	Reverence for the environment – stewardship and a sense of guardianship and accountability for the Earth and its inhabitants **Justice, fairness, and equity** – prioritising the needs of vulnerable communities and future generations in environmental decision-making and resource management.	**Truthfulness** – virtue of speech satya	Pristine Awareness: शुद्ध जागरूकता (Shuddh Jaa-grookta)				**Prudence** – Wisdom in decision-making and discernment of what is morally right **Temperance** – Moderation and self-control, especially in areas like eating, drinking and desires.	

Source: Author.

The relational ethical dimension of ubuntu shows connections with a much more recent Western tradition of care ethics (Noddings, 2015) in which caring relationships require moral effort and responsibility to complement those which form 'naturally'. Originally focused on relationships between humans, like ubuntu, this also advocates that our caring relationships should embrace the natural environment (e.g. Tronto, 2013).

All the above approaches to defining virtuous living, if applying a Greek categorisation of ethical thinking (and accepting the limitations of this as only one framework) refer to an aretological dimension (*arete* – Greek for virtue) to ethics. This is one which focuses on the motives and dispositions of individuals. In the context of this book, this would be the motivations and values held by researchers.

This book has asked authors as researchers to reveal insights into the motivations and values which help explain their decision-making. These will be antecedent to their behaviours, on which a second, deontological dimension related to duty (*deon* – Greek for duty) and forms of action by individuals focuses. This is also explicated in the book's chapters. To consider the consequences of researcher actions, there is also a third teleological (*telos* – Greek for end or consequence) dimension to consider. Staying with the focus on seeking guidance, and aretology, researchers might ask, 'Whose guidance should we therefore seek?' Options include drawing on the cultural heritage of the researcher and of those in the setting of the proposed research, as well as reaching out to the academe to seek the guidance of researchers as laid down in publications.

Have we heard everyone's perspectives?

The virtues captured in Table 1.2 are principally those associated with individuals and may, or may not, align with the values of groups of people involved in research, who might not place such priority on individualism. When people come together, we should look towards including, rather than excluding, what is valued. Even within an individual, these values might not be clearly articulated, but this does not justify making assumptions. Spaces might need to be created within the research for such exploration.

One source of bias to look for within published literature is to question the positionality and positioning of who are considered key authors – to be explored further, in particular in Chapter 4. Whilst we can look for those who are writing and being cited, it is less easy to see those who have not caught attention within the canon of philosophy, or are oral traditions of knowing.

There are calls growing for absences to be redressed (e.g. Jones and Wilson, 2021; Smith and Garrett-Scott, 2021). What we, in the West, have decided to term *philosophy* might not even be recognised as such in other cultural systems, and we should note our blind spot. We know even less about the aspirations of those who are not vocal and visible in any particular society. This leaves us with the important question 'Whose voices and therefore values are we, as researchers, not hearing and hence not valuing?' Originally ascribed to Fricker in 1999 (Fricker, 2007), this imbalance in knowledge of one another and of one another's knowledge is classed as 'epistemic injustice' or, more strongly termed, 'epistemicide'.

> Epistemicide is the killing, silencing, annihilation, or devaluing of a knowledge system … epistemicide happens when epistemic injustices are persistent and systematic and collectively work as a structured and systemic oppression of particular ways of knowing. (Patin et al., 2021: 1,306)

In particular, 'Where are the female voices?' Whilst male voices are usually dominant in the historical development of philosophy, it is women who have been prominent in bringing back attention to virtue ethics as an attractive moral theory to offer ways forward (Stohr, 2015). As part of decolonising our ethical curriculum, we should recognise the contributions of philosophers such as Elizabeth Anscombe (1958), Philippa Foot (2002) and Rosalind Hursthouse (1999)[2] who have taken on the challenge to re-evaluate theories originally constructed and articulated by men. Whilst being aligned with a feminist tradition of philosophy, these philosophers have sought theories which encompass the breadth of moral experience and are inclusive of the experience of the marginalised and underprivileged, beyond seeking only to highlight and advocate against injustices to women. Such authors argue for the importance of including emotion in making moral judgements. In seeking to be guided by inclusion of 'the personal as political, recognition of gender-based oppression and inequality, challenging patriarchal power structures, intersectionality, and the pursuit of emancipation and social transformation' (Ulug'bek qizi Rasulova et al., 2024: 56), feminism makes a contribution to thinking about the virtuous life. This book is authored by over 80 per cent of those who identify as female, and feminist thinking has particularly influenced authors in Chapters 7 and 12.

'Where are the voices not articulated in English?' 'Who is not hearing who, through the colonial domination of English as a lingua franca in so much of academic publishing and dissemination?' Linguistic hegemonies constrain cross-cultural exchange of views on ways of living. Translation can lose much of the meaning attributed to particular concepts and ways of being. Table 1.1 offers a clumsy attempt at pointing to equivalence in meaning. In this book, multilingualism and language preferences affecting ethical decision-making are covered, in particular, in Chapters 5 and 20. The choice or assumptions made about language options can also affect research in practice, as articulated by Corbett, a co-researcher in a multinational project quoted in:

> The question is always whether the choice of a particular language facilitates and empowers or excludes and disempowers. Sometimes, however, it does both and one needs to find compensatory support for anyone who is disadvantaged. (Holmes and Rajab, 2022: 256)

If we pick 'off-the-shelf' ethical guidelines (level two, Table 1.1) and, even if we seek to explain our actions with reference to the theories and principles on which these are underpinned (level three, Table 1.1), researchers are in danger of doing so in a procedural and potentially unethical way. If we stop to recognise our own heritage and open our awareness that this is likely to be different to that of others, we can proceed to make decisions (level one, Table 1.1) cautiously. We can ask ourselves 'Are we prepared to challenge assumptions that we need to follow the canon of visible thought-leaders?' and 'Are we open-minded enough to explore what virtuous behaviour might mean to others, and hence of us as researchers?' 'Is there common ground on which we can agree?'

Are there global virtues which can guide research?

To tackle challenges which are not only affecting local communities but extend globally, whether environmental, demographic, economic or technological, there is a sense that 'we are all in this together'. In adopting this stance, international policy makers and global movements such as the United Nations (UN) call for us all, wherever we are, to work towards attaining seventeen Global Sustainable Goals by 2030,[3] and presumably their successor, and to follow agreed Conventions such as the fifty-four articles which make up the Rights of the Child.[4] We are expected to buy-in personally as a citizen of countries signing up to the Conference of Parties (COP) summit commitments and agreements towards tackling Climate Change, such as after the global stocktake at COP28 in Dubai, 2023.[5] In the UK, this is influencing research funders who are calling all research-active institutions to sign up to the Concordat for Environmental Sustainability in Research and Innovation (UKRI/Wellcome, 2019). Together, these organisations combine into a call for us to connect locally and globally, to think 'glocally'. There is even a peer-reviewed, open-access and cross-disciplinary journal *Glocalism* established in 2013 dedicated to 'stimulating increased awareness and knowledge around the new dynamics that characterise both globalisation and glocalisation'.[6]

One solution to this globalisation, in terms of ethical guidance for research, has been the creation of a Global Code of Conduct.[7] In 2018, a code based on four principles – fairness, respect, care and honesty – was presented widely, for example, to the UN, the European Parliament and the Vatican. These principles were not plucked out of the air but can be found embedded in the values and virtues presented earlier in the chapter within Table 1.2 as held within different moral traditions. The argument is made that these values can be held across traditions. A series of engagement workshops seeking to embody equitable involvement from a wide range of stakeholders in research across low- and middle-income settings developed the framework into its final form. Originally termed a Global Code of Conduct for Research in Resource-Poor Settings, in 2023 it was renamed The TRUST Code – A Global Code of Conduct for Equitable Research Partnerships. European Commission funding has adopted this as a reference document for its recent calls. The code has received funding from Horizon 2020 and, under the leadership of Doris Schroeder, fifty-six authors are named as contributors, alongside six research funders and six industry partners. The code is articulated as twenty-four articles aimed at countering ethics dumping from one setting to another, to recognise and seek to overcome power, resources and knowledge imbalances towards long-term equitable research relationships. Here we see the caring relational application of virtue ethics in action (e.g. Noddings, 2015). Chapter 21 maps this code against the BERA ethical guidelines in order to look for commonalities with and insights from the code for UK educational researchers.

Whilst widely adopted, an argument has been made about the need to recognise and negotiate 'pluriversal' ways of knowing and living (Leeming, 2023) and counter attempts to seek a one-world answer. In particular, a decolonial approach to any search for a universal or global ethics is called for which challenges normative assumptions and calls out injustices (Hutchings, 2019). This places emphasis on the process by which the TRUST code of conduct was developed, rather than on its product, and leaves us as researchers needing to take the spirit of this into our own research relationship-building.

Negotiating a mean path

> in every continuous and divisible quantity there is an excess and a deficiency and a mean ... The mean relative to us is the best, for this is the way science and reason command ... and this is what makes the best habit ... Consequently moral virtue must be about certain means and be a certain mean state. (Simpson, 2013: 27 – translation of Aristotle)

In his treatise Nicomachean Ethics, Aristotle refers to seeking 'the doctrine of the mean' as an aspiration for moral behaviours which would achieve someone 'living well'.

This notion of avoiding excesses and deficits and searching for a mean (see Figure 1.1) is a tool we could use as we tread the path of meeting with one another to negotiate where ethical consensus might be found.

For those who want to start from a Western/Greek interpretation of what makes for virtuous behaviours, we can turn to Bruce Macfarlane (2009) and his re-interpretation of the virtues of Aristotle for the contemporary Social Science researcher. Each of six virtues (courage, respectfulness,

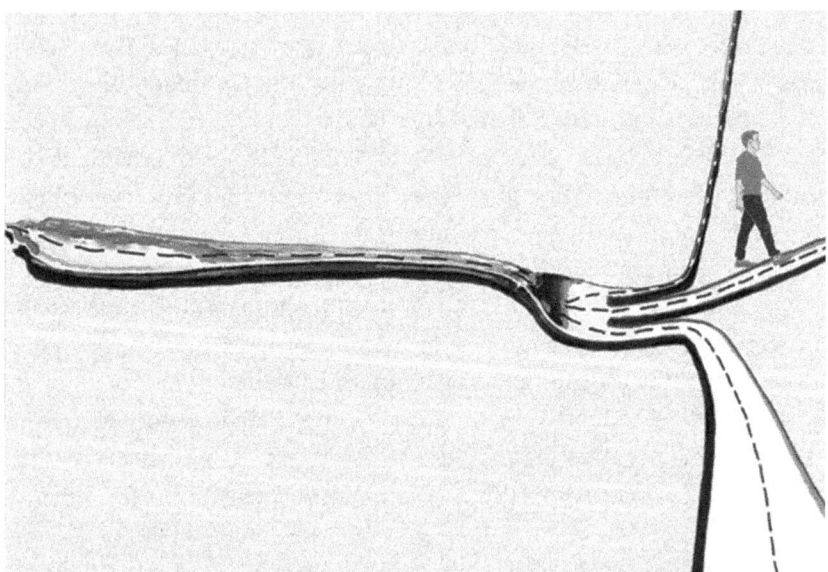

Figure 1.1 A representation of avoiding non-virtuous forks in the path – of excess or of deficit.

Source: Image with thanks to Alex Fox.

resoluteness, sincerity, humility and reflexivity) are mapped against six phases of the research process (framing, negotiating, generating, creating, disseminating and reflecting) to identify excesses and deficits to be avoided (see Table 1.3).

If a researcher wanted to adopt the TRUST code of conduct for example, a framework could be co-created which sought agreement about the limits of ethical conduct in relation to the four virtues identified. In adapting this to a researcher's setting, this might start to look something like Table 1.4.

As the author of this chapter, my heritage and upbringing are with the philosophies of Greek histories, and I accept that this chapter has remained biased to the language and values of these traditions. Authoring the chapter has led me to look outside my locale into the worlds, values and languages of others, whilst, apologetically, circling back to the frameworks closer to home.

Table 1.3 The Virtues and Vices of Research according to Macfarlane.

Phase	Vice (deficit)	Virtue	Vice (excess)
Framing	Cowardice	*Courage*	Recklessness
Negotiating	Manipulativeness	*Respectfulness*	Partiality
Generating	Laziness	*Resoluteness*	Inflexibility
Creating	Concealment	*Sincerity*	Exaggeration
Disseminating	Boastfulness	*Humility*	Timidity
Reflecting	Dogmatism	*Reflexivity*	Indecisiveness

Source: Table 3.2, page 42, Researching with Integrity The Ethics of Academic Enquiry, Macfarlane, B. © 2009. Reproduced by permission of Taylor & Francis Group. This framework could be adapted to any set of virtues, such as those outlined in Table 1.2, and is one which could be populated through dialogue and coming to know those to be involved in the research.

Table 1.4 Virtues and Vices interpolated from the TRUST code.

Vice (deficit)	Virtue	Vice (excess)
Inequity	*Fairness*	Partiality
Disrespect	*Respect*	Dependence
Carelessness	*Care*	Smothering
Deception/Dishonesty	*Honesty*	Bluntness

Source: Author.

Final thoughts

There is a need to remember that values underpin behaviours and that people will be judging the behaviours of others based on their own assumptions and values. These judgements place often unspoken expectations on researchers approaching others to become involved in research – whether funders, stakeholders, gatekeepers, participants or future readers of the published research. Alertness to our values and heritages means we should consider the value systems of others. This chapter has argued that exploring what is valued as virtuous by others might offer a means for this, as long as this can be through the languages or media of preference of others to express themselves. Whether accepting pluriversality of views or seeking to work within frameworks of commonality, researchers can seek to enter research without exerting privilege and hence demonstrating a commitment to decoloniality. Chapter 21 will pick up these ideas and the value of the TRUST code as a meta-ethical reification of values which might explore what is universal to us all in seeking 'glocal' approaches to ethical research.

Reflective questions

1. Identify any experiences when others have expected something of you (or of another researcher) which have surprised you.
2. From your perspective, why do you think there was this contradiction to what you expected?
3. How could you go about finding out what others expect of you as a researcher?
4. Choosing a virtue from Tables 1.2, 1.3 or 1.4, think through what would constitute (a) an excess and (b) a deficit of researcher behaviour in relation to this.

Further reading

1. Carpenter, D. (2013). Generic ethics principles in social science research discussion 'stimulus' paper for symposium 1 (Principles). *Generic*

Ethics Principles in Social Science Research, 3, 3–6. https://acss.org.uk/wp-content/uploads//Generic-Ethics-Principles-in-Social-Science-Research-2013.pdf.

You can read the fuller paper David Carpenter presented to the Academy of Social Sciences for developing Generic Ethics Principles based on the notion of a virtuous researcher via the link above.

2. Hammersley, M. (2013). Response I to '*Generic Ethics Principles in Social Science Research*', 6–9. https://acss.org.uk/wp-content/uploads//Generic-Ethics-Principles-in-Social-Science-Research-2013.pdf.

Using the same link, you can read Martyn Hammersley's critique of the case David Carpenter makes, challenging how feasible or desirable this is. He argues for the need to accept pluriversal views and the situated nature of decision-making within any discussion of principled guidance for research ethics.

3. Kara, H. (2020). *Research ethics for independent researchers*, blog post. 22 July 2020. https://helenkara.com/2020/07/22/research-ethics-for-independent-researchers/.

Helen Kara offers a range of resources about approaches to research ethics which seek to be inclusive and applicable across research contexts. In this blog post she encourages independent researchers to seek resources which help them make situated ethical decisions, either with or without access to a research ethics committee.

4. Kara, H. (2023). *Epistemic freedom, creative research methods and ethics*, blog post. 24 November 2023. https://researchwhisperer.org/2023/11/24/epistemic-freedom-creative-research-methods-and-ethics/.

In this blog post Helen Kara explains how she came across the concept of epistemic freedom and realised it had already been infusing her views of what was needed for the future of ethical research. She reflects on what this means for researchers, being careful to be part of a solution, rather than contributing to the epistemic violence.

5. Kaur, K., Grama, B., Chaudhuri, N. R. and Recalde-Vela, M. J. (2023). Ethics and epistemic injustice in the global South: A response to Hopman's human rights exceptionalism as justification for covert research. *Journal of Human Rights Practice*, 15(2), 347–73. https://doi.org/10.1093/jhuman/huad008.

This empassioned article is a critical response to another article in the same journal. It demands that researchers should be 'honouring knowledge, agency and voice' by engaging in 'cross-cultural ethical dialogue', rather than compounding epistemic injustices. Whilst written in the context of socio-legal research, the notions of reflexivity and reciprocity to redress power imbalances have a wider relevance.

Notes

1. BCE = Before Common Era.
2. The use of first names is a deliberate act, taking advice about how to redress gender balance in our citations – see: https://www.open.edu/openlearn/citational-politics.
3. https://www.un.org/sustainabledevelopment/sustainable-development-goals/.
4. https://www.unicef.org.uk/what-we-do/un-convention-child-rights/.
5. https://unfccc.int/cop28/5-key-takeaways#:~:text=COP%2028%20closed%20with%20an,cuts%20and%20scaled%2Dup%20finance.
6. https://riviste.unimi.it/index.php/glocalism/about.
7. https://www.globalcodeofconduct.org/wp-content/uploads/2023/06/The_TRUST_Code.pdf.

References

Academy of Social Sciences (2015). *Developing generic ethics principles for social science research.* https://acss.org.uk/wp-content/uploads//Developing-Generic-Ethics-Principles-for-Social-Science-Research-2015.pdf.

Angle, S. C. and Slote, M. (2013). *Virtue Ethics and Confucianism.* New York: Routledge.

Anscombe, G. E. M. (1958). Modern moral philosophy. *Philosophy,* 33(124), 1–19.

BERA (2024). *Ethical Guidelines for Educational Research* (5th ed.). London: BERA. https://www.bera.ac.uk/publication.

Carpenter, D. (2013). Generic ethics principles in social science research discussion 'Stimulus' paper for symposium 1 (Principles). *Generic Ethics Principles in Social Science Research,* 3, 3–6. https://acss.org.uk/wp-content/uploads//Generic-Ethics-Principles-in-Social-Science-Research-2013.pdf.

Foot, P. (2002). *Virtues and Vices and Other Essays in Moral Philosophy.* Oxford: Oxford University Press.

Fricker, M. (2007). *Epistemic Injustice: Power and the Ethics of Knowing.* Oxford: Oxford University Press.

Goodman, C. (2015). Virtue in Buddhist Ethical Traditions. In L. Besser-Jones, and M. Slote (Eds.), *The Routledge Companion to Virtue Ethics*, London: Routledge (pp. 89–98).

Holmes, P. and Rajab, T., 2022. An ethic for researching multilingually in transnational, multilingual, multidisciplinary research teams. In Critical Intercultural Pedagogy for Difficult Times. London: Routledge (pp. 228–249).

Hursthouse, R. (1999). Virtue ethics and human nature. *Hume Studies*, 25(1), 67–82.

Hutchings, K. (2019). Decolonizing global ethics: Thinking with the pluriverse. *Ethics & International Affairs*, 33(2), 115–25.

Jones, L. and Wilson, M. (2021). Decolonising the academic library: Reservations, fines and renewals. In J. Crilly and R. Everitt (Eds.), *Narrative Expansions: Interpreting Decolonisation in Academic Libraries*, London: Facet Publishing (pp. 57–71).

Kitchener, K. S. and Kitchener, R. F. (2009). Social science research ethics: Historical and philosophical issues. *The Handbook of Social Research Ethics*, 10(9781483348971), n1.

Leeming, W. (2023). Negotiating pluriversality. *Public*, 34(68), 19–27.

Macfarlane, B. (2009). *Researching with Integrity: The Ethics of Academic Enquiry*. New York: Routledge. ISBN:9780415429030.

Macfarlane, B. (2010). Values and Virtues in Qualitative Research. In M. Savin-Baden (Ed.), *New Approaches to Qualitative Research*, London: Routledge (pp. 35–43).

Matolino, B. (2020). Ubuntu: A Traditional Virtue Ethics Contribution to Economic and Social Development in Southern Africa. In K. Ogunyemi (Ed.), *African Virtue Ethics Traditions for Business and Management*, Cheltenham: Edward Elgar Publishing (pp. 12–29).

Noddings, N. (2015). Care Ethics and Virtue Ethics. In L. Besser-Jones, and M. Slote (Eds.), *The Routledge Companion to Virtue Ethics*, London: Routledge (pp. 401–14).

Patin, B., Sebastian, M., Yeon, J., Bertolini, D. and Grimm, A. (2021). Interrupting epistemicide: A practical framework for naming, identifying, and ending epistemic injustice in the information professions. *Journal of the Association for Information Science and Technology*, 72(10), 1306–18.

Perrett, R. W. and Pettigrove, G. (2015). Hindu Virtue Ethics. In L. Besser-Jones, and M. Slote (Eds.), *The Routledge Companion to Virtue Ethics*, London: Routledge (pp. 51–62).

Pinsent, A. (2015). Aquinas: Infused Virtues. In L. Besser-Jones, and M. Slote (Eds.), *The Routledge Companion to Virtue Ethics*, London: Routledge (pp. 141–54).

Sim, M. (2015). Why Confucius' Ethics Is a Virtue Ethics. In L. Besser-Jones, and M. Slote (Eds.), *The Routledge Companion to Virtue Ethics*, London: Routledge (pp. 63–76).

Simpson, P. L. P. (2013). *The Eudemian Ethics of Aristotle*. New York: Transaction Publishers.

Smith, C. A. and Garrett-Scott, D. (2021). 'We are not named': Black women and the politics of citation in anthropology. *Feminist Anthropology*, 2(1), 18–37.

Stohr, K. (2015). Feminist Virtue Ethics. In L. Besser-Jones, and M. Slote (Eds.), *The Routledge Companion to Virtue Ethics*, London: Routledge (pp. 271–82).

Tronto, J. C. (2013). *Caring Democracy: Markets, Equality, and Justice*. New York: New York University Press.

UK Research and Innovation (UKRI) and Wellcome (2019). *Concordat for Environmental Sustainability in Research and Innovation*. Concordat for the Environmental Sustainability of Research and Innovation Practice (last accessed: 9 November 2024).

Ulug'bek Qizi Rasulova, D., Qizi Turobova, O. O. and Akmalxonov, S. F. A. (2024). Fundamental principles and development of feminist theory. *International Conference on Modern Development of Pedagogy and Linguistics*, 1(11), 56–61. https://universalconference.us/universalconference/index.php/icmdpl/article/download/3293/4750 (last accessed: 6 June 2024).

White, N. (2015). Plato and the Ethics of Virtue. In L. Besser-Jones, and M. Slote (Eds.), *The Routledge Companion to Virtue Ethics*, London: Routledge (pp. 3–16).

2

Ethical Guidelines in Educational Research: The State of Play

by *Sin-Wang Chong and Qi Liu*

Introduction

This chapter aims to shed light on the state-of-play of ethical research practices by analysing twenty major international ethical guidelines for conducting educational and social sciences research. Some of these guidelines refer to specific countries such as Australia, Canada, New Zealand, UK and the United States, while others have a broader (e.g. Europe) and international focus (Table 2.1). Specifically, this chapter focuses on nine topics of educational research ethics: (1) digital research; (2) ethics of publication; (3) human rights; (4) inclusivity for neurodiversity of researchers and participants; (5) inter-university collaborative research; (6) international and intercultural research; (7) practitioner and independent research; (8) sensitive issues and vulnerable groups; (9) sustainability and environmental responsibility. The themes are ordered to reflect a logical progression, starting with the vibrant area of digital research, which introduces new ethical challenges, and then moving to established topics and more niche areas such as sustainability and environmental responsibility. This chapter will first present the coverage of these nine topics in these twenty ethical guidelines. Then, recommendations will be made in light of the analysis. Information pertaining to selection process and content analysis can be found on the BERA website/Bloomsbury website that accompanies the book.

Table 2.1 A summary of the 20 ethical guidelines reviewed.

	Name of the guideline	Learned society	Geographical location	Year of publication[i]	Edition analysed	Publication year of 1st edition
1	American Educational Research Association's (AERA) Code of Ethics	American Educational Research Association	United States	2011	2nd	1992
2	Australian Association for Research in Education's (AARE) Code of Ethics	Australian Association for Research in Education	Australia	1993	1st [ii]	1993
3	British Educational Research Association's Ethical Guidelines for Educational Research (4th ed.)	British Educational Research Association	United Kingdom	2018	4th	1989
4	British Psychological Society (BPS) Code of Human Research Ethics	British Psychological Society	United Kingdom	2021	2nd	2010
5	British Sociological Association's (BSA) Statement of Ethical Practice	British Sociological Association	United Kingdom	2017	3rd	1992
6	British Sociological Association's (BSA) Ethical Guidelines and Collated Resources for Digital Research	British Sociological Association	United Kingdom	2017	1st	2017
7	Ethical Decision-Making and Internet Research: Recommendations from the AoIR Ethics Working Committee (Version 2.0)	Association of Internet Researchers	International	2012	2nd	2002

	Name of the guideline	Learned society	Geographical location	Year of publication[i]	Edition analysed	Publication year of 1st edition
8	Generic Ethics Principles in Social Science Research	Academy of Social Sciences	United Kingdom	2015	1st	2015
9	Montreal Statement on Research Integrity in Cross-Boundary Research Collaborations	World Conferences on Research Integrity Foundation	International	2013	1st	2013
10	National Foundation for Educational Research (NFER) Code of Practice	National Foundation for Educational Research	United Kingdom	2022	Not specified	1993
11	Research Charter for Aotearoa New Zealand	Royal Society Te Apārangi	New Zealand	2020	1st	2020
12	RESPECT Code of Practice for Socio-Economic Research	RESPECT Project funded by the European Commission	Europe	2004	1st	2004
13	Social Research Association's (SRA) Research Ethics Guidance	Social Research Association	United Kingdom	2021	1st	1980s
14	Social Policy Association (SPA) Guidelines on Research Ethics	Social Policy Association	United Kingdom	2009	1st	2009
15	Society for Education & Training (SET) Code of Ethics and Conduct	Society for Education & Training	United Kingdom	2022	2nd	2014
16	Scottish Educational Research Association's (SERA) Ethical Guidelines for Educational Research	Scottish Educational Research Association	United Kingdom (Scotland)	2005	1st	2005

	Name of the guideline	Learned society	Geographical location	Year of publication[i]	Edition analysed	Publication year of 1st edition
17	Singapore Statement on Research Integrity	2nd World Conference on Research Integrity	International	2010	1st	2010
18	Starting Points for Research in Schools by SERA-SEED Research in Schools Working Group	Scottish Educational Research Association	United Kingdom (Scotland)	2007	1st[iii]	2007
19	Tri-Council Policy Statement (TCPS): Ethical Conduct for Research Involving Humans	The Canadian Institutes of Health Research (CIHR), the Natural Sciences and Engineering Research Council of Canada (NSERC), and the Social Sciences and Humanities Research Council of Canada (SSHRC)	Canada	2018	2nd[iv]	1998
20	UKRI Framework for Research Ethics	UK Research and Innovation	United Kingdom	2022	Not specified	Not specified

Source: Author.

i This refers to the years of the publications of the edition that was analysed.

ii Multiple revisions have been made to the document but there is no specific information about additional formal editions beyond the 1993 publication online.

iii The 2nd edition was published in 2020 (https://www.sera.ac.uk/wp-content/uploads/sites/13/2020/11/SERA-Starting-Points-for-Educational-Research-in-Scotland-2020.pdf), which was not included in this review because of the lack of access at the time the analysis was conducted.

iv The 3rd edition was published in December 2022 (https://ethics.gc.ca/eng/documents/tcps2-2022-en.pdf). This version was not included in the review because it was published after the analysis.

Coverage of the nine topics

The topic *digital research*, sometimes referred to as online research or internet-based research, is covered by nine out of the twenty ethical guidelines (45%). This emerging topic in research ethics, partly as a result of Covid-19, is covered in more recent ethical guidelines such as the British Psychological Society's *Code of Human Research Ethics* (2021) and Social Research Association's *Research Ethics Guidance* (2021). In the past decade, there have been ethical guidelines developed specifically for conducting digital or online research, such as *Ethical Decision-Making and Internet Research: Recommendations from the AoIR Ethics Working Committee (Version 2.0)* (2012) and British Sociological Association's (BSA) *Ethical Guidelines and Collated Resources for Digital Research* (2017b).

Ethics of publication, or ethics in research dissemination, is a topic that is discussed in the majority of the ethical guidelines reviewed. Fourteen out of the twenty ethical guidelines (70%) include dedicated sections or paragraphs on ethical issues related to publication, output and dissemination. The ethical guidelines that do not include *ethics of publication* are those that focus primarily on teachers (Society for Education and Training *Code of Ethics and Conduct*, 2022) and digital research (e.g. BSA's *Ethical Guidelines and Collated Resources for Digital Research*, 2017b). For the latter, the purpose of these ethical guidelines is to underscore specific issues peculiar to conducting digital research. Therefore, these guidelines do not include a section on ethics of publication, which is perceived as an aspect of research ethics that is well understood by the research community.

Human rights, or rights of participants, is discussed in sixteen of the twenty ethical guidelines (80%), making it one of the most common issues covered in the ethical guidelines. Ethical guidelines not covering this aspect of research ethics are those that specialise in a particular type of research or a specific area of research ethics. For instance, the *Starting Points for Educational Research in Scotland* by SERA-SEED Research in Schools Working Group (Shanks et al., 2020) document that focuses on practitioner research; *Montreal Statement on Research Integrity in Cross-Boundary Research Collaborations* (2013) concerns international collaborative research endeavours by universities.

Regarding *inclusivity for neurodiversity of researchers and participants*, which considers cognitive diversity and equitable research processes, it is only mentioned in nine of the ethical guidelines (45%). The ethical guidelines that do not discuss researching human participants with a diagnosed cognitive impairment or children are those that focus on a specific type of research (e.g. *RESPECT Code of Practice for Socio-Economic Research*, 2004, considers socio-economic research) and a particular ethical topic (e.g. the remit of *Montreal Statement on Research Integrity in Cross-Boundary Research Collaborations*, 2013, is on inter-institutional research). An ethical guideline that is relatively dated does not cover this topic (i.e. Australian Association for Research in Education's *Code of Ethics*, 1993). Neurodiversity is used here in lieu of neurodivergence to refer to a broader concept that frames neurological differences (i.e. neurodivergence) as part of the natural diversity of human beings. It challenges the view that certain cognitive abilities or developmental pathways are 'normal' or superior, promoting the idea that all neurotypes should be valued equally.

Inter-university collaborative research, which features in academic research partnerships, is one of the least discussed topics in the twenty ethical guidelines. Only four ethical guidelines have a dedicated section or paragraph(s) on the topic (20%). This topic is mentioned in the *Generic Ethics Principles in Social Science Research* (2013), *Montreal Statement on Research Integrity in Cross-Boundary Research Collaborations* (2013), *Tri-Council Policy Statement: Ethical Conduct for Research Involving Humans* (2018) and UKRI *Framework for Research Ethics* (2022). In particular, the *Montreal Statement on Research Integrity in Cross-Boundary Research Collaborations* (2013) is a document dedicated solely to the issue of inter-institutional research, covering a wide range of topics.

Thirteen out of the twenty ethical guidelines cover the topic *International and intercultural research* (65%), a crucial area in transnational research collaboration. This topic is not discussed in some of the more dated guidelines, such as Scottish Educational Research Association's *Ethical Guidelines for Educational Research* (2005) and guidelines that focus on a particular form of research where international collaborations are not common. Seven out of the twenty ethical guidelines reviewed cover the topic *practitioner and independent research* (35%), referring to research that may be conducted without institutional oversight. There are ethical guidelines that are developed solely for practitioner research, including the *Starting Points for Educational Research in Scotland* (Shanks et al., 2020). In addition to teachers, practitioners referred to in some guidelines include practitioners in other professions (e.g. psychologists in the British Psychological Society's *Code of Human Research Ethics*, 2021).

Sensitive issues and vulnerable groups, which focus on researching on/with marginalised populations, are another key ethical issue, covered in fourteen ethical guidelines (70%). The six ethical guidelines that do not currently discuss this topic are 'specialist' guidelines that concern a particular type of research (e.g. digital research in *Ethical Decision-Making and Internet Research: Recommendations from the AoIR Ethics Working Committee Version 2.0,* 2012) or a specific topic of research ethics (e.g. inter-institutional research in *Montreal Statement on Research Integrity in Cross-Boundary Research Collaborations,* 2020). The topic of 'sensitive issues and vulnerable groups' is discussed in all 'generalist' guidelines, such as the American Educational Research Association's *Code of Ethics* (2011).

Sustainability and environmental responsibility, defined as the integration of environmentally conscious practices and long-term considerations for the planet into the research process, is the least discussed topic in the twenty ethical guidelines, only mentioned in three guidelines (15%). The three ethical guidelines that cover the topic are: British Psychological Society's *Code of Human Research Ethics* (2021), *Research Charter for Aotearoa New Zealand* (2020) and Society for Education & Training *Code of Ethics and Conduct* (2022). The coverage of this topic by these three guidelines appears to be brief, including general principles in lieu of specific suggestions about how researchers can consider sustainability and environment protection in their research process.

Recommendations

Drawing from the content analysis of the twenty ethical guidelines, this section makes recommendations for ethical practices in conducting educational research based on the nine areas. As a caveat, it is important to view these recommendations using a reflexive and critical lens, and emphasise the dangers of using these guidelines with any sense of ethics dumping on another context, especially when most of these guidelines are developed by educational researchers from the Global North. These recommendations should be treated as ideas for further discussions with your own research community.

Digital research

As an emergent form of research, what constitutes *digital research* in the broad field of education needs to be clarified; for example, the one definition by *Ethical Decision-Making and Internet Research: Recommendations from the AoIR Ethics Working Committee (Version 2.0)* (2012), which includes seven characteristics of digital research (e.g. studying how participants use the internet), can be referred to.

Second, additional topics on digital research need to be considered, such as researchers' competence to conduct digital research and confidentiality/privacy of digital data (see also Chapter 7). It is the researchers' responsibility to ensure they are well-versed in conducting research using digital tools or analysing 'big data' such as those available on social media platforms (see also BERA, 2024, paragraph 4, 66).[1,2] Educational researchers need to consider ways confidential data and information are protected in storage, delivery or transfer using the internet or other electronic conduits. Given the nascent nature of digital research, it is crucial that educational researchers emphasise situationality and reflexivity in digital research ethics. The former refers to a contextualised approach to reviewing digital research ethics while the latter focuses on the experiences and roles of researchers in identifying potential ethical issues and risks pertaining to digital research. Chapters 7 and 9 provide in-depth discussions on conducting online interviews and researching the use of artificial intelligence in education, respectively.

Ethics of publication

Educational researchers need to consider ethical practices in scholarly publishing and journal peer review, a topic discussed in the included guidelines as well as more broadly by the Committee on Publication Ethics and publishers. As a case in point, in the American Educational Research Association's *Code of Ethics* (2011), Section 16.01 Submission of Manuscripts for Publication, there is a detailed description of ethical issues associated with submission of manuscripts for publication (e.g. avoid submitting the same manuscript to multiple journals), duplicate publication of data and roles of journal editors. American Educational Research Association's *Code of Ethics* (2011) also includes a separate section on the roles and responsibilities of journal peer reviewers. Such information is useful for doctoral students and early career researchers who do not have much experience navigating the journal peer-review process. The importance of supporting novice researchers in the peer-review process should form an integral part of publication ethics (see the case study presented in Chapter 16). Peer review needs to be an inclusive process that involves young researchers so that they are adequately prepared to take up a more active role in the system in the long run. Supporting early career researchers to gain experience in responding to peer reviewers' comments and reviewing manuscripts needs to be perceived as part and parcel of ethics in publication. Additional insights on ethical publication and dissemination can be found in Chapter 15.

Human rights

Educational research must align with broader human rights frameworks to ensure ethical practices that respect the dignity and welfare of all involved. Internationally recognised documents such as the United Nation's *Universal Declaration of Human Rights*[3] and UNESCO's *Universal Declaration on Bioethics and Human Rights*[4] provide a foundation for protecting human rights in research. Additionally, the United Nations *Convention on the Rights of the Child*[5] emphasises special protections for children, which are particularly relevant to educational research, where minors are often key participants. In line with the above, researchers' responsibility to protect human rights in the research process needs to be emphasised. For example, it should be the priority of educational researchers to protect the rights and dignities of participants and other stakeholders involved in the research. Educational researchers need to devise concrete plans to ensure research participants' rights and welfare are protected. Human rights extend to researchers' rights, which also need safeguarding. For instance, Scottish Educational Research Association's *Ethical Guidelines for Educational Research* (2005) advises that research staff, who are to collect data at a new location, visit the company.

Inclusivity for neurodiversity of researchers and participants

It is necessary to stress that the fundamental principle of including participants with diverse needs is to provide equal opportunities for participants to be involved in research and have their voices heard. It is also associated with one of the basic human rights, that is, the right to participate in research. When considering children as participants, the research process needs to be age-appropriate (see Chapter 6 on how research process is informed by children's rights); it refers to the importance and best practices of developing artefacts (e.g. short clips, animations, pictures) that are appropriate to the literacy level and cognitive maturity of children to aid children's understanding of the objectives and process of the research. There are alternative ways through which children can provide assent. For example, the British Psychological Society's *Code of Human Research Ethics* (2021) suggests allowing children to choose between smiley/sad faces in lieu of ticking boxes. Discussions need to be had on the role of parents or guardians in providing consent on behalf of children and the situations where such consent may or may not be appropriate.

Obtaining informed consent from those who have limited cognitive capacity may be a challenge, and a proxy (e.g. caretaker of the participant) may need to act on behalf of the participants. However, it should be clear that educational researchers do not make assumptions about participants' capacity to provide consent until it is medically proven. Moreover, ethical guidelines can outline the need for educational researchers to continuously monitor participants' willingness to participate in research, such as through non-verbal cues; this is especially important when conducting research with neurologically diverse participants who may not be able to express discomfort or distress verbally.

Inter-university collaborative research

Collaborative research needs to outline responsibilities of institutional research partners in establishing and sustaining collaboration, responsibilities in maintaining collaborative relationships and responsibilities in collaborative outcomes (see Chapter 19 for an example of UK-Ukraine research collaboration). Specific responsibilities can resemble those mentioned in the *Montreal Statement on Research Integrity in Cross-Boundary Research Collaborations* (2020). More importantly, the overarching principle of constant and candid communications among research partners needs to be emphasised. In addition to communication, the importance of mutual recognition of common ethical requirements needs to be noted. Educational research partners, including universities, professional organisations, funders, the public sector and industries, need to agree on a set of ethical standards that are consistently observed across the international research team.

Institutional conflict of interest needs to be reported to ethics review committees of university research partners, and where it is necessary to disclose such conflict of interest to participants when seeking informed consent. On the topic of ethics review of inter-institutional collaborative research, the *Tri-Council Policy Statement: Ethical Conduct for Research Involving Humans* (2018) can be referred to in their proposal for alternative models of ethics review. These models suggest a more inclusive approach to ethics review to include the establishment of review boards that include representatives from the institutions involved in the research.

International and intercultural research

International research involves studies that cross national boundaries, while intercultural research focuses on understanding and interacting with different cultural groups within or across countries. In both cases, researchers must be cautious of ethical issues such as ethics dumping – the imposition of unethical research practices in under-regulated settings – and helicopter research, where studies are conducted with little regard for the researched community's needs or contributions. Although it is an educational researcher's right and responsibility to publish findings, careful consideration is necessary to avoid harm, particularly when researching marginalised groups or sensitive topics. Published work should not reinforce stereotypes or discrimination; using non-judgemental language is essential.

Ethical guidelines, such as those in the *Tri-Council Policy Statement* (2018), emphasise documenting experiences with culturally diverse groups. Ethics committees should assess whether researchers have an appropriate understanding of the culture being studied. While resources like the BERA *Ethical Guidelines for Educational Research* (BERA, 2024) are useful, they should not be imposed rigidly but considered alongside local contexts, as discussed in Chapter 1. Further advice on ethical conduct in international and intercultural research is detailed in Chapters 3, 4 and 20.

Practitioner and independent research

Practitioner research holds significant value as a means for teachers and other professionals to engage in continuous professional development and generate ecologically valid insights relevant to their practice (Wilkinson and Dokter, 2023). This type of research must have direct relevance to local contexts and benefit the community involved, such as students, while recognising the ethical challenges inherent in researching one's own professional setting (see Chapter 10). It is also essential to note that not all practitioners work in traditional classroom settings; independent researchers, particularly those outside institutional contexts, may face additional challenges in accessing ethics review support. In such cases, guidelines from learned societies such as BERA offer valuable (although not definitive) advice to ensure ethical integrity in the absence of institutional ethics committees.

To enable meaningful and ethical practitioner research, practitioners must receive appropriate training from experienced researchers. While formal workshops and seminars are useful, hands-on mentorship programmes offer more personalised support, guiding practitioners through each stage of their research and providing access to resources typically available to university-based researchers. Additionally, workplace support is crucial – schools or other organisations should promote evidence-based practices and provide 'protected time' for research. Involvement of senior staff can amplify the impact of practitioner research, influencing areas such as curriculum planning. Ethical review services, tailored to practitioner and independent researchers alike, are essential (see Chapters 17 and 18).

Sensitive issues and vulnerable groups

Vulnerable groups in research are typically individuals or communities who may be at greater risk of harm, exploitation or marginalisation due to factors such as social, economic, physical or mental conditions. Their vulnerability can stem from power imbalances, diminished autonomy or heightened exposure to risks. In research, this vulnerability can be exacerbated by the ways findings are presented, potentially making these groups even more susceptible to negative consequences. From the analysis, two additional groups should be recognised as vulnerable: whistle-blowers and early career researchers. While the goal is not to encourage a whistle-blowing culture in academia, whistle-blowers' rights must be protected, including safeguarding their identities and providing channels for seeking advice before making formal complaints. Early career researchers are also vulnerable due to their limited experience and precarious positions. Principal investigators should clarify how junior researchers contribute to projects and how they will be supported and nurtured (see Chapters 12 and 13).

The rationale for conducting research on vulnerable groups is to maximise direct benefits and reduce harms. Unlike research with other populations, promoting general social good is insufficient to justify studies on sensitive topics or minority groups. Research involving vulnerable populations must be justified by the direct benefits it provides to participants and their communities. Additionally, efforts should be made to minimise potential negative impacts, including how findings are communicated, which could further increase the group's vulnerability.

For informed consent, similar to the British Psychological Society's *Code of Human Research Ethics* (2021), researchers should consider additional consent procedures when dealing with sensitive topics, especially when using video/audio recordings or online data, where participant identities may not be fully protected. Chapter 14 offers further suggestions for conducting research with vulnerable participants.

Sustainability and environmental responsibility

Among the twenty ethical guidelines reviewed, the topic of sustainability and environmental responsibility is only briefly discussed in three: the *Research Charter for Aotearoa New Zealand* (2020), the British Psychological Society's *Code of Human Research Ethics* (2021) and the Society for Education & Training *Code of Ethics and Conduct* (2022). The limited focus on this area may reflect a broader gap in the integration of environmental concerns within research ethics, an omission highlighted in the BERA's fourth edition of its ethical guidelines (BERA, 2018), which identified the need for guidance on sustainability to lead efforts in addressing the climate crisis. These three associations likely include this guidance due to regional leadership in environmental responsibility or the pressing need to address sustainability within specific research contexts.

Educational researchers must cultivate an awareness of their research's environmental impact and its connection to sustainable development. Clear definitions of terms such as 'sustainable development' are needed, and concrete steps must be outlined for promoting sustainability in research practices. For example, the British Psychological Society's *Code* (2021) suggests digital alternatives for information sheets and informed consent.

To further support sustainable research practices, documents such as the *Concordat for Environmental Sustainability in Research and Innovation* (Wellcome Trust, 2024) offer additional frameworks. Chapter 11 provides an example of how researchers can actively embrace environmental sustainability.

Final thoughts

This chapter documents the results of a text analysis conducted on twenty ethical guidelines. In relation to nine topical areas in research ethics, this report identifies areas covered in the ethical guidelines. Under each topical area, more specific sub-themes are discussed in the appendices. Another objective of this chapter is to identify emergent areas of ethical importance that need to be considered. Based on this analysis, recommendations are made, and the relevant chapters of the book are referred to. The analysis intends to serve as a framework for advancing discussions on established and embryonic topics on ethical practices in educational research. It is acknowledged that there are limitations inherent in the analysis. First, the analysis was conducted in 2022, and newer guidelines were not included (e.g. BERA's *Ethical Guidelines for Educational Research*, 5th ed.). Second, while the corpus of ethical guidelines includes those from the Global North and South, the majority of the guidelines are from Euro-American countries. We must adopt a decolonial and contextualised approach when discussing the issues outlined in this chapter (see Chapters 1 and 4). We invite future attempts to analyse ethical guidelines used in under-represented countries, especially in the Global South, such as radical ethics or indigenous ethics, which may not have explicit guidelines but are increasingly important, especially in educational research, where the emphasis lies with amplifying marginalised voices. Another worthy pursuit is to conduct a follow-up study where educational researchers are invited to share their experiences in how the principles in the guidelines are operationalised in practice.

Acknowledgement

This chapter is based on the following unpublished report that was commissioned by the British Educational Research Association: Chong, S. W.

(2022). *Researcher's Report for BERA Ethical Guidelines Review* [Unpublished report]. British Educational Research Association, UK.

Reflective questions

1 Referring to the nine themes in this chapter, how similar/different are ethical guidelines in your country/context?
2 How can the benefits of scholarly publishing be maximised for both researchers and the researched?
3 What are some ethical considerations when conducting research online or using data from the internet in your context?
4 In your experience, what are some good practices of environmentally responsible and sustainable ways for conducting educational research?
5 How can practitioners be supported to conduct research about their own practice ethically?

Further reading

1. Buchanan, E. A. and Zimmer, M. (2023). **Internet Research Ethics.** In E. N. Zalta, and U. Nodelman (Eds.), *The Stanford Encyclopedia of Philosophy* (Winter 2023 ed.), https://plato.stanford.edu/archives/win2023/entries/ethics-internet-research/.

   This concise guide is updated periodically, with the first edition published in 2012; it has undergone fourteen revisions. It provides the most up-to-date overview of ethical issues related to conducting internet research. Internet research ethics are discussed with reference to specific technologies such as big data and cloud computing, and trends in the IT industry.

2. Samuel, G. and Richie, C. (2023). **Reimagining research ethics to include environmental sustainability: A principled approach, including a case study of data-driven health research.** *Journal of Medical Ethics*, 49(6), 428–33. https://doi.org/10.1136/jme-2022-108489.

   This open-access article presents a research ethics framework informed by bioethics and sustainability that underscores respect not only for people and communities but also the environment. Although the case study presented focuses on health research, the principles outlined in the framework can be applicable to educational research.

3. Birch, C. (Ed.) (2020). *Independent Researchers: The Challenges of Accessing Ethical Approval.* A BERA Blog Special Issue. Retrieved from https://www.bera.ac.uk/blog-series/independent-researchers-the-challenges-of-accessing-ethical-approval.

This collection of blog posts, which is based on an BERA event on the same topic, illustrates independent researchers' experiences and challenges in conducting research beyond academia. Although not based on empirical studies, the richness of the personal narratives provides an insider's perspective for understanding ethical dilemmas faced by practitioner and independent researchers in education.

Notes

1   Paragraph 4, BERA (2024). Digital/online research, as well as the use of artificial intelligence, is a rapidly developing area, therefore conventions as to what constitutes good ethical practice are not as well established as in most other areas of educational research. Nevertheless, the fundamental principles apply. Where research draws on social media and online communities, it is important to remember that digital information is typically generated by individuals. Researchers should not assume that the names given and/or identities presented by participants in online forums or other sites are 'real', but should consider whether and how these potential participants might be traceable and indeed whether it can be proven that they exist at all.

2   Paragraph 66, BERA (2024). Attribution should include explicitly recognising authors of any type of content, in all cases in which an author (or creator) can be identified. As well as text, this includes images, diagrams, presentations and multimedia content. Researchers need to be aware that a great deal of content is subject to copyright, and cannot be freely reused or modified unless it is explicitly licensed as such – for example, by means of one of the 'Creative Commons' (CC) licences. Authors retain copyright of CC-licensed material (which may be published hard copy or digitally), but have chosen to permit reuse, distribution and sometimes adaptation, depending on the licence terms; any copies or modifications have to be made available under the original licence terms and must link to that licence. Researchers have the responsibility of checking the conditions for reuse, and for attributing the author(s) in all cases. Researchers are advised to regularly check the latest guidance from COPE as digital technology develops.

3 Universal Declaration of Human Rights | United Nations.
4 Universal Declaration on Bioethics and Human Rights | UNESCO.
5 Convention on the Rights of the Child | OHCHR.

References

References with an asterisk (*) are ethical guidelines included in the review.

*American Educational Research Association (2011). Code of ethics: American educational research association approved by the AERA council February 2011. *Educational Researcher*, 40(3), 145–56. https://doi.org/10.3102/0013189X11410403.

*Australia Association for Research in Education (2005). AARE Code of ethics. https://www.aare.edu.au/research-and-advocacy/research-ethics/.

BERA (2024). *Ethical Guidelines for Educational Research* (5th ed.). London: BERA. https://www.bera.ac.uk/publication/ethical-guidelines-for-educational-research.

*British Education Research Association (2018). *Ethical Guidelines for Educational Research* (4th ed.). London: BERA. https://www.bera.ac.uk/publication/ethical-guidelines-for-educational-research-2018-online.

*British Sociological Association (2017a). *BSA Statement of Ethical Practice*. https://www.britsoc.co.uk/media/24310/bsa_statement_of_ethical_practice.pdf.

*British Sociological Association (2017b). *Ethics Guidelines and Collated Resources for Digital Research*. https://www.britsoc.co.uk/media/24309/bsa_statement_of_ethical_practice_annexe.pdf.

*Canadian Institutes of Health Research, Natural Science and Engineering Research Council of Canada, Social Science and Humanities Research Council (2018). *Tri-Council Policy Statement: Ethical Conduct for Research Involving humans*. https://ethics.gc.ca/eng/policy-politique_tcps2-eptc2_2022.html.

*Economic and Social Research Council (2022). *Framework for Research Ethics*. https://www.ukri.org/councils/esrc/guidance-for-applicants/research-ethics-guidance/framework-for-research-ethics/.

*Lewis, J., Dingwall, R., Iphofen, R., Oates, J. and Emmerich, N. (2013). *Generic Ethicsprinciples in Social Science Research*. Academy of Social Sciences. https://acss.org.uk/wp-content/uploads//Generic-Ethics-Principles-in-Social-Science-Research-2013.pdf.

*Markham, A. and Buchanan, E. (2012). *Ethical Decision-Making and Internet Research: Recommendations from the AoIR Ethics Working Committee (Version 2.0)*. Association of Internet Researchers. https://aoir.org/reports/ethics2.pdf.

*National Foundation for Educational Research (2022). *NFER Code of Practice*. https://www.nfer.ac.uk/media/cgpl42av/nfer_code_of_practice.pdf.

*Oates, J., Carpenter, D., Fisher, M., Goodson, S., Hannah, B., Kwiatkowski, R., Prutton, K., Reeves, D. and Wainwright, T. (2021). *BPS Code of Human Research Ethics*. The British Psychological Society. https://doi.org/10.53841/bpsrep.2021.inf180.

*Resnik, D. B. and Shamoo, A. E. (2011). The Singapore statement on research integrity. *Accountability in Research*, 18(2), 71–5. https://doi.org/10.1080/08989621.2011.557296.

*Royal Society (2020). *Researcher Charter for Aotearoa New Zealand*. https://www.royalsociety.org.nz/assets/A3-Research-Charter-Aotearoa-NZ-complete-text.pdf.

*Scottish Educational Research Association (2005). *Scottish Educational Research Association Ethical Guidelines for Educational Research*. https://www.sera.ac.uk/publications/sera-ethical-guidelinesweb/.

*Shanks, R., Jaap, A., Darling-mcquistan, K. and Adams, P. (2020). *Starting Points for Educational Research in Scotland*. Scottish Educational Research Association. https://www.sera.ac.uk/wp-content/uploads/sites/13/2020/11/SERA-Starting-Points-for-Educational-Research-in-Scotland-2020.pdf.

*Social Policy Association (2009). *Social Policy Association Guidelines on Research Ethics*. https://social-policy.org.uk/social-policy-guidelines-on-research-ethics/.

*Social Research Association (2021), *Research Ethics Guidance*. https://thesra.org.uk/SRA/SRA/Ethics/Research-Ethics-Guidance.aspx.

*The Institute for Employment Studies (2004). *RESPECT Code of Practice for Socio-Economic Research*. UNESCO's International Institute for Educational Planning. https://etico.iiep.unesco.org/sites/default/files/2017-09/respect_code.pdf.

*The Society for Education and Training (2022). *SET Code of Ethics and Conduct*. https://set.et-foundation.co.uk/help/set-policies-and-procedures/set-code-of-ethics-and-conduct-and-procedures/set-code-of-ethics-and-conduct.

*The World Conferences on Research Integrity (2020). *Montreal Statement on Research Integrity in Cross-Boundary Research Collaborations*. https://www.wcrif.org/downloads/main-website/montreal-statement/123-montreal-statement-english.

Wellcome Trust (2024). *The Concordat for Environmental Sustainability in Research and Innovation Practice*. April. Retrieved from https://cms.wellcome.org/sites/default/files/2024-04/Concordat%20for%20the%20Environmental%20Sustainability%20of%20RI%20Practice.pdf.

Wilkinson, D. and Dokter, D. (2023). *The Complete Guide to Practitioner Research* (2nd ed.). London: Routledge.

Section 2

Case Studies

Section 2-1 Foreword – Responsibilities to Participants

by *Aimee Quickfall*

In this sub-section, the book is exploring researchers' responsibilities to participants through a number of different lenses and fictionalised experiences. Often, as researchers, our major concern and focus is on participants, but as will be described in this book's case studies, sometimes it is not clear on the most ethical course of action in terms of our responsibilities. As authors, we aim to explore dilemmas that have come about because of our responsibility for participants and show that as a researcher, you are not alone if you are grappling with these issues. In the chapters, the classic challenges around consent, informing participants, withdrawal from the study and doing no harm are examined as well as exploring themes around researching with participants who have a different first language than the researcher, intercultural issues, positionality and decolonial approaches, researching with children and their rights, and methodological considerations of collecting research data with participants online. This sub-section of the book takes as its starting point guidelines 1–49 of the BERA ethical guidance (BERA, 2024).

In Chapter 3, Felicity Hasson and Una Connor-Bones carefully consider the cultural, political and social sensitivities of research in international and intercultural settings. They provide an insightful and critical lens on the BERA *Ethical Guidelines for Educational Research* (BERA, 2024) from an international and intercultural research perspective, using two case studies to highlight the dilemmas in enacting ethical practice and process in each study. The authors present an effective road map for navigating international and intercultural research projects, ensuring that respect, adaptation and resilience are key elements for consideration by researchers in their responsibility for participants.

In Chapter 4, (Carol) Azumah Dennis provides a thorough and fascinating exploration of positionality and decolonial approaches to research ethics. The author takes us through the origins of decolonial thought before applying this lens to research ethics in the form of a detailed case study, following a researcher who is investigating conceptions of quality in a further education college. Dennis uses the tangible case study to give meaningful examples of how decolonial ethics can be incorporated into the design and execution of a research project. Dennis' premise is that decolonial research ethics has four defining features: (1) exercising critical reflexivity, (2) reciprocity and respect for self-determination, (3) embracing 'Other(ed)' ways of knowing and, finally, (4) embodying a transformative praxis.

In Chapter 5, Phil Wood, Aimee Quickfall and Kaisa Pihlainen take another look at international research, and this time, through a complexity lens. They point out, through long experience in the field, that management, travel, different expectations due to research systems with contrasting histories and navigation of different research ethics processes and requirements are all areas which need to be taken into account when planning and managing projects. They also signal that language is fundamental to the research process and to the care of participants and reflect on the use of language as an ethical issue. Two case studies are presented, relating to issues affecting participants and inter-researcher collaboration and decision-making.

In Chapter 6, Carmel Capewell, Helen Hanna and Chawin Pongpajon focus on placing children's rights central to researcher decision-making, arguing that fulfilling children's rights is essential to ethical decision-making for researchers. As three experienced researchers, the authors present three case studies from different educational contexts across the globe, including the UK, South Africa and Thailand. Like the other chapters in this subsection, Capewell, Hanna and Pongpajon illustrate how ethical dilemmas are complex, context-specific and go beyond basic ethical expectations.

In Chapter 7, Aimee Quickfall and Phil Wood explore the ethical issues that research methodology can present when considering our responsibilities as researchers to our participants. For their case study, the growing use of online data collection methods is explored from the researcher point-of-view, following unexpected events during an online interview. The practical benefits of online methods are juxtaposed with the ethical challenges that these can present, and alternative courses of action for the fictionalised researchers are explored in depth.

3

Applying BERA Principles to International and Intercultural Research

by *Una Connor-Bones and Felicity Hasson*

Introduction

The increasing globalisation of research requires researchers to have a comprehension of the multidimensional factors that can influence the research process. Ethical guidelines, including those set out by BERA, typically provide guidance for research undertaken nationally and internationally. They accommodate a continuum of social and ethno-cultural diversity which has proliferated as the twin paradigms of pluralism and globalisation permeate much of contemporary life. Such guidance draws on reciprocal norms or principles that adhere to a humanist commitment *to protect the dignity, rights and wellbeing of research participants* (WHO, 2024[1]). The universality of these standards further advocates normative values of honesty, openness, objectivity, fairness and accountability in the conduct of research.

This chapter will critically consider the applicability of BERA guidelines in the context of international and/or intercultural research. Recognising that both concepts can have singular and dual interpretations, the chapter will examine these issues in their contextual and situational relevance. Adopting a case study approach, the chapter will use two research studies as the basis to explore ethical dilemmas of research practice. Exploration of these dilemmas includes ethical issues anticipated before the research began and ethical issues that arose during the research, along with consideration of how the researchers navigated these.

The chapter will outline two international case studies that illustrate the interplay between individual, social, professional and political issues that can affect ethical application within the field. Both cases present real-life studies and the assumptions that underline westernised ethical principles in culturally diverse locations. Each case highlights the importance of understanding what constitutes locally acceptable research and the socioecological factors that researchers must navigate. The influence of gatekeepers, effect of political environments and power differentials on ethical procedures are explored, in addition to recognising the wellbeing and safety risk faced by both the participants and the researcher.

In the spirit of self-reflexivity, the positionality of the authors is presented to enable the reader to understand how our very being may have influenced the presentation of this work. Both authors are middle-class white women, with experience of undertaking and leading international and intercultural research. A key consideration is the positionality of the researcher as insider-outsider. The lead author is an international educationalist and practitioner researcher with a research focus on improving educational outcomes for children and young people, with a particular emphasis on social inclusion, community cohesion and policy reform. The second author is a social researcher with experience of engaging in research within the field of health and social care. Both are board members of several research ethics committees, leading and overseeing decisions on complex and challenging research ethics applications from several fields of study. As a result, they have a theoretical familiarity of the issues facing researchers engaging in international research projects.

Case Study One: Education in north-east Syria: An analysis of the educational policies run by the autonomous administration

Background

The original focus of this research was an illustrative case study on the reformed education system put in place by the Kurdish autonomous administration in 2015, specifically its impact on relationships between the diverse community groups living in north-east Syria. Since 2011, Syria has experienced conflict resulting in the geopolitical fragmentation of the country, with a non-state actor developing its own governance system in north-east Syria. At the time of the study, north-east Syria was polyethnic and dependent on humanitarian assistance. In response to the right of a child to receive education and the need for multilingualism, the autonomous administration in north and east Syria reformed the pedagogy, structure and atmosphere of the education system (BERA, 2024, paragraph 1).[2] The objective of the reformed system was to allow the teaching of the Kurdish language for the first time in Syria and the promotion of democratic values. A new curriculum was designed, along with associated teacher training, and pupils had the opportunity to study in their own mother tongue as classes in the three main languages (Kurdish, Arabic, Syriac) were offered in schools.

However, against a backdrop of political instability, the educational reforms have faced several challenges with regard to a lack of infrastructure, workforce and integration within the wider educational curriculum and government ethos. Some community members have refused to enrol their children in these schools, seeking instead placement in schools that continue to teach the Syrian government curriculum. Concerns exist towards the lack of recognition of certificates delivered by the education system at a national level as well as the politicisation of the new curriculum (BERA, 2024, paragraph 22).[3] The main research question was: In what ways has the introduction of new educational policies by the Kurdish autonomous administration in northeast Syria impacted inter-community relationships? Secondary research questions included the content of new educational policies, the extent to which they have the potential to generate inequalities among diverse community groups, the main contentious educational issues negatively impacting on community relationships (e.g. language, separationist setting, representation of diversity in practices and policies), the purpose of the new education policies, and the educational interventions that could contribute to enhancing inter-community relationships. To address these questions, it was planned to collect primary data through a series of in-depth open qualitative interviews and focus group discussions conducted with policymakers, education practitioners and community members to better understand the peoples' experiences of education policy and practice. In addition, an analysis of curriculum and policy documents available was also planned.

Fulfilment of the research was dependent on several inter-related factors that would ethically guide the research, with specific consideration of responsibilities for researchers' wellbeing and development and responsibilities to participants (BERA, 2024). In the developmental stage, a series of ethical issues emerged in the institutional review process that informed its refinement and implementation. These are related to the researcher's situational and contextual familiarity with the educational, social and political economy of the region; researcher safety; access to participants; and participant safety.

With little research existing in this area, the research study sought to explore the perceptions and perceived impact of the introduction of these reforms from the perspective of multi-stakeholders (Table 3.1). The research team consisted of two academics and one doctoral researcher. Due to welfare and security concerns, the student was not given ethical approval to visit Syria. In response, the research team utilised both online and face-to-face data collection methods. The researcher led online methods whilst she identified and trained data collectors (n=3) currently living in north-east Syria to assist face-to-face data collection.

The lead academic, a white male, is a senior researcher with experience in the management of multiethnic societies and international development

Table 3.1 Original overview of stakeholders and methods.

Setting	Individual interviews	Focus groups
In Northern Iraq	With non-governmental organisation workers, journalists, academics, officials from the autonomous administration	With teachers and parents from the Kurdish community group
In north-east Syria (with the help of data collectors)		With teachers, school directors and parents from diverse ethnic and religious communities
Online (video interviews, phone interviews, email interviews)	With NGO workers, journalists, academics, officials from the autonomous administration in Northern Iraq and north-east Syria	

Source: Authors.

with an interest in the Middle East. The second academic, a white female, is a senior researcher with experience in undertaking research in conflict-divided societies, including Syria. The doctoral researcher is a multilingual (French, English and Arabic) female student, who has worked as a peace builder in Iraq and Syria. At the time of the study, she was learning Kurmanji Kurdish (the dialect spoken in north-east Syria). Between 2004 and 2019, the researcher lived and worked in the Middle East – including periods spent in Northern Iraq and north-east Syria – and developed a substantial network of contacts from national and international civil society organisations, including those engaged in work around education and peacebuilding, community representatives from diverse religious and ethnic communities, journalists, researchers, government officials and community members. She had access to a well-established professional network which was deemed an important preparatory consideration in introducing and promoting the research across cultural and linguistic boundaries. To enhance her understanding of the context, she engaged in several field trips to understand the delivery of educational policies and attend local debates among community members (paragraph 22).

The ethical dilemma

Several ethical issues were considered by the team prior to and during the study.

Ethical approval

The team gained ethical approval from a higher educational institution which required two independent committee peer reviews to be undertaken. This highlighted the issues relating to the potential physical and/or psychological threat or abuse of the researcher to be considered (BERA, 2024, paragraph 47).[4] From a university perspective, this reflects a moral duty of care but also a national and European professional requirement (Universities UK, 2019; All European Academics, 2023). Consequently, prior to entering the field, the research team adapted the design and conduct of the study in line with the constraints of the security environment.

Situational and contextual familiarity

The proposed research was set within the territories in north-east Syria controlled by the Kurdish autonomous administration. Researcher travel to north-east Syria was a key consideration in undertaking the study, and the ethical implications of conducting research in a fragile, conflict-affected region were carefully scrutinised. The research team remained attuned to the highly volatile security situation and its potential impact on planned data collection (BERA, 2024, paragraph 74).[5] Consequently, the study's initial design incorporated built-in flexibility with appropriate alternative scenarios should they be required.

Researcher safety

The research was adapted to take place in two locations: Northern Iraq and north-eastern Syria. A security assessment was undertaken before the researcher travelled to Northern Iraq, supplemented with daily security updates from INSO – the International Non-governmental Organisation (NGO) Safety Organisation which provides up-to-date information to guide the operational work of international NGOs. Additional information was received from the large network of contacts, NGO workers and community members, living and working in the areas that the researcher might visit. In preparation, the researcher also completed conflict-specific training, including two United Nations (UN) security trainings that led to an advanced certification to work in hostile environments. The researcher stayed in a UN Department of Safety and Security (UNDSS), security-approved accommodation and transport was arranged with a designated driver rather than reliance on local taxis. Further precautions were applied whereby the researcher avoided predictable routines and varied routes and times of daily travel. A daily log of movement, including a schedule of meetings and locations, was shared with the wider research team and a security check was completed at the end of each day. Selection of the Northern Iraq region ensured continuity in addressing the research aim and objectives. Many Kurdish community members from north-east Syria had taken refuge there, and civil society representatives (including NGOs, journalists, researchers as well as autonomous administration officials) regularly visited the region. This made it possible for the researcher to conduct several face-to-face interviews in an alternative location, with written confirmation from local organisations to support the researcher 'on the ground'.

Engagement of local knowledge

In the original proposal, it was planned that three data collectors from the three main community groups living in northeast Syria (Kurdish, Arab and Christian) would be identified and trained to facilitate data collection. Such local knowledge was a crucial consideration as data collection on political issues in a conflict zone can become biased as well as become a source of threat, particularly if engagement becomes politically motivated. It was therefore essential for the researcher to become fully aware of existing risks and constraints and to adapt the research design as needed (paragraph 47).

Subsequently, the researcher, in consultation with the data collectors, agreed that conducting focus groups *in situ* was not suitable given the sensitivity of the geopolitical context. Instead, the data collectors were used as gatekeepers to widen the researcher's contacts within their respective community groups. In these circumstances, the established network of civil society and community members representing diverse community groups and political positions maximised opportunities for the researcher to reach out to diverse participants in a fair and balanced manner (paragraph 74).

Access to participants and participant safety

Data collection was predicated on safe researcher access to participants in each region, the safety of participants and representative participation among the various interviewees. Access to participants was subject to changing political, social and health restrictions. Consequently, a range of flexible scenarios was considered with regard to data collection whereby different forms of interviews would be used as necessary, including online interviews, email interviews, face-to-face interviews and/or focus groups. Participant access and personal safety were key considerations. For online participation, the chosen online platform had to be one commonly used and familiar to participants in the region, whilst maintaining an acceptable level of security. This was maximised with specific security measures, including a required password to enter the meeting, a virtual waiting room so that only invited interviewees were admitted and the meeting would be 'locked' to prevent any other person from entering.

The level of trust that is created between researcher and participant, particularly in fragile, conflict-affected areas, is a precursor to meaningful engagement. Researcher fluency in the two languages (English and Arabic) used to conduct interviews ensured an in-built process of verification across the interviews in each location. Nonetheless, challenges presented in seeking to gain in-depth insights about the impact of educational policies on relationships between different community groups. The sensitivity of the topic required a level of researcher-interviewee trust which was difficult to achieve in online meetings. As a result, the research adapted to explore how education choices are made by community members as this was considered a less sensitive subject matter.

In terms of participant safety, information sheets provided assurances of data anonymity. This was a critical acknowledgement, particularly where concerns may exist around collected data that may put participant(s) at risk (paragraph 47). In this study, it was decided to use verbal rather than written consent. The rationale for this is that written consent is deemed culturally and politically sensitive in Syria and Iraq, where participants may be wary of signing any document. In place of this, email replies and acceptances to participate would be considered as consent. Verbal consent was sought following provision of the information sheet and again before commencing interviews.

This approach corresponds with the best ethical practice which states that researchers should state the contents of the consent form to the participant and request their consent to each statement.

Courses of action

Whilst the team had gained ethical approval across the research process, they experienced additional challenges during the implementation of the study.

Contextual challenges

Several challenges were highlighted. First, the impact of the conflict had consequences on access which was limited to safer/controlled areas. Second, the disruption of educational information infrastructure meant limited availability and completeness of data, impacting data quality. Finally, an absence of Syrian government support for the educational structure may have created security concerns, potentially impacting participants' willingness to engage in the study and the quality of the data obtained (paragraph 47). Given this, the use of face-to-face data collection methods questions the safety of the researcher and the participant.

Methodological challenges

First, data collection was shared between the researcher and a local research team who had different degrees of training which may impact the quality and rigour of the study. Second, the use of online data collection may have resulted in the researcher engaging with a participant they did not know, potentially missing the non-verbal dimensions arising from community engagement and inhibiting engagement.

Alternative courses of action

Reflecting on the project, several alternative courses of action are proposed.

Ongoing ethical lens

The ethical review for most studies occurs prior to data collection; however, the reality is that harm/challenges can emerge at any stage of the research process. Research undertaken in a conflict-affected context may require ongoing ethical reflection, where a shift in geopolitical positions can impact the reach and scope of intercultural relationships. In circumstances like this, ongoing engagement between researchers, government(s), gatekeepers and funders is essential to maintain awareness of the situation and respond appropriately as and when necessary. This can involve a continuum of response options. In some instances, a fragile conflict situation might lead to a pause or delay in the research process until relative security and safety are assured and restored. In other instances, it may require recalibration of the research lens, involving, for example, revision of original questions, exclusion of an existing population sample or relocation of the research to an alternative setting. In each situation, the advantages and limitations of a revised approach must be carefully evaluated to ensure researcher and participant safety and to assess its feasibility in meeting the research goals.

Conflict and disadvantage

Undertaking research in countries experiencing political instability requires researchers to be aware of the actual and perceived notions of power imbalances between the researched population, local researchers and the research team. In these situations, it is incumbent on researchers to be cognisant of their position within the lives and communities of affected people. For independent, skilled research, collaboration with Syria-based educational researchers is an option to add face validity to the research process. Maximising the involvement of local researchers can provide an additional informed layer of contextual expertise. As evidenced in this project, partnership with local researchers provided valuable insider knowledge that suggested mistrust between participants and divergent viewpoints that could compromise the validity of focus group data. Such insights demonstrate how academic-operational collaboration can be nurtured in a real-world setting, promoting the relevance of the research at a local level and maximising chances of access to the end users.

Cultural sensitivity

Engaging in inter-cultural research requires empathetic awareness of the complex social, cultural, political and economic interactions that permeate a society and how these impact the immediate and longer-term needs of a population (paragraph 22). The challenge of being seen as an 'outsider' is a key consideration for researchers whose race, ethnicity, religion or linguistic background differs from the research population. Efforts to ameliorate any cultural resistance to research engagement are dependent on the level of familiarisation and preparation undertaken in advance of field work. In these circumstances, the logistics of identifying cultural sensitivities is time well spent and is integral to ensuring open and respectful relationships. In this case study, it may have been helpful to consider the creation of study materials in audio and video formats, which may have impacted engagement.

Accessibility and participation

In the digital era, the use of social media is increasingly incorporated as integral to the research process. Its widespread availability across regions and time zones offers a versatility to initiate, maintain and protect the organisation and conduct of research, although the threat to cybersecurity is acknowledged. In volatile research landscapes, the option for secure messaging platforms as a tool to conduct remote interviews may become the primary standardised option to overcome security challenges and improve access considerations. Use of social media platforms as a means of communication during times of conflict and crisis can buttress any challenges to the objectivity of the research process, ensuring that access to a diversity of voices – including hard-to-reach people and places – and perspectives is maintained.

Case Study Two: Birth across the borders: Exploring contextual education as a catalyst for change for improved maternal health

Background

This case study adopts a wide narrative lens to describe the undertaking of a research project in Myanmar. In detailing the steps taken by project team members, it demonstrates how the research was strategically pivoted in response to a series of unprecedented and volatile challenges whilst adhering to ethical principles. The original research premise sought to explore the realities and challenges of the critical maternal health situation in four regions of eastern and central Myanmar. Maternal mortality and morbidity are complex global challenges that can precipitate wider consequences, including increased poverty, reduced health outcomes, family breakdown and emotional and psychological trauma. The rate of maternal deaths due to pregnancy or childbirth-related issues is significantly higher in middle- to low-income countries and more so in fragile conflict and post-conflict contexts. Country data for Myanmar (WHO, 2018) shows a maternal mortality rate of 178 per 100,000, with only 36 per cent of deliveries in the poorest households having a skilled attendant at birth, although this data is limited due to reduced access in remote ethnic areas. At the time of the project's development, Myanmar was experiencing a political and organisational transition from a military dictatorship towards a form of ethnic federalism. However, poor relations between the central government and diverse ethnic groups were negatively impacting the wellbeing and livelihoods of people and communities, with ongoing risks of conflict, and breaches of human rights and humanitarian law. Within this multiethnic country, education is challenging, and a 'one-size-fits-all' approach does not accommodate the multiple layers of contextual, cultural and economic influences that can deter women from seeking support for their maternal health.

Development of the research was informed by previous studies conducted in the region; this provided relevant comparative data to generate a further research programme in remote communities where a critical lack of antenatal education, service and resource provision was reported (paragraph 22). The aim of the project was to identify and implement a contextually designed, community-based educational meta-intervention to have a positive impact on reducing harm to maternal health in remote communities of Myanmar. The objectives were to co-develop culturally relevant networks and partnerships at the national, regional and community levels; build community capacity to address health and socio-economic challenges influencing maternal health; analyse contextual factors influencing education and maternal health within ethnic groups in remote and post conflict regions; co-design and evaluate innovative, culturally relevant educational initiatives to address development challenges with regional and local communities; identify common and unique cultural components to inform the design, and equality screen the proposed interventions; and contribute to development research through the co-design of a theoretically innovative, holistic and contextually adaptable maternal health education model.

Regions were selected for their remote location, their broad similarities, but also their unique ethnic cultures and contexts. A meta-level approach, using evidence-based research, was designed to create cost-effective, integrated and innovative maternal health educational resources. These were to be completed across four work packages and in three phases: baseline, data collection, pre- and post-intervention (Table 3.2). Data collection would be completed by four regional teams of six data collectors from partner organisations; these teams were trained in ethics, research methods, data collection methods, community needs assessment and communication skills. Data analysis was undertaken by staff and students from two local universities, with supervision and mentorship provided by the lead university. Regional teams were trained and supported in the delivery of the meta-intervention comprising three educational programmes. These teams

Table 3.2 Overview of stakeholders and methods.

Work packages (WP)	Phases		
WP 1 Partnerships and Processes (Governance and oversight of project)			
	Phase 1 – Data collection	*Phase 2 – Analysis and design*	*Phase 3 – Intervention*
WP 2 – Mothers in Myanmar	Data collected from mothers, fathers, TBAs and family members: surveys, focus groups, interviews and community needs analysis	Analysis and triangulation of data to understand cultural and contextual factors influencing decision-making and health-seeking behaviour Design of three educational units for remote communities to address contextual challenges	Translation of three educational units. Cascade training of trainer's programme Implementation of intervention in two village tracts per region
WP 3 – Saving Lives, Saving Babies	Data collected from medics, midwives, EMOC workers and health departments (survey, focus groups and interviews) Mapping of EMOC centres and healthcare services	Analysis and triangulation of data to understand cultural and contextual factors influencing EMOC care in remote areas Design of comprehensive EMOC healthcare training programme for HCWs in remote areas.	Design of thirteen-unit EMOC training programme Training of EMOC healthcare workers
WP 4 – Enterprising Myanmar	Data collected from village tract leaders, village and community leaders, business owners and entrepreneurs	Analysis and triangulation of data to understand cultural and contextual factors influencing entrepreneurship Design of two units to promote entrepreneurial traits and programmes, including business development and community development projects	Cascade training for business and community leaders Delivery of intervention in two village tracts per region

Source: Authors.

included ten trainers from each region working in partnership at local levels to implement the educational programme whilst building local capacity by training community leaders, health workers and other beneficiaries in each region.

The research was funded by the UKRI Global Challenges Research Fund through a call that positioned education as a driver for sustainable development. Its design and scope were informed by partnerships and collaborations between higher education institutes in the UK, Thailand and Myanmar, as well as a range of international and local partners working in maternal, public and ethnic health, and community development networks. An international advisory panel from South East Asia (SEA) and the UK would oversee governance and management of the project. The project structure comprised partners from the UK, Thailand and Myanmar and was divided into a series of research teams, each with responsibility for discrete work packages. Researchers involved in the work packages comprised four academics, two project partners, four international academics and one research fellow who was based between the UK, Thailand and Myanmar. The four lead researchers (one male and three female) are all senior academics with extensive research experience; three have antenatal and maternal health, and emergency obstetric care – including working in conflict related contexts – and one has experience in social enterprise. International activities and operational teams collaborated in the delivery of the project in the regions; regional teams comprising project staff were responsible for operational activities; and a research management team was responsible for the overall delivery of project objectives.

The ethical dilemma and courses of action

The research team was awarded funding in November 2019, and the project started on 1 February 2020. Just over a month later, the full impact of the Covid-19 pandemic became clear, and in March, countries across the world were in full societal lockdown. Ethical approval had already been secured by the lead higher educational institution and an agreed collaborative ethical approach between the UK, Thailand and Myanmar was established, enabling knowledge exchange of in-country ethical processes, international ethical standards and project policies. However, considering the immediate restrictions and sanctions imposed during the pandemic and a shift in the fragile political situation in Myanmar, the research team were required to navigate a series of ethical dilemmas from the outset (paragraph 22).

The impact of Covid-19

The societal restrictions during the Covid-19 pandemic presented the most immediate challenge to the research team. All international travel was halted, impacting the scale and scope of planned research activity. In response to this, the research team prepared a comprehensive risk register in the early months of the project which was consistently monitored and updated as the impact of the pandemic unfolded. The register identified a number of governance, external, regulatory and compliance, financial and operational risks; these were analysed and scored according to the likelihood of them happening and their potential impact. Crucially, the process included identifying a target risk score that the team would be happy to accept. Measures already in place to reduce and control each risk were then used to re-score the likelihood and potential impact; if these did not reduce the risk to a satisfactory level, identification of additional actions was required to provide ongoing assurances that risks were being controlled effectively. This included identifying a risk owner (named individual/group) and a timeframe and process for review. For example, a governance risk of interruptions to scheduled face-to-face advisory board and project management meetings due to Covid-19 was initially highly scored. However, responsive measures, including the use of online training arrangements and ensuring all project stakeholders had access to appropriate technology, significantly reduced the risk, with the primary investigator (risk owner) taking responsibility to monitor online attendance and follow up any team absences.

Budget cuts

A secondary impact of Covid-19 was a reduction in project financing due to cuts in the overseas development budget, through which the project was funded. A loss of funding will inevitably affect the extent to which the original objectives of the research can be fulfilled, and so a positive relationship with the funders and partners was crucial at this juncture to identify and agree on refined outcomes that would still deliver key elements of the project. A redesign of the budget enabled completion of only Phase One in the first instance, with further changes made once the funding situation was clarified.

Cuts to the project budget also necessitated scaling back of the selected regions to focus on three remote ethnic regions. Operational teams were formed in each region, and accompanying new partnership agreements were put in place. These teams, which included key in-country stakeholders, were critical to the ethical and governance processes of managing teams of more than eighty people across the three regions. In two regions, the projects were led by ethnic health departments and in one region, it was managed by a key regional stakeholder who facilitated the partnership with the ethnic health organisation.

Political shifts

Human rights are a fundamental ethical principle, and within a conflict setting, this is even more critical. The context and governance structures of this project were multilayered and complex due to Myanmar's complicated political and ethnic history, so key members of the advisory committee provided training to the UK-based team to support a better understanding of the complex sociopolitical situations between the different regions. Training sessions focused on the history, political context and ethnic considerations unique to each region of Myanmar (paragraph 74).

Initial project agreements were in place with Ethnic Health Organisations (EHO) – who lead healthcare within their own areas – and regional stakeholders. However, there was some caution from these partners, particularly in relation to information and data sharing, due to long-standing tensions between the Burman military and government and the ethnic regions, as well as the project's involvement with the Ministry of Health and Sport.

Caution was exacerbated further by a surge in political unrest, requiring immediate strategic pivoting of the research design (paragraph 47). As the national election approached in 2020, communication and activity ceased in the Government-controlled regions following a coup in February 2021. This resulted in stalled relationships and one region withdrawn from the project. Regional ethnic stakeholders, who operated their own healthcare structures and governance processes, were approached to recommence the work following a cessation in violence across the three remaining regions. To offset the possibility of further changes in the political situation which might hold up or stop the research in one or more selected areas, several additional research sites were held in reserve.

Conflict impact assessment

The ongoing sociopolitical tensions across the lifetime of the project required the creation of a Conflict Impact Assessment (CIA) tool, an extension of the risk registry, to manage governance and decision making during critical phases of data collection. The CIA tool included risk assessment, decision making and reporting within a changing environment designed to support the mitigation of risks to inform real-time project activities before commencement (BERA, 2025, paragraph 74). This process was designed by the SEA Research Lead and managed by the Research Fellow and SEA Research Lead. An integral part of this was a review of the implementation of the distress protocol, completed after data collection (if necessary), to ensure participant follow up, and to check that any issues had been addressed and recorded appropriately, given the sensitivity of the topic.

Situational context and researcher safety

Researcher safety was a priority in this project due to the multiple contextual factors and volatile political situation in Myanmar. At the time of the study, the UK's Foreign, Commonwealth & Development Office (FCDO) advised against all travel to parts of Myanmar, which led to both the SEA Research Lead and Research Fellow travelling regularly to Thailand to meet with stakeholders and regional teams before, during and after the project (paragraph 22).

Culturally acceptable pseudonyms were used in local and wider communication and the teams were brought to a neutral setting outside the country for team meetings, enabling open and honest conversations on the conduct of the research. This reciprocal approach was very much in keeping with the relational culture within SEA, and the consistency of such engagement was instrumental in maintaining strong relationships and partnerships over the duration of the project. A social media restriction around project activities was agreed upon, implemented and maintained by project staff to maintain researcher and participant safety, as it was known that national actors often monitored social media activity. Physical challenges to data collectors were managed through avoidance of conflict areas, avoidance of lone working and engagement of local staff at all stages through local partnerships. Team members working in the field checked in frequently while travelling, and meetings were set up as requested to support all project activities. This facilitated a quick response and decision-making process for teams, and although it was at times challenging for the small Ulster team to manage, it allowed the avoidance of potential issues in real time and served us well.

Partners and champions: The importance of communication

Project partners have been a vital force in facilitating the project, and their engagement underlined the relational context within which the research was undertaken. Many of the relationships had been built by the SEA Research Lead over an extended period prior to the project commencement, with trust and transparency maintained through close working practices with regional teams. Another key component of the project's success was the existence of at least one champion in each region who was actively committed to facilitating the relationships and processes needed to improve maternal health. Due to the instability of the sociopolitical climate, clear communication strategies were set up to monitor and manage ethics, governance and project management in Phases One, Two and Three (paragraph 22). These were designed to support team decision making and included secure, encrypted messaging services, established to maintain continuous communication between the SEA Research Lead and Research Fellow, and with regional teams; this ensured communication in hard-to-access areas, as well as between regional and local teams.

Contextual barriers

Transport and access in remote areas were a significant barrier, and the project's regional and operational teams consistently leveraged partnerships to facilitate access at the local health level and village level. The data collection and intervention phases were both carried out during the rainy season in years two and three of the project; whilst this made transport more challenging, the sociopolitical situation was more stable due to the monsoon weather. Since the completion of the project, the conflict has escalated across all regions, with enforced conscription; the impact on local communities has resulted in an exodus from many areas and a significant increase in internal displacement and refugees, although many borders remain closed. This has impacted the current sustainability of the project in some areas, but all partners will have access to the final resources to implement across the regions and all EHOs have committed to future partnerships once the situation has stabilised.

Data security

Data security and back up was a particularly important consideration, not least its potential political sensitivity within a conflict setting. Considerations around data related to the way it was collected but also its storage and network security (paragraph 47). To address this, a risk analysis and data-sharing policy was agreed by the funder and all staff were trained in ethical and data management processes which was reviewed throughout the project lifetime. All participants were informed of data storage methods during the information and consent phases of data collection.

All data was anonymised as soon as possible and was uploaded and erased from local devices before project teams travelled to another site. This was to reduce the risk of data being accessed en route or putting teams at risk. All consent forms and other identifying materials were kept separate from data files. Due to the remote areas, there was a lack of access to electricity, so electronic devices were bought which could operate offline and be uploaded with an internet connection. All communities were anonymised to reduce the risk of harm, and only the EHOs, core regional and lead university team had records of these. This information was kept on a password-protected, cloud-based university system with restricted access.

It was possible that sensitive data might be collected within the context of the research due to the ongoing political and ethnic tensions. In addition to the HEI data-sharing policies, the international research team of co-investigators agreed on several steps specific to the different ethnic contexts. These included creation of a project-level data management and sharing policy agreement between partners; adoption of a 'need-to-know' basis for data sharing that was limited between ethnic health organisations, partner organisations and others; anonymisation of all data at individual village and village tract level, prior to analysis; creation of additional data-sharing restrictions where necessary or requested.

Permissions processes, confidentiality and consent

Within the post-conflict setting of Myanmar, the confidentiality of participants and their data was an ongoing priority (paragraph 1). The process of obtaining consent was carefully designed to be contextually sensitive and culturally relevant. As a community-based culture, collective decision making is the norm and is multilayered, involving a sequential gradient of permission. In each area, permission was sought initially from the relevant health organisations and regional stakeholders, local health authorities within each district, community leaders and then village tract leadership teams. Finally, permission was given by the village leaders and leadership teams. The process was facilitated by regional co-ordinators and research assistants with support from the SEA Research Lead and Research Fellow.

All data was anonymised, and consent forms and other identifying materials were kept separate from data files. Consent forms were gathered and confirmed by the research fellow, but these were managed by the regional teams to ensure the safety and security of the participants, the research teams and the local communities who contributed to, or took part in, the research. In a community-based culture, individual informed consent looks different from that provided in a western culture. This highlighted two crucial considerations. Firstly, due to the challenging and potentially dangerous political and conflict setting, people were often nervous to write an identifiable name. Secondly, low literacy levels could also prohibit the collection of meaningful signatures. Awareness of these obstacles enabled the project team to opt for the collection of informed consent in three ways: signed, fingerprint or verbal, with two witnesses (data collectors), all of which are customary in this culture. All data collectors were trained in ethical values, including informed consent, respect and confidentiality. Data collectors were also trained to observe and respect the preferences of any participants.

Alternative courses of action

Reflecting on the development and delivery of this complex project, the research team identified two alternative courses of action – one retrospective and one forward-looking to further iterations of the research.

The impact of Covid-19 affected the delivery of training within the project. Initially, all training was to be held in person, but due to the pandemic, this was moved to online provision. On reflection, the research team considered that recorded and translated sessions may have been a better option, as access to these would have allowed the data collectors to review the sessions as a reinforcement of their learning.

Within the project plan, the original aim was that the research fellow would be based between SEA and the UK to maintain a close working relationship and oversight role between the multiple partners. The combined impact of Covid-19 and the unstable sociopolitical situation meant that this was no longer a realistic option, and so more frequent travel was required by the research fellow and SEA research lead. It is unclear if this approach had any influence on the management or if it interrupted the strength of the partnerships, co-production and trust that was consequently built up between the project teams. Therefore, special consideration of the potential impact of online data collection is required on immersion and trust building, fundamental to research in conflict-affected settings.

Final thoughts

The intricacies described in the two case studies illustrate how the intersection of political and cultural practices can deepen the ethical complexities of the research process. Case Study One was a doctoral study and inevitably smaller in scale and scope compared to the operational and management expectations required in Case Study Two. Nonetheless, individually, they offer a unique perspective on the distinctive characteristics and realities of conducting international/intercultural research. Collectively, they provide a valuable roadmap for other researchers that signposts not only the diversity of inherent potential challenges but also how an adaptive and responsive approach can safeguard the integrity of research practice in these contexts.

Ethical guidelines provide a framework of the overarching principles; however, a more nuanced understanding of how to mitigate identified ethical concerns in the field and the implications of these need careful consideration.

Firstly, the situational and positional status of the researcher(s) in fragile, conflict-affected states required careful consideration of the sociocultural contexts in which both case studies were undertaken. The research teams of both case studies were drawn from largely peaceful societies, from another institution, country and culture; therefore, the need to engage in preliminary field work, to innately understand the dynamics of conflict and reduce perceptual gaps were necessary. Accountability in the ethical conduct of the research was based on the normative values of openness, honesty and objectivity to recognise differences and potential challenges (paragraph 22). It was important, therefore, that any situational interaction within and between researcher(s) and participant(s) was underpinned by an understanding of, and respect for, how others behaved, communicated and perceived the world around them. Similarly, researcher positionality was influential in the navigation and management of participant recruitment, engagement and data collection, and so it was necessary to ensure personal subjectivities were identified and addressed. In these instances, risk-assessment protocols had a pivotal function in identifying and offsetting potential oversights – for example, failure to familiarise with the host culture – which could have led to power imbalances or potential participant exploitation that would have ultimately rendered the research biased.

Secondly, the issue of researcher safety created challenges to both the internal and external validity of the research in both case studies. The contextual implications of undertaking research in conflict-affected regions underlined the strategic procedural importance of establishing what activity is reasonable in the conduct of research in politically febrile regions. The research design in each case study identified practical and logistical constraints as well as alternative courses of action that would still allow for data collection. The development of contingency (communication and action) plans that were reactive and adaptive to the realities of the field work was evident from an individual, methodological and organisational standpoint. In some respects, alternative methods could be viewed as a trade-off – albeit a necessary one – for the researcher; however, ethical guidelines relate as much to the researcher as to those being researched and should be applied with equal diligence.

Thirdly, research partnerships were a key consideration in the design and delivery of the projects, and the intricacies of co-ordinating these in an ethically safe manner underlined the sociocultural sensitivities involved. In each instance, researcher-participant engagement required communication that resonated on a humanist level (where the welfare and wellbeing of the individual was at the heart of decision-making) and at a situational level (where the contextual backdrop affected research relationships and, consequently, the research process and outcome). Further, the utilisation of local actors as co-generators of research facilitated collaboration and the building of relationships. Such approaches may also mitigate harm to local communities done by extractive data collection techniques.

Finally, any research engaging in international/intercultural research must acknowledge that initial plans may need to be revised and that a degree of adaptation and flexibility is integral to ensuring ethical principles are upheld. Gaps in the applicability of westernised ethical guidelines to international fieldwork exist. The need for a *culturally competent ethical framework* can help address perceived inequities and imbalances of power that may undermine the integrity of the research process (Gray et al., 2017: 24). For example, some indigenous groups have challenged the universal codes that researchers adhere to, citing them as not aligning to their cultural, social, religious and ethnic requirements and developing their own protocols, codes or guidelines. Such culturally tailored guidance cannot aspire to respond to all situations or questions that researchers face within the field. In these instances, balancing perspectives that illuminate understanding of, and respect for, other cultures as well as clear communication are essential criteria. Doing so may aid the transparent exchange of information and ideas and the development of mutually positive relationships between researcher and participants.

Reflective questions

1. How might your positionality (gender, race, class, ethnicity, geographical location, etc.) impact the way you understand and/or engage with international/intercultural research?
2. What do you consider to be the key feature of good practice in international/cross-cultural research?
3. When embarking on intercultural research, how would you consider issues of power intersectionality, inequality and ethics?
4. As a researcher, what approaches would you adopt to be inclusive of marginalised groups and communities or those living in difficult circumstances?
5. How can we support researchers who, operating in a global environment, co-create relevant culturally ethical principles and practice?

Further reading

1. Cossham A., Bidwell P., Pai L. (2024). Research ethics and international and cross-cultural research: Fiji and Aotearoa New Zealand. *Journal of the Australian Library and Information Association*, 1–8. https://doi.org/10.1080/24750158.2024.2359153.

   This article presents a critical appraisal of the complexities of cross-cultural, international and collaborative research from both the perspective of the researcher and the ethical approving body.

2. McMahon, E. and Milligan, L. O. (2023). A framework for ethical research in international and comparative education. *Compare: A Journal of Comparative and International Education*, 53(1), 72–88. https://doi:org/10.1080/03057925.2021.1876553.

   This article provides a framework to facilitate the enactment of international and comparative education ethics in research. It identifies five 'universal' ethical values which may help researchers navigate ethics in a global world.

3. Shanks, K. and Paulson, J. (2022). Ethical research landscapes in fragile and conflict-affected contexts: Understanding the challenges. *Research Ethics*, 18(3), 169–92. https://doi.org/10.1177/17470161221094134.

   Drawing on the researchers' experience of conducting research in fragile contexts and the challenges experienced, ranging from funding, research design, dissemination and ethical gatekeeping.

4. Wefers H., Krüger V., Iza Simba N. B., Guandinango Y. A. (2023). Ethical challenges of cross-cultural research – the example of a psychological research project in the andean context. *Journal of Empirical Research Human Research Ethics*, 18(4), 233–45. https://doi.org/10.1177/15562646231181880.

   This article presents a psychological research project as a case study to highlight the ethical challenges of engaging in a cross-cultural empirical research project.

Note

1. https://www.who.int/activities/ensuring-ethical-standards-and-procedures-for-research-with-human-beings.

2   *Paragraph 1*: Individuals should be treated fairly, sensitively, and with dignity and freedom from prejudice, in recognition of both their rights and their differences arising from age, gender, sexuality, ethnicity, class, nationality, cultural identity, partnership status, faith, disability, political belief or any other significant characteristic (BERA, 2024, paragraph 1).

3   *Paragraph 22*: The application of [ethical] principles in different social, cultural and political contexts may require careful negotiation, adaptation and sensitivity, and there is ultimately no substitute for the integrity and ethical code of the individual researcher (BERA, 2024, paragraph 22).

4   *Paragraph 47*: In an international context, researchers should be aware that it may not be possible to protect data stored within some jurisdictions from scrutiny (BERA, 2024, paragraph 47).

5   *Paragraph 74*: In some circumstances, research findings will be regarded as sensitive information by sponsors, commissioners or other research stakeholders (for example, because they raise politically or culturally controversial issues) (BERA, 2024/2025 paragraph 74).

References

All European Academics (ALLEA) (2023). *European Code of Conduct for Research Integrity*. Germany: ALLEA.

British Educational Research Association (2024). *Ethical Guidelines for Educational Research* (5th ed.). London: BERA. UK: BERA. https://www.bera.ac.uk/publication/ethical-guidelines-for-educational-research-fifth-edition-2024.

Gray B., Hilder J., Macdonald L., Tester R., Dowell A. and Stubbe M. (2017). Are research ethics guidelines culturally competent? *Research Ethics*, 13(1), 23–41. https://doi.org/10.1177/1747016116650235.

Universities UK (2019). *The Concordat to Support Research Integrity*. London: Universities UK.

World Health Organisation (2018). Myanmar RMNCAH Factsheet July 2018. *South East Asia: World Health Organization South East Asia, Regional Office*. http://cdn.who.int/media/docs/default-source/maternal-health/rmncah-fs-mmr.pdf?sfvrsn=4576662a_2.

World Health Organisation (2024). *Ensuring Ethical Standards and Procedures for Research with Human Beings*. Geneva: WHO. www.who.int/activities/ensuring-ethical-standards-and-procedures-for-research-with-human-beings.

4

Decolonising Research Ethics, Exemplifying Definition and Principles

by *Carol Azumah Dennis*

Case Study Introduction: Conceptions of quality in a Further Education college

This chapter presents a case study to illustrate the definition and principles of important considerations and what might be involved in *decolonising research ethics*.

A cisgendered Global North female doctoral candidate, Natasha has recently been promoted to the position of quality manager in a Further Education college in the south-east of England. This is a large City Centre College that over the last few years has grown in size through mergers and acquisitions to become the sole provider across multiple sites of post-16 vocational education. The staff in the college are 75 per cent white British and 25 per cent other, other made up of several different groups, including white non-British Europeans. There is substantial variation in how this mix is replicated depending on curricular area, hierarchical positioning and site location (BERA, 2024, paragraph 1).[1]

Given that Natasha works for the college, she considers herself an insider researcher. Her research explores conceptions of quality in Further Education college teaching. The work connects well with her professional responsibility, part of which includes helping the college recover from a recent OfSTED inspection (BERA, 2024, paragraph 19).[2] Having been classified as failing with a 'requires improvement' headline, the college has an institutional action plan charting their journey to a successful good or outstanding grade. The college has twelve months to prepare for re-inspection.

The teachers with whom Natasha works and who will form a significant part of her research participants are demoralised and fearful for their jobs after what they all agree was an eviscerating inspection process. Many object to the way they were treated by the OfSTED team and felt the criticism was unfairly and disproportionately directed (by the college if not OfSTED directly) at specific members of staff (BERA, 2024, paragraph 37).[3] They point out that they have between them decades of teaching experience both in the UK and in the various international contexts in which they have previously worked (BERA, 2024, paragraph 1). Natasha suspects that in part, their willingness to engage with the research is driven by their desire to speak back to the OfSTED process and feel that their voices – that is, their version of the world and the college – have been heard (BERA, 2024, paragraph 3[4]; paragraph 22).[5]

The college management was ambiguous about granting Natasha permission to undertake her research. Agreement was secured amidst much discussion and negotiation. Fearful that her presence would dissipate and misdirect energy, senior managers ultimately agreed to the research on the basis that it might reasonably help raise the profile of the college in a positive way. In part, they were influenced by the many publicly available turnaround quality case studies provided by the Education and Training Foundation. They envision the college providing a shining, publicly celebrated example, objectively certified by a doctoral thesis from a prestigious university, of how to turn an institution around from failing to excellence (BERA, 2024, paragraph 3; paragraph 6).[6]

The research underpinning this case study draws on multiple methods – documentary analysis, focus groups, analysis of artefacts, interviews and autoethnography to answer the question, 'What counts as quality when teaching in a Further Education college?'

The politics of location: Author and positionality

The case study is a composite based on various authorial experiences as a doctoral researcher, examiner, supervisor, practitioner and academic working in various UK-based colleges and universities. This location provides the template through which the imprint of what is considered interesting, necessary, convincing, relevant and worthy of attention is filtered.

I write about the issue of decolonial research ethics from the perspective of a diasporian, a child of the African diaspora. I am one of the UK's too few Black British academics, born in the UK with Jamaican parentage. I engage in such positionality statements with a high degree of reluctance. I'd like to imagine that what I say is more significant than what or who I am. But this, this is not a possibility. The privileged stance of the universal unmarked scholar is only obtainable through the supremacist delusion associated with specific kinds of bodies: white, male, cisgendered, heterosexual, able. All other bodies are bound to speak from an ethnographic location. The discussion this leans into is one that confronts the question of *who* is part of an ethical dialogue and *on what basis* they enter the discussion? This contested negotiation between different forms of inter-subjectivity is an irredeemable ethical question. The reflexivity implied by introducing a discussion of decolonial research ethics with a statement of the author's own positionality is a deliberately (though not exclusively) decolonising move. My own positionality is part of my institutional profile.[7]

Decolonisation with a view to pedagogic intervention is a frequently invoked discussion (C. Dennis, 2018). The exploration of decolonising research ethics is less well pronounced in comparison to these other adjacent concerns. To illustrate, a cursory Google search on 'decolonising the curriculum' with restricting quote marks, returns 3,700 results; a parallel search on the term 'decolonising research ethics' returns 51 results. There are, of course, seminal and significant texts in this space, which will be drawn upon during the discussion.

A decolonised approach to research ethics works from the premise that all knowledge, including ethical knowing, is local. The significance of this stance is profound. It challenges the overrepresentation of man as standing in for human (Wynter, 2003). This is perhaps the trouble with Decolonising

Research Ethics. It is not a discrete field of enquiry that enables a laser-like exploration of a neatly contained matter of concern. It is a struggle that must be encountered on multiple overlapping fronts. What surrounds decolonisation is a history of empire and its legacy enshrined in racialised social hierarchies.

Defining *decolonial research ethics*

The first dilemma encountered for *decolonial research ethics* is a definitional one. Colonisation and decolonisation are historical parallels; both movements trace their beginnings to the same moment.

As an expansive global movement, decolonisation theorises inequalities, violence and injustice that constitute global knowledge production along multiple axes of social, intellectual and material relations. In encountering this terrain, we also encounter empire, imperialism and other world epochal forces as woven into the fabric of the social sciences. No aspect of our social, cultural and intellectual lives is out of scope. The significance of this is sharpened when we are reminded that knowledge production in the field of education as a subset of the social sciences has traditionally been handmaidens of colonial and imperial interests (Swartz et al., 2024), inextricably linked to European colonialism, imperialism and eugenics (Andrews, 2018). The reminder that all knowledge is geopolitical is a reminder that European attempts to represent provincial experience as if it were universal, and its assumption of holding the space as the 'sovereign theoretical subject in the social sciences' (Swartz et al., 2024) has been thoroughly disrupted in the decolonisation process.

Despite the all-inclusive pervasive potential encoded in 'decolonisation', a meaningful exploration of the associated research ethics needs parameters and definition. The extensive historical and global dimension nonetheless sits behind this focus even if they are not directly and explicitly referenced in the discussion. There is no prescribed standard, model or practice that delimits and defines decolonised research ethics. Scholarly conversations in this space are ongoing and contested, as are their theoretical foundations, constituent elements and practice. Running throughout this discussion is the suggestion that decolonial research is at its sharpest, most critical edge when it includes either Indigenous groups or 'Other/ed' communities who are potentially vulnerable and whose lives deserve to be treated with respect.

The argument put forward here is that decolonial research ethics does not only become relevant only when racialised or minoritised others are part of the process. Indeed, in unsettling the supremacy of colonial legacies, a legitimate defining aspect might be accepted as unsettling the dominant epistemic order.

Put plainly, decolonised research ethics foregrounds a particular set of research dynamics, but the discussion may comfortably be inflected and considered in multiple scenarios, including that of a Global North cisgendered researcher working with Global North cisgendered research participants. Put plainly, decolonisation does not cease to be relevant when racialised others are not directly part of the encounter (Davies and Burrell, 2020).

The suggestion here is that the first tentative step towards decolonising research ethics is the unveiling of hegemonic notions rooted in colonisation. It is a response to an invitation to explore one's own context positioning and complicities, to unlearn privilege and to establish an ethical relationship to difference – an invitation to learn from below (Andreotti, 2007). The centring of subaltern voices disrupts Eurocentric epistemologies. The Global North researcher working in a Global North university with research participants who may also be from the Global North is thus invited to transgress the abyssal divide (Santos, 2014) and accept the otherness of the other, rendering their voices as relevant and existent. In the geopolitics of knowledge, the decolonial embrace allows epistemologies cultivated in the Global South to shed light on the Global North. This is of particular interest here as the current interest in decolonisation might reasonably be located in the single act of protest by University of Cape Town student, Chumane Maxwele (Ahmed, 2017) which has continued to resonate across the globe.

The discussion becomes meaningful when tangible suggestions are made about how to incorporate decolonial ethics in research projects. Inspired by Thambinathan and Kinsella (2021), this chapter suggests that *decolonial research ethics* is premised on four defining features.

These are suggested here as: (1) exercising critical reflexivity; (2) reciprocity and respect for self-determination; (3) embracing 'Other(ed)' ways of knowing, and finally; (4) embodying a transformative praxis.

The case study and its variations are explored using the above definitional account of what it means to decolonise research ethics. Some of these characteristics have already been threaded through the contextualising discussion. They are now deployed more explicitly to underline the salient aspects of research practice.

Exercising critical reflexivity

The first group of research participants with whom Natasha conducts a focus group and interviews seem to speak with one voice. They are adamant in their rejection of the OfSTED judgement and view it as unfair. They feel that they have been 'pushed under a bus' by the college management and compelled to take responsibility for decisions that were not of their making. Natasha finds she has plenty of data for exploration but can't help feeling there is a degree of performativity in what they are saying. She is aware of her position and role in the college and has a sense that research participants invest much more power in her role than she is able to wield in the organisation. Her fear is that her research has become a way for them to 'talk back' to OfSTED and the college. This is closely followed by an anxiety that she is simply not positioned to enable the research to offer any degree of fidelity to their aspirations.

The participants in the research are in a vulnerable position, and it is debatable whether the proposal is one that should be operationalised. The college and the careers of research participants are held in an uneasy balance, and it is possible that research in this context is a distraction. The hierarchical positioning of colleagues who have already experienced a humiliating public critique is exaggerated when they are already racialised as belonging to communities whose status with the structures they work with is precarious.

Critical reflexivity requires the researcher to consider how her research is implicated within the wider sociopolitical relations within which her project is located (Patel, 2014). A decolonised research ethic is an all-encompassing ethic that exceeds the specific procedural conduct of any given research project. It draws attention to the ontologies, epistemologies and axiology associated with the research itself. What this leans into is a view of decolonial research ethics as requiring an inelegant portmanteau: an onto-axio-epistemology (Watson and Knight-Manuel, 2020) enquiry.

With reference to the case study provided, this implies particular lines of ethical enquiry. An organisation – the further education college – implicated in the reproduction of structural inequalities along lines of race, gender, heteronormativity and class (Youdell, 2006) falls within the ethical frame. An organisation – OfSTED – whose purpose is to flatten and fold the social and structural dynamics of unequal educational outcomes into the individual pedagogic prowess of specific teachers or departments or colleges (C. Dennis, 2014) is likewise within ethical scope. The purpose here is not to argue a specific line of critique in relation to a research subject as such, but within a decolonial research ethic to require a critically reflexive exploration of research approaches, questions, subject matter and how the research/er is inextricably entangled within them.

The questioning continues – how / Is education in general and OfSTED in particular implicated in the reproduction of structural inequalities; how does the research/er position herself in relation to these social dynamics? How is the research/er positioned within the neoliberal flattening of the social and cultural undercurrents that determine educational outcomes? How does this research/er position itself in relation to research participants, racialised professionals in the most precarious positions in institutional hierarchies, often the lesser paid and most expendable. And how are these broader dynamics articulated in and through this research? It is hard to overestimate the ramifications of this stance. It implies ethics as shaping not only the day-to-day quotidian conduct of research but having disruptive implications for what research is undertaken and the conclusions it explores, as well as the procedural aspects of how the research is conducted.

Decolonial research ethics amplifies the voice of the subaltern – those less likely to be heard. But as the project progresses and the researcher becomes increasingly aware that research participants are telling a performative tale, how is this to be negotiated? The critical reflexivity invited here is one that explores whose world view the researcher subscribes to? Which voices are incorporated with or without question? Whose version of the college and quality is accepted as rational and true? And how is the researcher herself, her stance, privilege and positionality implicated in this swirling vortex?

Reciprocity and respect for self-determination

Within a *decolonial research ethic*, reciprocity is not limited to 'reporting back' to the community (Smith, 2021). It plays a pivotal role in reshaping ethics into a relational encounter. Grounded in trust, mutuality and respect, an anti-colonial understanding and answerability, decolonising ethics takes the form of an ongoing epistemic conversation involving the active seeking of guidance and reiterative feedback (Taha, 2018).

There is an issue here that extends beyond the confines of this brief chapter that considers the extent to which some methodologies are inherently more ethical than others and whether the scope for decolonisation is writ large in some approaches but less well pronounced in others. This discussion is beyond scope. However, when Sandoval defines a methodology of the oppressed, she includes sign reading; deconstruction and reconstruction of signs; an ethical commitment to justice; and the differential movement that keeps all aspects of being in motion and mutation. Decolonial ethics in relation to method and methodology is by definition an ethics which includes 'an ethical commitment to justice' (Sandoval, 2013: 130).

Mindful that her research is being hijacked in uncomfortable and unanticipated ways – to speak back when this was not what she had encouraged, Natasha decides to change her approach. She is deeply invested in her project but decides she would like to work more collaboratively with research participants. She returns to her university ethics committee with a revised set of proposals. Instead of focus groups and interviews aimed at understanding approaches to quality, she wants to broaden the project to incorporate a more collaborative approach. Her intention is to set out the situation as she sees it, including her hesitation in viewing the project as facilitative of 'talking back', and then to invite interested others to participate more fully in the project. This will mean inviting them to offer their perceptions of what research is necessary, helpful and interesting in the quality space, exploring with them the best questions to ask and how to answer those questions. Through a series of open meetings, she aims to redefine the project and what it needs to explore.

Focussing on the case study presented, a decolonising research ethic utilises a principle of reciprocity to drive a collaborative approach from conception of the study to its end, establishing collective ownership over the entire research process, data analysis and dissemination. This is not without its challenges or dilemmas.

In participatory research, the researcher gains amongst other things a doctoral degree, a prestigious publication, or a step up the career ladder. The research participants contribute towards this gain, while perhaps receiving a £25 gift voucher, a digital badge or something else less tangible. The anthropologist MacLeod (2009) in the spirit of ethnographic confessional awareness claims sensitivity to the issue of 'using' the young men who were part of his study for his own ends. His research participants share his awareness, inflecting his gaze to instead focus on the extent to which he enjoys a lucrative monetary gain from their stories. He is acutely aware that the gain is more than monetary. In persuading savvy and reluctant young men to tell him about their experiences, he confesses to feeling like a 'manipulative bastard' (MacLeod, 2009: 492). His gain is not restricted to money, it includes 'the power, privilege, and prestige', the book in which he tells their stories brings him.

The ethical challenge here is that the approach is an extractive one. It uncomfortably replicates relationships fashioned on neo-colonial exploitation. Research participants provide the raw data; the researcher transforms this into valuable intellectual material: theory. But what if research participants are repositioned, accepted as equitable intellectuals even if they are not granted enjoyment of the societal positioning associated with being an 'intellectual' (Gramsci, 1988). Educational research, as an arm of state-sanctioned positioning of intellect, profits from, and is therefore dependent on, a mythology that grants the status of intellectual to a specifically defined and employed group of people. A decolonial ethic which ascribes to a value of reciprocity and respect for self-determination challenges this stance.

This gestures towards an interrogation of the extent to which research can be non-extractive. Patel (2014) suggests this is related to a decolonial ethic that seeks answerability rather than accountability. That is one that refuses the notion of knowledge as property, a resource for which we are all locked in insatiable competition to consume. It instead positions the researcher and each utterance 'as primarily a response to preceding utterances of the given sphere' (Patel, 2014: 371): an ongoing conversation over time.

The stance explored here is one that gestures towards possibility for respect, mutuality and reciprocity between researcher and research participants. There are no straightforward or unequivocal answers here. The researcher may think carefully about the different power dynamics, how she is implicated within them and the deep institutional or structural inequalities within which she is embedded.

The exploitative risk is less pronounced if her participants are the more senior managers in the organisation. But this silences those in the more precarious situation. She will then have to carefully consider how their voices are brought into the study and on what terms and possibilities of working towards equitable dialogic engagement.

McGranahan and Rizvi (2016) point out that the people amongst whom we conduct our research are much like us. A sentiment that may be caught in the Igbo proverb, 'Different peoples speak different languages, but the sound of their coughing is the same.' This is not quite a retreat to the universalism it may echo. It instead implies that people may have knowledges, sophisticated understandings of the world and embedded within these are theories. Yet these utterances are embroiled within a hierarchy that renders them as vernacular or raw data or description; non-reciprocal relations of appropriation, expropriation mean they are only conferred the status of theory when emanating from *the researcher*. A decolonial research ethic avoids the researcher as the only significant decision-maker while reducing *informants* to mere sources of empirical data who are incapable of producing knowledge and theory (Castillo et al., 2023).

Embracing 'Other(ed)' ways of knowing

A third feature of decolonial ethics is an embrace of other(ed) ways of knowing. Without this embrace, it is hard to see how these others might become co-researchers, or their ideas anything other than the raw materials for extraction, refinement and exploitation.

If the challenges of working across difference are muted in the case study suggested, this is because the research participants are skilled cultural code-switchers. Able to adapt, assimilate, blend in or erase in order to fit in. Were the researcher to travel and conduct similarly framed research in an international context, the issues would quite suddenly become more intensely pronounced. The difference is arguably one of degree rather than substance.

If the case study presented placed research participants in an international context, there would be previously articulated and well-rehearsed ethical guidelines. The European Commission Directorate-General for Research and Innovation (EC, 2016) reminds researchers of the need to avoid ethnocentricity in migrant research. Researchers are advised to pay attention to their overarching frameworks and processes. They are challenged to abandon Western methods and theories if they prove prohibitive. In 1974, the Tapp report (Tapp et al., 1974) advised that cross-cultural research can only be undertaken ethically when done in collaboration and partnership with members of the cultural community.

The case study presented may be viewed from multiple perspectives and locations. In its original form, it assumes Natasha is working in a UK context with which she is familiar. This might be changed slightly to reposition her as UK based, undertaking a research degree awarded by a European university, with having secured temporary employment as a lecturer in West Africa. She has decided to undertake her research project in Accra, Ghana. The research focus remains the same, an exploration of different conceptions of quality, but in the absence of an international institutional counterpart, the threat and stigma associated with OfSTED is removed. Her research participants are not entirely free from micro-political aggressions, but the tensions between kinship groups do not encode the toxicity associated with colonisation, racialised oppression and inferiorisation.

The suggestion here is that an approach which might be standard when a Global North scholar is undertaking research in the Global South, or any global context with which she is unfamiliar, might usefully be replicated as a decolonising strategy. Indeed, there are many methodologies that advise the use of a *critical friend*. A 'critical friend' (Costa and Kallick, 1993) is someone who joins a research team on the basis that they more closely align with the bodily lived experience of research participants when these are at odds with that of the researcher; their acknowledged contribution might be that of a cultural broker. Along with member checking, this is an approach that might usefully guard against *thingification* in academic research (Césaire, 2004). This guards against the risk present in the exemplar case study that the colonised and their diasporic descendants are viewed as little more than objects, the raw materials whose epistemic DNA might be extracted, refined and commodified by the academic.

While the idea of a critical friend, in the form of a *cultural broker* (Rasing, 2022), to mediate research and points of difference, whether with international or home research contexts, is a welcome operationalisation, it is by no means sufficient. A cultural broker may well represent a quotidian practice for a decolonised methodology, but unless what sits behind it is a willingness to listen and embrace other(ed) epistemologies, it is unlikely to be successful. The cultural broker, similar to the research participants for whom they facilitate an exchange, might quite easily be subject to the same conflation that links the value of knowledge to the value ascribed to the knower. If a researcher is unable to hear the voice of research participants, is it possible that they might similarly be unable to hear the voice of their cultural broker?

The embrace of other(ed) epistemologies requires a more fundamental shift away from a capitalist market, commodification, competitive individualism and hierarchies. It requires the researcher to realise that the people who make their research possible – as the Igbo proverb says – 'cough just like us'. They have sophisticated understandings of the world, and embedded in those understandings are theories. The researcher can only absorb and speak with (rather than for) research participants and their cultural situation when they decentre themselves. This speaks to methodology. With or without a cultural broker, a decolonised research ethic explicitly rejects western-centric colonial frameworks. It amplifies research practices and knowledges that the academy has excluded, silenced, manipulated and 'epistemically demeaned as intellectually inferior and lacking credibility' (Johnstone, 2021: 637). It aims to 'understand and prioritise local conceptions of local realities, without filtering those realities through the interpretive machinery of elite European social theory' (Bejarano et al., 2019: 8).

This is of course a disruption. Slow, ethical relation-building through space and time is more radical, in its own quiet way, than generating endless decolonial 'products' (Castillo et al., 2023). It is the mechanism through which an embrace of other(ed) ways of knowing becomes possible. A *decolonial research ethic* invites the exploration of holistic ways of knowing; narrating, storytelling and sharing, reflective and reflexive practices; deep engagement; connecting mind, body and soul (Lamichhane and Luitel, 2023). The multiple, diffuse and diverse approaches stand as a challenge to disrupting the hegemonic presence of Western-modern post/positivist epistemologies, reconnecting researcher and their participants with the lifeworld of research participants.

The approach is one replete with risks of appropriation, tokenism and simplifying patronage. Ideas may be decoratively picked up and used to adorn the necks of colonial masters going native. Somewhere between handwringing apologetic caution and blustering supremacy is a space where the researcher might.

> dance among the diverse perspectives to unmask the complexity and chaos embedded in the phenomenon under study. (Lamichhane and Luitel, 2023: 442)

Embodying a transformative praxis

Decolonial research ethics calls for researchers to be respectful, sensitive to the context in which they are operating, paying attention to understanding and abiding by the beliefs of the group. It also calls for an alertness to how the findings from research are used which may include considering the extent to which research participants and their affinity groups benefit from research.

The case study may be developed to illustrate this point.

Natasha successfully completes and defends her thesis at viva. Within a few months, she publishes her work in a few high-profile key journals. While she might have preferred open access publishing, it was not financially an option available to her. Informally she hears news of the college and colleagues who participated in her research. Once the re-inspection was completed and the institution had secured its highly sought-after outstanding OfSTED grade, research participants were still in a difficult situation. There have been dramatic overnight redundancies and restructures.

An embodied transformative praxis boundaried by theories, values and practice (Freire, 1968) refuses the idea of research as a pure intellectual undertaking. There is no knower who stands distinct and separate from a world about which they are imbued with knowledge. There is a kind of knowing that is as affective, emotional and embodied as it is intellectual. Imbricated in a world, a decolonial research ethic is barely distinguishable from activism, albeit an activism that implies serious critical reflection and scholarship. *Decolonial research ethics* involves the full body as participant in meaning. The mind/body separation has no place here – after all, the colonisation of the mind was physically encoded in race and only made possible through bodily subjugation.

Embodying transformative praxis assumes a holistic thought-action-reflection-action regarding each aspect of the research process, from positionality, place of enunciation, privileges and biases. The scholar committed to transformative praxis does more than respect and reflect the struggles of research participants and their affinity groups; she stands with them.

There are several ways in which Natasha might have made her research accessible to her former colleagues:

She might, for instance, have chosen to offer a series of seminars and workshops in which the learning as process and outcome is explored, presenting alongside research participants.

She might have chosen her publications carefully and deliberately drafted research reports for practitioner-focused journals. Formal and informal publication spaces might include blogs, podcasts or videos hosted on social media platforms.

She may well have acceded to managers' desire for high-profile success stories for the college, and on the basis of her research ensured that the high profile included a fair account of the role key members of staff have played – even if they are anonymous.

It is not impossible that colleges may be willing to waive anonymity and feel that a full and named credited involvement with the project enhances their professional profile.

To maintain a faithful adherence to the insight the research offers, while protecting identities, Natasha might consider other modes of research presentation – an allegorical tale featuring mythical characters in another world – space and time – context.

She might have spent time specifically with research participants and, based on her study, shared with them insights that might strengthen their institutional or professional positioning.

There is a risk here of Natasha seeming openly partisan. An embodied transformational praxis is an activist, rather than a bystander, orientation.

Ethical challenges: An expected disclosure and an unwelcome request

Natasha thought through the intricacies of her research with meticulous care, but is not surprised when the unexpected and unanticipated emerge. Occupying as she does the space between insider/outsider, college employee and postgraduate researcher, the challenges were inevitable and plenty.

Her employment was project focussed and short term, and so while as an *insider* she explored an aspect of professional practice in which she was implicated, she was simultaneously an *outsider* who reads policy documents, institutional action plans and engages in work-a-day discussion but does so with the critical mindset of someone who is both enacting and analysing these texts. This might not be a position she publicly assumes, but her insider/outsider status is one her colleagues might well ascribe to her anyway. She has in some ways become a confidante as colleagues share insights and experiences with her that they might not have articulated in any other space. What this leads to is a series of sometimes unexpected conversations.

Natasha returns to the college post-viva and post peer-reviewed publication for a social event: a successful re-inspection celebratory drink. She had heard through informal conversations that the outcome of inspection was finely balanced between an outright fail or good, but with little context. During the evening, a senior manager begins to chat with her about the recent visit. She discloses the nature of the fine balance between two dramatically different OfSTED outcomes and explains how the department managed to secure the positive grade. Ultimately, she in a matter-of-fact way discloses that the department had fabricated evidence. The nature of the fabrication is peripheral at this stage. It simply changed the name of the qualification that had been awarded to particular students to comply with a recent policy change. Natasha is stunned.

This uncomfortable disclosure is here framed in one way but might have been framed in several different and competing ways. This was an intense evening for Natasha. An unanticipated and uncomfortable disclosure was followed by a request. I have geo-located her project elsewhere – in Accra, Ghana. In this instance, a senior manager is aware of her project and has asked if he may read it. This seems ideal to her. After all, she wants to impact on practice, and this senior manager is well placed in the institution to make a huge difference to the potential impact of her work. Having carefully considered the comments her research participants have made, she can find nothing controversial or likely to lead to discomfort.

Each of these dilemmas is explorable within the confines of BERA guidelines. And in the space between right and wrong, the researcher will need to locate a preferred stance. In this discussion, they are reviewed in terms of how a decolonial ethical stance might address them.

Ethical decision-making: Activist, advocate and a methodology of friendship

While confidentiality and anonymisation are fundamental to the research encounter, there are moments when that confidentiality and anonymisation have to be compromised. Most obviously safeguarding, an actual or potential crime or whistle blowing. There will be other moments when the compulsion to intervene (B. Dennis, 2009) is inescapable; the researcher may have to live with a nagging doubt: 'Did I do the right thing?'

The intention here is to propose a stance consistent with a *decolonial research ethics* in relation to both dilemmas. The conclusion reached may well cohere with conclusions arrived at by other means. It is the justification that sits behind the chosen course of action that matters.

In this chapter, the defining features of decolonial research ethics were enumerated along four lines – reflexivity, reciprocity, embracing other(ed) epistemologies and transformative praxis. Gonzalez (2003) suggests a less concrete notion of braiding: accountability, context, truthfulness and community. One cannot create decolonial research by reference to ethics. A decolonial research stance produces a particular set of ethical considerations. Hence the somewhat inelegant portmanteau: an onto-axio-epistemology (Watson and Knight-Manuel, 2020).

Natasha considers the political and policy context within which the OfSTED inspection takes place. This includes not only a local context within which provision of the sort provided by the college is limited and depriving the area of this provision would have undesirable impacts – no ITE provision in a vast geographical area. Nor is it limited to an acceptance that while college leaders, OfSTED, students and policy makers use a common language about quality, but have vastly different meanings. In other words, her focus here is not simply on the right or wrong of fabrication but the broader contextual cloth into which the fabrication is sewn. This situates the research as thoroughly part of the context. Not simply because of her insider/outsider status, but by her being part of a research community in the broadest sense. In her judgement, OfSTED as the ultimate arbitrators of what counts as quality is rightly contested. Their being thoroughly implicated in an education system that reproduces inequality (Patel, 2014). This convinces Natasha, after weighing things up in several directions, that there is no ethical imperative to disclose the fabrication.

Natasha's second dilemma is more ambiguous. Ostensibly, there is nothing wrong with a member of the research site reading a research report, which is in any case already in the public domain, albeit via a heavily paywalled peer reviewed journal.

Natasha is confident that the identity of her research participants is suitably obscured – she has used pseudonyms, relocated them institutionally within other departments, hierarchical positions or roles and structures that might locate them, she has also masked other identification features – gender, ethnicity, race, etc. – ensuring that changing these demographic locators does not impact on the tone, tenor or texture of their contributions. She is nonetheless mindful that the work does include comments that might be viewed as critical of senior managers. Before responding, she contacts research participants to ask if they mind the work being shared within the institution.

To her surprise, they are vehemently opposed to the idea. They voice their objection in loud, unambiguous and at times accusatory tones. They feel betrayed. And given the precarity of context, fearful. Natasha reassures them that nothing has been revealed about her work, apart from what was required for permission to access the site. They know she has done the work, but nothing about her methodology, who she has spoken to, what contributions they have made or conclusions she has drawn. It is striking in this exchange that Natasha's research participants held a very different sense of risk and danger from that held by Natasha. She listens to and responds to their anxieties in a respectful way, addressing their concerns carefully. With these reassurances, her research participants are less anxious.

Here, the advice offered by Madison (2020) is helpful. She envisions the academic as both advocate and activist; having embraced other(ed) ways of knowing and committed to transformative praxis, her first obligation is to her research participants.

Obligated to respect the preferences of her research participants, Natasha decides against making her research public within the institution. After months of close work, sharing of confidences and building mutual trust, she had become a friend (rather than merely a researcher). A methodology of friendship could not countenance betrayal. To soften senior managers' disappointment, she refers to her guidance on creative approaches to dissemination and considers other approaches to sharing her research which actively involves research participants. This negates any sense of disclosure that is not with their complete agreement.

Final thoughts

This chapter identifies *decolonial research ethics* as bounded by four principles:

1   exercising critical reflexivity;
2   reciprocity and respect for self-determination;
3   embracing 'Other(ed)' ways of knowing, and;
4   embodying a transformative praxis. (Thambinathan and Kinsella, 2021)

This is however a fluid space whose points of anchorage are in the process of being cast. The chapter frames principles are more important than any definitive guidelines, as they provide a template for navigating so far unexplored spaces. There is always risk associated with a journey, not the unknown; the perspective of research participants may differ radically from the perspective assumed by the researcher. Reciprocal respect and active listening are fundamental. Decolonisation is an ethical rather than pragmatic commitment. It is not promoted simply because it leads to better research with deeper disclosure. It does these things, but more importantly, it is consistent with a broader ethical commitment to equity and social justice.

Its relevance is expansive and extends beyond global majority researchers working with global majority research participants.

Reflective questions

The approach to decolonisation offered in this chapter is open to contestation.

1 Can you outline your view of the relevance of decolonisation in research ethics?
2 We have located the protagonist in this case study in some detail, along lines of sex, gender and race. To what extent are these locations explicitly and unambiguously relevant to the research process?
3 The practice of positioning the researcher so clearly in the research is widely accepted, but is it necessary, or of value? What does it add to or obscure about research?
4 The writer of this chapter assumes a particular stance in relation to coloniality and equity, one that frames them as ethical wrongs associated with epistemic violence: Do the four defining characteristics argued as *decolonised research ethics* adequately counter those ethical wrongs and their associated epistemic violence?
5 What concrete strategies might it be possible for a researcher to adopt to step beyond the limits of their own positionality and – ethically live the research with their participants.

Further reading

1. Cupples, J. and Grosfoguel, R. (Eds.) (2019). *Unsettling Eurocentrism in the Westernized University*. Abingdon: Routledge.

   This book beautifully curates a rich resource of ideas and approaches to what it might mean to decolonise research.

2. Smith, L. T. (2021). *Decolonizing Methodologies: Research and Indigenous Peoples*. London: Bloomsbury Publishing.

   This is a seminal text in which the writer's cogent critique of the Western concept of research articulates an indigenous approach aimed at replacing Western academic methods.

3. Mignolo, W. D. and Walsh, C. E. (2018). *On Decoloniality: Concepts, Analytics, Praxis.* Durham, NC: Duke University Press.

   The writers bring together other(ed) ways of theorising other(ed) conceptual instruments and other(ed) genealogies to transcend dismantling the master's house and instead build our own decolonial houses of thought.

4. *Savage Minds – notes and queries in anthropology* (from 2017 – anthro{dendum}) Savage Minds | Notes and Queries in Anthropology and anthro{dendum}

   Savage Minds (Anthro{dendum} from 2017) is a group blog that has, since 2005, been writing about sociocultural anthropology. The last blog entry was posted in January 2024. Committed to public anthropology, the site includes a series of blogs by Carole McGranahan and Uzma Z. Rizvi, about Decolonising Anthropology.

Notes

1   BERA believes that educational researchers should operate within an ethic of respect for all persons – including themselves – involved in or affected by the research they are undertaking. Individuals should be treated fairly, sensitively, and with dignity and freedom from prejudice, in recognition of both their rights and their differences arising from age, gender, sexuality, ethnicity, class, nationality, cultural identity, partnership status, faith, disability, political belief or any other significant characteristic (BERA, 2024, paragraph 1).

2   An important consideration is the extent to which a researcher's reflective research into their own practice impinges upon others – for example, in the case of power relationships arising from the dual roles of teacher/ lecturer/ manager and researcher, and their impact on students and colleagues. Dual roles may also introduce explicit tensions in areas such as confidentiality. These may be addressed appropriately by, for example, making the researcher role very explicit, involving an independent third party in the research process and seeking agreement for politically controversial research. Researchers who are researching their own practice should also consider how to address any issues arising as a result of collecting data for different purposes – for example, using data collected for evaluation purposes for research purposes, or vice versa (BERA, 2024, paragraph 19).

3   Researchers should recognise concerns relating to the time and effort that participation in some research can require – the long-term involvement of participants in some ethnographic studies, for example, and the repeated

involvement of particular participants in survey research or in testing for research or evaluation purposes. Researchers should consider the impact of their research on the lives and workloads of participants, particularly when researching vulnerable or over-researched populations. Equally, researchers should do what they can to ensure that relevant individuals and communities are not, intentionally or otherwise, excluded from participation in their research (BERA, 2024, paragraph 37).

4   Participants in research may be actively or passively involved in such processes as observation, experiment, auto/biographical reflection, survey or test. They may be collaborators or colleagues in the research process, or they may simply be implicated in the context in which a research project takes place. (For example, in a teacher's or lecturer's research into their own professional practice, students and/or colleagues will be part of the context but will not themselves be the focus of that research.) It is important for researchers to take account of the rights and interests of those indirectly affected by their research, and to consider whether action is appropriate – for example, they should consider whether it is appropriate to provide information or obtain informed consent. In rare cases – such as some politically volatile settings, or where researchers are investigating illegal activity – covert research can be defensible (BERA, 2024, paragraph 3).

5   BERA expects UK researchers to apply the same ethical principles to research they undertake outside of and within the UK. The application of these principles in different social, cultural and political contexts may require careful negotiation, adaptation and sensitivity, and there is ultimately no substitute for the integrity and ethical code of the individual researcher. In some countries it is advisable to work with a local person as a co-researcher/co-investigator in order to establish adequate levels of trust with prospective local participants. Appropriate permission should be sought from relevant authorities (such as community or religious leaders or local government officials) in cultures that adopt a collective approach to consent. However, in such cultures it should not be assumed that individuals cannot make their own informed decisions about whether or not to take part in the research (BERA, 2024, paragraph 22).

6   Researchers have a responsibility to determine the most relevant and useful ways of informing participants about the outcomes of research in which they are or were involved. Researchers should consider whether and how to engage with participants at the conclusion of the research, for example, by debriefing them in an audience-friendly format or by eliciting feedback on the findings. Should conflicting interpretations arise, researchers should normally ensure when reporting the research that participants' views are presented. Researchers may wish to offer

participants copies of any publications arising from projects in which they have participated, and/or to produce reports or summaries specially tailored for the research context, taking into consideration potential subsequent uses of this material, including by the participants' institutions. A project website can be a way of reaching and engaging with participants and others (BERA, 2024, paragraph 6).

7   My positionality is further elaborated upon at: https://www.open.ac.uk/people/cd9469.

References

Ahmed, A. K. (2017). #RhodesMustFall: Decolonization, praxis and disruption. *Journal of Comparative and International Higher Education*, 9(Fall), 8–13. https://www.ojed.org/index.php/jcihe/article/view/890.

Andreotti, V. (2007). An ethical engagement with the other: Spivak's ideas in education. *Critical Literacy: Theories and Practices*, 1(1), 69–79. https://blog.ufes.br/kyriafinardi/files/2019/08/Critical-Literacy-Lynn-Mario-Andreotti-cljournalissue2volume1.pdf.

Andrews, K. (2018). The Black Studies Movement in Britain: Becoming an Institution, Not Institutionalised. In J. Arday, and H. S. Mirza (Eds.), *Dismantling Race in Higher Education Racism, Whiteness and Decolonising the Academy*, London: Palgrave McMillan (pp. 271–88).

Bejarano, C. A., Juárez, L. L., García, M. A. M. and Goldstein, D. M. (2019). *Decolonizing Ethnography Undocumented Immigrants and New Directions in Social Science*. Durham, NC: Duke University Press.

BERA (2024). *Ethical Guidelines for Educational Research* (5th ed.). London: BERA. https://www.bera.ac.uk/publication/ethical-guidelines-for-educational-research-fifth-edition-2024.

Castillo, R. C. A., Rubis, J., and Pattathu, A. G. (2023). Critical research ethics as decolonial praxis: A comment and responses. *International Quarterly for Asian Studies*, 54(1), 21–37. https://doi.org/10.11588/iqas.2023.1.21746.

Césaire, A. (2004). Discourse on Colonialism (J. Pinkham, Trans.). In D. Brydon (Ed.), *Postcolonialism: Critical Concepts*. London: Routledge (pp. 310–39).

Costa, A. L. and Kallick, B. (1993). Through the lens of a critical friend. *Educational Leadership*, 2(51), 49–51. https://mlcp.co.uk/userfiles/files/Through%20the%20Lens%20of%20a%20Critical%20Friend.pdf.

Davies, A. and Burrell, K. (2020). 'They Call It "White Guilt: The Module"' Reflections on Teaching Postcolonial and Decolonial Geographies. In D. Bendix, F. Müller, and A. Ziai (Eds.), *Beyond the Master's Tools?: Decolonizing Knowledge Orders, Research Methods and Teaching*, Lanham, MD: Rowman and Littlefield Incorporated (pp. 143–62).

Dennis, B. (2009). What does it mean when an ethnographer intervenes? *Ethnography and Education*, 4(2), 131–46. https://doi.org/10.1080/17457820902972762.

Dennis, C. (2014). Positioning further education and community colleges: Text, teachers and students as global discourse. *Studies in the Education of Adults*, 46(1), 91–107. https://doi.org/10.1080/02660830.2014.11661659.

Dennis, C. (2018). Decolonising Education: A Pedagogic Intervention. In G. K. Bhambra, D. Gebrial, and K. Nişancıoğlu (Eds.), *Decolonising the University*, London: Pluto Press (pp. 190–207).

European Commission (EC) (2016). *Guidance Note – Research on Refugees, Asylum Seekers and Migrants*. Directorate-General for Research and Innovation. https://ec.europa.eu/research/participants/data/ref/h2020/other/hi/guide_research-refugees-migrants_en.pdf.

Freire, P. (1968). *Pedagogy of the Oppressed* (M. Bergman Ramos, Trans.). New York: Continuum.

Gonzalez, M. C. (2003). An Ethics for Postcolonial Ethnography. In R. P. Clair (Ed.), *Expressions of Ethnography: Novel Approaches to Qualitative Methods*, New York: State University of New York Press (pp. 77–86).

Gramsci, A. (1988). Intellectuals and Hegemony. In D. McLellan (Ed.), *Marxism: Essential Writings*, Oxford: Oxford University Press (pp. 264–82).

Johnstone, M. (2021). Centering social justice in mental health practice: Epistemic justice and social work practice. *Research on Social Work Practice*, 31(6), 634–43. https://doi.org/10.1177/10497315211010957.

Lamichhane, B. R. and Luitel, B. C. (2023). Postcolonial autoethnography: healing wounded humanities. *Cultural Studies ↔ Critical Methodologies*, 23(5), 437–46. https://doi.org/10.1177/15327086231188040.

MacLeod, J. (2009). *Ain't No Makin' It, Aspirations and Attainment in a Low-Income Neighborhood*. London: Routledge. https://doi.org/10.1201/9780429495458.

Madison, D. S. (2020). *Critical Ethnography: Method, Ethics, and Performance*. Thousand Oaks, CA: SAGE Research Methods. https://doi.org/10.4135/9781071878965.

McGranahan, C. and Rizvi, U. Z. (2016). *Savage Minds: Notes and Queries in Anthropology*. Blog post, Decolonizing Anthropology Blog. https://savageminds.org/series/decolonizing-anthropology/.

Patel, L. (Leigh) (2014). Countering coloniality in educational research: From ownership to answerability. *Educational Studies*, 50(4), 357–77. https://doi.org/10.1080/00131946.2014.924942.

Rasing, W. C. E. (2022). People, places, and practices in the arctic. In C. Buijs, K. van Dam, and F. Laugrand (Eds.), *Anthropological Perspectives on Representation*, Abingdon: Taylor and Francis (pp. 171–84).

Sandoval, C. (2013). *Methodology of the Oppressed* (Vol. 18). Minneapolis, MN: University of Minnesota Press.

Santos, B. de S. (2014). *Epistemologies of the South, Justice against Epistemicide*. London: Routledge. https://doi.org/10.4324/9781315634876.

Smith, L. T. (2021). *Decolonizing Methodologies: Research and Indigenous Peoples*. London: Bloomsbury Publishing.

Swartz, S., Nyamnjoh, A-N. and Mahali, A. (2024). Visibility, Voice and Emancipation: Suggestions for Decolonising Research Ethics in the Sociology of Youth. In J. Bessant, P. Collin, and P. OKeeffe (Eds.), *Research Handbook on the Sociology of Youth*, Cheltenham: Edward Elgar Publishing (pp. 416–28). http://hdl.handle.net/20.500.11910/23367.

Taha, D. (2018). Methodology, reflexivity and decolonizing refugee research: reflections from the field. In K. Grabska, and C. R. Clark-Kazak (Eds.), *Documenting Displacement, Questioning Methodological Boundaries in Forced Migration Research*, Montreal, QU: McGill-Queen's University Press (pp. 56–80).

Tapp, J. L., Kelman, H. C., Triandis, H. C., Wrightsman, L. S. and Coelho, G. V. (1974). Continuing concerns in cross-cultural ethics: A report. *International Journal of Psychology*, 9(3), 231–49. Doi: 10.1080/00207597408247108.

Thambinathan, V. and Kinsella, E. A. (2021). Decolonizing methodologies in qualitative research: Creating spaces for transformative praxis. *International Journal of Qualitative Methods*, 20, 1–9. https://doi.org/10.1177/16094069211014766.

Watson, V. W. M. and Knight-Manuel, M. G. (2020). Humanizing the black immigrant body: Envisioning diaspora literacies of youth and young adults from West African Countries. *Teachers College Record: The Voice of Scholarship in Education*, 122(13), 1–28. https://doi.org/10.1177/016146812012201304.

Wynter, S. (2003). Unsettling the coloniality of being/power/truth/freedom: Towards the human, after man, its overrepresentation-an argument. *CR: The New Centennial Review*, 3(3), 257–337. https://doi.org/10.1353/ncr.2004.0015.

Youdell, D. (2006). Diversity, inequality, and a post-structural politics for education. *Discourse: Studies in the Cultural Politics of Education*, 27(1), 33–42. https://doi.org/10.1080/01596300500510252.

5

International Research and the Ethics of Language

by *Phil Wood, Aimee Quickfall and Kaisa Pihlainen*

The ethics of language in research

Where research is developed which includes researchers from more than one country, there may well be a need to use more than one language. Holmes (2016: 91) argues that,

> Multilingual research also implies intercultural research.

This means that researchers bring their own languages, but with this, also contrasting assumptions and worldviews. Researchers might bring different social, political and cultural contextual knowledge which needs to be worked with to create a coherent approach to a research project. Therefore, time may need to be spent understanding the starting positions and sometimes initially hidden assumptions or perspectives which individuals may bring to the research. As part of this finding of common ground, Christians (2011, cited in Holmes 2016) argues that work in international projects should make use of multilingual dialogue as it opens up the unseen and unheard, as researchers and participants are able to use their first language through which they are more able to voice their perspectives. Holmes (2016) sees this as a way of ensuring that all participants have a possibility of participation.

The role of language in engaging with participants needs careful consideration, as to ask them to engage in languages other than their own brings with it important questions and considerations. Beyond the basic issue of potential misunderstandings or difficulties in engaging in a second, third or fourth language, Eaton (2020), analysing official research ethics guidance from several countries, highlights the complexities concerning informed consent. Can informed consent be given if a participant is attempting to read information in a language other than their own, particularly when ethics-related documentation may be complex and long in nature? The participant information sheets developed in many UK universities are overly technical and legalistic as they are as, if not more, concerned with risk management and legal protection than they are with ethics. In addition, dependent on the focus of the research, it might be the case that research requires engagement with participants who have poor literacy or who may even be illiterate. In this case, it might be more realistic to ask for verbal consent. This shows the situational complexity of ethical processes and decisions.

The presence of situational complexity when developing ethical decision-making is especially important when developing research projects in an international context. Christians sees ethics committees as working on the basis of the Enlightenment project, resulting in ethics codes which are stale, and attempting to work within a 'values-free' Social Sciences. Christians (2011, cited in Holmes, 2016: 94) also states that

> [Research ethics] *is also hierarchical (demonstrating a scientist-subject positioning) and glosses over the way the researcher is embedded in the research site and research culture.*

Hence, whilst ethics committees tend to work to a deontological, rules-based system which universalises the issues and questions relating to the ethics of a project, this becomes problematic in international contexts. As research cultures vary, and the situatedness of social research exposes the complexity of engaging with people from different cultures, the simplistic universality of committee systems may become barriers to ethical practice 'on the ground'.

Linguistic problems and the importance of context are highlighted by Smith et al. (2008), who were involved in public health research carried out in China. Research data was captured in Chinese and was then translated so that all researchers could engage with it. But translation causes issues. Firstly, it can be expensive and time-consuming. Secondly, meaning can be lost, as there are sometimes no words to express in one language when compared to the original used for data collection. As Smith et al. (2008: 1) reflect

> *The grammatical structure of Mandarin differs substantially to the English language which means the narrative of an interview might not be captured accurately.*

One way of dealing with this might be to use an interpreter, but if they become the interviewer, then the researcher may lose control of the process. Smith et al. (2008: 3) further go on to say that

> *The risk of misinterpretation, misunderstanding and loss of a respondent's intended meaning is high unless the translator is familiar enough with the dialect to convey 'conceptual equivalence'.*

These reflections demonstrate the complexities of engaging with the BERA guideline (2024) statement (the relevant element is underlined below) that:

> *The institutions and settings within which the research is set also have an interest in the research, and ought to be considered in the process of gaining consent. Researchers should think about whether they should approach gatekeepers before directly approaching participants, and whether they should adopt an institution's own ethical approval and safeguarding procedures; this is usually a requirement. (Furthermore, in some circumstances researchers may have a statutory duty to disclose confidential information to relevant authorities; see paragraph 48.)* <u>*Particularly when researching in more than one language or culture, researchers should consider the effects of translation and/or interpretation on participants' understandings of what is involved.*</u> *(paragraph 11)*

Berman and Tyyska (2010) also focus on the use of translators and interpreters, in their case, within feminist and community-based research. They argue that translators are generally seen as occupying a role which eliminates error, a technical position which ensures accuracy. But in their study, Berman and Tyyska believe that translators should be part of the research team, engaged with the wider understanding of the research to ensure that they play a role in design as well as execution. This will allow them to have a better understanding of the research context and how participant reflections relate to the research, an important context in creating meaningful translation.

Holmes and Rajab (2023) take a different approach and argue that, where possible, research should take place in the local language and hence that any decisions concerning language use should be decided at the beginning of a project, with more reflexivity during a project, including resisting the hegemony of English as the sole medium for research activity. However, whilst this is an important ethical point, it is unfortunate that English has become a lingua franca in both academia and wider culture, meaning that there is an implicit assumption in teams that it will be the medium for communication, often as across a multinational team, English might be the only language that is common, at least to some degree, to all.

As the issues above amply demonstrate, whilst there might be clear points in terms of ensuring fair and ethical language use, as with other ethical issues, the situated messiness of research and communication does not always resolve so easily. Meier, van der Voet and Yau (2024) reflect that

> *many authors believe that there are rarely straightforward ethical decisions to make in research because ethical codes do not always follow the complexity and specificity of research in social science for instance. Instead researchers often need to mark informed decisions on a 'case-by-case basis'.*

They therefore distinguish between two foci for ethics:

1 Procedural/professional research ethics. This is the formal, institutional research ethics set out in codes of conduct.
2 Research ethics. Decisions relating to a particular project in a specific context, that is, the practical application of ethics to real-world, complex contexts.

They then go on to highlight that, as a result of both the procedural ethics of committees, but also the research ethics of particular projects, research ethics must be a thread running through a whole project, leading to constant reflexivity about the process. Therefore, we argue that this leads to the need for situated ethics to be a clear element of the wider ongoing ethical process, but also in relation to linguistic issues and challenges.

This means that ethical decisions when working in multilingual contexts require researchers to reflect on the issues which are set out above, such as the need to consider how language is used, the loss of accuracy and nuance in translation, how participants are to be engaged in ways that are ethical via informed consent and the language in which their views are captured. This complexity is rarely caught by the formal ethical procedures of research ethics committees, as they tend to work on a deontological foundation of 'ethical rules' which are seen as universal. However, the literature above suggests that we need a much more situational approach, which is an ongoing reflexive process throughout the project, and which may require regular recalibration.

Finally, beyond the research process itself, there is the issue of publication. The BERA guidelines (2024) state that:

> Where research is conducted in a setting in which English is not the prevalent (or only) language, researchers should make the fruits of their research available in languages that make it locally accessible. (paragraph 71)

This is a very direct statement suggesting that the ethical route to research is to ensure that reporting is done in other languages as well as English. This is a positive statement which attempts to ensure that participants and the wider community have the opportunity to engage with research in their own language. However, whilst it is a positive and wholly reasonable general statement, as we will outline in the case studies below, the situated ethics of research projects makes this a more complex issue to unpick. For example, researchers from other countries may well wish to publish research in English as it may have more utility for them in terms of career progression. However, this might be in tension with the ethical practice of ensuring participants have access to the outcomes of research. Hence, again, this is an issue which needs to be navigated within the complexity of projects, with the statement above perhaps being seen as a loose guide rather than the command it is written as.

Case Study One: Researching with participants in multilingual contexts

David and Mike teach a master's degree which predominantly recruits international students from Asian countries. They lead a module on research methods and have felt that the students struggle with some of the content each year. They want to help students gain a better understanding of these areas of the module. To do this, they decide to use action research to explore two aspects of student learning: the philosophical basis for research and collecting and using quantitative data.

They begin by reflecting on the problems students have had in the past, based on previously submitted assignments. This shows that the philosophical foundations of research methods (e.g. ontology, epistemology, paradigms) are poorly understood, and students often show confusion in their written work. They therefore think about what the learning challenge is and develop a two-hour seminar designed to help students gain a better understanding. The same approach is taken when considering basic quantitative research. They have observed that many students appear to avoid using quantitative techniques, and often their use of even basic statistics is poor.

They apply for ethical approval from the university ethics committee, involving observation of the sessions, followed by inviting a group of six students to share their notes, before completing both a focus group and individual interviews. They discuss the notes the students have taken and their more general understanding of the areas covered.

Having designed each of the sessions, David and Mike teach each in turn. During each session, they observe the reactions of students, especially how they engage with activities, and after the seminars, they carry out a focus group and then the individual interviews. All materials, both for the project (for example participant information sheets and consent forms) and the seminars themselves, are taught using English materials and the medium of communication.

Students are willing to take part in the research and share their experiences and reflections in focus groups and interviews conducted in English. Some of their notes are in their first languages, and the discussion of these in the interviews tends to focus on translation with less focus on the meaning and processes involved in the students making these notes. On occasion, there is some difficulty in making the meaning of some technical terms clear, mainly those around philosophy, and both David and Mike are conscious that these discussions about terms become a little confused.

The focus group meeting is quite informative, but three of the students tend to dominate, all with strong abilities in English, whilst those with weaker abilities and/or less confidence in their use of language tend to be quiet, and when they do offer responses, they tend to be short and generally descriptive.

Once they have analysed the results, David and Mike use the data to present at a large national conference in the UK and submit a paper on their findings to a well-known academic journal which publishes in English.

Ethical dilemmas – case study one

A number of issues emerge from this case study relating to participants and the issue of language. Firstly, the researchers develop the areas they deem important based on their own reflections on students' submitted materials. Whilst this might be a good starting place for the identification of areas for concern, it assumes that they fully understand the issues faced by the students. They cannot be certain about the nature of the issues students face in these areas; is there a lack of understanding because of the fact that students will be writing in a second, third or more languages; it might be that the core issue is one of language and expression rather than a deep misunderstanding of concepts. However, it is only possible to begin to gain insight into these questions if the researchers first talk to students in an attempt to understand their perspective. Similarly, designing a seminar without input from students may make more assumptions about the type of activity students find most useful in aiding the development of their understanding.

Given the lack of linguistic knowledge David and Mike have, they could consider including an extra member in the research team. In some universities, international students will have in-session seminars with an English as a Foreign Language (EFL) tutor, or support for English for Academic Purposes (EAP). If such an expert could be added to the research team, they would be able to mediate and develop aspects of the research to minimise the potential barriers between the research team and the students, as they will have a great deal more knowledge and understanding about the particular needs of the students from a linguistic perspective.

The inclusion of an EFL tutor would also aid in minimising problems relating to the second issue in this case study, that of potential problems with understanding ethics paperwork. Even though students must have a relatively good command of English to be studying in a UK university, the technical and legal language used in research ethics may be beyond their full understanding. If this is the case, then can they give fully informed consent? If an EFL tutor is part of the team, they can play a role in working with potential participants to ensure that they do understand what the research will include, what they are being asked to do and what their rights are in terms of withdrawing from a study or making complaints.

The third issue which needs to be considered is that of the use of a focus group. Focus groups are often not easy to run as they can tend to prefer the inclusion of some voices at the expense of others unless carefully managed. Some participants will always be either more confident or more enthusiastic to be involved and to make their views known. It is also the case that intercultural issues may be important. Some students might find it disrespectful to make negative comments about their work, particularly when discussing their learning in front of other students and with their lecturers. In addition, there may well be a differential in the ability of participants to make themselves understood in English. As a consequence of this, some students may wish to remain largely quiet, only offering brief responses or responses when directly asked to contribute. This means that they might not have a full opportunity to feed back to the researchers about their new teaching approaches and how successful they have been for the students. It is difficult to correct these problems, but there are ways in which disparities might be minimised. One way in which the team could do this is to give the questions they will use to participants in advance. This will allow them to reflect, possibly translate questions into their own languages and formulate some ideas they wish to talk about. To facilitate this process, the EFL tutor might even be able to offer individual support to help students navigate this process. Such an approach, whilst imperfect, might allow for a more in-depth discussion and greater confidence for some students to engage and offer deeper reflections, particularly if the EFL tutor is present at the focus group to support.

Similar difficulties lay at the centre of the fourth issue, that of exploring philosophical and technical language in individual interviews. If the main issue that students are encountering concerning philosophical aspects of research is the meaning of core concepts, then attempting to discuss them in an interview adds an extra layer of complexity. If a student is unable to explain a concept, is it because they do not understand, or is it that they do not have the English language to explain? Similarly, there may be technical language relating to statistics that they are not able to clearly explain, whilst being able to carry out the statistical manipulations to complete a task. As with the focus group issues above, some extra support might help, but ultimately, it might be the case that researchers need to accept that they might not be able to capture detailed reflections from participants and that this becomes a recognised restriction in the research design.

What the issues above demonstrate is that many of the decisions made are situational. They can be reflected on and written into a research design ahead of time, but the way in which the researchers actually develop the details of the project will depend on contextually specific characteristics. The linguistic ability of those who agree to take part in the research cannot be known ahead of time, the degree to which assistance will impact on their ability to take part, and the degree to which they will have the confidence to develop full answers in focus groups and interviews must all be navigated and reflected on in real time. This may even require the research team to alter the details of how they engage with participants to ensure that they retain an ethical approach to the research. A rules-based approach to research ethics can offer a coarse framework within which the research team should operate, but it is the emergent, situational space in which they operate with participants which will be crucial to acting ethically.

Finally, there is the issue of research dissemination and publication. In their plan, David and Mike intend to report back to other researchers through a conference presentation and publication of a paper. The researchers will report in English, in part due to the fact that they cannot report in another language, and also because their audience is predominantly UK-based. In this situation, it is perhaps not surprising that this is the plan. However, there appears to be a missing element, reporting back to the students who participated in the research project. Given that this project focuses on the development of pedagogic approaches with international students, it is surely an ideal case study to use with the students themselves, perhaps as they begin to plan for their dissertations. By reporting back in this way, they can ensure that the students get the opportunity to engage with and understand the research in which they have been a part.

Case Study Two: Negotiating the complexities of working in multilingual research teams

Sarah, Neelam and Dan have had a keen interest in wellbeing research for some time. They have completed small-scale research projects in the UK over a number of years, focusing on the wellbeing of teachers and on university lecturers. A couple of years ago, they met two lecturers from a university in France at a conference dinner who had a similar set of interests. They have kept in contact, and in the meantime have also created a mutual contact with three academics in the Netherlands. It is suggested by the English team that they could apply for a research grant to do some joint research work focused on creating a resource kit to support schoolteachers and their wellbeing.

The planning for the project occurs through the use of online meetings, and the researchers use English at all times when they are talking to each other. The bid form is also an English medium document, and therefore any editing done by the team is done in English. The bid they develop has a three-part design.

1. Initial literature review and baseline research to inform the resource development
2. Development of resources, including the use of user experience sessions to gain feedback on draft resources for further development
3. Evaluation research to gain feedback on the use of the resources once complete.

The bid is eventually successful, and the project begins with an initial face-to-face meeting over two days, held in England, to plan and agree on the first step of the research. It is decided that each partner will carry out a literature review in their own language and then provide a presentation and a written summary to the other teams in English. Research will then be carried out locally in each partner country in the first language. The data collected will also be decided locally. Once the baseline research is complete, the three teams again present to each other and provide written summaries.

Using this baseline work, the team decides on the foci for resource development and each team takes responsibility for two or three elements of the total kit. All members develop the draft resources using English and, over twelve months, create a detailed set of resources. At another team meeting, this time in the Netherlands, they invite local teachers to come to engage with the resources and give feedback. From this feedback, delivered in English to the French and English teams, though in Dutch to the local team, further development of the resources is made. At a final meeting, the final draft of the resources is tested again, and as with the workshop in the Netherlands, the resources are demonstrated in English, with participants feeding back in English or French.

The final resources are now finished, and the project has funding to ensure that the full resource kit is translated into both French and Dutch. This ensures that all resources are available in the first languages of the three partners. A website is built to allow access to users, and again, all three languages are used to ensure that teachers can easily engage in their own languages.

Six months after the resources are made publicly available, the team carries out an evaluation by using a questionnaire with teachers to gauge their opinions of the resources they have used. The questionnaire is developed in English by the team and then translated into French and Dutch by local teams for use in those countries. This results in a large dataset that the team analyses.

In an online meeting, the team decides to write three papers to explain the process, resources and the results, focusing on teacher use of the resources they have had. The French and Dutch teams are keen to publish in English-medium journals as they have a greater impact index and are important for their promotion prospects. However, local conference opportunities are identified in all three countries which will be presented in local languages.

Ethical dilemmas – case study two

This project has a number of issues which need to be considered in relation to language due to the international nature of the work involved. Firstly, at the planning stage of the project, it appears that English has become the core language with little or no discussion. This might be, in part, due to the bidding document being presented in English, but this should not then implicitly determine the medium for future work with no discussion. Instead, there should be a discussion concerning the use of language throughout the project, including media for meetings, paperwork and research activity. This is done to some extent, as the team decides that baseline and evaluation research will be conducted in local languages, thus allowing participants to engage in their own languages. However, within the team, there is an assumption that English becomes the main language of communication. If this were discussed, then it might well be the case that English would still be used, but at least this would be a conscious choice rather than an assumption.

In a similar way, there is also a use of English in resource development. Again, this is likely the result of all team members being able to speak and work in English. As it is useful for the teams to be able to comment and give feedback on each other's work, English becomes a natural medium for development.

However, the team appreciates that this might cause problems as some concepts might not translate easily, and therefore it becomes important for the teams to communicate regularly to recognise and overcome potential misunderstandings. The use of English may also lead to some team members being sidelined, because their English is not as strong. This needs to be considered, and care taken over ways to create as inclusive an approach to team communication as possible.

Once the draft resources have been created, there is another issue in terms of trialling the emerging resources. As stated in the case study, on two separate occasions, teachers in the Netherlands and France were given the opportunity to trial the resources and provide feedback on their utility. However, because the resources are written in English, this will impact those who are able to engage in a positive and consistent way, and also in giving useful feedback. Teachers who are not able to read English to a relatively high level will be unable to take part in the user experience work, and hence it might be the case that the feedback gained becomes skewed. However, it is difficult to develop an alternative approach once English has been chosen for the draft work. Translation of the resources at this stage, whilst they are being developed, would be prohibitively expensive and therefore, whilst this might be the best solution, it is not sustainable. Therefore, whilst there is a better solution, the use of English as the sole medium may have to be accepted. Again, whilst perhaps not the most deontologically sound ethical solution, it is nevertheless a reasonable situational ethical solution; there may be those who are unable to engage well with the materials, but at least some reflections can be captured to help with further development which is better than having no feedback from which to work.

The final issue in this case study is that of publication. There are several dimensions to the publication of materials from the project. The baseline data and literature were summarised in English, even though research and literature had been engaged with in first languages. From these summaries, final reports were created, again in English. Ideally, these reports would be published in all three languages. This requires the financial resources to do this, as a report written in English would need to be translated into French and Dutch. This would be the best option, but finances did not allow for this, so the team discussed the issue and agreed that these reports were the least important part of the project for translation, so they decided that they would not pursue this.

Once the project was concluded, there was then the issue of publishing the data that had been collected. Again, there is pressure here to publish in English as this is often an important step in the promotion potential for those working in academic systems other than in the UK. Therefore, there is pressure to publish in English-medium academic journals. Again, this is a situational issue. Whilst the BERA guidelines (BERA, 2024) state a preference for publishing in languages other than English for at least some of the outputs, the situation here is to prefer English journal papers. However, whilst this is the case for academic publication, money was deliberately claimed for the project to translate the resources themselves into all three languages. This ensures that those who have participated in the research are at least able to engage with the applied outputs in their own language. In addition, it would be possible to make some of the data available across the teams to allow for national teams to publish in their own languages if they wished to pursue this, using the English-medium reports, translation of some of the original data if they wish to do this as ways of being able to work in their own languages.

Final thoughts

The above discussion makes it clear that it is important to consider language as an ethical issue in research activity. This is not just something to reflect on when working with researchers and participants in international projects but also when working in the UK with participants for whom English is not their first language. At the core of this consideration is the need to reflect on how we allow the greatest opportunity for participants, and where applicable, international colleagues to have an authentic voice in our research. We may not always be able to accommodate an ideal in this respect, but we do need to consider what is possible, and where this is the case, how it can be facilitated. In addition, when we do consider language, we also need to be aware that this might also entail intercultural issues, the language being the most obvious manifestation of different ways of understanding and engaging with the world. Therefore, in altering and creating a more inclusive approach to our research, we need to not see it only as a simple process of language, but the assumptions and worldviews which may spring from this linguistic heterogeneity.

As Meier et al. (2024) highlight, when considering the linguistic aspects of a research project and the desire to act ethically, we should not see it as a single decision at the start or planning phase of the process but as an ongoing process which informs our work throughout a project. There are discussions and decisions which need to be made at all steps, and the eventual direction a project moves in cannot be predetermined but needs to be made situationally. As we can see in the two case studies, decisions could have been made in different ways which would then have taken the projects in potentially different directions. By being cognisant of the range of issues which need to be identified and considered, researchers should be able to make more confident and informed choices about how the complexities of language can be accommodated.

Following on from the need to reflect constantly on language as a medium of communication, there then arises how any written materials are created and used. Ethical paperwork can be difficult to engage with, even for some native English speakers, so how ethics forms are presented to and engaged with by those for whom English is not their first language becomes important if we are to claim that participants are fully informed in giving their consent for involvement in a research project. Similarly, the use of questionnaires and other written resources needs to be reflected upon so that we can ensure that participants can be confident when engaging with research tools if we are to gain high-quality data and give the participants as full an access as we can to the process. However, we must also consider that imperfect understanding and engagement due to language barriers should not be a bar on developing research, as this would remove any chance of having a voice for those who wish to participate, but we should at the same time try to create as many support strictures as it practically possible to help minimise those barriers.

As with written resources, so with verbal communication. As set out above, there are ways in which data collection methods might impinge on the full inclusion of some participants, as they find interviews or focus group dialogue difficult. We should try to minimise the problems which might occur, through careful planning, and where possible through additional support, such as that offered by EFL/EAP tutors and/or translators. However, if any of these language professionals are to act as critical and supportive members of a research project, then they should be given the opportunity to be part of the team itself rather than just being brought in for a merely technical purpose; deeper inclusion in the research process will give then more context and an opportunity to see weaknesses in research approach and design at an early stage so that its practical impact can be minimised.

Publication and outputs have also been raised as creating potential ethical dilemmas. Whilst the BERA guidelines (2024) strongly advocate for the production of outputs in languages other than English in those contexts where researchers and/or participants speak other languages, the particular contexts of projects can make such decisions more complex. What if a team only has English speakers? What if partners from other countries themselves desire English publications, as this suits their professional purpose? These are genuine questions, but it should nevertheless be the case that teams should find ways of reporting back to the groups who have participated in their research in ways that will engage them, even if this means, on occasion, that this needs to be done in English. And to maximise the impact of finding ways to successfully engage participants in either their own language or English requires that planning occurs early in the project and is revisited regularly throughout the life cycle of the research.

Finally, what the discussion of language and research ethics above does demonstrate is that whilst it is useful to have 'ethical rules', deontological guidance as a general framework to help us think about the ethical decisions and paradoxes we might face, it is nevertheless crucial to remember that the practical ethics of developing and completing a research project will require frequent situated ethical decisions. We can plan as carefully as we want, and this is important, but ultimately we will always be in a position where we need to reflect on the circumstances we find ourselves in as our research emerges, and it is only through reflecting on the problems which emerge as our work progresses that we can develop ethical responses which help all those concerned, researchers and participants alike, to navigate a positive route through the research.

Reflective questions

1 How does your experience of research ethics fit with the experiences in case studies one and two?
2 How can researchers, supervisors, mentors and ethics board members keep ahead of changes in how researchers work across borders and languages?
3 If research teams cannot afford translation and interpretation services, should the research go ahead?
4 How can research teams be supported to make their methods and practices equitable?

Further reading

1. Eaton, S. E. (2020). Ethical considerations for research conducted with human participants in languages other than English. *British Educational Research Journal*, 46(4), 848–58. Doi: 10.1002/berj.3623.

    This is an accessible and wide-ranging reflection on the ethics of language and research.

2. Holmes, P. and Rajab, T. (2023). An Ethic for Researching Multilingually in Transnational, Multilingual, Multidisciplinary Research Teams. In P. Holmes, and J. Corbett (Eds.), *Critical Intercultural Pedagogy for Difficult Times*, London: Routledge (pp. 228-49).

We recommend a practical, empirical paper which explores the complexities of working in multilingual and multidisciplinary research teams. Open access at https://durham-repository.worktribe.com/output/1621950

3. Meier, G., van der Voet, P. and Yau, T. (2024). Research ethics in a multilingual world: A guide to reflecting on language decisions in all disciplines. *Diametros*, 21(80), 1-21. Doi: 10.33392/diam.1926.

This is an interesting paper which considers the ethical implications and issues at every step of a research project.

References

Berman, R. C. and Tyyska, V. (2010). A critical reflection on the use of translators/interpreters in a qualitative cross-language research project. *International Journal of Qualitative Methods*, 10(1), 178-90.

British Educational Research Association (2024). *Ethical Guidelines for Educational Research* (5th ed.). https://www.bera.ac.uk/publication/ethical-guidelines-for-educational-research-fifth-edition-2024.

Christians, C. G. (2011). Ethics and Politics in Qualitative research. In N. Denzin, and Y. S. Lincoln (Eds.), *The Sage Handbook of Qualitative Research* (4th ed.). Thousand Oaks, CA: Sage (pp. 61-80).

Eaton, S. E. (2020). Ethical considerations for research conducted with human participants in languages other than English. *British Educational Research Journal*, 46(4), 848-58. https://doi.org/10.1002/berj.3623.

Holmes, P. (2016). Navigating Languages in the Research Process: The Ethics and Positionality of the Researcher and the Researched. In M. Dazli, and A. R. Díaz (Eds.), *The Critical Turn in Intercultural Communication Pedagogy: Theory, Research and Practice*. London: Routledge (pp. 91-108).

Holmes, P. and Rajab, T. (2023). An Ethic for Researching Multilingually in Transnational, Multilingual, Multidisciplinary Research Teams. In P. Holmes, and J. Corbett (Eds.), *Critical Intercultural Pedagogy for Difficult Times*, London: Routledge (pp. 228-49).

Meier, G., van der Voet, P. and Yau, T. (2024). Research ethics in a multilingual world: A guide to reflecting on language decisions in all disciplines. *Diametros*, 21(80), 1–21. https://doi.org/10.33392/diam.1926.

Smith, H. J., Chen, J. and Liu, X. (2008). Language and rigour in qualitative research: Problems and principles in analyzing data collected in Mandarin. *BMC Medical Research Methodology*, 8(44), 1–8. https://doi.org/10.1186/1471-2288-8-44.

6

Placing Children's Rights at the Centre of Ethical Researcher Decision-Making

by *Carmel Capewell, Helen Hanna and Chawin Pongpajon*

Introduction

This chapter considers the importance of putting children's rights at the centre of how we conduct ethical education research through looking at three reflective case study examples from UK, South Africa and Thailand. It argues that fulfilling children's rights is essential to ethical decision-making in research (BERA, 2025, paragraph 36),[1] underpinned by Article 12 of the UN Convention on the Rights of the Child that concerns the child's right to express their views and have them taken into account, and Article 3 that states that the child or young person's 'best interests' should be our primary concern (BERA, 2025, paragraph 23).[2] As part of this commitment, while we used different research methods as part of our 'aim[s] to put participants at their ease and to avoid making excessive demands on them' (BERA, 2025, paragraph 34),[3] we have all been influenced by the famed 'Lundy model' of child participation (2007), that involves consideration of the four inter-related elements of space, voice, audience and influence. 'Space' indicates that children must be given the opportunity to express a view; 'voice', that children must be facilitated to express their views; 'audience', that the view must be listened to; and 'influence', that the view must be acted upon, as appropriate. Researchers like us, who work with children and young people (CYP), are normally concerned with the fundamental principles of informed consent, confidentiality, addressing adult-child power imbalances and finding research methods that are CYP-friendly but also robust (BERA, 2025, paragraphs 56 and 57).[4] But we contend that the real-life ethical dilemmas researchers face are much more complex and 'messy' than this. Drawing on different elements of the Lundy model in various ways and to varying degrees, in each case study the author considers their own positionality, which 'reflects the position that the researcher has chosen to adopt within a given research study' (Savin-Baden and Major, 2013: 71) – in terms of age, ability, professional standing, race, language and other characteristics – how that influenced the power dynamic between us and our younger participants, and the realities of enacting Lundy's model in an ethical way in research spaces with CYP.

In the first case study, Capewell draws on her examples of working with CYP with auditory processing difficulties across a range of projects. She considers issues arising when trying to put CYP at the heart of the research process, especially negotiating issues of control and authority between adults and CYP. The case study explores ways of making the expectations and possibilities of research accessible to children of all age ranges and with different communication needs, using a structured diary format with children aged 3–8 years. This includes consulting a Young Person's Advisory Group (YPAG) to develop appropriate age-friendly research methods.[5]

In the second case study, Hanna explores her experiences of researching with migrant children in primary schools in South Africa, analysing a scenario whereby she had to deal with the silence that she faced from participants when using picturebook activities and discussion around migration, discrimination and race. She focuses on Lundy's principle of 'voice' and how she came to understand that it should take account of silence, and how her positionality as a white adult may influence the research.

In the third and final case study, Pongpajon reflects on his research with secondary school students in conflict-affected southern Thailand that used draw-and-write techniques and interviews. He considers the difficulty posed by gatekeepers' inappropriate intervention in data-collection processes and exercise of power over the students, and how he dealt with the ethical dilemma of whether and how to intervene. Drawing on Lundy's principles of 'space' and 'voice' and understanding of himself as holding multiple positionalities, he discusses how he created a safe space for students to express their opinions, to ensure their full consent for participation, and to balance the power dynamics between the researcher and students.

Case Study One: Making participation accessible (Carmel Capewell)

Background

The research described in this first case study focuses on understanding the extent of the impact that hearing loss has on young children aged 3–7 years with continuous Glue Ear. This causes intermittent hearing loss and, for those children in whom the condition is recurring, results in repeated hearing tests and visits to the audiologist and Ear, Nose and Throat (ENT) surgeons (Bluestone and Klein, 2007). Because it occurs in about 80 per cent of all children under the age of seven years (Bluestone and Klein, 2007), it is not generally regarded as requiring adjustments in educational settings. Usually, the child's parent speaks on behalf of the child, and the children comply with what actions the health care professionals ask of them. The child is not usually consulted about the day-to-day impact of their hearing loss or the situations which help them or are barriers to understanding what a specific person is saying to them.

This case study explores research carried out by me (Carmel Capewell) and centres on the importance of acknowledging the perceived power differentials between adults and children (BERA, 2024, paragraph 2).[6] As Lowe (2012) explores, children as young as three to four years are very aware of the power imbalance between adults and children, with the latter perceiving the former with greater power than themselves. This can be seen happening in home, educational and healthcare settings. Although the language of adults may imply choice, such as when an adult says, 'Would you like to join us?', the intention is a command from the adult which the child is expected to obey. This can present particular issues for researchers who wish to gain insight into children's views/experiences and perspectives. In order to minimise the child feeling like there is a 'right' answer required by an adult, the data collection needs to have the child's participation at the centre.

Ethical issues anticipated

How could the adult-child power differentials be reduced to elicit children's experiences?

Before research begins, an Ethics Research Committee must give ethical approval. Their remit is to protect the interests of potentially vulnerable participants (Harcourt and Quennerstedt, 2014). In the UK, and many other countries, adult agreement (Informed Consent) is required before children are invited to participate in the research process. Potentially, the children are 'pressured' into participation rather than actively giving their informed consent/assent (Capewell, 2023). Obtaining children's assent was part of the planning stage in my research. I did not want them to feel obliged to comply due to the power differentials between themselves and adults (BERA, 2024, paragraph 31).[7]

As outlined in the introduction to this chapter, Lundy's (2007) Model of Participation for children in educational research has four basic tenets. Firstly, space – whereby children must be provided with a place to both form and express their opinions. From previous research, I realised that spending time building rapport with child participants was important, as was providing them with opportunities to make choices and demonstrate that their opinion and thoughts mattered to me. In the Participant Information Sheet for the adults, I explained that this rapport-building stage was important to gaining the child's trust and that their views mattered. As part of the research, the children were asked to provide a name that they wished to be known as. One child said that he wanted to be known as 'Unhearable'. His mother considered this to be a 'silly name' but I reassured her it was his choice and it did make sense as he explained he felt he could often not hear what others were saying to him (BERA, 2024, paragraph 27).[8]

Secondly, voice – children are supported and encouraged to express themselves. A structured diary format was used (Capewell, 2015). The child was asked to specify, in situations in which they were trying to understand what a specific person was saying to them, one of three options. Could they understand *all/most* of what the person was saying;

could they understand *some* of what the person was saying; or could they understand *little/none* of what the person was saying? They were encouraged to complete the diary in a range of situations, although a specific number of entries was not required. If no data was produced, it was assumed that they wished to withdraw from the research. The adult was encouraged to act as scribe if the child wished so, but adult contribution was limited to anything the adult said/did, rather than interpreting on behalf of the child.

Thirdly, audience – the experiences and thoughts expressed by children are listened to. By sitting with the child and the parent, a worked example of the diary format was completed.

Fourthly, influence – what children say is valued and respected, rather than tokenistic. As the researcher, I wrote what the child said in the worked example and did not reinterpret what they said. It was important to keep my face neutral and not show my own estimation of the situation being described as to which option was chosen. The diary format enabled the child to complete information in a structured way, which encouraged analysis by them. This leads to consideration of the second ethical issue.

What methods would legitimately encourage the active participation of children?

Bird, Culley and Lakhanpaul (2013) identify that children are excluded from the research process due to the application of methods that were developed with adults, rather than taking children's capabilities/preferences into account (BERA, 2024, paragraph 56).[9] Such misunderstanding can lead adults to assume that children are not cognitively competent to analyse and communicate difficulties that may arise for them, particularly regarding their lived experience (BERA, 2024, paragraph 23).[10] Consequently, children may be excluded as active contributors to the research process.

As part of the development of the research method, I consulted a Young People's Advisory Group (YPAG). The members are trained to support researchers in developing ways of including children in research to ensure the child participants' understanding of the research goal and ongoing assent.

Ethical issues that arose during research

It is ethically important to ensure researchers match what they say with what they do and consider perceived power relationships when working with children (BERA, 2024, paragraph 19).[11] Upon the suggestions from the YPAG, I had initially used emoji faces to represent the three options describing the understanding of the speech of a specific person. However, some of the children liked to create a pattern with the emojis or had a preference for a smiley face. To minimise power differentials, I had not initially included adult voices. But there were times when the child did not realise the actions that an adult took to gain the child's attention. This was a balance between respecting the child's perspective and gathering data effectively (BERA, 2024, paragraph 57).[12]

Course of action

Once I became aware of the above situations, I made changes to the process with further participants. This avoided causing any upset to the participants (BERA, 2024, paragraph 34).[13] Instead of using emojis, I gave the children a choice of five colours from which they could choose three and allocate a colour to each of the conditions and provide a key for this. This accords with adjusting the method in a way to better meet the child's cognitive skills (Bird, Culley and Lakhanpaul, 2013) while maintaining the integrity of the data quality (paragraph 57).[14] In a similar way, a column was added to the diary format which provided an opportunity for the adult to identify any action they had taken to support the child's understanding. For example, one adult wrote that they had seen the child was not listening to what they were saying and had attracted the child's attention by using his name, then repeated the instructions.

Alternative courses of action

The research discussed in this case study was built upon previous research that I had conducted with older children with glue ear. That had highlighted the importance of taking time to get to know the children, which had ensured that I played a game of the child's choice as a way of getting to know them. It was important that I supported the adults around the child in this research, both in terms of their legal responsibility for their child (BERA, 2024, paragraph 24)[15] and also in terms of not undermining them or causing discomfort as to what their child says (paragraph 34).[16] It might have been better if I had talked to the parent separately regarding the choice of names and how, if the name was not offensive, then it would be accepted.

Case Study One – concluding section

When working with children as research participants, it is important that they are active participants in the research process so that their experience and perspective can be understood (paragraph 23).[17] This includes the right of children to contribute their experiences and opinions in a way that enables them to express what they think/feel rather than this being filtered through an adult perspective. However, it is important to respect the role of parents/carers' legal responsibilities in giving their informed consent (paragraph 24).[18] It is ethically important to think about whether the method being used is appropriate for the children to ensure that they can be included in the research process (BERA, 2024, paragraph 37).[19]

Case Study Two: Taking account of positionality, silence and voice (Helen Hanna)

Background

In this section, I (Helen Hanna) reflect on my experiences of researching with migrant children in primary schools in South Africa, and what influenced my decisions from a research ethics perspective. Migrant children are often considered to be multiply marginalised in post-apartheid South Africa, both because they are children in a deeply divided and highly paternalistic society (Bray and Moses, 2011) and also because they are migrants, and therefore are considered 'outsiders' and among the least powerful members of society (Palmary, 2009) (paragraph 2).[20] There is little research that focuses on primary-age children's experiences from their perspective, hence my decision to work in this field and my desire to offer such learners a 'voice'.

Between 2016 and 2019, I completed three periods of fieldwork in primary schools in the Western Cape, South Africa, using picturebooks and photography to explore migrant children's experiences of school, and what can be done to support them (Hanna, 2021; 2022; 2023). Normally, I worked with a small group of around six children aged nine to ten years old, who had been born overseas (such as in the Democratic Republic of Congo, Zimbabwe) over a period of three-six weeks, once per week for around one to one-and-a-half hours. In this chapter, I will focus on the parts of my research where the wordless picturebook *The Arrival* by Shaun Tan (2006) was used.

The scenario I will analyse in this chapter relates to how I tried to deal with the silence that I was met with from children when I used picturebook activities and discussion around migration, discrimination and race, and the ethical dilemma this presented for me: whether to push children to respond to my questions by using different approaches and whether to change the book. Below, I describe the details of the dilemma, the rationale behind the approach I took, and reflections on my other options (what I would do differently), particularly taking account of my now better understanding of children's silence as part of 'voice' and my positionality as a white adult.

The ethical dilemma

The scenario I will analyse in this chapter section is as follows: I employed *The Arrival* as a way to engage children in the topic of migration and to encourage them to share their own experiences. One of the tasks was to 'read' a double-paged spread showing the main protagonist (the migrant man) arriving at 'immigration' (the border) in a new and strange country after a long journey. In the scene, he is depicted as having pieces of paper stuck to his clothing, seemingly to indicate different aspects of his identity. The man shows confusion and eventually despair on his face and through his body language, as he appears to be trying to communicate. The task I gave the children was to use post-it notes to write or draw responses to two questions: what is the man feeling? And how could someone help him? I had thought the children would connect well with the man's experience as someone from a migration background and would have a lot of responses, but they did not. So I faced a twofold ethical dilemma: whether to push children to respond to my questions by using different approaches and whether to change the book.

Before I did the research, I had anticipated the ethics of using this book that considered migration. I had felt it was an ethically and methodologically sound decision to use the book that met the 'needs' of the research (paragraph 56),[21] as I believed it would connect with the children's experiences, offering them a unique and potentially powerful way to see their own experiences reflected in children's literature. This is something that is of prime concern in the field of multicultural children's literature, a field I have been engaged with for some time. I was influenced, also, by how it had been used by other scholars whom I admired, such as Evelyn Arizpe and colleagues (2014), and how much it had been used by teachers in the classroom (Kucharczyk and Hanna, 2020). Wider than that, I had been heavily impacted by the work of Helen Kara on creative research methods (2015), particularly her call for research methods to be fit for purpose. I was convinced that using a methodological approach that linked to children's own lives was the most ethical choice, as, in line with the Lundy model, it would offer a 'space' for children to share their experiences and express their 'voice', and I believed that I was 'competent' to complete such work (BERA, 2024, paragraph 7).[22]

However, what I had not anticipated was how little the children would connect on a personal level with the main protagonist – the man. Their responses in the task and follow-on discussions I tried to strike up resulted in much silence. This was especially the case when I mentioned anything relating to race and discrimination. So I was left with the dilemma of whether to push the children to write more responses and potentially contradict my ethical aim of putting them 'at their ease' (paragraph 34)[23] or find other ways to discuss race, including changing the book or to allow them to be silent and accept this as a potential sign that they had made 'non-verbal signs' of withdrawing their consent (BERA, 2024, paragraph 8)[24] from participating in the project in the ways I wished them to.

Course of action

My response to the 'problem' of children's silence in the face of my questions was not immediate, although I did have to make a quick decision in the moment: I decided to retain the book as I did not have time or resources to buy another set of books, and I persisted with some lines of enquiry although I eventually gave up when the topic was changed so often by the children. My less immediate but more informed response evolved over many months (and – as I began to write up the research for publication – years), and involved learning to listen to children's silence as part of their 'voice' or 'meaning-making', and taking better account of my positionality as a white adult.

In going back to the research on children's rights and participation in research, I came across articles that looked at children's silence, particularly the writings of Mazzei (2003) and Spyrou (2016). Mazzei (2003: 364–6) argues that silence can be found not only in omissions but in evasions, denials, pauses and signs, and that there are many different types of silences (polite, privileged, veiled, intentional and unintelligible). Spyrou (2016) sees silence as an inherent part of voice that is too often overlooked, despite the fact that it is intrinsic to meaning-making in normal conversation. He argues compellingly that, 'far from being absences or lack of data, children's silences are pregnant with meaning and a constitutive feature of their voices; childhood researchers who need to account for children's voices must therefore attend to their silences rather than merely their voiced utterances' (2016: 7). Therefore, I needed to think differently about 'silence'.

Over time, reading and reflection, as well as formulating my ideas on paper during writing and peer review for publication, I came to reframe how I viewed children's silence in the research space: moving away from seeing it as a methodological problem to be solved, towards seeing it as part of voice, imbued with meaning, and therefore an opportunity to be embraced on my journey towards better understanding migrant children's experiences and better fulfilling children's rights to be involved in research on topics that affect them – in other words, better meeting the principles of the Lundy model.

But it wasn't only about the children's voice; it was also about my 'powerful' position, a key topic of debate among adult researchers working with CYP, who are keen to avoid dominating them, in order to better ensure that their views can be expressed and shared (paragraph 23).[25] It is possible that the child participants' silence was compounded by my own identity; I am a white adult researcher from one of the former colonisers of South Africa (and some of the other countries where the learners' heritage lay), my adult and racial identities perhaps marking me as someone with whom, for Black children, it wasn't acceptable or polite to discuss topics such as race. Indeed, they may have been concerned that I would be offended – and perhaps respond negatively – if they hinted that the lack of white teachers had racist undertones, given the racialised past and current reality of South Africa, with 'race' further compounding the adult–child power differential that must also be acknowledged. (I discuss alternative potential reasons for this in Hanna, 2022.) It was through being challenged on this point at conferences and seminars, as part of a supportive 'community of educational researchers' (BERA, 2024, paragraph 58),[26] that I started to become more aware of my blind spot. However, I also had to accept that I will never know the full effect of my position as a white adult.

Alternative courses of action

So, what could I have done differently in order to better (more ethically) work with child participants and better capture their perspectives? Coming to more fully recognise and accept my positionality as a white adult from a former coloniser, in a previously colonised space, has been part of that process. This has meant that I believe I might do two things differently if I did this type of research again, one in terms of practice and the other in terms of the interpretation of findings.

Firstly, on the practical side, I might use a different book with the research participants: one that still told a story of migration (in order to prompt children's ideas and memories) but that better represented the participants in terms of age and race and ethnicity. For example, the book *The Day War Came* (Davies and Cobb, 2018) depicts a 'brown' child who escapes war in her home country, or *My Two Blankets* (Kobald and Blackwood, 2014) that tells a similar story and whose protagonist is a Black migrant child (for more books, see 'Further reading' at the end of this chapter). My aim would be to better ensure that they felt 'at ease' and that the task wasn't excessively demanding (paragraph 34).[27] However, the potential drawback would be that these books require some understanding of English in order to follow the story (whereas *The Arrival* is wordless). Even though I would change the book and might also try to find other methods to access the children's knowledge and experience, I would still attempt to discuss sensitive issues such as race and discrimination in the South African context, as I know it remains a dominant societal challenge. I believe that addressing such issues, as part of the movement to overcome them, remains a key ethical responsibility of educational researchers.

Secondly, in terms of interpretation of the findings, I would consider more deeply my position as a white adult and how that was influencing the participants. This might involve more in-depth conversations with Black colleagues in South Africa, including those from migration backgrounds, and potentially inviting a co-researcher on board. It is true that this would require me to be very open to (hopefully constructive!) critique, as it is a vulnerable space. Nevertheless, I feel that it could help with interpreting the children's responses, at least to offer another perspective that I might not have considered, contributing to 'the community spirit of critical analysis and constructive criticism that generates improvement in practice and enhancement of knowledge' (BERA, 2024, paragraph 59)[28] and continuing my development as an ethical researcher. Here, I have not been knowingly influenced by anything I have read but rather by a long period of attending conferences, engaging with children's research methodology scholars, watching documentaries and reading analysis about the history of migration and colonialism in and by the UK, and coming to terms with my own implicated position as a white person within these difficult, racist and discriminatory times that extend to today.

Even as I write this, when the fieldwork has long since come to an end, I carry the burden of regret that I hadn't realised these things before, as perhaps I could have done a better job while with the children. I find this is always the case when doing this kind of research, however, a feeling of loss and missed opportunity that is rarely talked about openly in research circles. Maybe we *should* talk about that more, and in this way come to accept that as part of our 'self-care' as researchers (BERA, 2024, paragraph 82),[29] while we wish so desperately to do research in as ethical a way as possible, and use models such as Lundy's to guide us, there will always be some new things we won't have thought of before, and some things that, ultimately, we cannot control. Having a supportive research community where we can discuss ethical issues openly is key.

Case Study Two – concluding section

Overall, my research with Black migrant children in schools in South Africa has led me to realise the importance of taking better account of positionality and voice. I learned the value of reflecting on my position as a white adult from a country that colonised South Africa, how I may have affected how and what the children shared with me, and also that the concept of 'voice' is not straightforward and that we need to broaden our understanding of how children and young people may communicate with us, in both verbal and non-verbal ways. This experience also underlined the importance of drawing in others from the educational research community who might bring a critical perspective on research findings, in the spirit of openness and support – something that is challenging on a personal and professional level but also something that could ensure a more ethical way of doing educational research.

Case Study Three: Reclaiming students' power and voice from school gatekeepers (Chawin Pongpajon)

Background

Education in challenging contexts has become a global concern due to significant increases in environmental adversities, economic crises, sociocultural inequalities and geopolitical tensions. According to the UN (2020), lack of educational access in conflict-affected areas in the Global South has been the most critical hindrance to achieving inclusive and equitable quality education for all. This includes southern Thailand, where the conflict is deeply rooted and multifaceted, centring around identity politics between the Thai-Buddhist state and Malay-Muslim minority (McCargo, 2008; Chambers, Jitpiromsri and Waitoolkiat, 2019). Schools and children, regardless of ethno-religion, have been victims of, or witnesses to, violence perpetuated by state military and Malay-Muslim insurgents. Therefore, they study within fearful and unsafe environments (Human Rights Watch, 2010; UNICEF, 2014; Pherali, 2021).

Based on this context, in this section, I (Chawin Pongpajon) share my experience in dealing with unexpected ethical dilemmas that emerged during this research with marginalised students with varying identity backgrounds in conflict-affected areas of southern Thailand. In order to understand the students' perceptions of peace and experiences in school peace practice, I employed a draw-and-write technique followed by a semi-structured interview to talk about sensitive issues with them (Mitchell, Theron, Stuart, Smith and Campbell, 2011). The draw-and-write method is intended to provide students, whose ability to communicate complex ideas might be limited by their ages and linguistic competencies, with opportunities to express their ideas through a collaborative meaning-making process of creating artwork with descriptions (Fargas-Malet,

McSherry, Larkin and Robinson, 2010). The interviews based on what the students drew/wrote were also conducted so that the voices and creativity of the students would be fully and carefully listened to and understood, avoiding misinterpretations (Mitchell, Theron, Stuart, Smith and Campbell, 2011). Therefore, in exploring the ethical dilemmas faced, this section will focus on the 'space' and 'voice' elements of Lundy's (2007) model.

The ethical dilemma

The ethical dilemma I experienced during my research arose in my encounters with gatekeepers and relates to their and my differing understandings of students' right to participate in research to the extent and in the way that children themselves choose. Before the fieldwork, I had made personal visits to the potential participant schools to talk about the research with the school principals as gatekeepers (BERA, 2024, paragraph 18).[30] Once they gave me permission to collect the data with the students at their schools, I used this written permission as part of my ethical approval application to my institution. I visited the schools once again about six months later with information sheets and consent forms differently designed for the principals and students (paragraph 8).[31] In line with institutional protocol, due to the fact that the young people were over sixteen years old, they could give consent without their parents'/guardians' permission. Nevertheless, the schools still informed parents about their involvement (paragraph 27).[32] The principals or teachers selected the students on my behalf, based on the selection criteria I had suggested. They were expected to have ensured that the students understood the research process described in the information sheet and consent form before the students joined me in a private space on the school premises.

But I was challenged by unexpected situations. While I had intended to offer 'space' to the students to freely express their views, my attempts were to an extent thwarted when one of the gatekeepers insisted on staying in the same room during the fieldwork, making it difficult for the students to discuss sensitive issues and breaking confidentiality. This also concerns consent and power. For the former, most students were not well-informed about the research, neither by the schools nor by me before the interviews. Some joined the session as they thought that this was a special channel for admission to the university where I work. For the latter, most students reported that they 'worked' under pressure in the research since they were requested by the gatekeepers to work well and respond 'properly' as they were representing the school. Subsequently, they did not freely draw what they wanted and copied text from Google so as to avoid making the drawings 'messy' or saying something 'wrong'.

These situations created an ethical dilemma for me: I needed to follow the ethical protocols approved by my institutional ethics review board, and I also wanted to sincerely conduct my research in an ethical way, yet, I was also in a less powerful position in relation to the gatekeepers. Would it be possible for me to both follow the ethical guidelines while also accommodating the gatekeepers' wishes?

Course of action

I responded to the ethical dilemma in a number of practical ways. To address the space issues, where the gatekeeper appeared to be trying to control the research space and the students' participation, I made a conscious effort to make the interviewing room a comfortable and safe zone for them, in line with good practice in ethical research. I decided to sit at the opposite corner of the room from the gatekeeper and asked the students to position themselves so as to avoid eye contact with the gatekeepers. Moreover, because I did not have a chance to get to know the students via the introductory and artwork sessions, I made the interviewing room young person-friendly by providing snacks, desserts and drinks for them to have during the interviews or to take home with them. I also used small talk to break the ice and let them decide when to begin, only whenever they felt ready. Whereas the students called me 'อาจารย์' (Ajarn) or 'professor' in English, I called myself 'พี่' (Pêe) or 'elder brother' instead of other pronouns that in Thai language and culture would show power or distance; in this way I tried to create a sense of comfort by narrowing down the hierarchy both between age and social status. While we were not still totally equal, I was in a position where the students could see me as their elder but to whom they were not culturally required to respond formally and politely (paragraph 34).[33] These acts were to promote the space element of Lundy's model, where safe, inclusive chances must be physically and psychologically given to students (Lundy, 2007).

For the consent-related issue, as I was not confident that the gatekeeper had explained the research adequately to the students, before I began recording the conversations, I asked the students what they understood from the information sheet and consent form (BERA, 2024, paragraphs 24 and 25).[34] I already knew from published research (UNICEF, 2016) and my previous research experience in the region that, as non-native speakers of Thai, my participants might struggle with vocabulary and reading comprehension and that they might be shy to reveal their misunderstanding or ask questions. Therefore, to better ensure they genuinely understood what participation would involve, I asked them to read both documents aloud, and together with them, I clarified each point before asking them to make a decision about whether to proceed with the interviews (BERA, 2024, paragraph 9)[35] (UNICEF, 2016). This was despite the fact that they had already completed draw-and-write tasks. Although I believed that there would be no students daring to refuse participation due to structural powers between themselves and gatekeepers (paragraph 2),[36] the space for students' rights to make a decision should be made safe and respected (Lundy, 2007).

For the power-related issue, because students had been instructed to work 'properly' as a way of preserving the school image, to subvert the inappropriately powerful influence of the gatekeeper, during the interviews I checked the students' understanding of the task and what they should produce, together with their inspirations, imaginations, opinions and experiences behind the work. When I found that the students did not draw what they wanted, I offered them an opportunity to either re-draw, add further detail or explain their original ideas. Without responding negatively, I also asked them to highlight the part of the writing that they copied from Google and talked about their own opinions and experiences instead. Moreover, throughout the interviews, I switched my multiple-positionality to relate to the different groups of students, as and when appropriate. My intertwined identities of national majority Thai-Buddhist, regional minority Thai-Buddhist, a university lecturer, an international doctoral student and an outsider researcher with a focus on Malay-Muslim grievances had been purposefully employed to balance my power with the students (BERA, 2024, paragraph 22).[37] Their freedom of expression was, thus, to the best of my ability, protected and encouraged through multiple methods (BERA, 2024, paragraph 35),[38] in a sincere attempt to fulfil the 'voice' element of Lundy's model (2007).

Alternative courses of action

I have engaged in a process of iterative self-reflection on what I did and what I could have done differently to address the ethical dilemmas that arose in this research. Below, I will consider what I believe was under my control and that, if I had another chance to do it again, I would do more ethically and hopefully with better outcomes.

Firstly, I would try to insist more on the information sheet being shared by the gatekeepers with the potential participants and negotiate with the gatekeepers to give me time to run an introductory and artwork session by myself. I would ask for after-school or weekend time and subsidise travel and food expenses for the students and gatekeepers. If this space would not be allowed, I would record a video clip explaining data collection processes and ask the gatekeeper to share it with the students (paragraph 25).[39] Despite additional costs or work, the students would be better informed about the research tasks prior to starting, thereby better ensuring informed consent.

Secondly, I would increase the number of participants so that these would replace the students who did not want to participate in the research but who did not feel they could directly refuse their gatekeepers' selection (paragraph 31).[40] Given the power imbalance between students and gatekeepers, I would interview these 'non-participating' students without recording and would not analyse the data. This would be to prevent undesirable consequences that the gatekeepers would directly and indirectly cause the students if the former knew that the students had not wanted to participate (BERA, 2024, paragraph 16).[41]

Finally, I would carefully revise the information sheet and the direction of the draw-and-write task in order to try to avoid the gatekeeper's manipulation (paragraph 24)[42] and, hopefully, reduce the students' discomfort.

However, such alternatives would be more time- and energy-consuming and therefore add to costs. In some conflict-affected areas, this would be impossible, as the time spent in the field needs to be intensive due to the risks to researchers and the participants (Goodhand, 2000; Helbardt, Hellmann-Rajanayagam and Korff, 2010). This underlines the complexity of doing ethical research with CYP in conflict-affected societies (paragraph 82).[43]

Case Study Three – concluding section

Ethical dilemmas during the fieldwork can be hugely challenging for a novice researcher, especially in conflict-affected areas where there are so many sensitivities relating to education, children and society. Due to the deeply segregated environment of the Deep South of Thailand, I experienced problems with the school gatekeepers trying to intervene unhelpfully in data collection processes and exercising their power over the students with the aim to manipulate the responses and thereby control the researchers' perceptions and findings (paragraph 59).[44] With critical and ethical concerns for placing students' rights at the heart of my decision-making, the challenge for me was not only how to negotiate with gatekeepers but also how to work under the pressure they exerted on myself and the students while also ensuring children and young people's rights to express their views (paragraph 25).[45] Lundy's Model focuses on 'space' and 'voice' which were key to my reflections here. While I used strategies such as creating a comfortable environment for students to express themselves, trying to encourage participation through drawing-based methods and drawing on different aspects of my positionality to facilitate an open environment for discussion, still there were alternative courses of action that I could have taken. Although it should be remembered that often finding the 'right' and ethical solution is complex and not without additional costs, I nevertheless believe it is worth striving for.

Final thoughts

This chapter considered the importance of putting children's rights at the centre of how we conduct research through looking at three reflective, case study examples from education in UK, South Africa and Thailand. It argued that fulfilling children's rights is essential to ethical decision making in research, underpinned by Article 12 of the UN Convention on the Rights of the Child that itself informed the 'Lundy model' of child participation (2007): that educational research should consider space, voice, audience and influence (paragraph 23).[46] It also took account of the role of positionality in research, particularly in terms of age, ability, professional standing, race and language. Through the case studies based on our own research with CYP in different educational contexts across the globe, we illustrated that real-life ethical dilemmas researchers face are highly complex, context-specific and go beyond informed consent, confidentiality and finding research methods that are robust and CYP-friendly (paragraph 24).[47]

Capewell drew on her research with CYP auditory processing difficulties, highlighting the challenge of negotiating issues of control and authority between adults and CYP. She explored ways of making the expectations and possibilities of research accessible to children of all age ranges and with different communication needs, including consulting a Young Person's Advisory Group (YPAG) to develop appropriate age-friendly research methods. Hanna reflected on her experiences of researching with migrant children in primary schools in South Africa, analysing a scenario whereby she had to deal with the silence that she faced from participants when using picturebook activities and discussion around migration, discrimination and race. She focused on Lundy's principle of 'voice' and how she came to understand that it should take account of silence and how her positionality as a white adult may influence the research. Finally, Pongpajon drew on his experience of research with secondary school students in conflict-affected southern Thailand using draw-and-write techniques and interviews. He considered the difficulty of gatekeepers' inappropriate intervention in data collection processes and exercise of power over the students, and how he dealt with the ethical dilemma of whether and how to intervene. Drawing on Lundy's principles of 'space' and 'voice' and understanding of himself as holding multiple positionalities, he discussed how to create a safe space for students to express their opinions, to ensure their full consent for participation, and to balance the power dynamics between the researcher and students.

As a group, we believe we have 'a responsibility to support the next generation of educational researchers' (paragraph 58)[48] and have therefore tried, through this reflective chapter, to communicate what we have found 'in a clear, straightforward fashion' (BERA, 2024, paragraph 70).[49] We hope this chapter has offered a candid and useful look at researching ethically with children and young people which will encourage others to take such an approach with both confidence and humility.

Reflective questions

1. How can the need to gain adult consent (parent/carer and/or stakeholder) be negotiated with the CYP's right to assent?
2. What are some of the ways in which you can ensure that CYP have the right to withdraw?
3. Why is it important to consider using non-traditional research methods when working with CYP?
4. What parts of your identity do you think are relevant to thinking about your positionality in relation to young research participants, and how might they influence how you do research with them?
5. How could you use the Lundy Model (space, voice, audience, influence) to help you ensure children's rights are met through your research?

Further reading

1. United Nations Convention on the Rights of the Child, 1989: https://www.unicef.org.uk/what-we-do/un-convention-child-rights/.

   This is the basis for the Lundy model and any research that involves working with children and young people.

2. National Society for the Prevention of Cruelty to Children (NSPCC) guidelines for ethical research with children: https://learning.nspcc.org.uk/research-resources/briefings/research-with-children-ethics-safety-promoting-inclusion.

3. https://www.scottishbooktrust.com/book-lists/10-picture-books-about-refugees-and-migration.

   The Scottish Book Trust has put together a list of children's books about migration that researchers might find helpful to use as research tools.

4. https://inee.org/resources/conceptual-framework-education-research-conflict-and-protracted-crisis-ericc.

   The Conceptual Framework for Education Research in Conflict and Protracted Crisis (ERICC) project run by a consortium researching in conflict-affected societies.

5. https://www.open.edu/openlearn/health-sports-psychology/understanding-research-children-and-young-people/content-section-overview?active-tab=description-tab.

   Free Open Learn course on Understanding Research with Children and Young People.

6. https://inee.org/resources/conceptual-framework-education-research-conflict-and-protracted-crisis-ericc.

   The Conceptual Framework for Education Research in Conflict and Protracted Crisis (ERICC) project run by a Consortium researching in conflict-affected societies.

7. https://www.open.edu/openlearn/health-sports-psychology/understanding-research-children-and-young-people/content-section-overview?active-tab=description-tab.

   Free Open Learn course on Understanding Research with Children and Young People.

Notes

1. The rights of individuals should be borne in mind along with any potential social benefits of the research, and the researcher's right to conduct research in the service of public understanding. The researcher's obligations to the wider research community and to the public good may, in some circumstances, outweigh the researcher's obligations to act in accordance with the wishes of those in positions of economic, legal or political authority over the participants (such as employers, headteachers or government officials) (BERA, 2024, paragraph 36).
2. Principles of consent apply to children and young people as well as to adults. This is termed assent for those under the age of legal consent in the setting/culture. However, children of different ages vary in their capacity to make informed decisions. BERA endorses the United Nations Convention on the Rights of the Child (UNCRC);5 the best interests of the child are the primary consideration, and children who are capable of forming their own views should be granted the right to express those views freely, and have them taken into consideration, in all matters affecting them, commensurate with their age and maturity. Information sheets and consent forms should be appropriately designed for participants who may differ in such factors as age, reading ability and attention span. Researchers should be aware of issues to do with neurodiversity, as referenced in paragraph 2 (BERA, 2024, paragraph 23).
3. Ethical research design and implementation aim to put participants at their ease and to avoid making excessive demands on them. In advance of data collection, researchers have a responsibility to think through their duty of care in order to recognise potential harms, and to prepare for and be in a position to minimise and manage any distress or discomfort that may arise. Researchers should immediately reconsider any actions occurring during the research process that appear to cause emotional or other harm. The more vulnerable the participants, for whatever reasons, the greater the responsibilities of the researcher for their protection (BERA, 2024, paragraph 34).
4. These guidelines should not be interpreted as privileging particular research methods over others: the Association respects the diverse range of possible methods. Researchers who prefer or promote specific methods, theories or philosophies of research should have knowledge of alternative approaches sufficient to assure sponsors that they have considered these, and that the needs of the research are being properly addressed. Sponsors should be offered a full, honest and accessible justification for the final choice of methods (BERA, 2024, paragraph 56).

Researchers should, within the context and boundaries of their chosen methods, theories and philosophies of research, communicate the extent to which their data collection and analysis techniques, and the inferences to be drawn from their findings, are robust and can be seen to meet the criteria and markers of quality and integrity applied within different research approaches (BERA, 2024, paragraph 57).

5   This case study appears in a slightly adapted form as a web case study. Research Ethics Case Studies 2024 | BERA.
6   The Association expects researchers to be mindful of the ways in which structural inequalities – including those listed above but also socio-economic status, parental status and neurodiversity (BERA, 2024, paragraph 2).
7   Researchers should recognise the right of all participants to withdraw from research ... participants should be informed of this right (BERA, 2024, paragraph 31).
8   Researchers should aim to be open and honest with participants and other stakeholder, avoiding non-disclosure (BERA, 2024, paragraph 27).
9   Researchers ... should have knowledge of alternative approaches sufficient ..., that the needs of research are being properly addressed (paragraph 56).
10 See note 2 (paragraph 23).
11 An important consideration is the extent to which a researcher's reflective research ... impinges upon others – for example, in the case of power relationships (BERA, 2024, paragraph 19).
12 Researchers should ... communicate the extent to which their data collection ... are robust and can be seen to meet ... the markers of quality (BERA, 2024, paragraph 57).
13 Ethical research design and implementation aim to put participants at their ease ... Researchers should immediately minimise and managed any discomfort (BERA, 2024, paragraph 34).
14 Researchers should ... communicate the extent to which their ... findings are robust (BERA, 2024, paragraph 57).
15 Researchers following the UNCR will take into account the rights and duties of those who have legal responsibility for children (paragraph 24).
16 Ethical research design and implementation aim to put participants at their ease ... (BERA, 2024, paragraph 34).
17 ... children who are capable of forming their own views should be granted the right to express those views freely, and have them taken into consideration, in all matters affecting them ... (BERA, 2024, paragraph 23).
18 Researchers following the UNCR will take into account the rights and duties of those who have legal responsibility for children ... parents ... who have responsibility for the welfare and wellbeing of the participants ... (BERA, 2024, paragraph 24).

19 Researchers should do what they can to ensure that relevant individuals … are not, intentionally or otherwise, excluded from participation in their research (BERA, 2024, paragraph 37).
20 The Association reminds researchers of the protected characteristics as defined by the Equality Act 2010 – age, gender reassignment, being married or in a civil partnership, being pregnant or on maternity leave, disability, race including colour, nationality, ethnic or national origin, religion or belief, sex and sexual orientation. Beyond this, the Association expects researchers to be mindful of the ways in which structural inequalities – including those listed above but also socio-economic status, parental status and neurodiversity – affect all social relationships, including those that are formed in the course of research. Where relevant, attention should be paid to the ways in which such inequalities specifically affect vulnerable individuals and their relationships. Sensitivity and attentiveness towards such structural issues are important aspects of researchers' responsibilities to participants at all stages of research, including reporting and publication (BERA, 2024, paragraph 2).
21 See note 4 (paragraph 56).
22 Researchers should not undertake work for which they are not competent (BERA, 2024, paragraph 7).
23 See note 3 (paragraph 34).
24 It is normally expected that participants' voluntary informed consent to be involved in a study will be obtained at the start of the study, and that researchers will remain sensitive and open to the possibility that participants may wish, for any reason and at any time, to withdraw their consent. The Association takes voluntary informed and ongoing consent to be the condition by which participants understand and agree to their participation, and the terms and practicalities of it, without any duress. It should be made clear to participants that they can withdraw at any point without needing to provide an explanation – this is detailed in paragraphs 31 and 32 below. Researchers should be alert to non-verbal signs that individuals who previously consented to participate may no longer wish to. In such circumstances, renewed consent should be sought (BERA, 2024, paragraph 8).
25 See note 2 (paragraph 23).
26 The 'community of educational researchers' is considered to mean all those engaged in educational research – including, for example, students following research-based programmes of study, independent researchers and practitioners who undertake research, as well as staff who conduct educational research in their employment within organisations such as universities, schools, local and national government, charities and commercial bodies. Established educational researchers, and the

community as a whole, have a responsibility to support the next generation of educational researchers, including independent and practitioner researchers. The Association is supportive of the Researcher Development Concordat in this respect (BERA, 2024, paragraph 58).
27 See note 3 (paragraph 34).
28 All educational researchers should aim to protect the integrity and reputation of educational research by ensuring that they conduct their research to the highest standards. Researchers should contribute to the community spirit of critical analysis and constructive criticism that generates improvement in practice and enhancement of knowledge (BERA, 2024, paragraph 59).
29 Safeguarding the physical and psychological wellbeing of researchers is part of the ethical responsibility of employers and sponsors, as well as of researchers themselves. In general, there should be an ethics of care for researchers, including self-care. Safety can be a particular concern in certain circumstances, for example when fieldwork is undertaken in situations that are potentially risky. Researchers should be aware of the legal responsibilities as well as the moral duty of institutions towards the safety of staff and students. Institutions, sponsors and independent researchers should consider whether an in-depth risk assessment and ongoing monitoring of researcher safety is advisable, especially for those undertaking fieldwork, working in certain jurisdictions and/or investigating sensitive issues; this may be required by employers and sponsors. Principal investigators, other researchers, students undertaking research and their supervisors should ideally be offered training on researcher safety. Specialist training should be made available to researchers entering conflict or post-conflict settings, or areas with high levels of infection or other risks (BERA, 2024, paragraph 82).
30 Specific issues also arise with respect to consent within large-scale research across multiple settings. Institutional leaders may agree to take part, acting as gatekeepers on behalf of members (such as teachers and students in schools). In order to ensure that all participants are as fully informed as possible about the benefits and potential costs of the study, researchers should offer both information and support. This may result in participants exercising their right to opt out within the parameters of the intervention. Where stratified random sampling is used, it may be appropriate to select additional participants so that where institutions or individuals withdraw, they can be replaced (BERA, 2024, paragraph 18).
31 See note 24 (paragraph 8).
32 Researchers should aim to be open and honest with participants and other stakeholders, avoiding non-disclosure unless their research design

specifically requires it in order to ensure that the appropriate data are collected, or so that the researcher or participants are not put at risk. Decisions to use non-disclosure in research should be the subject of full, principled deliberation and subsequent disclosure in reporting (BERA, 2024, paragraph 27).

33 See note 3 (paragraph 34).
34 Researchers following the UNCRC will take into account the rights and duties of those who have legal responsibility for children, such as those who act in guardianship (for example, parents) or as 'responsible others' (that is, those who have responsibility for the welfare and wellbeing of the participants, such as social workers). This may involve gaining the consent of those responsible for children, such as parents, guardians or others in loco parentis (BERA, 2024, paragraph 24).

In the case of potential participants whose capacity, age or circumstances may limit the extent to which they can be expected to agree voluntarily to participate, researchers should fully explore ways in which they can be supported to participate with assent in the research. Care should be taken to ensure that documentation and oral information is as intelligible as possible. In such circumstances, researchers should also seek the collaboration and approval of those responsible for such participants (BERA, 2024, paragraph 25).

35 Researchers should do what they can to ensure that all potential participants understand, as well as they are able, what is involved in a study. They should be told why their participation is desired, what, if anything, they will be asked to do, what will happen to the data they provide and how and to whom the data will be reported. They also should be informed about the retention, sharing and any possible secondary uses of the data (BERA, 2024, paragraph 9).
36 See note 20 (paragraph 2).
37 BERA expects UK researchers to apply the same ethical principles to research they undertake outside of and within the UK. The application of these principles in different social, cultural and political contexts may require careful negotiation, adaptation and sensitivity, and there is ultimately no substitute for the integrity and ethical code of the individual researcher. In some countries it is advisable to work with a local person as a co-researcher/co-investigator in order to establish adequate levels of trust with prospective local participants. Appropriate permission should be sought from relevant authorities (such as community or religious leaders or local government officials) in cultures that adopt a collective approach to consent. However, in such cultures it should not be assumed that

individuals cannot make their own informed decisions about whether or not to take part in the research (BERA, 2024, paragraph 22).
38 Researchers should make known to the participants (or their guardians or responsible others) any predictable disadvantage or harm potentially arising from the process or reporting of the research. Any unexpected harm to participants that arises during the research should be brought immediately to their attention, or to the attention of their guardians or responsible others as appropriate. Researchers should take steps to minimise the effects of research designs that advantage or are perceived to advantage one group of participants over others. For example, in an experimental design (including a randomised controlled study), the intervention made available to one group, while being unavailable to the control or comparison group, may be viewed as desirable. In mitigation, for example, an intervention found to be effective can typically be offered to control groups after the end of a trial (BERA, 2024, paragraph 35).
39 See note 34 (paragraph 25).
40 Researchers should recognise the right of all participants to withdraw from the research for any or no reason, and participants should be informed of this right and how to exercise it. In most cases the appropriate course of action will simply be for the researchers to accept a participant's decision to withdraw, but there are circumstances in which researchers can appropriately discuss with the participant whether a course of action might be taken that would enable the participant to re-engage. Any decision to attempt to persuade a participant to re-engage should be taken with care, and coercion, duress of any form or additional incentives (see paragraph 33) must not be used. However, in cases in which participants are required by a contractual obligation to participate (for example, when mandated as part of their employment to facilitate an evaluation study), researchers may have proper recourse to a third party (the employing authority in this example) to request compliance (BERA, 2024, paragraph 31).
41 In circumstances in which some members of a group (such as students in a class or their parents/guardians) have not given consent to participate, for example in class observation, researchers should decide whether this was an active refusal of consent, in which case they would need to respect this and find a practical solution. For those whom it is not possible to contact to obtain consent, a decision should be taken as to how it might be appropriate to proceed, in conjunction with gatekeepers or other stakeholders (BERA, 2024, paragraph 16).
42 See note 34 (paragraph 24).
43 See note 29 (paragraph 82).

44 All educational researchers should aim to protect the integrity and reputation of educational research by ensuring that they conduct their research to the highest standards. Researchers should contribute to the community spirit of critical analysis and constructive criticism that generates improvement in practice and enhancement of knowledge (BERA, 2024, paragraph 59).
45 See note 34 (paragraph 25).
46 See note 2 (paragraph 23).
47 See note 34 (paragraph 24).
48 See note 26 (paragraph 58).
49 Educational researchers should communicate their findings, and the practical significance of their research, in a clear, straightforward fashion, and in language judged appropriate to the intended audience(s). Researchers have a responsibility to make the results of their research available for the benefit of educational professionals, policymakers and the wider public, subject only to the provisos indicated in subsequent paragraphs. They should not accept contractual terms that obstruct their exercise of this responsibility (BERA, 2024, paragraph 70).

References

Arizpe, E., Colomer, T. and Martinez-Roldan, C. (2014). *Visual Journeys through Wordless Narratives*. London: Bloomsbury.
Bird, D., Culley, L. and Lakhanpaul, M. (2013). Why collaborate with children in health research: An analysis of the risks and benefits of collaboration with children. *Archives of Disability Childhood Educational Practice Education*, 98(2), 42–48.
Bluestone, C. D. and Klein, J. O. (2007). *Otitis Media in Infants and Children* (4th ed.). Hamilton, ON: BC Decker.
Bray, R. and Moses, S. (2011). Children and participation in South Africa: Exploring the landscape. *Perspectives in Education*, 29(1), 6–17.
British Educational Research Association (BERA) (2024). *Ethical Guidelines for Educational Research* (5th ed.). London: BERA. http://www.bera.ac.uk/publication/ethical-guidelines-for-educational-research-2024.
Capewell, C. (2015). Hearing maps: Documenting a child's speech comprehension in noise. *Audacity*, 7, 20–2.
Capewell, C. (2023). Involving Children in Research: Active Participation and Ongoing Assent. In C. Brown, and M. Wild (Eds.), *Ethical Dilemmas

in Educational Research Considering Challenges and Risks in Practice, Maidenhead: Open University Press (pp. 61–73).

Chambers, P., Jitpiromsri, S. and Waitoolkiat, N. (2019). Conflict in the Deep South of Thailand: Never-ending stalemate? *Asian International Studies Review*, 20(Special issue), 1–24.

Davies, N. and Cobb, R. (2018). *The Day the War Came*. Somerville, MA: Candlewick Press.

Fargas-Malet, M., McSherry, D., Larkin, E. and Robinson, C. (2010). Research with children: Methodological issues and innovative techniques. *Journal of Early Childhood Research*, 8(2), 175–92.

Goodhand, J. (2000). Research in conflict zones: Ethics and accountability. *Forced Migration Review*, 8, 12–15.

Hanna, H. (2021). Listening to Silence in the Quest to Offer Migrant Learners a 'Voice' through Picturebook Research in South Africa. In A. Fox, H. Busher, and C. Capewell (Eds.), *Thinking Critically and Ethically about Research for Education*, Abingdon: Routledge (pp. 78–91).

Hanna, H. (2022). Recognising silence and absence as part of multivocal storytelling in and through wordless picturebooks: Migrant learners in South Africa engaging with the Arrival. *Literacy*, 56(1), 40–9. https://onlinelibrary.wiley.com/doi/epdf/10.1111/lit.12269.

Hanna, H. (2023). Being a migrant learner in a South African primary school: recognition and racialisation. *Children's Geographies*, 21(3), 518–32. https://www.tandfonline.com/doi/full/10.1080/14733285.2022.2084601.

Harcourt, D. and Quennerstedt, A. (2014). *Ethical Guardrails When Children Participate in Research: Risk and Practice in Sweden and Australia*. SAGE open. July–September. 1–8. https://doi.org/10.1177/2158244014543782.

Helbardt, S., Hellmann-Rajanayagam, D. and Korff, R. (2010). War's dark glamour: Ethics of research in war and conflict zones. *Cambridge Review of International Affairs*, 23(2), 349–69.

Human Rights Watch (2010). *'Targets of both Sides': Violence against Students, Teachers, and Schools in Thailand's Southern Border Provinces*.

Kara, H. (2015). *Creative Research Methods in the Social Sciences. A Practical Guide*. Bristol: Policy Press.

Kobald, I. and Blackwood, F. (2014). *My Two Blankets*. New York: Little Clarion.

Kucharczyk, S. and Hanna, H. (2020). Balancing teacher power and children's rights: Rethinking the use of picturebooks in multicultural primary schools in England. *Human Rights Education Review*, 3(1), 49–68. http://doi.org/10.7577/hrer.3726.

Lowe, R. (2012). Children deconstructing childhood. *Children and Society*, 26(4), 269–79. Doi: 10.1111/j.1099-0860.2010.00344.

Lundy, L. (2007). 'Voice' is not enough: Conceptualising article 12 of the United Nations Convention on the Rights of the Child. *British Educational Research Journal*, 33(6), 927–42. http://dx.doi.org/10.1080/01411920701657033.

Mazzei, L. A. (2003). Inhabiting silences: In pursuit of a muffled subtext. *Qualitative Inquiry*, 9(3), 355–68.

McCargo, D. (2008). *Tearing Apart the Land: Islam and Legitimacy in Southern Thailand*. Ithaca, NY: Cornell University Press.

Mitchell, C., Theron, L., Stuart, J., Smith, A. and Campbell, Z. (2011). Drawings as Research Method. In T. Linda, M. Claudia, S. Ann, and S. Jean (Eds.), *Picturing Research: Drawing as Visual Methodology*, Leiden: Brill Academic Pub (pp. 19–36).

Palmary, I. (2009). *For Better Implementation of Migrant Children's Rights in South Africa*. UNICEF. http://www.migration.org.za/wp-content/uploads/2017/08/For-Better-Implementation-of-Migrant-Children%E2%80%99s-Rights-in-South-Africa.pdf.

Pherali, T. (2021). Social justice, education and peacebuilding: Conflict transformation in southern Thailand. *Compare: A Journal of Comparative and International Education*, 53(4), 1–18.

Savin-Baden, M. and Howell Major, C. (2013). *Qualitative Research: The Essential Guide to Theory and Practice*. Abingdon: Routledge.

Spyrou, S. (2016). Researching children's silences: Exploring the fullness of voice in childhood research. *The Child*, 23(1), 7–21.

Tan, S. (2006). *The Arrival*. London: Hodder.

UNICEF (2014). *Thailand Case Study in Education, Conflict and Social Cohesion*. Bangkok: UNICEF East Asia and Pacific Regional Office (EAPRO). https://deepsouthwatch.org/th/node/6408.

UNICEF (2016). *Bridge to a Brighter Tomorrow: The Patani Malay-Thai Multilingual Education Programme*. Bangkok: UNICEF Thailand. https://www.unicef.org/thailand/media/1291/file/Bridge%20to%20a%20Brighter%20Tomorrow%20(Summary%20Report).pdf.

United Nations (2020). *The Sustainable Development Goals Report 2020*. United Nations. https://sdgs.un.org/publications/sustainable-development-goals-report-2020-24686.

7

Dilemmas of Care in Online Interviewing

by *Aimee Quickfall and Phil Wood*

Introduction

Interviews are a classic data collection method across research paradigms, and typically, pre-Covid, would take place face-to-face with ethical considerations based on being in the same room. As researchers, we are very interested in how ethical processes and considerations need to be adapted to reflect the evolution of methods. In this chapter, we will share a case study which is fictionalised, but based on multiple experiences we had during the pandemic and post-pandemic period. We experienced this phenomenon in real life during the pandemic, as we undertook research with newly qualified teachers and head teachers about their Covid experiences (Quickfall et al., 2022; Quickfall and Wood, 2024). Previously, we had used interview methods in a number of studies, usually interviewing participants face-to-face, sometimes entailing long-distance travel for us as researchers (e.g. Quickfall, 2022). We both research experiences of teachers, student teachers and academics; Aimee often with a focus on well-being and mental health and Phil often with a focus on organisations, change and policy.

Online interviews did of course exist before Covid, with possibilities explored in the research literature, for example asynchronous interviews facilitated by email (James and Busher, 2006) and telephone interviewing (Sturges and Hanrahan, 2004; Nambiar and Benny, 2021) but the use of online interview tools was not well explored pre-pandemic (Gray et al., 2020). With the outbreak of the Covid-19 pandemic worldwide, the opportunity to carry out face-to-face interviews was removed for many months, and in some places, years (Torrentira, 2020). Researchers had to quickly adapt in order to continue with their projects, and many researchers also wanted to conduct research on the experiences of people during the pandemic (Saarijärvi and Bratt, 2021). The 'technology lag' in ethical guidelines reported almost twenty years ago (Hair and Clark, 2007) is an ongoing issue for researchers (Viljoen and Cilliers 2019; 2021). Whilst there is excellent ethical guidance on working as an online researcher (e.g. Association of Internet Researchers ethical guidelines 3.0, 2019), much of this relates to gathering data from internet sources rather than how to adapt traditional face-to-face methods for new online resources.

As many aspects of work and leisure adapted to the pandemic and lockdown, the proliferation in use of online conferencing tools such as Teams and Zoom gave the research community a way of continuing interviews with participants whilst ensuring that Covid restrictions and ethical requirements to protect the health of their participants could be maintained (Serekoane et al., 2021). Positive aspects of online interviewing include convenience and ease of use, accessibility and time-saving, meaning that participants with caring and work commitments are able to participate more easily, as well as those in remote locations (Gray et al., 2020; Serekoane et al., 2021). Online interviewing also can cut the costs of data collection, such as costs of travel, venue hire and refreshments, and mean that researchers can consider a wider geographical scope for studies and reach previously excluded participants, such as those with caring responsibilities and physical access challenges. Research participants can leave online interviews at the click of a button, arguably giving them more agency in participation (Seitz, 2015).

However, the use of online interviewing requires careful thought and planning, as it is not the same as a face-to-face interview, either in the experience of taking part (Thunberg and Arnell, 2022) or the ethical considerations required. The BERA Ethical Guidelines (2024) state:

> Digital/online research, as well as the use of artificial intelligence, is a rapidly developing area, therefore conventions as to what constitutes good ethical practice are not as well established as in most other areas of educational research. Nevertheless, the fundamental principles apply. (paragraph 4)

Some studies have suggested that online interview methods are not suitable when researching sensitive topics (Seitz, 2015) because of data storage security risks and the reduced capacity of the researcher in identifying distress in the participant. Surmiak, Bielska and Kalinowska's study (2022) suggests that some social researchers believed it was unethical to move sensitive studies online because of a reduced opportunity to build an 'atmosphere of mutual trust' (p. 218). Other studies suggest the opposite – that online interviews are suitable for sensitive topics because of the distance between researcher and participant (Thunberg and Arnell, 2022).

Some researchers recommend caution and careful consideration when using online data collection methods with participants who have disabilities or who are neurodivergent (Kim and Sutharson, 2021). Szulc (2022) gives the example of online interviews where video backgrounds can be very distracting for neurodivergent participants, and this is just one consideration to take into account. Szulc (2022) recommends involving participants in the planning process for research but also cautions that people are unique; certain accommodations may work for some, but not for others.

Other researchers have pointed to potential challenges around privacy, given that platforms used to host interviews are usually owned by third-party companies whose primary purpose is not to uphold research ethics (Seitz, 2015). Researchers may give reassurances about their own data management processes (such as storing downloaded data files on a secure hard drive) whilst the third-party companies themselves have no such guarantees on data security. This can vary greatly depending on the companies involved and the legal jurisdictions they are operating within.

Online interviews may appear to solve issues around geographical space and place, but the interviewer and interviewee both have environments to control, and consideration in advance is needed around colleagues, family members and strangers entering that environment during the interview, particularly where sensitive topics are being discussed (Adams-Hutcheson and Longhurst, 2017).

Whilst online methods 'need not be considered unilaterally riskier than in-person data collection' (Newman et al., 2021), they are not the same as face-to-face research interactions; they are different, as we will explore in our fictionalised ethical dilemma.

Ethic of care

The notion of an ethic of care threads through our dilemma. Ethic of care describes the way of thinking about caring that includes 'many of the everyday judgements involved in activities of caring for ourselves and others' (Tronto, 1998: 15). The theory of ethic of care has been a significant influence and aspect of feminist research since the 1990s (e.g. Held, 1993; Jaggar, 1995; Sevenhuijsen, 1998) and invites us to consider ethics as it was originally conceptualised, as knowledge of how to live a good and meaningful life. This means that the researcher has a responsibility to the participant and themselves for the research process to contribute to that sense of a good life and a meaningful experience. Whilst formal ethics processes uphold principles and rules of ethics in institutions, disciplines and nations, an ethic of care offers a view of a more complex and nuanced ethical approach to add to the valuable work of ethics committees and boards.

In a research context, it can be challenging to balance the ethic of care with formal ethical requirements and demands of universities and other organisations (Evans, 2016). However, it is possible for researchers to critically examine inequalities and power to protect their participants and themselves (Reich, 2021). Reich suggests that a research ethic of care should be reflexive and require the researcher to make decisions around their own and participant's vulnerability and harm (Reich, 2021).

The ethical dilemma

In this case study, we explore the fictionalised case of face-to-face planned interviews being adapted to synchronised online interviews at short notice, with three key considerations highlighted that make online interviews different to face-to-face equivalents: withdrawal from the interview, follow-up and aftercare. Whilst this dilemma is fictional, it draws upon our own experiences of research. It is worth noting that this fictionalised case is set in a university, with research ethics protocols and an ethics committee, and that this situation may 'play out' differently in a commercial, practitioner or independent research setting. In UK universities, each university has ethics protocols and an ethics review board or committee to uphold these protocols and to advise and support researchers. This structure is enacted to protect participants from exploitation but also to protect universities from reputational damage and legal consequences of unethical research practices (Quickfall, 2022).

Background and ethical preparation

Jo and Femi are successful in applying for external funding for their research project and are granted ethical approval in February 2020 to carry out face-to-face interviews with twenty participants who are teachers about their experiences of working in schools. The interviews are planned to be unstructured, with the participants invited to tell the researcher what it is like to do their job. Given the very open nature of the interview, Jo and Femi are aware that the interviews may cover sensitive and personal topics, and the ethical approval granted reflects this. As part of the ethics design:

- Participants will be contacted through school networks and invited to participate. If they respond, an information sheet and consent form will be sent to them.
- Interviews will be held in their school, on the university campus, or in another quiet public place (e.g. a library meeting room). Participants choose the venue.
- Participants will be sent a reminder before the agreed interview date and time to confirm and will be reminded of key information and consent before the interview starts.
- If the participant does not attend the interview, one email will be sent inviting them to re-arrange the interview. If no response is received, the researchers will cease to contact the participant.
- Participants can withdraw from the study at any point before or during the interview, and may request that their data be withdrawn from the study up to a month after their interview date.
- A debrief sheet will be given to participants during the face-to-face interview, sharing contact details for appropriate support services and charities and informing participants that disclosure of criminal activity or safeguarding concerns would lead to other agencies such as the police being informed.

By March 2020, it was clear that the interviews would not be able to take place face-to-face due to the ballooning infection rates from Covid-19 and university guidance on safe working. Jo and Femi decided to go ahead with the study, particularly as the funding for the project was for a fixed period and no one knew how long the pandemic would last. Amendments were made to the ethical approval to change the face-to-face interviews to online, and some thought was given to how this might change the study. For example, Femi thought about data analysis and how the interactions between participant and researcher may be different online, and of course because some data would not be captured (e.g. hand gesticulation off-screen). Femi decided that because they were not focusing on physical movement and gesture, the research design was not significantly disrupted.

However, the research protocols in terms of withdrawing from the interview were not adapted, and it was deemed that the previous face-to-face considerations would still apply to an online interview situation. Jo and Femi were not alone in taking this approach during the pandemic. Surmiak, Bielska and Kalinowska (2022) surveyed 193 researchers during the early months of the pandemic and found that they broadly fell into three groups: those who reported that nothing had changed and no additional thought on ethical issues was required, those who saw opportunities in the changes, and those who reported needing precautions in place to work ethically during the pandemic. Jo and Femi seem to take an approach to adapting their ethical design that assumes nothing has changed to a serious extent and that there are opportunities to change the design in order to retain funding and complete the project. The change they made was in the mode of interview, which was changed to online.

Ethical issues that arose during the research

The first two interviews went as planned and did not feel to Jo and Femi to be significantly different in terms of ethics from their face-to-face equivalent. Jo and Femi interviewed the participants separately, as per their research design, and then talked to each other following the interviews to debrief and make sure things were going well. The ethical protocols put in place for face-to-face interviews seemed to be adequate, and Jo and Femi had no concerns about the first two participants in terms of their care. However, during the third online interview, the participant, Ali, shared a personal story with Jo about being bullied by her current head teacher, to the point where Ali had become ill, suffered from depression and began to question whether they were fit for the job. Ali was visibly distressed, crying and at times struggling to get her words out. Jo was concerned about Ali and the potential harm caused by continuing with the interview. Jo asked if Ali wanted to pause or stop the interview. At that point, Ali left the online call without responding verbally to Jo.

Jo contacted Femi immediately for advice – should Ali be contacted, how should that contact happen, and what should Jo do if they could not get in touch with Ali? Both Femi and Jo were concerned about the welfare of the participant. The BERA Ethical Guidelines (2024) state that:

> Researchers should recognise the right of all participants to withdraw from the research for any or no reason, and participants should be informed of this right and how to exercise it. In most cases the appropriate course of action will simply be for the researchers to accept a participant's decision to withdraw, but there are circumstances in which researchers can appropriately discuss with the participant whether a course of action might be taken that would enable the participant to re-engage. (paragraph 31)

Jo and Femi felt that in this circumstance, they could not be certain that Ali had wanted to withdraw and were also concerned about her wellbeing.

Course of action

Contacting Ali

Both Femi and Jo felt that the right course of action was to contact Ali, although the ethics approval they had completed did not specify this as part of their process, and participants had not been informed that the researchers would contact them if they left during the online interview. Despite this potential hurdle, Femi and Jo felt that their duty of care to Ali justified an attempt to contact her. The researchers decided that an email to Ali would be less intrusive than a phone call or online call, and give Ali agency to decide whether to reply or not. Femi and Jo contacted the chair of their research ethics committee to let her know what they were planning to do and their rationale. Luckily, the chair of the committee was able to respond quickly and agreed with their plan to contact Ali. The BERA (2024) guidelines are useful here, as whilst ideally all participants would have been informed of follow-up communications following the termination of an interview meeting, as per paragraph 9:

> Researchers should do what they can to ensure that all potential participants understand, as well as they are able, what is involved in a study. They should be told why their participation is desired, what, if anything, they will be asked

to do, what will happen to the data they provide and how and to whom the data will be reported. (paragraph 9)

Paragraph 31 clarifies why researchers may contact participants:

In most cases the appropriate course of action will simply be for the researchers to accept a participant's decision to withdraw, but there are circumstances in which researchers can appropriately discuss with the participant whether a course of action might be taken that would enable the participant to re-engage. (paragraph 31)

Meanwhile, for the researchers, this was a stressful situation and an unfamiliar one. In previous research work, Jo and Femi's experiences of interviewing had always been face-to-face, where they felt adept at monitoring participant distress and taking action rapidly if needed. Both had experienced research interviews 'in person' that had been paused or stopped because of distress, interruptions and emergencies (even a fire alarm going off!), and both felt confident in negotiating these situations, but the online interview was new territory. Ali had quite literally 'disappeared' in the midst of sharing a distressing series of experiences, which had happened in the school where they had logged in for their interview. Femi began to wonder whether the participant had been overheard, and had terminated the interview because of fear of further bullying in their workplace, or whether the interview had just become too distressing, or whether something as simple as a power cut or Wi-Fi issue had occurred. Jo and Femi both felt regret that they had rushed to adapt their research design without fully reflecting on the potential differences with online interviewing, including their own self-care. Both questioned what their role was in safeguarding Ali, given that in previous research they had both undertaken projects with children, when the scenario covered in this case study would have triggered a safeguarding protocol, including raising a concern with relevant bodies (such as parents/guardians and institutions). Jo was upset by the experience and talked to Femi about whether they should continue with the project in any format. Femi felt that it was more important to understand and adapt their process than to stop the research as this would have ethical ramifications in its own right by curtailing the rights of other participants to tell their stories. Both were worried about Ali and her wellbeing in this situation.

Jo emailed the participant with the following message (Figure 7.1), drawing upon the debrief sheet, but in unexpected circumstances:

From: jo.k@WBU.ac.uk

Sent: Wednesday, 10.30am

To: Ali <ali.jones@bubbles.com>

Cc: Femi <femi.g@WBU.ac.uk>

Subject: Research Interview

Hi Ali

Just wanted to send a quick message to say that I hope you are ok.

Figure 7.1 Email from Jo (researcher) to Ali (research participant).

Source: Authors (fictionalised).

Both Jo and Femi were worried about the wording of the message and rewrote it several times, trying to maintain the participant-researcher relationship and professional distance, whilst feeling really concerned about Ali as a person in distress. Jo had a sleepless night after sending the email, checking her email inbox every ten minutes or so.

Two days later, Jo received a response from Ali, who explained that she had felt both overwhelmed by emotion after sharing her experiences and also fearful that she may be overheard crying in her classroom. She expressed a wish to continue as a participant, and Jo and Femi arranged to reschedule the interview for a time when Ali could log in from home, rather than needing to 'hold' the interview in a public place as the face-to-face protocol suggested. Jo and Femi were concerned that Ali was consenting freely, rather than feeling like she owed them an interview. When they met online a second time, Jo discussed this with Ali and was reassured that this was a free choice to participate. The interview was completed, with Ali logging in from home and appearing and reporting that she felt much more comfortable with this arrangement, which also enabled her to collect her children from school and have dinner with them before joining the meeting.

Alternative courses of action

Femi and Jo could have taken a few different courses of action at various points in the research design and implementation. In this section, some of these key action points are identified, with alternative choices explored. We have made an effort here to not only consider the choices that Femi and Jo made, as experienced researchers, but also the support and guidance they were offered (or could have been offered) by their employers and funders. It is important to us that the part of the wider system is acknowledged in ethical dilemmas and issues, rather than being reduced to a competency or legal problem for individuals.

Consideration of online/face-to-face differences

Hindsight is a wonderful thing, and in our fictionalised case, this is certainly true. Jo and Femi might have taken more time to consider the differences in their new data collection method. Jowett (2020) suggests that researchers 'take time to pause and reflect on whether data collection can be postponed' (p. 3) when methods are forced suddenly to be changed, for example, in the 2020/21 pandemic. Jowett acknowledges that for some researchers, such as master's students, there may be little opportunity to postpone data collection and we also suggest that this applies to funded research, where deadlines can be tricky or impossible to renegotiate. Jo and Femi would have felt pressure to stick to their funding timeline, despite the pandemic, and this may have exacerbated the issues with their research design.

Ideally, Jo and Femi would have spent time considering the differences in online interviewing, discussed this with the ethics leads in their institution, and read the guidance and literature in this area before deciding on a new protocol for the project. Whilst the literature concerning online interviews was decidedly scarcer pre-pandemic, there are insightful papers and books that pre-date the pandemic and discuss methodological and ethical considerations (e.g. James and Busher, 2007; Seitz, 2015; Gupta, 2017). Jo and Femi could have spent some time reviewing their processes and integrating some of the guidance and advice on offer, such as considering specific protocols for participant withdrawal in online scenarios.

However, it is important to consider the university's responsibility to its researchers in this situation. Whilst Femi and Jo are experienced researchers, during a fast-changing situation like the pandemic, particularly with funded or time-pressured projects, the university systems might have adapted to provide more support to those who were making rapid changes to methodologies, in terms of ethics and researcher health. Whilst many researchers would not have needed support to adapt projects and make decisions about funding, timelines and capacity in that situation (obviously with recourse to the ethics board and potentially re-application for approval), the offer of support from the employer, who has the overview of all projects given approval through the university, seems like a good way to support staff. It can be argued that the hierarchical 'hurdle jumping' nature of ethical approval often seen in universities (Fox and Busher, 2022) means that ongoing support with research projects, particularly in relation to ethics, is not easily accessed or organised. Jo and Femi did go back to the ethics committee for approval of the change to online interviews and did seek advice from the chair of the committee when their research protocol did not cover the situation with Ali – but we can imagine that the official nature of these roles and processes would dissuade some from jeopardising their ethical approval with further questions and problems. It is also important to reflect on the capacity of an ethics board, chair or committee to advise on the intricacies of ethics for methodologies that may be unfamiliar or rapidly emerging (Fallon and Long, 2007). The chair of the ethics committee may have little or no experience of their method, yet is expected to be able to offer advice and a judgement on what they should do next.

Jo and Femi might have decided, on reflection, to postpone their data collection and wait for the end of the pandemic and a return to safe face-to-face methods. However, as is demonstrated in this fictionalised case, online data collection can be more convenient and appealing for participants who would have faced practical issues in taking part, such as caregivers, and in the Covid-19 pandemic this would have likely resulted in them losing their funding and not completing the project.

Another consideration in this case is the extent to which Ali would have been aware of the setting of her online interview and the privacy level in her classroom:

> Researchers need to be aware that participants' understandings of their level of privacy in a particular place, especially in online spaces, may be inaccurate. (BERA, 2024, paragraph 44)

Whilst this guideline may naturally fit with online spaces as risky in terms of privacy, for Ali, her own classroom was not necessarily a safe space to share her story. Again, Jo and Femi might have considered this when re-applying for ethical approval, as their previous face-to-face protocols had required interviews in a public place, such as a classroom or library, but online interviews give a potential advantage in terms of privacy and participant choice, which they could have built into their redesign. Whether Femi and Jo would have ever wanted to override the participant choice of venue, as set out in their research design, is another matter.

Not contacting Ali

In the adaptation of face-to-face to online interviews, the protocol remained the same – that participants could withdraw at any point before or during the interview, with no questions asked and without the need for an explanation. This was the project information shared with Ali and other participants before their interviews, and therefore, the expected process that Femi and Jo would follow after Ali left the call. The BERA guidelines (2024) give researchers some valuable advice when considering these dilemmas in paragraph 34.

> Ethical research design and implementation aim to put participants at their ease and to avoid making excessive demands on them. In advance of data collection, researchers have a responsibility to think through their duty of care in order to recognise potential harms, and to prepare for and be in a position to minimise and manage any distress or discomfort that may arise. Researchers should immediately reconsider any actions occurring during the research process that appear to cause emotional or other harm. (paragraph 34)

It could be argued here that contacting Ali was an effort to manage distress or discomfort, by reconsidering the actions (which in this case, would have entailed no action).

The impact of taking this decision is an unknown; in our fictionalised case, we have the benefit of knowing that Ali was distressed at the time and place of the interview – and potentially, had Jo not reached out, may have got in touch with the researchers, or may not have done so. We don't know for certain that Jo's email did not exert pressure on Ali to reconsider taking part. Strictly following the planned ethics processes for this project, Femi and Jo should not have contacted Ali after she left the meeting, for this very reason – avoidance of pressure on the participant to continue. However, given the differences in online interviewing and the uncertainty around Ali leaving the meeting, it is understandable that the researchers were concerned about their participant's wellbeing and uncertain of Ali's motives for leaving the call. In a face-to-face equivalent, Ali may have left the room without giving an explanation – this was part of the ethics protocol, and perhaps something that, in retrospect, Femi and Jo would plan differently. For example, they could have planned to contact participants once if they left the interview, with no obligation from the participant to respond. Whilst this may seem a little clumsy for a face-to-face interview, the situation could still arise, and planning for this saves an ethical dilemma such as the one faced by Femi and Jo. There is a delicate balance to be struck between infantilising adult participants, who may have volunteered to participate because they wanted to speak frankly and emotionally with an outsider, and supporting researchers to feel content with their design.

Jo and Femi's wellbeing may also be a consideration here; whilst ethical protocols are often grounded in the notion of the researcher as an impartial, objective observer (Mortensen et al., 1996), Jo's obvious distress following the termination of the interview suggests further support for these researchers may have been needed. Whilst we would not want to argue that ethical protocols are changed to protect researcher wellbeing over and above responsibilities to participants (for example, justifying a change of communication protocol purely to reassure Jo that Ali was ok), researcher care is also important and should not be left to luck.

Not offering Ali a further interview

Another point where the case study may have taken an alternative path is in the offer of a further interview for Ali. Femi and Jo did not have this as part of their research protocol but talked through this with the chair of their ethics committee as a possibility for increasing Ali's options in terms of participation or withdrawal. When planning the face-to-face version of their data collection, Femi and Jo did not expect that participants would withdraw mid-interview and thought that in the unlikely event that this did happen, it would be obvious that the participant had deliberately ended the interview and therefore did not want to participate. Online, there are many reasons why a meeting may end unexpectedly, and an attendee leaving the meeting is just one.

It could be argued that offering a further participation opportunity puts pressure on Ali to accept, particularly when this was not part of the information sheet, and hence Ali would not be expecting this as part of withdrawing from the interview. An alternative view of this might suggest that Ali has invested time and effort into this interview so far, and that becoming upset or distressed should be an anticipated part of this sort of qualitative research for the research team and ethics reviewers. Ali has a right as a participant to finish her interview – and it may harm her if she is not allowed this opportunity, through frustration and confusion over her forced withdrawal from the project. Granted, this was not part of the research protocol for the study, and building in protocols retrospectively is considered dubious ethical practice; however, Femi and Jo were mindful of their responsibilities as set out in the BERA (2024) guidelines:

> Researchers should do what they can to ensure that relevant individuals and communities are not, intentionally or otherwise, excluded from participation in their research. (paragraph 34)

Different support structures for Jo and Femi

Femi and Jo find themselves in a position where ethical approval has been granted, but they still need support with ethics, even as experienced researchers. The pandemic brought about a sudden change for many of us in our ways of working as researchers – but experienced researchers may also find themselves in unforeseen situations, or using new methods, and require additional support. It can be difficult to re-engage with ethical issues once approval has been granted, and sharing ethical dilemmas is a potentially risky activity if your approval is then put in jeopardy. Normalising these discussions between researchers 'could bring about a research culture of shared dilemmas' (Quickfall, 2022: 9) and may have helped Jo and Femi.

Jo and Femi find themselves with a dilemma that causes stress and sleepless nights, and regardless of the ethical protocols in place, the situation could still arise and cause similar problems. For example, even if Femi and Jo had planned and communicated a plan to contact participants who withdraw during the interview, Ali might not have responded to that communication, leaving them with an ongoing concern for Ali and her situation. As stated in the BERA guidelines (2024):

> Safeguarding the physical and psychological wellbeing of researchers is part of the ethical responsibility of employers and sponsors, as well as of researchers themselves. In general, there should be an ethics of care for researchers, including self-care. (paragraph 82)

Femi and Jo's university have protocols on researcher safeguarding and wellbeing – but these focus on obvious threats to safety, such as entering conflict zones or infection outbreaks, or on support and care for early career researchers and student teachers, who are assigned a supervisor or mentor. Jo and Femi supported each other by discussing the dilemma and planning their next course of action.

Let's imagine that their employer has a different approach to researcher support and wellbeing. At the point when Ali leaves the online meeting, Femi and Jo discuss what has happened and then contact their research ethics mentor. They have a mentor despite being experienced researchers, who they meet with throughout the life of the project to discuss how things are going. Their mentor reassures them and helps them plan the next steps, liaising with the formal ethics structures of the university to make changes to the ethics protocol for the project together. Their mentor can call upon a group of mentors, who have expertise across methods and methodologies. Jo and Femi's mentor also feeds back to the group of research ethics mentors, voicing a concern about methodological changes brought about by the move online and bringing about university-wide guidance on switching research projects online and considerations for researchers at all levels. The mentor group also organises optional online training for researchers and facilitates a collection of hints and tips from researchers themselves on how they have negotiated ethical dilemmas in this area. This ongoing research ethics support means that the whole research community benefits from the discussion and exploration of a dilemma, rather than repeating the same situation across projects in the same institution, and provides researchers with opportunities to develop their own skills in a collegiate, democratic environment (Fox and Busher, 2022). Whilst this is a positive case study to imagine, the practical challenges of sourcing and resourcing mentors for this role in busy departments are significant. It is possible that careful reflection and review of research reports and feedback from researchers could achieve similar outcomes, with better and more up-to-date guidance for researchers.

Final thoughts

Here we summarise the lessons learned from our fictionalised case study, with specific regard to researcher decision-making around care of participants. You may also take other lessons from this case for your own research.

Care of participants

A central ethical thread through this case was the ethic of care for participants, which ultimately resulted in changes to the project protocol to facilitate inclusion and agency for the participants. In this case, as in many 'real-life' situations, the path to better care for participants is not a clear one. Here, contacting Ali might have caused her unnecessary distress or put pressure on her to continue participating, but equally, contacting her might give Ali options and provide signposting to support. The researchers had to think carefully about a course of action that would minimise harm, whilst protecting participant rights around consent, withdrawal and data use. In this example, as in our own experiences of interviewing, the participant's wellbeing was the priority, and the fictional researchers worked towards a solution from that starting point. Involving the chair of the ethics committee, and, in our alternative actions, having access to a research ethics mentor meant that the researchers were not making decisions in an echo chamber, and lessons learnt could be used to protect other project participants by informing and advising the wider research community.

Considerations when making changes to projects

Research designs often have to change, sometimes after ethical approval processes in universities and after equivalent ethical reviews and reflections in other settings. It is vitally important that researchers feel able to change their projects and have clear pathways for incorporating ethical thinking into making those changes. As we saw in the fictionalised case, research changes that were driven by a global crisis were primarily about methods and tools, and the ethical implications were not reflected upon properly until later. For researchers in the thick of a crisis, whether global, national or local, it might not be clear that there are ethical implications in the changes they wish to make. Whilst ideally researchers would take time to reflect on this carefully, with a very real option of not continuing the project (Jowett, 2020), there are practical reasons why this might not be realistic, including funding pressures and timelines for completion (with funded projects and student research). Universities and funders should build in systems to avoid the 'tick box' nature of ethical approval being granted, entailing that ethical reflection can stop (Fox and Busher, 2022; Quickfall, 2022). For example, having ethics support that continues throughout the life of the project may give researchers opportunities to explore ethical dilemmas before they happen and have a safe space to discuss ethical dilemmas as they occur.

Careful consideration when researching online

A clear lesson from the fictionalised case, and from our own experience, is that moving research online does not mean the face-to-face protocols will fit. Whilst online methods 'need not be considered unilaterally riskier than in-person data collection' (Newman et al., 2021: 11), they are not the same as face-to-face research methods and require 'thoughtful, reflexive, and deliberative approaches in order to identify and mitigate potential and dynamically evolving risks' (Newman et al., 2021: 11). For any researcher planning online methods or changing face-to-face methods to online during the project, it is vital to engage with the research literature that is specific to these tools (e.g. Franzke et al., 2020), rather than engaging only with general literature on, for example, interviews. Where technology is brand new, literature may be scarce or non-existent and therefore researchers must be supported by their institutions and employers to ensure they are not taking additional risks in using these tools. Where ethics committees and advisors are not familiar with new technologies and tools themselves, again, time needs to be given over to consulting experts, discussing advantages and disadvantages and, where possible, engaging with training to upskill the research community.

All of this takes time (and potentially additional finances), and the responsibility for developing and maintaining researcher capacity and skill has to be shouldered by the employer, rather than relying on 'experienced researchers' to be masters of every new development and tool in research. Research funders also need to make allowances in terms of timelines, where innovative methods are being used that require flexibility and often, additional training. We would not expect new technology to be used with medical patients without extensive training, trialling and evaluation, and the same principles should hold when it comes to research design and methods.

A case for ongoing researcher support

In our fictionalised case, Femi and Jo experience impacts on their own wellbeing because of their ethical dilemmas. We have experienced this first-hand with our own real-life research, because caring about your participants can very often mean that there are emotional loads for the researchers to bear, too. In the alternative actions section, we suggested ways in which Femi and

Jo's university could have restructured their ethics processes and people to better support research in action, and this has been explored thoroughly in the literature (e.g. Eliasson and DeHart, 2022; Fox and Busher, 2022; Folkes, 2023). Where these wider structures do not exist for the researcher, or are slow to change, it is important that researchers at any level of experience have routes to support with ethics, which extend beyond gaining ethical approval. With experience, some aspects of researcher self-care may become easier and more familiar, but even those with significant experience can find themselves wrestling with ethical issues or experience distressing situations during data collection. We expect protocols in place around safeguarding vulnerable participants, reporting criminal and abusive behaviour that is disclosed during research – but often the care of researchers in more nuanced circumstances is not covered. Researchers who are traumatised (Eliasson and DeHart, 2022) or experiencing anxiety (Todd, 2021) are not best placed to care for their participants, and an ethic of care should apply to everyone involved in the research process.

Reflective questions

1. How does your experience of research ethics fit with an ethic of care?
2. How can researchers, supervisors, mentors and ethics board members keep ahead of changes in methods and online data?
3. Is it realistic to expect members of the research community to understand rapidly changing technology, social media and ethical considerations?
4. If new methods, platforms and online opportunities are not well understood, should researchers use them?
5. How can experienced researchers be supported when situations change rapidly or they work in new fields?

Further reading

1. Newman, P. A., Guta, A. and Black, T. (2021). Ethical considerations for qualitative research methods during the COVID-19 pandemic and other emergency situations: Navigating the virtual field. *International Journal of Qualitative Methods*, 20, 1–12. https://doi.org/10.1177/16094069211047823.

In this open-access paper, Newman, Guta and Black outline a range of ethical considerations when working online, not limited to the Covid-19 pandemic. There are some really important considerations explored here, which would have been very helpful to Femi and Jo.

2. Fox, A. and Busher, H. (2022). **Democratising ethical regulation and practice in educational research.** *Education Sciences,* **12(10), 674. https://doi.org/10.3390/educsci12100674.**

This open-access paper introduces ideas for a democratising of ethical practice, including decolonisation, linking well to Chapters 1 and 21 of this book.

3. Thunberg, S. and Arnell, L. (2022). **Pioneering the use of technologies in qualitative research – A research review of the use of digital interviews.** *International Journal of Social Research Methodology,* **25(6), 757–68. https://doi.org/10.1080/13645579.2021.1935565.**

This open-access paper synthesises twenty-nine studies on using online interviews and considers positives and negatives, including ethical issues.

This open-access paper introduces ideas for a democratising of ethical practice, including decolonisation, linking well to Chapters 1 and 21 of this book.

4. Thunberg, S. and Arnell, L. (2022). **Pioneering the use of technologies in qualitative research – A research review of the use of digital interviews.** *International Journal of Social Research Methodology,* **25(6), 757–68. https://doi.org/10.1080/13645579.2021.1935565.**

This open-access paper synthesises twenty-nine studies on using online interviews and considers positives and negatives, including ethical issues.

References

Adams-Hutcheson, G. and Longhurst, R. (2017). At least in person there would have been a cup of tea. Interviewing via Skype. *Area,* 49(2), 148–55. https://doi.org/10.1111/area.12306.
British Educational Research Association (2024). *Ethical Guidelines for Educational Research* (5th ed.). London: BERA. https://www.bera.ac.uk/publication/ethical-guidelines-for-educational-research-fifth-edition-2024.
Busher, H. and Fox, A. (2021). The amoral academy? A critical discussion of research ethics in the neo-liberal university. *Educational Philosophy and Theory,* 53(5), 469–78. https://www.tandfonline.com/doi/full/10.1080/0013 1857.2019.1707656.

Cilliers, L. and Viljoen, K. (2021). A framework of ethical issues to consider when conducting internet-based research. *South African Journal of Information Management*, 23(1), 1552–1561. doi: https://doi.org/10.4102/sajim.v23i1.1215.

Eliasson, M. and DeHart, D. (2022). Trauma experienced by researchers: Challenges and recommendations to support students and junior scholars. *Qualitative Research in Organizations and Management*, 17(4), 487–97. https://doi.org/10.1108/QROM-10-2021-2221.

Evans, R. (2016). Achieving and evidencing research 'impact'? Tensions and dilemmas from an ethic of care perspective. *Area*, 48(2), 213–21. https://doi.org/10.1111/area.12256.

Fallon, D. and Long, T. (2007). Ethics Approval, Ethical Research and Delusions of Efficacy. In T. Long, and M. Johnson (Eds.), *Research Ethics in the Real World: Issues and Solutions for Health and Social Care Professionals*, London: Elsevier Health Sciences (pp. 139–56), ISBN: 9780443100659.

Folkes, L. (2023). Moving beyond 'shopping list' positionality: Using kitchen table reflexivity and in/visible tools to develop reflexive qualitative research. *Qualitative Research*, 23(5), 1301–18. https://doi.org/10.1177/14687941221098922.

Fox, A. and Busher, H. (2022). Democratising ethical regulation and practice in educational research. *Education Sciences*, 12(10), 674. https://doi.org/10.3390/educsci12100674.

Franzke, A., Bechmann, A., Zimmer, M. and Ess, C. (2020). *Internet Research: Ethical Guidelines 3.0, Association of Internet Researchers*. https://aoir.org/reports/ethics3.pdf.

Gray, L., Wong-Wylie, G., Rempel, G. and Cook, K. (2020). Expanding qualitative research interviewing strategies: Zoom video communications. *The Qualitative Report*, 25(5), 1292–301. Retrieved from https://nsuworks.nova.edu/tqr/vol25/iss5/9.

Gupta, S. (2017). Ethical issues in designing internet-based research: Recommendations for good practice. *Journal of Research Practice*, 13(2), D1. ISSN: 1712-851X.

Hair, N. and Clark, M. (2007). The ethical dilemmas and challenges of ethnographic research in electronic communities. *International Journal of Market Research*, 49(6), 1–13. https://doi.org/10.1177/147078530704900609 (Original work published 2007).

Held, V. (1993). *Feminist Morality: Transforming Culture, Society and Politics*. Chicago, IL: University of Chicago Press.

Jaggar, A. M. (1995). Caring as a Feminist Practice of Moral Reason. In V Held (Ed.), *Justice and Care: Essential Readings in Feminist Ethics*, London: Routledge (pp. 179–222). ISBN: 9780429499463.

James, N. and Busher, H. (2006). Credibility, authenticity and voice: Dilemmas in online interviewing. *Qualitative Research*, 6(3), 403–20. https://doi.org/10.1177/1468794106065010.

James, N., and Busher, H. (2007). Ethical issues in online educational research: Protecting privacy, establishing authenticity in email interviewing. *International Journal of Research and Method in Education*, 30(1), 101–13.

Jowett, A. (2020). Carrying Out Qualitative Research under Lockdown – Practical and Ethical Considerations. blog post, Impact of Social Sciences Blog. 20 April. Blog post. https://blogs.lse.ac.uk/impactofsocialsciences/.

Kim, H. N. and Sutharson, S. (2021). Concerns and needs of research participants with visual disabilities amid the COVID-19 pandemic. *Theoretical Issues in Ergonomics Science*, 23(3), 277–89. https://doi.org/10.1080/1463922X.2021.1940351.

Mortensen, P. and Kirsch, G. (1996). *Ethics and Representation in Qualitative Studies of Literacy*. Urbana, IL: National Council of Teachers of English. ISBN-0-8141-1596-9 96.

Nambiar, D. and Benny, G. (2021). Telephony and trade-offs in fieldwork with the 'unreached': On the conduct of telephonic interviews with indigenous study participants in southern India. *BMJ Global Health*, 6(Suppl 5), e006261.

Newman, P., Guta, A. and Black, T. (2021). Ethical considerations for qualitative research methods during the COVID-19 pandemic and other emergency situations: Navigating the virtual field. *International Journal of Qualitative Methods*, 20, 1–12. https://doi.org/10.1177/16094069211047823.

Quickfall, A. (2022). Reflecting on ethical processes and dilemmas in doctoral research. *Education Sciences*, 12(11), 751. https://doi.org/10.3390/educsci12110751.

Quickfall, A. and Wood, P. (2024). *Transforming Teacher Work for Retention and Recruitment: Reflections from the Pandemic*. Leeds: Emerald Publishing.

Quickfall, A., Wood, P. and Clarke, E. (2022). The experiences of newly qualified teachers in 2020 and what we can learn for future cohorts. *London Review of Education*, 20(1), 1–14. https://doi.org/10.14324/LRE.20.1.50.

Reich, J. (2021). Power, positionality, and the ethic of care in qualitative research. *Qualitative Sociology*, 44(4), 575–81. https://doi.org/10.1007/s11133-021-09500-4.

Saarijärvi, M. and Bratt, E. (2021). When face-to-face interviews are not possible: Tips and tricks for video, telephone, online chat, and email interviews in qualitative research. *European Journal of Cardiovascular Nursing*, 20(4), 392–6. https://doi.org/10.1093/eurjcn/zvab038.

Seitz, S. (2015). Pixilated partnerships, overcoming obstacles in qualitative interviews via Skype: A research note. *Qualitative Research*, 16(2), 229–35. https://doi.org/10.1177/1468794115577011.

Serekoane, M., Marais, L., Pienaar, M., Sharp, C., Cloete, J. and Blomerus, L. (2021). Fieldworker reflections on using telephone voice calls to conduct fieldwork amidst the Covid-19 pandemic. *Anthropology Southern Africa*, 44(4), 161–74. https://doi.org/10.1080/23323256.2021.2002701.

Sevenhuijsen, S. (1998). *Citizenship and the Ethics of Care*. London: Routledge.

Sturges, J. and Hanrahan, K. (2004). Comparing telephone and face-to-face qualitative interviewing: A research note. *Qualitative Research*, 4(1), 107–18. https://doi.org/10.1177/1468794104041110.

Surmiak, A., Bielska, B. and Kalinowska, K. (2022). Social researchers' approaches to research ethics during the COVID-19 pandemic: An exploratory study. *Journal of Empirical Research on Human Research Ethics*, 17(1–2), 213–22. Doi: 10.1177/15562646211055056.

Szulc, J. M. (2022). Towards more inclusive qualitative research: The practice of interviewing neurominorities. *Labour and Industry*, 33(2), 179–87. https://doi.org/10.1080/10301763.2022.2148853.

Thunberg, S. and Arnell, L. (2022). Pioneering the use of technologies in qualitative research – A research review of the use of digital interviews. *International Journal of Social Research Methodology*, 25(6), 757–68. https://doi.org/10.1080/13645579.2021.1935565.

Todd, J. D. (2021). Experiencing and embodying anxiety in spaces of academia and social research. *Gender, Place and Culture*, 28(4), 475–96. https://doi.org/10.1080/0966369X.2020.1727862.

Torrentira, M. (2020). Online data collection as adaptation in conducting quantitative and qualitative research during the Covid-19 pandemic. *European Journal of Education Studies*, [S.l.], 7(11) 1–10. http://dx.doi.org/10.46827/ejes.v7i11.3336.

Tronto, J. C. (1998). An ethic of care. *Generations: Journal of the American Society on Aging*, 22(3), 15–20. http://www.jstor.org/stable/44875693.

Viljoen, K. and Cilliers, L. (2019). *The Ethics of Conducting Research using Social Media: A Discussion Case*, Transforming society using ICT: Contemporary discussion cases from Africa, UNISA, Pretoria.

Section 2

Case Studies

Section 2-2 Foreword – Responsibilities to Sponsors, Clients, Stakeholders and the Environment
by *Matthew Courtney*

This sub-section explores the responsibilities educational researchers have towards individuals and organisations with a direct interest in their research, including funders, wider society and the environment. The chapters in this sub-section explore themes discussed in other chapters of the book, such as informed consent and bias, but here we consider these issues through the lens of our obligations to stakeholders and wider society. This sub-section of the book takes as its starting point guidelines 50–57 of the BERA ethical guidance (BERA, 2024).

Chapters 8 and 9 both explore areas of research which are emerging and developing: research involving large-scale quantitative data and the use of Artificial Intelligence in educational research. In Chapter 8, Sonia Ilie and Michelle Ellefson explore the application of core ethical principles of anonymity and confidentiality when interrogating large-scale datasets by drawing upon two case studies. This chapter highlights the importance of clear communication from researchers as well as the need to consider both legal and ethical responsibilities. The authors highlight the importance of a researcher's responsibility to their participants, whilst also considering their responsibility to data owners and other stakeholders when using large-scale quantitative data.

In Chapter 9, Robert Farrow and Wayne Holmes explore the ethical implications of researching an Artificial Intelligence-enabled learning management system in a fictional UK Higher Education institution. The authors highlight the importance of continuous reflection when working with emerging technology. The importance of in-depth knowledge of both research methodologies and the technology being used and/or researched is also highlighted.

Chapter 10 explores classroom observation, a well-established and extensively used research method that is underexplored in the research ethics literature. In this chapter, Daniel Muijs and Matthew Courtney present two case studies which consider the ethical dilemmas researchers need to consider when engaging in observational research. The first case study considers the dilemmas that insider researchers, such as practitioner-researchers, may face when conducting observational research. The second case study engages with the issue of observer bias and considers how this might influence classroom observation.

In Chapter 11, Lynda Dunlop and Lizzie Rushton explore a further area which is underexplored in the literature on education research ethics: environmental sustainability. In this chapter, the authors consider the intersection between research processes and environmental considerations. They highlight that, as some of the highest greenhouse gas emitters in society, educational researchers have an ethical responsibility to consider the impact of their work on the environment at all stages of the research process. This brings to life a new guideline – 54 – included in the fifth edition of the BERA Ethical Guidelines for Educational Research (BERA, 2024).

8

Working with Large-Scale Quantitative Data: Two Ethical Dilemmas around Anonymity

by *Sonia Ilie and Michelle R Ellefson*

Introduction

Education research benefits from increasing availability, scope and size of quantitative data. Large-scale quantitative data is routinely collected directly from research participants through surveys, assessments, online empirical tasks or social media. It is also made available to researchers by a variety of bodies and organisations that govern data collected in the process of monitoring their activity, providing a service or delivering a programme, or for a variety of other reasons – this administrative data is often linked to other primary data sources, including longitudinal surveys, cohort studies or further individual records.

Regardless of its source, large-scale quantitative data enables education researchers to explore educational phenomena in detail, to draw conclusions about groups of people and to understand complex relationships, from cause-and-effect to longitudinal trends and individual differences. Like all forms of data, large-scale quantitative data also has limitations in terms of the types of research questions it may answer. And like all forms of data, it requires that education researchers pay specific attention to how they generate and use such data ethically.

While education research with quantitative data is not new, recent developments around open science practices (Erb et al., 2021), digital data collection (Bamdad, Finaughty and Johns, 2022) as well as around new opportunities to access linked large-scale, often from governmental sources, datasets (Stiles and Boothroyd, 2015) give rise to new ethical considerations for education researchers. Such considerations include the core ethical principles of anonymity (BERA, 2024, paragraph 28)[1] and confidentiality (BERA, 2024, paragraph 39),[2] which raise new challenges when large-scale data are concerned (Grierson et al., 2023).

This chapter tackles two key ethical dilemmas around anonymity and confidentiality as they relate to the generation and use of large-scale data in contexts of open science and administrative data usage for research. We explore each dilemma within our context in the UK and use local examples, including practical opportunities and training that would support the proposed solutions to the dilemmas. We recommend that researchers contextualise their own solutions to relevant national, local and data landscapes.

The first dilemma centres on how participant data may be shared openly while retaining their anonymity and confidentiality against a backdrop of developments to support research transparency and replication.

The second dilemma centres, conversely, on tightly controlled large-scale data that can never be shared publicly and how potentially paradoxical issues of lack of anonymity may be addressed.

We frame both ethical dilemmas using four principles of ethical research: autonomy, justice, beneficence and non-maleficence (Varkey, 2021). Briefly, *autonomy* is the right for participants to make their own well-informed decisions about participating in research, while *justice* is to avoid unfair burdens and treating participants equally. *Beneficence* relates to the obligations that research should have benefits, while *non-maleficence* is about research not doing any harm, even inadvertently.

While not identical, these align to the BERA fundamentals for research in education (BERA, 2024).[3] More specifically, the ethic of respect for people, knowledge and the ethic of care for all those involved in research, including researchers, speak to the autonomy intrinsic to the research process, and it being guided by a sense of justice, whereby the rights of all are upheld. This applies to researchers, individual participants, as well as society as a whole, with non-maleficence as a guiding framework. The trust and an acceptance of responsibility for their research by researchers,[4] which the BERA fundamentals (BERA, 2024) also emphasise, relate to the above principle of beneficence. Applying these principles together ensures the quality of education research, emphasises respect for the environment and protects academic freedom.

We approach these two ethical dilemmas as researchers who predominantly do quantitative research using large-scale data. Across our research, we regularly use online platforms to run surveys and administer questionnaires that may include assessing attitudes, knowledge or skills. We also deploy experimental and quasi-experimental research methodologies in the lab, classroom and other settings, working both in controlled and naturally occurring educational environments. Our work often includes survey platforms to collect data online – these are an effective way to generate large-scale data across different educational settings and geographical regions in asynchronous ways. We also use data from cohort studies, longitudinal surveys and administrative sources such as the English National Pupil Database or the Higher Education Statistics Agency, with our research often requiring links between such datasets to answer our research questions. Across our research, we work with young children, students, teachers and other education practitioners who either individually consent to their participation in our studies or use data already collected about such individuals from administrative sources as those mentioned above. In our research, we emphasise transparency and replicability, and where appropriate, possible and relevant, make our research data or analytical code open or available to other researchers. As part of that, we think carefully about the rights of the participants whose data we engage with and ways to comprehensively support them while retaining the focus and authenticity of our research aims.

Aligned to the two research dilemmas we tackle, the chapter is structured as two case studies: both completely fictitious, and each reflecting on a key ethical dilemma and possible courses of action. The chapter then concludes, inviting reflective thoughts on the variety of issues addressed throughout.

How can participant data be shared openly while retaining participants' anonymity and confidentiality?

Background

In the wake of some high-profile research scandals (Świątkowski and Dompnier, 2017), there has been an increased interest in, and expectation of, sharing research data and findings more openly across the research community. Sharing data openly aims to allow other education researchers to scrutinise the findings and analytical approaches in ways that can improve research and research practices. The days of merely making 'data available upon request', sometimes hindered by relevant skills (Houtkoop et al., 2018), are ending, and researchers are now expected to share raw data and analytic code, sometimes alongside research protocols, statistical analysis plans or other pre-registration material outlining research plans.

Many academic journals are expanding their editorial teams so that all shared data and analytic code can be run and replicated before agreeing to accept a manuscript for publication. While such practices are not common across all types of education research, where large-scale quantitative data is concerned, they are increasing in popularity and advocated for by some scholars (van der Zee and Reich, 2018).

These changes are good for research transparency and reproducibility, but they do raise important ethical issues around consent and maintaining participant anonymity and confidentiality. Some early evidence on participant perspectives suggests that, *given* appropriate information around how anonymity would be preserved, individual participants are open to their data being shared, though primarily for research, and not commercial, purposes (Eberlen et al., 2019). This emphasises the need for anonymity approaches communicated to participants to be robust and practically implementable by researchers. This is precisely what the following case study addresses.

Case Study One

Emma is an early career education researcher looking to undertake research that would see her collect data using a commercial online survey platform, analyse the collected quantitative data using existing and freely available statistical software, and then look to publish her results in a peer-reviewed journal that adheres to principles of open science and requires the sharing of data and analysis code as a precondition for publication. Emma is keen for her research to include a sample that is representative of the wider population, so she includes in her data collection tool a series of questions around personal characteristics that may be deemed sensitive by participants and are part of the protected characteristics defined by the UK Equality Act 2010.

The ethical dilemma

Emma therefore faces an ethical dilemma: how can one ensure that when sharing participant data openly, this is done in a way that retains their anonymity and is not liable to later misuse?

Anticipated ethical issues

Ahead of starting to design her research, Emma is aware of both the BERA guidelines (BERA, 2024) for the ethical conduct of research and the local requirements of the ethics review board[5] of the higher education institution that employs her. She is concerned, however, that the future need to openly share her research data specifically may go against traditional assurances to participants that only the original research team would ever have access to data being generated in the course of the research and require steps towards data anonymisation that are cumbersome or may result in insufficient anonymity for participants.

First, Emma is aware that, traditionally, education researchers assured participants that the individual responses collected in the study would not be shared beyond the research team and that only group-level insights or findings would be disseminated. However, Emma also understands that this previous protocol goes against the open science principle of sharing raw data. Emma knows it would be a violation of consent for education researchers to tell participants that they will not share individual responses but then do so as part of the publication process (BERA, 2024, paragraph 42).[6]

Relatedly, Emma anticipates that she may have to consider carefully how identifiable the various types of information she collects about her participants in the course of her planned work would be. Few education researchers realise how easily participants could be identified from only a few bits of information, even when these are presented independently of each other. While most would acknowledge that having the school, gender and date of birth of a participant would enable participant identification with little effort, fewer realise the depth of information routinely collected when participants engage with digital data collection. Having previously worked with the online survey platform she intends to use for data collection, Emma understands that sharing unprocessed data from online survey systems jeopardises anonymity because those systems routinely collect IP addresses, type of Information Technology (IT) platform used to answer the questions being asked via the platform, and other geographic data that could easily identify research participants.

Unforeseen ethical issues

Emma applies for and receives ethical endorsement for her planned research and starts carrying out her study. The data collection goes well, she deploys appropriate skills and knowledge in anonymising the data, and at the end of her research, she publishes her findings in an open-science journal, sharing both appropriately anonymised data and her analytical code openly alongside the article. This data includes some, but not all, of the personal characteristics Emma has collected from participants during her research, rendering participants anonymous in the data and preserving the confidentiality of their individual answers.

One year later, Emma notices a new published research article that uses her openly shared data and that misinterprets how a particular variable in the quantitative data has measured a concept of interest and uses this alongside some of the individual personal characteristics included in the shared data. Emma is concerned about the validity of the findings of this new article and is particularly worried that the analysis around individual characteristics goes against her initial intentions around sample representativeness.

Therefore, Emma faces an unforeseen, but foreseeable, issue of potential misuse. This possibility is ever-present with openly shared data. Efforts to improve research generalisability across a wide range of populations have encouraged researchers to collect more detailed information from participants about their backgrounds, just as Emma has done, especially in terms of protected characteristics and other sensitive information that may enhance the representativeness of their data. Having more representative samples is important for education research, but sharing the characteristics of potentially marginalised individual participants could enable ill-meaning actors to misuse the data beyond the initial research questions. Emma does not assume the new paper she has encountered is deliberately misusing the data but is nonetheless concerned about the implications of this paper for her own research.

Courses of action

Addressing anticipated issues

Generally, education researchers should engage in research practices that both protect their participants and engage with open, transparent and reproducible research. Emma understands this and, as a result, knows that the key is to clearly ask participants for consent to share data openly with other researchers, including for research questions not included in the original study.

Emma uses clear and simple language to explain why sharing individual responses is important for the transparency of research (BERA, 2024, paragraph 27),[7] and for the potential of answering new research questions. She generates a participant information sheet that is comprehensive but concise, easy to understand but not condescending to participants. She informs participants of the purposes of her research in non-technical terms and explains that future research may have other aims. She tells participants how their data is going to be anonymised and informs them of all their rights from a data protection perspective. Emma does all of this in the online platform she is using for data collection, which allows her to require that participants indicate they have read and understood these terms ahead of providing their consent and starting with their participation in the study. She arranges via available platform options that individuals who refuse consent do not have any data collected (BERA, 2024, paragraphs 8 and 9).[8]

In relation to the data anonymisation process, Emma is proactive about her training, and she seeks to develop the technical skills that enable her to appropriately anonymise her data. She deploys these skills and takes steps to ensure that participants can't identify their own responses in the original data either, as this may mean that participants could be able to identify other participants with similar answers. Emma strips the data of immediately identifiable information such as Internet Protocol (IP) addresses and the general geographic location that can be inferred from this. She also removes some, but not all, of the personal characteristics she has collected from participants, ensuring that no combination of these characteristics renders any participant identifiable. Finally, Emma uses meaningless identifiers in the data that she ultimately shares openly, which are unrelated to original participant identifiers.

Addressing unforeseen issues

Having taken the above steps during her research to preserve individuals' anonymity, Emma now faces the possibility that her data has been (possibly inadvertently) misused. While she is not concerned that this is a breach of individuals' anonymity, Emma does want to ensure that she engages with the new article using her data.

Emma therefore writes to the authors of the article to gently query their use of both the specific measure, which she deems has been misconstrued (having first explored relevant literature around the ethics of measurement, e.g. Robson and Malette, 2023) and the individual characteristics that the authors have used in their analysis. The authors, also adopters of open science principles, explain their interpretation of the concept and measure that Emma is expressing concern about and are willing to include an addendum to their published piece where they justify and defend this interpretation further, pointing to other research that has taken a similar approach. While Emma disagrees with the authors on conceptual and psychometric grounds, she accepts their justification, and the journal publishes the brief addendum. This process takes over a year to complete, during which time Emma continues to expand her knowledge about best practices in open science. With hindsight, Emma realises that she might not have shared participant characteristics used to describe the sample but that were not essential for her data analysis, especially if those characteristics exposed marginalised populations.

Alternative courses of action

Had Emma not been able to engage ethically in open science principles, her approach would have been to prioritise her participants, engaging in as many open, transparent and reproducible practices as possible while still protecting her participants' anonymity and the confidentiality of their data.

Emma may have deemed that all data collected as part of her research would be ethically problematic to share openly. For example, instances where marginalised characteristics are a key part of the analysis, or where the responses themselves could give away participant identities. In those cases, Emma might have considered alternative methods for sharing. These include sharing metadata, histograms, raincloud plots or lines of best fit that approximate the pairwise relationships between relevant variable combinations.

Emma might have also considered sharing all her analysis code but none of her data. We both do this routinely in our own education research: either for early data management where the raw data is not yet fully anonymised but is useful to show the process of how the project went from the raw data to the openly shared data, or at final publication stage where the full analytical code that is completely non-identifiable of any individual observations is appended to the article or report.

In terms of anonymising data, Emma already considered how combinations of variables may have led to participants' anonymity being compromised. She may have gone further, removing other details of the research from publication, for instance, the date when the data was collected, or providing only minimal detail about the geographic location of participants (if at all relevant). This would allow Emma to share data critical to her analysis where exact information is essential, but its presence alongside another piece of data renders it ethically problematic.

Finally, and addressing the unforeseen issue of possible misuse, Emma might have considered not sharing these personal details of participants – and possibly only sharing the analysis code that uses them. This could have compromises on open science but does follow the key ethical principle of non-maleficence and takes steps towards the principle of justice.

Case Study One – concluding section

It is important for education researchers to engage in open science practices, but they do raise new ethical issues that need to be considered and planned for from the start of the project. It is important for researchers to be clear and transparent with their participants and to take great care in protecting anonymity and confidentiality. In instances where open science and ethics collide, then education researchers should consider alternatives that prioritise their participants while still allowing for some engagement with open science.

How can anonymity be retained when dealing with sensitive data and topics in large-scale administrative data research?

Background

The increasing availability of administrative data provides education researchers with the opportunity to explore complex phenomena and to do so with very large samples of individuals, and sometimes even full populations. This is particularly the case when government- and other organisation-provided datasets are linked together in an ecosystem of administrative data that is made available to researchers. The UK is at the forefront of such efforts (e.g. ADRUK, 2023) and research that uses administrative data has recently tackled challenging topics of high public interest in education (Leckie and Maragkou, 2024) and beyond (Robinson et al., 2024). Administrative data has allowed for this kind of research to be undertaken because it often includes a wealth of personal information in addition to the key variables of interest, including individual characteristics protected under the UK's Equality Act (2010). And although the scale of administrative data is often very large, the use of it in research raises significant ethical issues, including finer concerns around anonymity, even in the presence of large samples.

A key issue around administrative data in research, beyond the ethical principles that govern its use (e.g. Grierson et al., 2023), relates to education researchers possessing the data literacy to understand the complex ethical considerations at play (Mandinach and Jimerson, 2021).

These ethical considerations derive not only from BERA's guidelines (BERA, 2024) but are also closely related to legal data protection considerations. The UK General Data Protection Regulation (2018) and principles derived from it offer a framework for the ethical and safe use of administrative data for education research, but while these principles are necessary, they may not always be sufficient from an ethical perspective. This applies particularly to distinctions of what counts as sensitive from a legal and ethical perspective, and also relates to how the anonymity of individuals may not be upheld when categorical insights about the group they belong to are generated from such data.

Sitting behind these considerations are concerns about informed consent and the extent to which individuals understand that their data, originally collected for other purposes and potentially by agencies and organisations with no role in education research, may ultimately be used for education research.

The fictitious case study below tackles these issues and proposes possible courses of action to address an emerging ethical dilemma.

Case Study Two

Ella is a doctoral researcher looking to undertake research using linked administrative data for the first time, with access secured via the UK's administrative data access processes governed by the Office for National Statistics and similar organisations.[9] Ella's study would see her analyse data about educational processes that stems from several government departments and agencies, all linked together at the level of the individual. Some elements of this data relate to topics Ella deems sensitive. Ella's study would include a component of how the educational phenomena she is exploring manifest for individuals who have historically been under-represented in specific educational spaces and settings, and therefore she would look to engage with data that relates to individual characteristics protected under the UK Equality Act 2010.

The ethical dilemma

Ella's ethical dilemma addresses the sensitivity of the topic and personal characteristics being researched even as the research is being carried out with large numbers.

Anticipated ethical issues

Ella is fully aware of the requirements for training and accreditation that she must meet prior to her gaining access to the data relevant to her research. She engages early with the Research Accreditation process (ONS, 2024), participating in the training required by this process and beyond. She understands that a key part of that training is building her skills, data literacy and knowledge of ethical challenges and processes (BERA, 2024, paragraph 5)[10] to understand when her research may, possibly in subtle ways, pose ethical challenges and ethical risk to the individuals whose data she will be using in her research.

Ella is also attuned to the ethical issue that individual re-identification (BERA, 2024, paragraph 45)[11] may be possible, that is, that the results she ultimately presents in her published work may, independently or alongside information publicly available, lead to the identification of individuals. Ella is particularly concerned about this given the sensitivity of the topic she is tackling and the groups of individuals she is including in her work. Ella is aware that controls put in place by the organisation facilitating her access to data require that she engages with this and include a mechanism to protect against such re-identification risks, but she remains concerned that this may still occur in unforeseen ways.

Relatedly, Ella is concerned that while the individuals engaging with the education phenomena in her research were initially aware of how their data would be stored and shared and that potentially it would be used at a later stage for research, they may not have fully understood the reach of this data, particularly considering the linking across different governmental data sources (paragraph 28).[12] Ella is reassured by the legal protections in place and understands that her research would undergo a rigorous review process before she would be granted access to data, but the sensitivity of the topic and groups included in her work makes her think she would need to take additional steps, beyond the legal requirements, to ensure no harm comes to individuals whose data she is exploring, or indeed other members of their respective groups.

Unforeseen ethical issues

Ella dedicates ample time to the generation of her application for data, which she submits to the appropriate organisation that would facilitate her access. In the application, which includes a full account of the proposed research, she explains transparently and fully the data and sensitive information she is looking to engage with, provides comprehensive justification for her decisions, and outlines what she believes is the benefit from her research to both academic knowledge and the society in general. Ella also applies for, and receives, ethical endorsement for her proposed research. She includes this with her application for data, which is approved.

Ella commences her research, engaging with the data in appropriate ways. During her research, Ella's findings show stark contrasts in how the educational phenomena she is researching manifest for the different groups she is interested in. In one instance, she finds that members of a specific group, identified by a combination of sensitive personal information, always face a specific adverse educational outcome. Were her findings to be published showing this, they would disclose sensitive information about all members of that specific group in ways that may further marginalise or disadvantage them.

Ella has essentially encountered an issue of class disclosure. While Ella was aware of the possibility of class disclosure prior to the start of her research, she had deemed the risk of occurrence to be low. Ella is aware that this issue may limit what, and how, she reports on her results, and that she needs to balance this with an overriding duty to do no harm to individuals whose data she is accessing or are represented by that data.

Courses of action

Addressing anticipated issues

Education researchers who use linked administrative data require training and accreditation and take clear steps towards ensuring their research is both ethical and adheres to legal frameworks and rules. In doing so, they must balance the overall benefits that emerge from doing research with large-scale and often population-level data with the potential risks to the individuals from whom the data emerges. Ella understands this and behaves accordingly throughout her research.

First, Ella undertakes the required training in both the statistical skills and safe data access protocols but sees this as a minimum level of preparation. She reads widely around issues of ethical conduct of research with administrative data and engages with other researchers, at the doctoral level and beyond, who do similar work. She applies her training and knowledge to her engagement with the existing protocols around the publication of results from administrative data research. She follows the rules and guidelines closely and pays special attention to all legal requirements around engaging with sensitive personal information.

In addition to strictly adhering to protocols around publishing results from her work, Ella also considers the implications stemming from the topic of her research, which she deems to tackle sensitive issues. Ella therefore explores the best ways to report her results, both in terms of statistical approach and content and in terms of non-technical interpretation. She consults wide literature on how researchers engage with large-scale data (e.g. Favaretto et al., 2020) and sensitive topics (Decker et al., 2011), reflects on the use of language when discussing adverse outcomes and negative experiences, and balances these with a need to remain authentic to her research questions. This reflects in Ella's approach to the challenges of individual re-identification. Beyond the reporting requirements she must adhere to, Ella is careful to report only as much information as is strictly necessary to answer her research question, aggregated at the appropriate level. She therefore provides less background information on groups of individuals, where they are located, the types of educational institutions they engage with or other educational characteristics than she might have otherwise but describes the populations and samples in her study in sufficient detail for her findings not to be misinterpreted.

Finally, Ella engages early on with the data owners (BERA, 2024, paragraph 14),[13] the government departments and agencies who initially collected the data, to source where possible the exact information provided to individuals in relation to their data being shared for research purposes. She reassures herself that, beyond all legal requirements already in place, individuals were provided with clear and easily understandable information about how their data would be used. Ella also familiarises herself with how these organisations have taken steps to ensure changing data-sharing processes are re-communicated to individuals, including any changes to the law. She concludes that while more and better information can always be provided, this must be balanced with practicality and the minimising of burden on individuals. She is therefore personally satisfied that she has done all she can to understand how the data she uses has been collected.

Addressing unforeseen issues

In tackling the foreseeable, but unforeseen, class disclosure issue, Ella engages with the team checking her adherence to results publication rules currently in place and with her doctoral supervisor. Together, they restructure the group that Ella would be reporting results about in a way that eliminates the class disclosure problem. This sees Ella redefine the group slightly, choosing a variable from the available data that provides a slightly less specific disaggregation of the overall population but still retains the original intention of her work. In this new, slightly bigger group, the incidence of the adverse outcome generating the class disclosure issue is not 100 per cent. Therefore, Ella can safely report this result, knowing that conclusions cannot therefore be drawn about every single member of that group. This revised version of the result is cleared by the team, ensuring the adherence to reporting rules and guidelines, and Ella is able to publish her work in a relevant journal at a later stage.

Alternative courses of action

Had Ella not been able to take the approaches above, several alternatives would have been available to her. When deciding between them, she would have been guided by the BERA principles (BERA, 2024) of the ethic of respect for the knowledge being generated and for research participants, even in the absence of direct contact with them. She also might have been guided by the four principles of autonomy, beneficence, non-maleficence and justice and even been informed by the open science principles which, while not entirely applicable, provide a further framework for transparent and replicable research.

First, Ella might have taken a very early step of reframing her research questions by attempting to foresee the challenges to anonymity around class disclosure emerging from the use of sensitive data and abiding by the above principles. She might have refocused her research to align more closely with the principle of justice, shifting the focus to the structures which may have generated observed adverse outcomes in the first place. Or she may have chosen to focus on individual characteristics deemed less sensitive. Doing any of this would not have been straightforward.

Education researchers usually have very good reasons for wanting to address particularly sensitive research questions – the point of ethical principles is not to stop research from engaging with sensitive topics or sensitive personal information, but to make this kind of research as ethical as possible.

Ella might have also chosen to engage directly with members of the groups she was interested in, or those experiencing the adverse educational outcome, to understand their attitude towards this and towards her reporting of results about them. This would have had to be additional to the planned research, and therefore might have brought about timing challenges and potentially required a different set of research approaches from those that Ella was expecting to deploy in her work, including participatory approaches, qualitative interviewing or similar. This approach would have brought about even further challenges: it would be essential for such engagement to not be tokenistic, to remain authentic to the voices of individuals and to possible conflicting perspectives, anticipating and offering possible solutions. Despite these challenges, this approach may have informed Ella's approach to her research and may have supported her in identifying a way of reporting results that both adhered to the legal requirements in place and was acceptable to the individuals concerned.

Case Study Two – concluding section

The use of large-scale administrative data does not automatically eliminate the risk of individuals or groups of individuals being inappropriately identified and of their anonymity being compromised, especially when tackling sensitive topics or doing research with groups defined by sensitive personal information. While legal protections are in place and education researchers must engage with these when accessing and reporting on administrative data, these are only a first step towards the ethical conduct of research with such large-scale data. By remaining open to additional ways of engaging with individuals or groups whose data features in the research, education researchers may remain authentic to their aims of researching sensitive topics or analysing sensitive information and still minimise harm and maximise societal benefit from their work.

Final thoughts

Large-scale quantitative data enables education researchers to explore complex educational phenomena, draw conclusions from large numbers of participants, or reuse data collected for initially different purposes in search of new knowledge and insights. Against a backdrop of open science principles emphasising transparency, and of the growing availability of data from a variety of administrative sources being brought together for research purposes, research with large-scale quantitative data poses a series of challenges. This chapter has focused predominantly on issues of anonymity and confidentiality, touching upon related issues of informed consent, disclosure and potential misuse.

Consent remains a complex matter in research with large-scale data, and new educational spaces pose further challenges (e.g. Costello et al., 2023) on massive online open courses, where implicit assumptions around the data being generated by means of engagement with the educational act require further clarification and communication on the part of the researchers as well as relevant educational institutions. Anonymity is even more common of a concern, where issues of inadvertent reidentification may be made increasingly more likely by the proliferation of public data, the public sharing of personal information by participants themselves, and the growing availability of linked data sources that provide information on the same individuals from a range of perspectives. While such developments do not pose impassable ethical hurdles, they raise questions for researchers in terms of their technical skills and sensitivity of research topics and questions. The developing legal frameworks that accompany these developments also put the onus on researchers to make themselves aware of the legal implications of their work, to keep up to date with changing legislation, and also to understand where new technologies and analytical techniques fit within that. On some level, education, and all social science, researchers must become fluent in both ethical and legal principles and their application to education research.

In our own education research, we grapple with such issues regularly, constantly reflecting upon the ethical nature of analytical and reporting decisions, as well as on the very questions our research seeks to address and the overall approaches we take to do so. In doing so, we rely both on existing ethical guidelines, chief amongst which are the BERA guidelines (BERA, 2024) – the four previously mentioned principles of autonomy, justice, beneficence and non-maleficence – and balance the possible public good with individual risk (to anonymity but also more broadly). This is what the two case studies above have looked to illustrate, both in terms of the ethical dilemmas faced and practical ways of addressing both foreseen and now-foreseeable issues.

At the same time as emphasising and monitoring our responsibilities to our participants or individuals whose data our work engages with, we are acutely aware of the need to sometimes balance this with our responsibility to data owners and other stakeholders engaged with our research. Especially in relation to administrative data, but also relevant to newly generated data that may be linked to an institution, organisation or entity researchers may be connected to, these responsibilities may include early engagement and justification of the researchers' aims and purposes as well as the provision of detailed information surrounding their methods and approaches. Other responsibilities, which reinforce the ethical considerations above, relate to the need to protect individuals' anonymity, requirements around pre-publication controls (only in relation to potential breaches of anonymity, not the interpretation of results) and the explicit justification of the public benefit attached to the research and how this may be balanced against individuals' data-related rights. Taken together, these responsibilities may raise further ethical challenges to education researchers, particularly when they are looking to research topics deemed sensitive. We return to the principles we outlined at the start of the chapter, and to the BERA Guidelines (BERA, 2024), as useful tools in supporting education researchers in engaging with such responsibilities and responding to related ethical dilemmas.

Alongside the above responsibilities to participants, education researchers should also treat their large-scale quantitative data ethically because of their responsibilities to sponsors, clients, other stakeholders and the environment. For example, sponsors are increasingly requiring that education researchers justify how their use of large-scale quantitative data speaks to wider societal good, including social justice and environmental concerns, and how this is balanced with the rights of the individuals whose data is being used in the research. As such, education researchers must attend to beneficence shaping their research for societal good.

This chapter has not been able to tackle other complex ethical issues, such as the automated collection of data and its potential reuse for non-research purposes, research with secondary data collected in contexts of conflict or in jurisdictions where the confidentiality of individuals and their anonymity in data sharing are not overriding principles. These examples are recent innovations, where education researchers are still grappling with ethical approaches (e.g. Jeon et al., 2024). In framing these dilemmas, we have assumed that researchers engage with the ethical issues around the power (BERA, 2024, paragraph 19)[14] they hold when carrying out the types of research discussed above. Education researchers should be guided by the BERA fundamentals (BERA, 2024) of an ethic of respect and care to participants in how they handle any form of data, including large-scale quantitative data.

To all these challenges, we maintain that the ethical principles we outlined above, and those supported by BERA (2024),[15] act as crucial steers. Within this, a multitude of perspectives may be relevant, and different approaches to tackling ethical dilemmas may be appropriate, but as long as the ethical fundamentals around respect for participants, consideration of public good and commitment to transparent education research are upheld, the research, and ultimately, society, will benefit.

Reflective questions

Researchers looking to generate or engage with large-scale quantitative data in their education research may consider the following five reflective questions:

1. To what extent do my research questions rely on sensitive personal information? How can I ensure that were I to openly share my data, the anonymity of my participants would be retained?
2. Is the information I am providing my research participants sufficiently clear and comprehensive when it comes to how their data will be used in this, and possibly, later research?[16]
3. Am I mindful of the totality of my responsibilities to the research participants, regardless of how I have accessed their data?
4. Have I understood the range of ways in which breaches to anonymity may occur and put in place appropriate safeguards and controls that meet but possibly go beyond legal requirements?
5. Have I considered the possibility of misinterpretation or misuse of my findings, and what courses of action may be available to me?

Further reading

1. Lewis, C. (2024). *Data Management in Large-Scale Education Research.* Boca Raton, FL: CRC Press. https://datamgmtinedresearch.com/.

   An open-source e-book that tackles issues of data management while also exemplifying open science principles:

2. The Counting Project – Tim Harford: Oxford Mathematics https://www.youtube.com/watch?v=BHqxRC5fBTU.

   This public lecture by mathematician Tim Harford raises a series of questions and issues education researchers may want to reflect on. Note not all perspectives expressed here may reflect BERA ethical guidelines (BERA, 2024), and this is provided as food for thought rather than as a guide.

3. Harkness, F., Rijneveld, C., Liu, Y., Kashef, S. and Cowan, M. (2022). A UK-wide public dialogue exploring what the public perceive as 'public good' use of data for research and statistics. *Administrative Data Research UK (ADR UK) Office for Statistics Regulation.* https://osr.statisticsauthority.gov.uk/wp-content/uploads/2022/10/Public_perceptions_of_public_good.pdf.

   A report on public perspectives and attitudes to 'public good' uses of data.

Notes

1. See BERA Ethical Guidelines paragraphs 28 and 39, which emphasise that consent is relevant to research where data is to be reused; and that both institutions and individuals retain a right to privacy, including in relation to research that reuses data previously collected.
2. These guidelines refer to the secure storage of data, with a view to protecting the privacy and anonymity of research participants. They also cover instances where confidentiality may not be possible, and how researchers may handle complex cases where disclosures may be necessary to avoid harmful actions.
3. See the BERA Ethical Guidelines Fundamentals (pp. 7–8).
4. See BERA Ethical Guidelines' Aspirations of education researchers (pp. 9–10).
5. See the BERA Ethical Guidelines Fundamentals for the relationship between the BERA Guidelines and institutional mechanisms (pp. 7–8).

6   See BERA Ethical Guidelines paragraph 42, which outlines how research sponsors may require that data be made available; and that this may need early planning from researchers to ensure appropriate consents have been considered and given prior to any data collection.
7   See BERA Ethical Guidelines paragraph 27. This highlights the importance of transparency in researchers' communication with participants about their what their research design entails.
8   See BERA Ethical Guidelines paragraphs 8 and 9, which outline normal consent procedures, including what information prospective research participants should at minimum be given to inform their decision whether to participate. Please also consult the full section on Consent (paragraphs 8 to 26).
9   The Office for National Statistics and other organisations govern access to secure data in the UK. Similar institutions fulfil this role in other national contexts or across wider regions. While this chapter focuses specifically on the UK context, the issues addressed here are relevant to education researchers regardless of which context, or through which governing body, they may be accessing secure data.
10 See BERA Ethical Guidelines paragraph 5, which states that researchers who use data shared by an organisation have the responsibility to engage with the processes of consent that allowed the data to be collected in the first place, and to consider the authorship and ownership of the data, while keeping abreast of developments in data use regulations.
11 See BERA Ethical Guidelines paragraph 45, which state that researchers are required to comply with laws around data protection, data use and storage, as well as any data sharing or disclosures of research participants' data. These laws and their revisions place specific requirements on researchers in terms of data security and its monitoring.
12 See BERA Ethical Guidelines paragraph 28 that clarifies that both secondary data analysis by the same research team who initially collected data and the sharing of data with other researchers must be done only when initial consent has been given for such re-use and sharing.
13 Paragraph 14 outlines the minimal set of issues researchers must consider ahead of reusing data, including the original owners and creators of the data, the data sensitivity, and the original purpose and intentions for the data collection. Both paragraphs strongly emphasise that researchers looking to reuse data must satisfy themselves that research participants gave informed consent for such reuse, or that other appropriate and reasonable arrangements are in place.
14 See BERA Ethical Guidelines paragraph 19, which prompts researchers to consider situations where research into researchers' own practice may

have consequences for others, and to understand the power dynamics at play in such situations. Please review this paragraph in conjunction with the full Presidential Preamble to the BERA Ethical Guidelines, which also considers this point.

15 See BERA Ethical Guidelines Fundamentals on key principles (pp. 7–8).
16 See BERA Ethical Guidelines on Consent (pp. 13–18).

References

Administrative Data Research UK (2023). *Annual Report 2022–2023*. https://reports.adruk.org/annual-report-2022-2023/.

Bamdad, S., Finaughty, D. A. and Johns, S. E. (2022). 'Grey areas': Ethical challenges posed by social media-enabled recruitment and online data collection in cross-border, social science research. *Research Ethics*, 18(1), 24–38.

BERA (2024). *Ethical Guidelines for Educational Research* (5th ed.). London: BERA. https://www.bera.ac.uk/publication/ethical-guidelines-for-educational-research-fifth-edition-2024.

Costello, E., Brunton, J., Bolger, R., Soverino, T. and Juillerac, C. (2023). Massive omission of consent (MOOC): Ethical research in educational big data studies. *Online Learning*, 27(2), 67–87.

Decker, S. E., Naugle, A. E., Carter-Visscher, R., Bell, K. and Seifert, A. (2011). Ethical issues in research on sensitive topics: Participants' experiences of distress and benefit. *Journal of Empirical Research on Human Research Ethics*, 6(3), 55–64.

Eberlen, J. C., Nicaise, E., Leveaux, S., Mora, Y. L. and Klein, O. (2019). Psychometrics anonymous: Does a transparent data sharing policy affect data collection? *Psychologica Belgica*, 59(1), 373–92.

Erb, B., Bösch, C., Herbert, C., Kargl, F. and Montag, C. (2021). *Emerging Privacy Issues in Times of Open Science*. Preprint: Open Science Foundation Repository. https://doi.org/10.31234/osf.io/u236e.

Favaretto, M., De Clercq, E., Gaab, J. and Elger, B. S. (2020). First do no harm: An exploration of researchers' ethics of conduct in big data behavioral studies. *Plos One*, 15(11), e0241865.

Grierson, L., Cavanagh, A., Youssef, A., Lee-Krueger, R., McNeill, K., Button, B. and Kulasegaram, K. (2023). Inter-institutional data-driven education research: Consensus values, principles, and recommendations to guide the ethical sharing of administrative education data in the Canadian medical education research context. *Canadian Medical Education Journal*, 14(5), 113–20.

Houtkoop, B. L., Chambers, C., Macleod, M., Bishop, D. V., Nichols, T. E. and Wagenmakers, E. J. (2018). Data sharing in psychology: A survey on barriers and preconditions. *Advances in Methods and Practices in Psychological Science*, 1(1), 70–85.

Jeon, J., Kim, L. and Park, J. (2024). *The ethics of generative Ai in social science research: A qualitative approach for community-based Ai research ethics.* SSRN 4784555. https://papers.ssrn.com/sol3/papers.cfm?abstract_id=4784555.

Leckie, G. and Maragkou, K. (2024). Student sociodemographic and school type differences in teacher-predicted vs. achieved grades for university admission (Paper #04/23). *Bristol Working Papers in Education Series* (pp. 1–27). https://www.bristol.ac.uk/media-library/sites/education/documents/bristol-working-papers-in-education/Leckie%202023_Student%20Sociodemographic%20and%20School%20Type%20Differences%20-%20Working%20Paper.pdf.

Mandinach, E. B. and Beth, J. (2021). Data ethics in education: A theoretical, practical, and policy issue. *Studia Paedagogica*, 26(4), 9–26.

Office for National Statistics (2024). *Become an accredited researcher.* https://www.ons.gov.uk/aboutus/whatwedo/statistics/requestingstatistics/secureresearchservice/becomeanaccreditedresearcher.

Robinson, L., Curds, M., Abbasizanjani, H., Bedston, S. and Akbari, A. (2024). *Inequalities in Severe COVID-19 Outcomes in Wales, 2020 to 2022.* ADR Wales: Data Insight. https://www.adruk.org/fileadmin/uploads/adruk/Documents/Data_Insights/Inequalities_in_severe_COVID-19_outcomes_in_Wales_2020_to_2022.pdf.

Robson, K. and Malette, N. (2023). The Ethics and Bureaucratization of Data Management. In K. Robson and N. Malette (Eds.), *Handbook of Critical Education Research*. London: Routledge (pp. 675–94).

Stiles, P. G. and Boothroyd, R. A. (2015). Ethical use of administrative data for research purposes. In J. Fantuzzo and D.P. Culhane (Eds.), *Actionable Intelligence: Using Integrated Data Systems to Achieve a More Effective, Efficient, and Ethical Government.* New York: Palgrave Macmillan US (pp. 125–55).

Świątkowski, W. and Dompnier, B. (2017). Replicability crisis in social psychology: Looking at the past to find new pathways for the future. *International Review of Social Psychology*, 30(1), 111–24.

Van der Zee, T. and Reich, J. (2018). Open education science. *AERA Open*, 4(3), 2332858418787466.

Varkey, B. (2021). Principles of clinical ethics and their application to practice. *Medical Principles and Practice*, 30(1), 17–28.

9

Thinking It through or Thinking through 'It'? The Ethics of Research Involving Artificial Intelligence and Education

by *Robert Farrow and Wayne Holmes*

Case study background

This case study concerns research being undertaken at a fictional Higher Education Institution (HEI) in the UK (although the case study raises many issues of relevance elsewhere) about the impact of an Artificial Intelligence-enabled learning management system (LMS).[1] Note that we capitalise Artificial Intelligence to distinguish it as a field of enquiry or a type of technology rather than an intelligence that is artificial (Holmes and Tuomi, 2022). LMS (such as Blackboard and Moodle) are software platforms designed to deliver, manage and track educational courses, training programs or learning and development programs. They provide a virtual space for educators to create and deliver content, monitor student activity and assess performance. Incorporating AI technologies in an LMS nominally allows content and interfaces to be adapted to different learner needs, as well as making assessments and resource recommendations more responsive. Our fictional HEI hopes that this 'advanced' fictional LMS named 'STEMinus' will cost-effectively enhance student outcomes in STEM subjects (science, technology, engineering and mathematics), traditionally areas where some students struggle. STEMinus represents a fictional amalgam of AI-enabled tools that are increasingly widely used in K12 educational settings around the world and are beginning to be used in many Higher Education settings. STEMinus's functionality builds on existing functionalities of real AI-enabled tools, although it is important to note that few of those tools and their functionalities have been independently researched at scale for their effectiveness, safety or positive impact in educational contexts.

In this case study, STEMinus is currently being rolled out in a pilot program involving first-year STEM students. Initial feedback has been mixed. Some students have said that they appreciate what appears to be a 'personalised approach' that allows them to learn at their own pace. However, others find the system's suggestions repetitive and not always aligned with their learning needs. Lecturers also report a range of experiences, expressing concerns about reliability, the quality of recommendations and the lack of transparency in how the AI-enabled LMS operates. Currently, there is a lack of detailed guidance in UK Higher Education regarding such tools.

One of the key areas of disruption is assessment since traditional examination processes often rely on learners producing text, image or multimedia outputs which can now be convincingly created with a type of AI known as GenAI (generative AI). The misuse of GenAI tools for qualification assessment constitutes malpractice (JCQ, 2024) but may be extremely hard or even impossible to prove. 'AI detection' technologies are rarely accurate and often misidentify human-created text as AI-created (e.g. Elkhatat et al., 2023). The Department for Education has provided a position paper on the use of GenAI for education (Department for Education, 2023). This sets out some principles for the use of GenAI technologies in primary and secondary education contexts, but these are mostly framed as the key questions that require attention rather than a roadmap. The risks associated with AI are still being assessed (Slattery et al., 2024), and it has been shown that the use of AI in education remains largely absent from policy development (Schiff, 2022). In any case, the rapid pace of change means any AI guidance may quickly become outdated or inaccurate, and there remains a need to develop a distinctive institutional approach (BERA, 2024, paragraph 4).[2]

Dr Eleanor Thornton (known to her students and colleagues as 'Ellie' (she/her)) is a dedicated educator with over fifteen years of experience in teaching chemistry and integrating technology into education. After completing her

PGCE (Postgraduate Certificate in Education) and a short teaching career at a comprehensive school in East London, she moved into Higher Education. At St Catherine's University College, her current employer, she became an advocate for the use of educational technology to enhance learning outcomes, which led to her taking on the additional semi-formal role of Educational Technology Coordinator. During her sixteen years at St Catherine's, she also completed an Educational Doctorate based around her innovative practice as a science educator. Though her teaching and management duties account for the vast majority of her work plan, Dr Thornton regularly contributes to research and evaluation activities.

Ellie has been asked by her leadership to conduct some research over the next three months, leading up to the end of the exam period. The aim is to explore and evaluate the effectiveness of the AI-enabled LMS, as well as its other impacts on students, teachers and the classroom ecosystem. Ellie is an experienced researcher of educational technology. However, she is less familiar with AI technologies and how they work, though she is aware of some of the potential risks and benefits from things she has read in newspapers or seen on social media. She suspects that some students are already routinely using GenAI technologies, such as ChatGPT, to produce some or all of their coursework and agrees that research is needed.

ChatGPT is a well-known GenAI technology that was launched to the public in November 2022 and can be used to automatically generate text in response to a prompt. The use of GenAI tools like ChatGPT in educational settings is controversial – both because they might be used by students in their writing assessments, raising academic integrity concerns, and because the long-term effects of such tools on student progress, classroom practices, teacher agency, human rights, etc., remain unknown.

STEMinus has been presented to members of the St Catherine's community as the ultimate partner in fostering the next generation of engineers, scientists and mathematicians. The central selling point of STEMinus is that it doesn't just track the progress of learners in STEM subjects, but also predicts future performance, using complex algorithms to anticipate where students might struggle before they even start to experience a challenge. STEMinus then tailors content and assessments based on subtle inferences about each student's interactions with the system. By monitoring every click, keystroke and pause, STEMinus constantly refines its models. It then quietly adjusts curriculum materials, adding extra resources or adaptive quizzes, always careful to give the impression that the learners are the ones driving the pedagogical process.

STEMinus has been developed by ThisLMS, a well-known technology company. Their slick marketing emphasises how STEMinus can 'personalise education like never before' and uses futuristic graphics and buzzwords like 'precision learning' and 'algorithmic excellence'. The promotional literature also highlights ThisLMS's claims that STEMinus will increase student engagement, enhance learning outcomes and streamline the teaching process, but they are less forthcoming about the ethical grey areas, such as the vast amounts of data it harvests and the degree of surveillance involved. The company's ethos is a carefully constructed image of progress and student empowerment, though it never quite answers questions about where all that data goes, how it's used beyond the immediate scope of education or the subtle ways STEMinus might shape (or distort) educational practice.

The system monitors every interaction students have with the platform, collecting data not only on their academic performance but also on their behaviour, learning patterns and even emotional states. In fact, a close examination of the terms and conditions shows that STEMinus collects interaction timings, display notifications, data that is copied and pasted, screen captures, downloads, devices connected to the system such as personal computers and smartphones, apps, extensions, themes and any privacy-related settings a user has set. This level of surveillance raises significant privacy concerns, particularly regarding how this data is stored, who has access to it and how it might be used beyond the educational context. This ambiguity surrounding the data's end use, especially in the hands of a for-profit company like ThisLMS, has raised concerns among colleagues of Ellie's at St Catherine's University College. While they acknowledge that there is a need to improve STEM subject results, many are wondering whether all the data being captured and processed is really needed for the sake of learning.

Ethical dilemmas

There is a lot for Ellie to consider here. Research on AI, like most research, takes place within epistemologically contested spaces. AI in education is itself an interdisciplinary research field, for which multiple evidence types are relevant, and claims are often challenged for lacking evidence. Accordingly, researchers have a duty to fairly balance evidence types (BERA, 2024, paragraph 75)[3] but also to find productive routes through these tensions (BERA, 2024, paragraph 68).[4] In this example, researching the effects of the AI-enabled LMS requires gathering potentially sensitive data from various stakeholders, including students and teachers. Such data raises important privacy, data integrity and Intellectual Property concerns (BERA, 2024, paragraph 44).[5] Given the relative novelty of AI, it is also valid to question whether participants understand the technologies involved and their potential impact well enough to consider their views as informed (BERA, 2024, paragraph 3).[6] Power differentials between researcher and students also need to be taken into account (BERA, 2024, paragraph 20).[7] Finally, this research has been commissioned by the HEI leadership, who have an interest in specific metrics and outcomes. Inevitably, this will introduce potential conflicts of interest that need to be addressed (BERA, 2024, paragraphs 30 and 53).[8,9]

Navigating epistemic tensions

Research typically takes place within epistemologically contested spaces, and when novel technologies like AI are being brought to market, some of the claims that are made about their likely impact can sound more like marketing than evidence. For instance, it is frequently claimed that AI systems can provide 'personalised learning'; though there is little independent evidence at scale which supports this (Bhutoria, 2022). There is also little evidence that personalised learning is more effective than traditional or collaborative approaches to teaching and learning (Bernacki et al., 2021). Yet personalised learning is presented as one of the main benefits of the new LMS and has generated some excitement among students as well as managers.

Since the steps Ellie takes and the evidence that she produces may determine future strategies for pedagogy and learning design, the central challenge here is the fair and productive treatment of differing claims and the kinds of evidence that would substantiate them. For example, this research has been commissioned by the HEI leadership, who clearly have an interest in the outcomes (the leadership at St Catherine's has invested significant capital in its reputation as a technology leader in Higher Education, and perhaps they might try to influence the method to focus on LMS metrics rather than student voice). This could introduce potential conflicts of interest and might skew the research results. Conflicts of interest may be minor in nature, but the researcher needs to act with integrity (paragraph 30).[10] For the research to be widely accepted and useful, different epistemic spaces need to be navigated and aligned with the theoretical stance and conceptual commitments of the project.

Protecting research integrity

Research projects typically take place within a specified time frame using a determined set of resources, and this can limit scope. More generally, the competitive nature of academic research can pressure researchers to publish results quickly, which can lead to incomplete studies, ethical shortcuts and misleading information. In researching the use of an AI-enabled LMS, how can researchers ensure that they are able to avoid being compromised and uphold rigorous ethical standards? This can include taking the time to double-check findings, being circumspect about what has been learned, and communicating findings in accessible language to relevant parties (BERA, 2025, paragraph 70).[11] It can also be useful to seek out and compare findings with counterfactual evidence. However, all this requires time and resourcing. Navigating these constraints within a research project inevitably means that compromises are considered regarding the scope and feasibility of the 'perfect' research design.

Balancing risk and potential benefit

It is also frequently claimed that AI-enabled technologies have the 'potential' to improve teaching and learning. However, here, the word 'potential' may be misleading. Almost anything has potential. Without strong evidence, the positive 'potential' of AI is instead rather speculative. In fact, some AI-enabled technologies have been shown to cause harm and reinforce inequalities. AI has been identified with, for instance, social harms (Selwyn, 2022); environmental harms (Crawford, 2021); algorithmic injustices (Baker and Hawn, 2021); and violating the privacy of students (Akgun and Greenhow, 2022). Conversely, some AI technologies offer routes to ameliorating injustices by evidencing discrimination through mining large data sets. This could include providing insights into institutional decision making, such as analysing patterns of scholarships awarded, or refining application processes to make them fairer (Austin et al., 2023) (although AI-enabled application systems can embed hidden biases, Burke, 2020). Some of the benefits might be realised in the local community, while the harmful effects might be felt by people far away, or in the future. When there are real harms involved, how far should we go in researching and evaluating new technologies? Some would question whether we should be using AI technologies at all given such risks. At the same time, the potential benefits for the HEI need to be explored. An ethical approach requires careful balancing of the risks and benefits as a whole (BERA, 2024, paragraph 54).[12]

Collecting and managing evidence

Another complication with doing research into AI is that there is no one thing called 'AI'; we tend to bundle lots of different specific technologies into one category. This can lead to a lack of nuance and ambiguity in the way we speak about these technologies. Furthermore, to fully understand the potential impact of AI, it may be useful to consider (and triangulate) multiple types of evidence, both qualitative and quantitative. AI is an interdisciplinary research field, and multiple evidence types may be recommended. There is also an ethical obligation on the researcher to have a solid grasp of epistemology and practise epistemic justice (fair treatment of individuals, addressing issues of bias, marginalisation and power dynamics in knowledge production and dissemination). A solid conceptual framework which elaborates relevant research paradigms and their epistemological commitments (Farrow et al., 2021) may be helpful here since 'concepts such as "data", "reliability", "validity", "credibility", "trustworthiness", "subjectivity" and "objectivity" may [be] understood and legitimately applied in different ways' (BERA, 2024: 9). Researchers have a duty to fairly balance evidence types but also to find productive routes through these tensions (BERA, 2024, paragraph 68).[13]

Using sensitive data

The use of AI in adaptive learning systems depends upon the collection and analysis of large amounts of potentially sensitive personal data (which might include interaction data). This could include things like information about academic performance, data revealing how and when the LMS is accessed, metadata about personal messaging and so on. It is relevant to ask what kinds of expectations those that use the LMS have of the treatment of data on the platform. While this data might be used to inform the research, it also raises important privacy, data integrity, and Intellectual Property concerns. In researching the use of an AI-enabled LMS, Ellie is required to balance the need for data and the obligation to protect student privacy, academic integrity and intellectual property. In addition, care needs to be taken that this research data is kept confidential, including in any dissemination (BERA, 2024, paragraph 46).[14]

Informed consent

Further to the consideration of analytic and other data that can be drawn from the LMS, Ellie also considers collecting qualitative data (opinions and experiences) from stakeholders like students and lecturers. This data is potentially sensitive, and so obtaining informed consent is essential. However, it can be challenging to explain and/or demythologise the complex nature of AI and its potential impact – especially given that AI is fast developing, and its role and impact are often contested. In researching the use of an AI-enabled LMS, how can Ellie ensure that participants fully understand what they are consenting to and how their input will be protected, without overwhelming them with detail? To ensure that consent is informed, researchers need to be able to understand and communicate risks to participants (BERA, 2024, paragraph 9).[15]

Balancing stakeholder perspectives

The introduction of AI-enabled technologies and services is likely to impact everyone involved with the HEI. In other words, there are several stakeholder groups – students, educators, administrators, technologists, suppliers – each with their own distinct perspectives and agendas, some complementary and some contradictory. Nonetheless, all these different interests need to be represented in the research and balanced in the analysis. In researching the use of an AI-enabled LMS, how might Ellie ensure that the various stakeholder perspectives are fairly balanced and obligations to different stakeholders are equitably discharged? Researchers are required to act fairly and without favouritism (BERA, 2024, paragraph 74)[16] and to consider responsibilities to all stakeholders, including in how the research is communicated. It is also important to understand the difference between stakeholders and sponsors of research (paragraph 9).[17] While Ellie has been asked to conduct the study by her management, that does not mean that they should determine or influence the outcomes. In practice, balancing stakeholder interests is a matter of judgement for the researcher and depends on their reflective capacities and ability to take a holistic perspective.

Positionality

The history and experiences of the researcher are increasingly acknowledged as part of the conceptual framework for research. Researchers inevitably bring their own personal perspective to their research, consciously or unconsciously. Some epistemologies (approaches to knowledge and how it is acquired, e.g. positivist and post-positivist) see bias as something to be minimised or removed entirely in the interests of objectivity, while for others (e.g. interpretivist and critical studies researchers), personal bias is considered not just inevitable but a potential source of insight. Ellie is herself a member of St Catherine's, and so is also a stakeholder in the research rather than a 'disinterested' observer. She can offer personal insights into the context of the research – and might even choose a research method such as autoethnography that could facilitate this – but she needs to take care that her research positionality is transparent (BERA, 2024, paragraph 1 and 3).[18] Ravitch and Riggan (2017: 18–19) suggest six key framing questions for researcher positionality:

1. What do I want to study?
2. Who cares?
3. What literature do I need to include, and when have I had enough?
4. How do I know what kind of data to collect and how to analyse them?
5. How does my own position and way of seeing the world shape the framing and execution of my research?
6. How do I deal with surprises in the data or unexpected developments in the field?

In the context of Mixed Methods research in higher education studies, where the researcher also serves as a stakeholder – such as a faculty member, administrator or policymaker – rigorous reflexivity becomes critical to mitigate the inherent tensions in this dual positionality. This dual positionality may lead to conflicts of interest, where the researcher's personal investments influence the design, data collection and interpretation of results, potentially skewing findings to favour the interests of a particular stakeholder. Additionally, maintaining critical distance becomes challenging, as the researcher might struggle to separate their subjective perspectives from the need for impartial or reflective analysis. Ethical dilemmas are also more prevalent, as described above. To navigate these tensions, Ellie must engage in rigorous reflexivity, openly acknowledge her positionality and implement transparent methodologies to ensure that her dual roles do not undermine the credibility and validity of the research.

Reflexivity in this scenario involves a deep, ongoing examination of Ellie's own assumptions and influences throughout the research process. Ellie advocates for the use of educational technologies but also aims to bring a critical perspective on their use. When there are contradictory presentations of AI across traditional and social media, it can be hard to differentiate marketing hype from reliable evidence. As an expert in educational technology, Ellie is perhaps better placed than most to have a meaningful opinion about a new LMS. Accounting for her positionality reflexively is not a matter of removing her own insights from the research in the name of removing bias so much as embracing the tensions in her role as an insider-outsider (Dwyer and Buckle, 2009).

For example, when conducting surveys and interviews with students or colleagues, Ellie must remain acutely aware of how her insider status might affect the responses she elicits. Her familiarity with the institution could lead to leading questions or interpretations that unconsciously validate her preconceived notions or align with institutional goals. Furthermore, a researcher's stake in the outcomes they investigate (such as improving a programme they help manage or enhancing the reputation of their institution) might affect the data analysis, prioritising positive results over critical insights. To counter these risks, Ellie must document and critically reflect on every stage of her research, openly discussing how her positionality may have shaped her interactions with participants, data collection methods and interpretation of findings. Ellie might, for instance, engage in journaling, asking research participants for their feedback on preliminary outcomes to help ensure the validity of final outcomes, or collaborate with external auditors to ensure rigour and transparency. In Mixed Methods research, this reflexivity extends to how a researcher like Ellie integrates and triangulates qualitative and quantitative data, being mindful that her own interests or perspectives do not overly influence the synthesis of these different types of evidence. By systematically and transparently engaging in reflexivity, Ellie can navigate the complexities of her dual role, contributing to the trustworthiness and ethical integrity of her work in higher education studies.

The ethical practice of a researcher who is also a stakeholder is thus deeply intertwined with the principles of reflexivity and the recognition of positionality, particularly in relation to epistemology. Ethical research requires the researcher to be acutely aware of how their dual role might influence not just the research process but also the very foundation of knowledge production. From an epistemological standpoint, the researcher's positionality shapes what is considered valid knowledge and whose perspectives are prioritised (Soedirgo and Glas, 2020). In a higher education context, where Mixed Methods research is often employed, this dual positionality can affect the balance between qualitative and quantitative data, potentially leading to an overemphasis on findings that support institutional interests. Ethical practice demands that researchers critically reflect on how their embeddedness in the context they study could bias their interpretation of data and the conclusions they draw, ensuring that these biases do not undermine the reliability or validity of the research. This involves not only being transparent about their positionality but also actively seeking to minimise its impact through reflexive strategies, such as peer debriefing or engaging with alternative epistemological perspectives (Darwin Holmes, 2020).

Course of action

Ellie decides to take a methodical and transparent approach to her research on the AI-enabled LMS, STEMinus. First, she drafts a research plan that acknowledges her dual role as both a researcher and a stakeholder within St Catherine's University College. This plan includes a detailed positionality statement, where Ellie openly discusses her advocacy for educational technology and the advantages and disadvantages that might stem from her involvement in the project. The plan also describes some of the potential benefits that AI might bring to how teaching and learning are conducted at St Catherine's and acknowledges some of the fears and concerns that have been expressed among staff and students. This approach appealed to transparency as a way of engaging different stakeholders (BERA, 2024, paragraph 27).[19]

A research plan was developed that includes triangulating learning analytics data from the STEMinus LMS with interviews and observations and discussing the outputs with stakeholder focus groups (in particular, with students, educators and education administrators). As required, Ellie follows the ethical approval process for research at St Catherine's. This process sees the protocols for research written in detail and assessed by the Ethical Review Committee, a group of researchers experienced in dealing with ethical issues who must approve activities in advance (Guillemin, 2012; Head, 2018). Ellie prepares a detailed research protocol for review, which includes the study's objectives, methodology, recruitment strategies, consent forms, data collection methods and plans for data analysis. Getting approval from the Ethical Review Committee involves a thorough assessment of potential risks and benefits, with a focus on continuous ethical engagement throughout the research lifecycle. Ellie aimed to align her practices with the

St Catherine's institutional values and codes of conduct to help ensure that the research is trustworthy and credible. In recognition of the importance of the study for St Catherine's, she requested a full, unexpedited review from the Ethical Review Committee in order to draw on as much input from expert colleagues as possible.

Ellie knows that this protocol must clearly outline how participants will be protected and how the study will address ethical issues like privacy, confidentiality and potential risks. Rather than relying solely on people signing consent forms to indicate their informed willingness to participate in the research, Ellie decides to add a verbal consent process where she explains the research and checks verbally whether participants understand what they are consenting to (e.g. that they understand that their interactions with STEMinus will be recorded and analysed), offering a chance to discuss and inviting questions when the consent form is signed (Xu et al., 2020).

In her own time, Ellie had already begun to explore and experiment with AI tools designed to facilitate and support research. These included:

- ChatGPT (a commonly used GenAI tool) as a critical friend and conversation partner to refine the scope and central questions of a research project;
- AI-enhanced search engines to find and summarise relevant literature;
- GenAI tools designed to help with drafting and editing papers, or writing research instruments;
- Visualisation tools which can represent data in interesting ways.

Before being asked to lead the research into STEMinus, Ellie had only played around with such tools. She had also experimented a little with using other GenAI tools for various tasks to see what kind of uses they might have for learners at St Catherine's and what kind of implications this might have for assessment. Her initial subjective and unsystematic evaluation of such tools was mixed. Sometimes the results were highly impressive, while at other times basic errors (what are sometimes incorrectly called 'hallucinations') appeared in the results. But she wondered whether using AI tools for research might lead to more insightful results or allow the research to progress more efficiently when resources are limited. Might AI also help communicate results to the different stakeholders? Should the research plan include AI tools when it is AI tools themselves that are under investigation? Would people see the research outputs as less credible if they knew that some of them were drafted with the help of a chatbot? Is it wise to 'let the AI do the thinking'? These questions are challenging, especially given that there is currently little consensus on AI-systems' capabilities for research (e.g. do GenAI summariser tools summarise effectively, or do they just shorten, potentially losing important information or key aspects of the original arguments?).

Ellie decides that she should use all tools available to her and so integrate some AI-enabled tools into the research plan. To mitigate the potential risks involved, she limits the use of such tools to helping to find and summarise relevant literature for the development of the conceptual framework and streamlining the process of writing research instruments (such as interview prompts and protocols for observing the everyday use of STEMinus). Ellie does not want to risk using AI for analysis of the data because she is not yet confident it is capable of doing so accurately and is concerned about how this might be perceived by the research stakeholders.

She also resolves to be upfront about the use of AI by using the Academic Integrity and Transparency in AI-assisted Research and Specification (aiTARAS) Framework (Bozkurt, 2024) to acknowledge the limited use of AI and to transparently describe the specific ways in which AI tools were used in the research process. The aiTARAS framework allows researchers to describe the specific applications of AI tools during the research process and provides a protocol for reporting. Researchers can indicate any combination of the following: a direct contribution by AI, where a significant amount of content or writing was generated; general assistance by AI; drafting of a specific section of a paper by AI; using AI for developing ideas; using AI in the reviewing and editing of text; using AI to translate (or otherwise localise) text; using AI to analyse data; using AI for data visualisation; or using AI to generate or validate code or algorithms.

In developing her conceptual framework, Ellie expanded her ethical considerations to include stakeholders beyond the immediate research context. This included acknowledging the potential impacts on student safety (e.g. their mental health) and on the wider educational ecosystem and sociocultural perspectives, not just on the narrow question of whether learning could be shown to be improving. She also thought about the long-term implications of her work, including how future students and faculty members might be affected by the outcomes. These considerations fed into the conceptual framework for the research at a fundamental level. The decision was taken to include representatives from ThisLMS as part of the stakeholders potentially affected by the research project and to solicit input from them (particularly with respect to their management of learner data).

Ellie began by extracting learning analytics data directly from the STEMinus platform. This data included student engagement metrics such as login frequencies, time spent on various activities, participation in discussion forums and the completion rates of assignments. She also collected data on student performance in quizzes and exams, focusing on how AI tools within STEMinus might correlate with academic outcomes.

In parallel, Ellie conducted semi-structured interviews with a diverse group of participants, including students, faculty members and IT staff. These interviews were designed to explore user experiences with STEMinus, their perceptions of its strengths and weaknesses, any suggestions they had for improvement, and any concerns that they had with using a technology underpinned by AI. Ellie used a combination of open-ended questions and more specific prompts to ensure a thorough exploration of perspectives. As part of this, she explained in detail the data management system used by STEMinus and asked for feedback to gauge understanding.

To complement the interviews, Ellie also carried out observations in various classroom, blended and virtual settings where STEMinus was actively being used. These observations focused on how instructors integrated the LMS into their teaching, how students interacted with the platform during lessons, and the overall flow of classroom activities with the LMS in play. Finally, Ellie facilitated focus group discussions with key stakeholders, including university administrators and representatives from ThisLMS. These sessions were aimed at gathering feedback on preliminary findings and discussing potential implications for the broader community at St Catherine's.

To further strengthen the credibility of her findings, Ellie arranges for an external auditor to review her methodology and findings. This auditor, whose involvement had a financial implication for the project, provides an independent perspective, helping to ensure that the research process and conclusions are sufficiently robust (Carcary, 2021). Ellie also engaged indirectly with alternative epistemological perspectives by discussing the preliminary results with academic colleagues from different disciplines, broadening the scope of her analysis by giving them a chance to have input.

Ellie carefully designed a dissemination strategy that prioritised the impact on St Catherine's University College. Recognising the significance of the research for the institution, she aimed to ensure that the findings would directly inform and improve educational practices. To achieve this, Ellie planned a series of internal presentations and workshops tailored to different stakeholder groups, including faculty, administrative staff and students. These sessions were structured to not only share the findings but also to engage stakeholders in discussions about whether and how STEMinus might be integrated into teaching and learning practices, seeking ways to mitigate risks to stakeholders while more data was collected for a longitudinal study. Concerns around surveillance were brought to ThisLMS, who agreed to alter aspects of the contract regarding the types of data gathered and put into place additional policies regarding the anonymisation of analytic data.

Ellie also worked closely with the St Catherine's leadership team to develop actionable recommendations based on the research outcomes. These and other recommendations were designed to be practical and aligned with institutional strategic goals, addressing both the potential benefits and the concerns raised by the stakeholders. Professional development activities for staff and students focused on AI in education were offered. Additionally, Ellie collaborated with the communications department to create accessible summaries and infographics that could be shared across the university's internal communication channels, ensuring that the findings were communicated effectively to all members of the St Catherine's community as part of an ongoing dialogue about future strategy.

Alternative courses of action

Different strategic options available to Ellie have a range of ethical implications. Considering first the choice of research methods, instead of a Mixed Methods approach, Ellie could have employed a purely quantitative experimental design. By creating control and experimental groups, she could measure the 'effectiveness' of STEMinus through standardised test scores and learning outcomes. This method aligns with a positivist epistemology, emphasising objectivity and generalisability, and is likely to be most acceptable to policymakers. It also depends on a clear understanding of what 'effectiveness' means in this context (e.g. enhanced student outcomes, not undermining student human rights, positive benefits for the university's eco-system and relationships between staff and students). Conducting a quantitative experimental study would involve assigning participants to control and experimental groups. Ethical issues include ensuring informed consent, especially when participants may not understand that they might receive different treatments. There's also the challenge of dealing with potential disparities in access to STEMinus or educational support, which could raise concerns about fairness and equity. Additionally, reducing participants to mere data points could overlook their individual experiences and agency.

Alternatively, Ellie could have prioritised extensive consultation with a wide range of stakeholders, including external experts (e.g. Delphi-style study (Landeta, 2006)), making this the central approach to the research rather than attempting to triangulate qualitative and quantitative data. Alternatively, a more ethnographic approach could see Ellie immersed in the everyday experiences of students and teachers using STEMinus (including herself). An ethnographic study requires deep immersion in the lives of participants, which potentially raises ethical concerns around privacy, confidentiality and the researcher's impact on the community. Ellie would need to be vigilant about obtaining continuous informed consent, as the lines between observation and participation can blur. There is also a risk of unduly influencing the experiment due to the presence of the researcher, requiring attention to Ellie's identities as insider-outsider and stakeholder-researcher (Porisky and Glas, 2022).

Engaging the stakeholders in a different way, Ellie could have used Participatory Action Research (Baum et al., 2006), involving teachers, students, administrators and other staff as co-researchers in the study. This approach would emphasise collaborative inquiry and democratic knowledge production, valuing change and action over mere observation. Participatory approaches organise collaboration and co-ownership of the research process, which can empower participants but also ambiguate roles and responsibilities. There could still be a real benefit here in terms of bringing the stakeholders of St Catherine's together. Ellie would need to carefully navigate issues of power dynamics, ensuring that all voices are heard and respected, especially those of less powerful stakeholders such as students. The co-researcher status might blur boundaries, making it difficult to maintain robustness and to handle conflicts of interest.

To address issues around power and inequality more directly, Ellie might have chosen to analyse STEMinus through the lens of critical theory and the potential for AI tools to reinforce or exacerbate existing hierarchies (Kellner, 2003). This approach would involve critiquing the underlying assumptions of AI in education and exploring how different groups (e.g. marginalised students) experience these technologies differently. Similarly, a feminist research methodology could focus on exploring gender dynamics relative to STEM education, which could surface sensitive issues related to inequality, bias and discrimination (McDonald et al., 2013). Ellie would need to handle these topics with discretion, ensuring that participants feel safe and supported when discussing potentially traumatic or controversial experiences. There is a risk of reinforcing stereotypes or inadvertently excluding participants who do not conform to typical gender narratives. Ethical research in this context would require a careful balance between advocacy and respecting the diversity of participant experiences.

Some might also question the scientific credibility of such an approach. When working with critical approaches, there's a risk of alienating stakeholders who might feel accused or criticised, perhaps leading to resistance or defensiveness. Ethical considerations here also include maintaining respect for all participants, ensuring that the research does not inadvertently harm the reputations of individuals or the institution, and navigating the potential for skewed interpretations that align with Ellie's own critical stance and professional investment in educational technology. With such a range of considerations, it's easy to see why Mixed Methods research often seems an attractive approach (Cresswell, 1999). However, it's important to note that different combinations of research methods result in specific ethical and epistemological requirements. Whichever research approach is taken, developing an adequate conceptual framework can help describe and anticipate risks and mitigations.

Regarding the Ethical Review Committee, we might observe that Ellie opted for a more detailed and thorough review while making reflective practice a central support for her method. This may mean that the process takes longer, which can be a factor in time-sensitive research. A lighter touch might have involved relying solely on a traditional or generic checklist to assess risks and benefits and the possible impact on those who participate in the study. This could result in a less nuanced understanding of the impact of STEMinus due to the dynamic and evolving nature of AI technologies and risks overlooking emergent ethical issues (franzke et al., 2020). This approach can also limit opportunities for reflection. For the participants, this could lead to insufficient protection of their rights and privacy and failure to address individual concerns, especially if emergent risks in a scenario like this are not covered by standard research ethics checklists. When Ellie's approach foregrounds her epistemological standpoint, making space for reflection is essential.

Ellie could also have decided not to use AI-enabled tools to support the research process, maintaining a clear separation between the AI being studied and the research instruments. This could limit the scope and effectiveness of the research by slowing the process or limiting the review of literature in a project with a tight time frame. However, the use of AI to conduct research is itself yet to be supported by robust research. In addition, innovating the research process can result in risks, especially where new technologies are concerned. On the other hand, Ellie could have made greater use of AI tools throughout the research process, leveraging them not just for literature review and instrument design but also for data collection, analysis and dissemination (Bolanos et al., 2024). For instance, AI could have been used to analyse qualitative data by identifying patterns or themes within interview transcripts or observational notes (Zhang et al., 2023). Additionally, Ellie might have used AI-driven predictive models to forecast the potential impact of STEMinus on student outcomes, providing a data-driven basis for her conclusions. However, there is as yet little evidence to support the use of such approaches, and they also raise ethical concerns, such as the potential for algorithmic bias and the risk of dehumanising participants by relying too heavily on automated tools and metrics. Ensuring that AI tools are used responsibly and with full transparency would be crucial, including clearly communicating the extent of AI involvement to all stakeholders and continuously assessing the impact of these technologies on the integrity and validity of the research outcomes (Farrow, 2023).

Ellie used an external auditor to validate the outcomes of the research, but another option here would have been to consult an expert in AI who is not associated with ThisLMS. However, such an expert would also need to have knowledge of the research process and how to ascertain the reliability of research results.

Finally, to promote the transparency and reusability of her research, Ellie could consider releasing the data from the study as open data. Open data is important for science (van Dijk et al., 2021). When research involves human participants, however, great care must be taken to ensure that the data is adequately prepared before release. To maximise the value of her work, Ellie could also share the research instruments on open licences so that others could repeat the experiment in different contexts or at St Catherine's in the future.

Final thoughts

Managing the ethical challenges of researching new technologies demands a deep understanding of ethical principles and a commitment to reflective practice, together with in-depth knowledge of research methodologies and issues and of the particular technologies in question (both how they work and their human implications). In the context of AI in educational research, this challenge is heightened by the rapid pace of technological change, often outstripping existing ethical guidelines. Researchers must not only comprehend and apply ethical principles grounded in moral philosophy but also engage in continuous reflection to adapt these principles to new scenarios.

Ellie, the researcher, sought to align her work with the values of St Catherine's University College but quickly recognised the risk that traditional static checklists were inadequate for addressing AI's dynamic nature (Srikumar, 2022). To address this, she adopted a dialogic and reflexive ethical review process, engaging in ongoing dialogue with diverse stakeholders and reflecting on the broader impacts beyond just learning outcomes. This approach allowed her to consider a wider set of factors, including the sociocultural and human rights implications of AI on the educational environment and the long-term effects on students and faculty.

Ellie realised that traditional ethical review methods, which often rely on static risk checklists, were insufficient due to the evolving nature of AI. Instead, she employed a more fluid ethical review process, underpinned by a consistent research strategy that allowed for the adaptation of methods as new ethical challenges emerged. This approach not only ensured the integrity of her work but also facilitated a more authentic and comprehensive assessment of the AI-enabled LMS, STEMinus. Ellie also recognised that evaluating STEMinus could not be limited to measuring learning outcomes alone. She expanded her focus to consider the broader impacts on the classroom ecosystem, including interactions among students and between students and educators. Her aim was to ensure that the use of AI-enabled tools for data analysis and knowledge creation did not compromise ethical standards, particularly concerning data privacy and integrity. Given that the data analysis tools were provided by third parties, Ellie faced challenges in ensuring data protection. She conducted a thorough review of the terms and conditions associated with these tools, presented the findings to her leadership, and acknowledged that not all risks could be fully mitigated.

Some of the ethical challenges described in this scenario arise because the leadership at St Catherine's decided to start implementing STEMinus without conducting an evaluation first. This decision placed Ellie at the forefront of upholding ethical standards as she navigated the introduction of potentially disruptive technologies like AI. One approach to due diligence evaluation that has been proposed (Veletsianos, 2024) involves educational institutions asking five questions before they purchase any AI-enabled products: Which educational problem does the product solve? Is there evidence that a product works? Did educators and students help develop the product? What educational beliefs shape this product? Does the product level the playing field? Meanwhile, Ellie's approach underscores the importance of maintaining ethical vigilance and adaptability in the face of emerging technologies, ensuring that the pursuit of innovation does not come at the expense of ethical integrity.

Managing the ethical challenges generated by researching new technologies also requires a solid understanding of ethical principles that supports reflective practice on the part of the researcher. Navigating the complexities of AI in educational research requires adapting to rapid technological changes that may be outside the scope of existing ethical guidelines. Researchers must strive to understand, reflect on and continuously engage with research ethics principles and their grounding in moral philosophy. Not everyone has the time to become a moral philosopher, though ethical reflective practice can be supported by developing a better understanding of these principles and their application. In this regard, virtue ethics may have some guidance.

Virtue ethics focuses on the cultivation of moral character and practical wisdom (phronesis), which can be especially valuable in researching new technologies like AI (see, e.g. Ober and Tasioulas, 2024). Unlike rule-based ethical frameworks that rely on fixed principles or consequences, virtue ethics focuses on developing the moral qualities of the researcher – such as honesty, courage and integrity – which could enable them to negotiate complex, evolving scenarios with sound judgement. In the context of AI research, where rapid technological advancements often outpace existing ethical guidelines, virtue ethics might encourage researchers to develop a reflective and adaptive mindset. This approach helps them to make ethically informed decisions that consider not only the immediate impact of their work but also the broader implications for society, ensuring that their research contributes positively to human flourishing and upholds the trust placed in them. By fostering virtues like responsibility, empathy and transparency, researchers can better address the ethical uncertainties and challenges posed by AI, supporting more responsible and conscientious innovation. The characteristic feature of virtue ethics is that one's own moral development is seen as a work in progress, requiring constant and habitual ethical reflection and learning from experiences. This fits well with the theme of reflective practice in research (Banks, 2018). Similarly, researching newer technologies can be supported by keeping up to date with new developments where possible. Developing an improved understanding of AI can happen through targeted reading of trusted resources (e.g. Rough and Sutherland, 2024). Engaging with relevant policymakers can also be a way to ensure the relevance and timeliness of research into new educational technologies, and for this clear communication is essential (Schiff, 2021). When new and potentially disruptive technologies like AI emerge, it is the research community that bears responsibility for upholding ethical standards.[20]

Finally, while this case study has been situated in a UK HEI, the issues raised are broadly applicable elsewhere. However, while no AI-specific regulations have been developed or adopted in the UK (instead, regulation has been left to existing instruments such as the GDPR), AI systems and their use are being increasingly regulated elsewhere (the EU AI Act[21] and the Council of Europe's Framework Convention,[22] to name just two examples). That being said, currently, few if any of these regulatory approaches around the world specifically address the use of AI systems in education or in research. For LMICs (Low- and Middle-Income Countries), such as many in the global south, additional issues may arise (such as the impact of inequitable access to research resources and AI technologies and the underexplored AI 'neo-colonialism') that also need to be properly considered and robustly addressed.

Reflective questions

1. When conducting research into the impact of AI, how can the interests and perspectives of different stakeholders be balanced and/or integrated?
2. When new technologies are introduced, what is the role of research in ensuring that all students receive equitable educational opportunities?
3. How can research on AI be designed to responsibly balance immediate benefits with potential long-term risks for HEIs?
4. How much should we emphasise transparency and explicability of AI systems as part of ethical practice? Should such transparency be extended to learners too?
5. How can we ethically evaluate a technology that potentially affects many people but also is not necessarily well understood by them?

Further reading

1. Bozkurt, A. (2024). GenAI et al.: Cocreation, authorship, ownership, academic ethics and integrity in a time of Generative AI. *Open Praxis*, 16(1), 1–10. https://doi.org/10.55982/openpraxis.16.1.654.

   This paper discusses the evolving nature of academic authorship in a world where AI tools are being used. It calls for a fresh examination of standards and proposes a practical schema for addressing and acknowledging the use of AI in research.

2. Farrow, R. (2023). The possibilities and limits of XAI in education: A socio-technical perspective. *Learning, Media and Technology*, 48(2), 266–79. https://doi.org/10.1080/17439884.2023.2185630.

   Issues around AI ethics, transparency and explicability are critically explored with reference to the socio-technical ecosystems of production, assembly, programming, training, using and maintaining AI systems

3. Holmes, W. and Porayska-Pomsta, K. (Eds.) (2023). *The Ethics of AI in Education. Practices, Challenges, and Debates*. London: Routledge. https://www.routledge.com/The-Ethics-of-Artificial-Intelligence-in-Education-Practices-Challenges/Holmes-Porayska-Pomsta/p/book/9780367349721.

   This book identifies and confronts key ethical issues generated over years of AI research, development and deployment in learning contexts. Features expert perspectives from inside and outside the AIED scholarly community and provides questions, frameworks, guidelines, policies and regulations to ensure the positive impact of Artificial Intelligence in learning.

4. Holmes, W., Porayska-Pomsta, K., Holstein, Ken, Sutherland, E., Baker, T., Buckingham Shum, S., Santos, O. C., Rodrigo, M. M. T., Cukorova, M., Bittencourt, I. I. and Koedinger, K. (2021). Ethics of AI in education: Towards a community-wide framework. *International Journal of Artificial Intelligence in Education*, 32(4), 504–26. https://link-springer-com.libproxy.ucl.ac.uk/article/10.1007/s40593-021-00239-1.

   This paper introduces issues around the ethics of AI in education and discusses the complex issues raised by respondents to a survey of questions about ethics and the application of AI in educational contexts. Specific outcomes include the recognition that most AIED researchers are not trained to tackle the emerging ethical questions.

5. Srikumar, M., Finlay, R., G., Abuhamad, Ashurst, C., Campbell, R., Campbell-Ratcliffe, E., Hongo, H., Jordan, S.R., Lindley, J., Ovadya, A. and Pineau, J. (2022). Advancing ethics review practices in AI research.

Nature Machine Intelligence, 4(12), 1061–4. https://doi.org/10.1038/s42256-022-00585-2.

This paper discusses how successful ethics review processes depend on coordinated community efforts, experimentation with different ethics review processes and opportunities for diverse voices from the community.

Notes

1. This case study appears in a slightly adapted form as a web case study. Research Ethics Case Studies 2024 | BERA.
2. Digital/online research, as well as the use of artificial intelligence [*sic*], is a rapidly developing area, therefore conventions as to what constitutes good ethical practice are not as well established as in most other areas of educational research (BERA, 2024, paragraph 4).
3. Researchers must not bring research into disrepute by in any way falsifying, distorting, suppressing, selectively reporting or sensationalising their research evidence or findings (BERA, 2024, paragraph 75).
4. Assessment of the quality of the evidence supporting any inferences is an especially important feature of any research (BERA, 2024, paragraph 68).
5. Researchers need to be aware that participants' understandings of their level of privacy in a particular place, especially in online spaces, may be inaccurate (BERA, 2024, paragraph 44).
6. It is important for researchers to take account of the rights and interests of those indirectly affected by their research, and to consider whether action is appropriate (BERA, 2024, paragraph 3).
7. In some cases, potential participants may not be in a social position vis-à-vis the researcher that enables them to give voluntary informed consent. This can occur, for example, when the researcher and potential participant are family members, or if the researcher is the participant's teacher/lecturer. Researchers need to consider carefully how to deal with such situations and, if possible, should reassure potential participants that non-participation is entirely acceptable (BERA, 2024, paragraph 20).
8. Researchers should not undertake work in which they can be perceived to have a material conflict of interest, or in which self-interest or commercial gain might compromise the validity of the research. Any potential conflicts of interest should be declared to relevant parties at various stages of the research, including in any publications (BERA, 2024, paragraph 30).
9. Researchers are encouraged to think carefully about how they position themselves and their research design, analysis and interpretation in

relation to the interests of their sponsors and other stakeholders. Any conflicts of interest or compromises to the integrity of the research must be made clear and open to scrutiny (BERA, 2024, paragraph 53).

10   It is even possible that Ellie should decline the offer to lead the research project. See note 8 (BERA, 2024, paragraph 30).

11   Educational researchers should communicate their findings, and the practical significance of their research, in a clear, straightforward fashion, and in language judged appropriate to the intended audience(s). Researchers have a responsibility to make the results of their research available for the benefit of educational professionals, policymakers and the wider public, subject only to the provisos indicated in subsequent paragraphs. They should not accept contractual terms that obstruct their exercise of this responsibility (BERA, 2024, paragraph 70).

12   Researchers should consider the implications of their research for the global community and the environment more generally, bearing in mind the interests of non-humans and broader issues to do with sustainability, climate change and biodiversity (BERA, 2024, paragraph 54).

13   See note 4.

14   Researchers should ensure that data are kept securely, and that the form of any publication or dissemination (for example, at a conference) does not directly or indirectly lead to a breach of agreed confidentiality. Accepted practices for keeping data secure change over time but currently include: the use of secure computer networks; ensuring that hard copy data are stored under lock and key on secure premises; digitising resources and destroying the originals; the use of password protection and/or data encryption for electronic data; using courier or secure electronic transfer when moving data; and ensuring that any third-party users of the data agree to an appropriate data-sharing agreement. Researchers should be aware that some online services, such as automated transcription, may compromise confidentiality (BERA, 2024, paragraph 46).

15   Researchers should do what they can to ensure that all potential participants understand, as well as they are able, what is involved in a study. They should be told why their participation is desired, what, if anything, they will be asked to do, what will happen to the data they provide and how and to whom the data will be reported. They also should be informed about the retention, sharing and any possible secondary uses of the data. (BERA, 2024, paragraph 9)

16   In some circumstances, research findings will be regarded as sensitive information by sponsors, commissioners or other research stakeholders (for example, because they raise politically or culturally controversial issues, or because they may result in negative publicity for an organisation). When researchers become aware that research findings

are likely to be sensitive, they should aim to inform stakeholders prior to publication, and negotiate with those stakeholders a fair publication strategy that takes into consideration the public interest in the findings, the researchers' need to publish and the stakeholders' concerns. Particular care should be taken to guard against publication or dissemination leading to discrimination against marginalised or otherwise disadvantaged groups or particular individuals, including whistleblowers, or to negative impressions being formed or reinforced about such groups or individuals (BERA, 2024, paragraph 74).

17 Researchers should do what they can to ensure that all potential participants understand, as well as they are able, what is involved in a study. They should be told why their participation is desired, what, if anything, they will be asked to do, what will happen to the data they provide and how and to whom the data will be reported. They also should be informed about the retention, sharing and any possible secondary uses of the data. Where appropriate, researchers who are BERA members may include a declaration of membership in information sheets and consent forms, to make explicit the fact that members are expected to follow BERA guidance as part of the Association's code of conduct (which contains a complaints procedure that may be helpful) (BERA, 2024, paragraph 9).

18 BERA believes that educational researchers should operate within an ethic of respect for all persons – including themselves – involved in or affected by the research they are undertaking. Individuals should be treated fairly, sensitively, and with dignity and freedom from prejudice, in recognition of both their rights and their differences arising from age, gender, sexuality, ethnicity, class, nationality, cultural identity, partnership status, faith, disability, political belief or any other significant characteristic (BERA, 2024, paragraph 1).

Participants in research may be actively or passively involved in such processes as observation, experiment, auto/biographical reflection, survey or test. They may be collaborators or colleagues in the research process, or they may simply be implicated in the context in which a research project takes place. (For example, in a teacher's or lecturer's research into their own professional practice, students and/or colleagues will be part of the context but will not themselves be the focus of that research.) It is important for researchers to take account of the rights and interests of those indirectly affected by their research, and to consider whether action is appropriate – for example, they should consider whether it is appropriate to provide information or obtain informed consent. In rare cases – such as some politically volatile settings, or where researchers are investigating illegal activity – covert research can be defensible (BERA, 2024, paragraph 3).

19 Researchers should aim to be open and honest with participants and other stakeholders, avoiding non-disclosure unless their research design specifically requires it in order to ensure that the appropriate data are collected, or so that the researcher or participants are not put at risk. Decisions to use non-disclosure in research should be the subject of full, principled deliberation and subsequent disclosure in reporting (BERA, 2024, paragraph 27).

    A stakeholder of research is considered to be any person or body who has a direct interest in its framing and success. A sponsor of research is considered to be a stakeholder that funds or commissions research (such as a research charity or philanthropic foundation, a national research council or other government body, or a commercial or nongovernmental organisation), or that facilitates it by allowing and enabling access to resources needed to carry out the research, such as data and participants (for example, an examinations body) (BERA, 2024, paragraph 50).
20 Dr Eleanor 'Ellie' Thornton, St Catherine's University College, STEMinus and ThisLMS are fictional entities created by ChatGPT 4.0. No resemblance to anyone or anything non-fictional is intended.
21 Regulation (EU) 2024 of the European Parliament and of the Council of laying down harmonised rules on artificial intelligence and amending Regulations https://www.europarl.europa.eu/doceo/document/TA-9-2024-0138-FNL-COR01_EN.pdf.
22 Council of Europe Framework Convention on Artificial Intelligence and Human Rights, Democracy and the Rule of Law. https://search.coe.int/cm?i=0900001680afb122.

References

Akgun, S. and Greenhow, C. (2022). Artificial intelligence in education: Addressing ethical challenges in K-12 settings. *AI Ethics*, 2, 431–40. https://doi.org/10.1007/s43681-021-00096-7.

Austin, T., Rawal, B. S., Diehl, A. and Cosme, J. (2023). AI for equity: Unpacking potential human bias in decision making in higher education. *IntechOpen*. https://doi.org/10.5772/acrt.20.

Baker, R. S. and Hawn, A. (2021). Algorithmic bias in education. *International Journal of Artificial Intelligence in Education*, 32(4), 1052–92. https://doi.org/10.1007/s40593-021-00285-9.

Baker, R. S. and Hawn, A. (2022). Algorithmic bias in education. *International Journal of Artificial Intelligence in Education*, 32, 1052–92. https://doi.org/10.1007/s40593-021-00285-9.

Banks, S. (2018). Cultivating Researcher Integrity: Virtue-Based Approaches to Research Ethics. In Emmerich, N. (Ed.), *Virtue Ethics in the Conduct and Governance of Social Science Research* (Advances in Research Ethics and Integrity, Vol. 3), Leeds: Emerald Publishing (pp. 21–44). https://doi.org/10.1108/S2398-601820180000003002.

Baum, F., MacDougall, C. and Smith, D. (2006). Participatory action research. *Journal of EpideMiology and Community Health*, 60(10), 854–7. https://doi.org/10.1136/jech.2004.028662.

BERA (2024). *BERA Ethical Guidelines for Educational Research* (5th ed.). London: BERA. https://www.bera.ac.uk/publication/ethical-guidelines-for-educational-research-fifth-edition-2024-online.

Bernacki, M. L., Greene, M. J. and Lobczowski, N. G. (2021). A systematic review of research on personalized learning: Personalized by whom, to what, how, and for what purpose(s)? *Educational Psychology Review*, 33, 1675–715. https://doi.org/10.1007/s10648-021-09615-8.

Bhutoria, A. (2022). Personalized education and artificial intelligence [sic] in the United States, China, and India: A systematic review using a human-in-the-loop model. *Computers and Education: Artificial Intelligence*, 3, 100068. https://doi.org/10.1016/j.caeai.2022.100068.

Bolanos, F., Salatino, A., Osbourne, F. and Motta, E. (2024). Artificial intelligence for literature reviews: Opportunities and challenges. *arXiv*. preprint arXiv:2402.08565. https://doi.org/10.48550/arXiv.2402.08565.

Borenstein, J. and Howard, A. (2021). Emerging challenges in AI and the need for AI ethics education. *AI Ethics*, 1, 61–5. https://doi.org/10.1007/s43681-020-00002-7.

Bozkurt, A. (2024). GenAI et al: Cocreation, authorship, ownership, academic ethics and integrity in a time of generative AI. *Open Praxis*, 16(1), 1–10. https://doi.org/10.55982/openpraxis.16.1.654.

Bradley, V. M. (2021). Learning Management System (LMS) use with online instruction. *International Journal of Technology in Education*, 4(1), 68–92. https://doi.org/10.46328/ijte.36.

Burke, L. (2020). The death and life of an admissions algorithm. *Inside Higher Ed*. Retrieved 12 October 2024, from https://www.insidehighered.com/admissions/article/2020/12/14/u-texas-will-stop-using-controversial-algorithm-evaluate-phd.

Carcary, M. (2021). The research audit trail: Methodological guidance for application in practice. *Electronic Journal of Business Research Methods*, 18(2), 1–12. https://doi.org/10.34190/JBRM.18.2.008.

Crawford, K. (2021). *The Atlas of AI: Power, Politics, and the Planetary Costs of Artificial Intelligence*. New Haven, CT: Yale University Press. https://doi.org/10.2307/j.ctv1ghv45t.

Creswell, J. W. (1999). Mixed-Method Research: Introduction and Application. In G. J. Cizek (Ed.), *Handbook of Educational Policy*, Cambridge, MA: Cambridge Academic Press (pp. 455–72). https://doi.org/10.1016/B978-012174698-8/50045-X.

Darwin Holmes, A. G. (2020). Researcher positionality – A consideration of its influence and place in qualitative research – A new researcher guide. *Shanlax International Journal of Education*, 8(4), 1–10. https://doi.org/10.34293/education.v8i4.3232.

Department for Education (2023). *Policy Paper: Generative Artificial Intelligence [sic] (AI) in Education*. UK Department for Education. https://www.gov.uk/government/publications/generative-artificial-intelligence-in-education/generative-artificial-intelligence-ai-in-education.

Dwyer, S. C. and Buckle, J. L. (2009). The space between: On being an insider-outsider in qualitative research. *International Journal of Qualitative Methods*, 8(1), 54–63. https://doi.org/10.1177/160940690900800105.

Elkhatat, A. M., Elsaid, K. and Almeer, S. (2023). Evaluating the efficacy of AI content detection tools in differentiating between human and AI-generated text. *International Journal for Educational Integrity*, 19(1), 17. https://doi.org/10.1007/s40979-023-00140-5.

Farrow, R. (2023). The possibilities and limits of XAI in education: A sociotechnical perspective. *Learning, Media and Technology*, 48(2), 266–79. https://doi.org/10.1080/17439884.2023.2185630.

Farrow, R., Iniesto, F., Weller, M., PittR., Algers, A., Baas, M., Bozkurt, A., Cox, G., Czerwonogora, A., Elias, T., Essmiller, K., Funk, J., Mittelmeier, J., Nagashima, T., Rabin, E., Rets, I., Spica, E., Vladimirschi, V. and Witthaus, G. (2021). *The GO-GN Guide to Conceptual Frameworks*. UK: Open Education Research Hub. The Open University. CC-BY 4.0. https://oro.open.ac.uk/81508/.

Franzke, A. S., Bechmann, A., Zimmer, M., Ess, C. (2020). And the association of internet researchers. *Internet Research: Ethical Guidelines 3.0*. https://aoir.org/reports/ethics3.pdf.

Giroux, H. A. (2023). Critical Theory and Educational Practice. In A. Darder, K. Hernandez, K. D. Lam, and M. Baltodano (Eds.), *The Critical Pedagogy Reader*, London: Routledge (pp. 50–74). https://doi.org/10.4324/9781003286080.

Guillemin, M., Gillam, L., Rosenthal, D. and Bolitho, A. (2012). Human research ethics committees: Examining their roles and practices. *Journal of Empirical Research on Human Research Ethics*, 7(3), 38–49. https://doi.org/10.1525/jer.2012.7.3.38.

Head, G. (2018). Ethics in educational research: Review boards, ethical issues and researcher development. *European Educational Research Journal*, 19(1), 72–83. https://doi.org/10.1177/1474904118796315.

Holmes, W., and Porayska-Pomsta, K. (Eds.) (2023). *The Ethics of AI in Education. Practices, Challenges, and Debates.* London: Routledge. https://www.routledge.com/The-Ethics-of-Artificial-Intelligence-in-Education-Practices-Challenges/Holmes-Porayska-Pomsta/p/book/9780367349721.

Holmes, W. and Tuomi, I. (2022). State of the art and practice in AI in education. *European Journal of Education: Research, Development and Policies,* 57(4), 542–70. https://doi.org/10.1111/ejed.12533.

Holmes, W., Persson, J., Chounta, I.-A., Wasson, B. and Dimitrova, V. (2022). *Artificial Intelligence and Education a Critical View through the Lens of Human Rights, Democracy and the Rule of Law.* Council of Europe. https://rm.coe.int/artificial-intelligence-and-education-a-critical-view-through-the-lens/1680a886bd.

Holmes, W., Porayska-Pomsta, K., Holstein, K., Sutherland, E., Baker, T., Shum, S. B., Santos, O. C., Rodrigo, M. T., Cukurova, M., Bittencourt, I. I., Koedinger, K. R. (2021). Ethics of AI in education: Towards a community-wide framework. *International Journal of Artificial Intelligence in Education,* 32(3), 504–26. http://dx.doi.org/10.1007/s40593-021-00239-1.

Joint Council for Qualifications (2024). *AI Use in Assessments: Protecting the Integrity of Qualifications (Revision 1).* London: Joint Council for Qualifications. https://www.jcq.org.uk/wp-content/uploads/2024/07/AI-Use-in-Assessments_Feb24_v6.pdf.

Kellner, D. (2003). Toward a critical theory of education. *Democracy and Nature,* 9(1), 51–64. https://doi.org/10.1080/1085566032000074940.

Landeta, J. (2006). Current validity of the Delphi method in social sciences. *Technological Forecasting and Social Change,* 73(5), 467–82. https://doi.org/10.1016/j.techfore.2005.09.002.

Macfarlane, B. (2009). *Researching with Integrity: The Ethics of Academic Enquiry.* London: Routledge. http://www.routledge.com/books/details/9780415429047/.

McDonald, K. E., Kidney, C. A. and Patka, M. (2013). 'You need to let your voice be heard': Research participants' views on research. *Journal of Intellectual Disability Research,* 57(3), 216–25. https://doi.org/10.1111/j.1365-2788.2011.01527.x.

Ober, J. and Tasioulas, J. (2024). *AI Ethics with Aristotle (White Paper).* Stanford University Human Centred Artificial Intelligence/University of Oxford Institute for Ethics in AI. https://www.oxford-aiethics.ox.ac.uk/sites/default/files/2024-06/Aristotle%20and%20AI%20White%20Paper%20-%20June%202024.pdf.

Porisky, A., and Glas, A. (2022). Insiders, outsiders, and credible visitors in research. *PS: Political Science and Politics,* 56(1), 51–5. https://doi.org/10.1017/S1049096522001172.

Ravitch, S. and Riggan, M. (2017). *Reason & Rigor: How Conceptual Frameworks Guide Research* (2nd ed.). New York: Sage. https://doi.org/10.12698/cpre.reasonandrigor.

Rough, E. and Sutherland, M. (2024). *Artificial intelligence: A reading list.* House of Commons Library. https://commonslibrary.parliament.uk/research-briefings/cbp-10003/.

Schiff, D. (2021). Education for AI, not AI for education: The role of education and ethics in national AI policy strategies. *International Journal of Artificial Intelligence in Education*, 32(3), 527–63. https://doi.org/10.1007/s40593-021-00270-2.

Selwyn, N. (2022). The future of AI and education: Some cautionary notes. *European Journal of Education*, 57(4), 620–31. https://doi.org/10.1111/ejed.12532.

Soedirgo, J. and Glas, A. (2020). Toward active reflexivity: Positionality and practice in the production of knowledge. *PS: Political Science and Politics*, 53(3), 527–31. https://doi.org/10.1017/S1049096519002233.

Slattery, P., Saeri, A. K., Grundy, E. A., Graham, J., Noetel, M., Uuk, R., Dao, J., Pour, S., Casper, S. and Thompson, N. (2024). *The AI risk repository: A comprehensive meta-review, database, and taxonomy of risks from Artificial Intelligence*. arXiv preprint. arXiv:2408.12622.https://doi.org/10.48550/arXiv.2408.12622.

Srikumar, M., Finlay, R., Abuhamad, G., Ashurst, C., Campbell, R., Campbell-Ratcliffe, E., Hongo, H., Jordan, S. R., Lindley, J., Ovadya, A. and Pineau, J. (2022). Advancing ethics review practices in AI research. *Nature Machine Intelligence*, 4(12), 1061–4. https://doi.org/10.1038/s42256-022-00585-2.

van Dijk, W., Schatschneider, C. and Hart, S. A. (2021). Open science in Education Sciences. *Journal of Learning Disabilities*, 54(2), 139–52. https://doi.org/10.1177/0022219420945267.

Veletsianos, G. (2024). *OpEd: 5 questions schools and universities should ask before they purchase AI tech products*. 16 April. https://www.veletsianos.com/2024/04/16/oped-5-questions-schools-and-universities-should-ask-before-they-purchase-ai-tech-products.

Xu, A., Baysari, M. T., Stocker, S. L., Leow, J. L., Day, R. O. and Carland, E. (2020). Researchers' views on, and experiences with, the requirement to obtain informed consent in research involving human participants: A qualitative study. *BMC Medical Ethics*, 21, 93. https://doi.org/10.1186/s12910-020-00538-7.

Zhang, H., Wu, C., Xie, J., Lyu, Y., Cai, J. and Carroll, J. M. (2023). *Redefining qualitative analysis in the AI era: Utilizing ChatGPT for efficient thematic analysis*. arXiv preprint. arXiv:2309.10771. https://doi.org/10.48550/arXiv.2309.10771.

10

Ethical Dilemmas in Observational Research

by *Daniel Muijs and Matthew Courtney*

Introduction

Classroom observation has long been a key part of educational research. It is the basis of teacher effectiveness research, in which teacher behaviours are related to student outcomes, controlling for background characteristics and prior attainment (Muijs et al., 2014). In this type of observational research, we typically use a form of behaviour checklist or rating scales, on which observers score a range of items. This was the approach used in the large-scale Measures of Effective Teaching project, for example (Kane et al., 2012), in which observations were compared with teachers' value-added attainment scores and pupil questionnaires, and is common in quantitative studies of teaching, even being used to make comparisons across countries (e.g. van de Grift et al., 2024). But observation has also been used in a range of more qualitative research traditions. Parker and Bickmore (2020), for example, used qualitative observation to study the use of Peace Circles to facilitate dialogue about conflict.

Classroom observation allows researchers to observe actual classroom practices rather than relying on self-reported data, which may be biased or inaccurate (Wragg, 2012). Observation can reveal the nuances of teacher-student interactions and how different learning environments influence student behaviour. Additionally, classroom observation can be a valuable tool for understanding the complex dynamics that influence learning and can complement other research methods like interviews or surveys, offering a more holistic understanding of educational phenomena (Muijs, 2006; Jentsch et al., 2024). A significant advantage of qualitative observation in particular is the ability to observe non-verbal communication, such as body language or social cues, which are often missed in other data-collection methods. This can provide a more in-depth understanding of classroom dynamics. Quantitative observation allows us to use replicable standardised instruments. By using structured observation protocols, such as the Classroom Assessment Scoring System (CLASS) or the Flanders Interaction Analysis Categories (FIAC), researchers can ensure consistency in data collection across different classrooms or time periods (Pianta et al., 2012; Bell et al., 2018). This allows for the comparison of different instructional methods or the identification of patterns that correlate with student outcomes, providing a clear link between observed behaviours and educational effectiveness (Good and Lavigne, 2017).

Classroom observation is popular in research on teaching because it is often seen as providing a realistic perspective on what teachers and students do and is therefore seen as the most valid way of getting at teacher behaviours (Muijs, 2006). This is something of an oversimplification, however. Studies show that it is hard to achieve high levels of interrater reliability (where different observers come to the same rating of a classroom behaviour), suggesting that there is a fair amount of subjectivity in observer judgements, and this is one of the issues we will look at in one of the two cases described below. The presence of an observer itself influences and changes the behaviour of the observed, and that is true of both teachers and students (Muijs et al., 2014; Chi, 2023). And as we cannot realistically observe everything, there are inevitably choices to be made regarding what we look at. There is also evidence of halo effects in observation, in that observers sometimes make an overall judgement on their views of the lesson and then extrapolate from there to the individual items in the observation schedule (Casabianca et al., 2015). Another methodological issue in classroom observation includes sample size issues, as the number of observations needed to reach reliability can be problematic in what is a labour-intensive and therefore expensive methodology. The extent to which we have actually carefully and accurately defined the constructs we are measuring (e.g. 'teaching effectiveness' or 'cognitive activation') is also an issue in a lot of classroom observation research (Charalambous et al., 2025; White and Klette, 2024).

Classroom observation is of course commonly used outside of research as well. There is the extensive use of observation for coaching and professional development (O'Leary, 2020), with schools using observation systems such as IRIS-Connect for video analysis and feedback (Whewell et al., 2021). Observation is also widely used for accountability purposes, for example in inspection (Hofer et al., 2020) or for internal accountability in schools (Bernhard et al., 2024). In fact, these are the contexts in which teachers will most commonly encounter observation, which is one of the challenges when we use this approach for research, as it strengthens the impact of observation on behaviour (BERA, 2024, paragraph 19).[1]

It is interesting that when we look at the literature as a whole, the issue of ethics in classroom observation is not that frequently discussed (e.g. Charalambous et al., 2015; Bell et al., 2019). Where it is, the main issue to be highlighted is usually consent. As with any research, consent must be obtained from all those being observed, including pupils and their parents if underage. Participants need to be fully aware of the nature of the observation, its purpose, the data being collected, and how the data will be used. For minors, special care must be taken to communicate in an age-appropriate way to ensure they understand their participation is voluntary (BERA, 2024, paragraph 8).[2] This can cause particular issues in classroom observation, as it is likely that we may receive consent from some but not all pupils and their guardians. Where this happens, care needs to be taken to ensure that those pupils who have not opted in are not observed. This can cause us some practical difficulties, as we want to observe natural classroom behaviour. That means we would not want those pupils not to be present in the classroom (also as this may affect their learning), so most commonly seating arrangements are adapted to accommodate those pupils and make sure they are not filmed, for example. However, this in itself is a change to regular classroom patterns, which may affect behaviour.

Classroom observation research, especially where lessons are filmed as is usually the case in educational research, particularly quantitative studies (Chan and Jazby, 2022), also presents some challenges to privacy and data protection. Privacy and confidentiality are critical in classroom observation, as both teachers and students are vulnerable to having their behaviours, interactions and possibly sensitive information recorded. This is particularly important when sharing findings or publishing research, as the misuse of classroom observation data can lead to reputational damage, stigmatisation or other negative consequences for participants. It is often impossible to guarantee the anonymity of the observed teacher fully, especially where data is intended for broader use, so this needs to be made very clear as part of the consent process. Researchers also need to be very cautious in relation to the filming of children and young people, and what consent has been given in that regard (BERA, 2024, paragraph 41).[3]

Researchers must consider how and where the data is stored, ensuring it is protected from unauthorised access. This is especially important in this digital age, where video or audio recordings could be easily distributed if not properly secured.

In this chapter, we will focus on two specific ethical issues in classroom observation research: power imbalances and observer bias. In our first case study, we will look at the example of a teacher/observer being put in a difficult situation by a senior manager. In the second case, we look at a case where an observer's views on classroom practice start to impact their observations.

Case Study One: Observational research and accountability – Conflicting pressures?[4]

Background

Sarah has been a primary school teacher for ten years. Alongside her teaching commitments, she is also completing a part-time master's degree in educational assessment at a local university. As part of her studies, Sarah is exploring teachers' use of formative assessment and feedback to improve pupil outcomes. She is particularly interested in ways in which primary practitioners provide feedback to children about their writing. The research question for her small-scale study is: 'How do primary school teachers use written and verbal feedback to improve children's writing?'

Sarah conducts interviews with primary school teachers to understand their perceptions of their use of feedback to improve children's writing. She then observes each participant teaching a writing lesson to see this in action. Sarah also collects anonymised samples of pupils' work, some of which include written feedback from their class teacher.

Sarah has received ethical approval from her university for the study. She follows the consent procedures required by her university and provides all potential teacher participants with an information sheet outlining the aims of her study and what their participation involves. Sarah successfully recruits twelve teacher participants from her own school and other schools within the same local authority. Headteachers are provided with a gatekeeper consent form and an information sheet that outlines the expectations of taking part in the study. Participants are provided with an information sheet that outlines how responses from the interviews and notes from the teaching practice observed will be treated confidentially and, when disseminating findings from the research, names and revealing characteristics of teachers, school staff and pupils will be altered to ensure anonymity.

After successfully recruiting twelve teachers, Sarah provides an information sheet to the parents of pupils in their classes. Sarah obtains opt-in consent from the parents, in line with the consent procedures required by her university.

The ethical dilemma

One of the participants, Tom, is a year two teacher working at Sarah's own school. As part of her study, Sarah incorporates lesson observation as a research method. In preparation for the research, Sarah considers the complexities of teacher observations, pre-thinks possible scenarios of distress or harm to the participants and how they can be minimised, and describes such information in the project information sheet to clarify expectations (BERA, 2024, paragraph 34).[5] When observing him teaching a writing lesson, Sarah notices that the majority of Tom's class appear not to be listening to his feedback. Several children are displaying disruptive behaviour, which includes talking over Tom and not following his instructions to discuss the feedback with their peers.

One child then leaves their seat and begins intentionally ripping the lettering from a display board and discarding this on the floor. Tom tells the child to stop, and the child refuses. The noise level in the class continues to rise, and Tom says that the entire class will be missing their playtime, contradicting the school's behaviour policy. Tom appears visibly stressed during this interaction.

Sarah is concerned about the children's behaviour and the manner in which Tom attempts to manage this. Based on her own experience as a practitioner, Sarah feels Tom needs support to develop effective strategies to manage behaviour in his classroom which will enable the class to focus on Tom's teaching. She is also concerned for Tom's wellbeing. During the observation, Tom appears to be under a significant amount of stress. Sarah finds it difficult to draw firm lines between her researcher role and her everyday capacity as a colleague of Tom.

However, in both her written and verbal communication to the participants, Sarah has highlighted that the aim of the study is to observe teaching to support her understanding of current practice for providing feedback on writing in primary classrooms (BERA, 2024, paragraph 9).[6] She has stressed, verbally, that she is not there to make a subjective judgement on the quality of the teaching and learning she observes. The participant information sheet has also made it clear that Sarah's notes from the teaching practice observed will be treated confidentially and that participant anonymity will be ensured. She worries that taking any action to support Tom or raise her concerns with the school's leadership team would undermine this and may negatively impact his career (BERA, 2024, paragraph 37).[7]

Sarah is also concerned that her role as a primary teacher and an insider supported the recruitment of colleagues. She worries that they may have consented to their participation in part because they positioned Sarah as a fellow practitioner and trusted colleague. She worries that voicing her concerns to Tom's leadership team may damage their professional relationship (BERA, 2024, paragraph 19).[8] Sarah is concerned that raising this issue with the school's leadership team may cause damage to her professional relationships, her status in her workplace and the trust between herself and her colleagues after the research is complete.

Course of action

Sarah is concerned about the situation and is unclear if it warrants breaking the terms of consent with her participant, by making a judgement on the quality of the teaching practice she has observed and sharing this with the school's senior leadership team. In line with her university's ethical guidance, Sarah decides to raise this issue with her master's supervisor (BERA, 2024, paragraph 48).[9]

Sarah's supervisor praises her for voicing her concerns, highlighting the importance of researcher self-care. Her supervisor reinforces the importance of researcher wellbeing and of sharing any distress or potential distress brought about by the research process (BERA, 2024, paragraph 92).[10] Sarah's supervisor advises her not to report her judgement on the quality of teaching and classroom management to her school's senior leadership team.

Her supervisor reminds her that she was present in Tom's classroom in the capacity of a researcher and not as a member of staff. Although her dual roles of researcher and member of the staff team could potentially introduce tension into this decision, the participant information sheet and Sarah's verbal communication with Tom made her role as a researcher, and not as a teacher, in this study very explicit (BERA, 2024, paragraph 19).[11] Sarah is reminded that she was only present in Tom's classroom because of his consent.

Sarah's supervisor highlights that no one present in the classroom was at risk and that she did not have any concerns related to safeguarding. Therefore, it would not be appropriate to break the terms of consent agreed with Tom as a participant. However, Sarah's supervisor agrees that the situation appeared to be stressful for Tom and was perhaps made more so with Sarah's presence in his classroom. Given Tom and Sarah's effective professional relationship, Sarah and her supervisor decide it would be appropriate for Sarah to discuss the incident with Tom in a supportive manner.

Sarah speaks to Tom and explicitly states that she is talking to him as a supportive colleague, rather than in her role as a researcher. Sarah raises her concerns about Tom's wellbeing during the lesson she observed. Tom tells Sarah that his class's teaching assistant was unwell and absent on the day of Sarah's classroom observation, which he feels significantly contributed to the children's behaviour in the lesson and his feelings of stress as a result of this behaviour. Tom assures Sarah that the behaviour she witnessed, and his response to this behaviour, was out of the ordinary. Sarah reminds Tom that his colleagues, and the school's senior leadership team, are there to support him if needed. Tom thanks Sarah for having a supportive, professional discussion with him.

Alternative courses of action

Sarah could have spoken to the school's senior leadership team about the teaching practice and classroom management she observed in Tom's classroom. This may have negatively impacted Tom's career and the senior leadership team's perception of his competence (BERA, 2024, paragraph 37).[12] It would also constitute a break in both the terms of consent with her participant and the ethical approval obtained from her university. After discussion with her supervisor, Sarah felt this would not only be an unethical way to proceed, but it would also be a break in trust between herself and

Tom that would likely impact negatively on their professional relationship as colleagues. This may have led to damage to her standing with her colleagues across the school after the research was complete.

Sarah could have decided not to recruit participants from her own school. This would have allowed Sarah to protect herself from the conflict of interest that arose from her insider status due to her dual roles of researcher and member of staff within the school (BERA, 2024, paragraph 30).[13] Deciding not to recruit participants from her own school would have also provided an extra safeguard to ensure that potential participants were in a social position vis-à-vis Sarah, as the researcher, that would have enabled them to give voluntary informed consent (BERA, 2024, paragraph 20).[14]

Case Study One – concluding section

This case study highlights some of the ethical dilemmas involved in insider research. Teacher-researchers, and other researchers with dual roles, such as lecturers and managers, need support to think through and anticipate potential conflicts of interest which may arise when conducting insider research. This includes support to ensure their role as a researcher is made explicit in written and verbal communication with participants, potential participants and other key stakeholders.

Researchers with dual roles also need support to understand their responsibilities to their participants and other stakeholders when working in the capacity of researcher and support to anticipate where potential tensions between their roles may arise.

Case Study Two: Observer bias – avoidable, inevitable or both?

Background

Shabnam leads a small team of researchers conducting a classroom observation study at a secondary school to evaluate the effectiveness of a new student-centred teaching method. The goal was to compare the traditional teacher-led approach with the new method to determine its impact on student engagement and learning outcomes. The researchers selected two classrooms for observation, both taught by experienced teachers with similar student demographics. Over the course of a semester, they observed each classroom once a week, documenting teacher-student interactions, student engagement and instructional methods.

Shabnam and the team adopted a structured observation approach, using predefined criteria to measure engagement levels (such as hand-raising, eye contact and active participation in discussions). They also conducted informal interviews with students and teachers to supplement their observations.

In each class, teachers, pupils and their parents received a detailed information sheet and were asked for consent to participate. Not all parents or guardians consented, so seating arrangements were adapted to ensure that those pupils were not observed a part of the study. Observations were conducted live, as Shabnam from previous experience felt that analysing recorded lessons would mean that too much of what happened in class would not be captured, and she wanted to make sure that observers saw all consenting pupils. Nevertheless, lessons were filmed for quality assurance purposes.

Classroom A employed the traditional teacher-led approach, where the teacher directed the lessons, and students were expected to follow instructions and complete assigned tasks. Classroom B, on the other hand, followed the new student-centred method, where students worked in small groups and were encouraged to take an active role in their own learning.

The research team consists of three observers, Peter, Catherine and Thandi, who are each assigned to a classroom. Peter, who was a former teacher and vocal advocate of the student-centred approach, was assigned to Classroom B. Catherine had a neutral stance and was assigned to Classroom A. Thandi rotated between both classrooms as a secondary observer to cross-check the data.

The ethical dilemma

As the study progressed, Shabnam began to notice a pattern in the data that raised concerns. Peter consistently rated student engagement in Classroom B highly, even when the students in Classroom B appeared distracted or disengaged during some lessons (BERA, 2024, paragraph 59).[15] Catherine, in contrast, provided more balanced ratings for Classroom A, noting both strengths and areas where engagement was lacking. Thandi, who rotated between the two classrooms, also recorded higher engagement in Classroom B but was more critical of some aspects of the student-centred approach, such as the frequent off-task behaviour during group work.

Upon reviewing the observation logs, videos and interviews, Shabnam found discrepancies in how the observers interpreted student behaviours. For example, in one observation, students in Classroom B were engaged in group work, but several groups were 'off-topic'. Peter noted this as 'creative problem-solving', interpreting the off-task behaviour as part of the collaborative learning process. Thandi, however, recorded this as a 'lack of focus', citing students' visible disinterest in the assigned task.

When Shabnam brought the team together to discuss their findings, an argument ensued. Peter questioned the observation findings from Classroom A, where Catherine often recorded student silence during teacher-led instruction as on-task behaviour during teacher explanation. Peter saw this as a sign of disengagement.

Course of action

Following the team meeting, Shabnam felt she had to directly address the issue of observer bias with Peter (BERA, 2024, paragraph 57).[16] Observer bias, where an individual's personal beliefs influence their data collection, is a critical issue in classroom observation. Peter seems to be interpreting student behaviour in Classroom B more favourably, even when objective observations suggest disengagement. Shabnam talked with Peter about this directly but diplomatically. She explained the importance of minimising personal bias in research to ensure the credibility of the study. She highlighted that differences in interpretation are normal, but they must be discussed and resolved to maintain the integrity of the findings (BERA, 2024, paragraph 59).[17]

Shabnam felt that she needed a second meeting to facilitate a reflective and open dialogue among the team members. This discussion focussed on clarifying how the predefined observation criteria needed to be applied and interpreted. For example, what constitutes 'engagement' or 'on-task behaviour' should be agreed upon to avoid subjectivity. She decided to do this by reviewing the videos together and discussing instances where discrepancies occurred. The goal was to ensure consistency in data collection across all observers.

To foster a more neutral discussion, Shabnam presented anonymised case examples from a separate set of classroom observations from a video archive to prompt the team to collaboratively analyse the behaviours. There was some heated discussion, but in the end, the team was able to reach a consensus on how to interpret similar situations in the future.

Finally, as these discrepancies had appeared in the original observation coding, Shabnam reported the issue explicitly in her research report so that there was transparency around the process. She felt that, as there is no way to guarantee objectivity in classroom observation research, it was important to show how observer bias may have influenced the findings and discuss the steps taken to mitigate it. By doing so, Shabnam ensures the integrity of the research, even if it complicates the study's conclusions. It will also contribute to the literature on the challenges of observational research in educational settings (BERA, 2024, paragraph 75).[18]

Alternative courses of action

Additional training

To reduce discrepancies, Shabnam could consider organising additional observer training and calibration sessions. These sessions can help the team align their interpretations of engagement behaviours with the predefined criteria. Calibration involves the team members observing the same lesson or scenario and then comparing their ratings to ensure consistency.

Reassignment

Given Peter's advocacy for the student-centred method, Shabnam may want to reconsider his assignment to Classroom B. Although his teaching background might initially seem like an asset, his strong personal views appear to be affecting the objectivity of his observations. Reassigning Peter to Classroom A or rotating the observers more frequently between the two classrooms could help balance any biases and cross-verify the data.

Thandi, who has demonstrated more balanced and critical assessments of both classrooms, could take a lead role in observing Classroom B to provide a more neutral perspective. This change in roles should be framed as a strategy to enhance the study's credibility, rather than a critique of Peter's abilities.

Triangulation

Shabnam could triangulate the findings of the observations by using data from multiple sources, such as observation logs, student interviews, teacher interviews and potentially student performance data. This multi-source approach can help mitigate individual biases and provide a more comprehensive understanding of classroom engagement.

For example, Shabnam could analyse student interviews in relation to the observational data to see whether students themselves felt engaged during specific activities. This can help determine whether Peter's interpretation of group work as 'creative problem-solving' aligns with students' perspectives or if Thandi's critique of disengagement is more accurate.

Case Study Two – concluding section

This case study highlights the issue of observer bias and how it can influence classroom observation. One of the challenges in educational research is that all of us have views and opinions that influence our thinking.

In this case, Peter's strong belief in the value of student-centred learning led to skewed data that initially suggested the new teaching method was more effective than it truly was. By recognising and addressing the bias through methodological adjustments, the research team was able to produce more accurate and reliable findings. This case underscores the importance of reflexivity, observer training and methodological rigour in minimising the impact of observer bias.

Final thoughts

Ethical issues are often under-discussed in research using classroom observation. This is unfortunate, as it is a research method that can throw up a number of dilemmas for researchers.

We have framed the first case study as an issue of insider research, which it is, but it also throws up a number of other ethical issues.

Power differentials are an issue in much research, but can come to the fore in classroom observation. There are a number of reasons for this. The experience of many educators is of observation being used as a management or accountability tool. This can lead to misconceptions, such as in the case presented, where there is an attempt to use hierarchy in relation to observation findings. There are also often actual or perceived power differentials between observer and observed. This can be the case, for example, in contexts where university researchers are perceived to have high status, and are seen as potentially wanting to see a particular type of teaching.

The other ethical dilemma hinted at in the first case related to what the observer should do if they observe a problematic practice. The answer here is dependent on what is observed. Any issues that raise safeguarding concerns, especially in relation to children, should lead to immediate action on the part of the researcher, be that reporting to management, or in some cases even direct intervention. The safeguarding of children and young people ethically overrides any other issues or assurances given. This is not the case, however, where the behaviour observed may be somewhat problematic but is not directly harmful from a safeguarding point of view. Here, the balance needs to be struck with the assurances made to participants. This can be difficult for the researcher, but we do need to take into account that there is an element of subjectivity to what we consider good or bad practice, as education research is not an exact science.

The second case is clearly an issue of bias which is a common occurrence in classroom observation research, and is methodologically one of the most difficult issues to deal with.

Several factors contributed to observer bias in that case:

1 **Pre-existing Beliefs:** In our case, Peter's advocacy for student-centred learning likely influenced his interpretation of behaviours, leading them to favour Classroom B and downplay its shortcomings.
2 **Selective Attention:** Peter paid more attention to moments that supported his belief in the effectiveness of student-centred learning, such as when students were actively discussing ideas, while overlooking periods of distraction or confusion.
3 **Confirmation Bias:** Peter sought out evidence that confirmed his preconceptions about the new method's superiority. When students were engaged, it reinforced their belief, but when students were off-task, he reframed the behaviour in a positive light.

4 **Expectation Bias:** Peter may have unconsciously expected Classroom B to perform better due to his belief in the new teaching method, leading him to record observations that aligned with this expectation.

Bias is hard to avoid in classroom observation, as most of us have quite entrenched views on what good teaching looks like, either as teachers ourselves, education researchers or from our own experience of being taught. Methodologically, this is one of the causes of the difficulty in achieving interrater reliability in classroom observation. The findings of the Measures of Effective Teaching project, one of the largest ever attempts to look at ways of measuring teacher effectiveness, concluded the following:

Even with systematic training and certification of observers, the MET project needed to combine scores from multiple raters and multiple lessons to achieve high levels of reliability. A teacher's score varied considerably from lesson to lesson, as well as from observer to observer. For four out of five observation instruments, we could achieve reliabilities in the neighbourhood of 0.65 only by scoring four different lessons, each by a different observer. Many have commented on the volatility (i.e., lack of reliability) in value-added measures. However, in our study, a single observation by a single observer was often more volatile (and, therefore, less reliable) than value-added: in our study, single observations produced reliabilities ranging from 0.14 to 0.37. By comparison, researchers typically report reliability of value-added measures between 0.30 to 0.50 (Kane et al., 2012: 9).

There is therefore a close relationship between ethics and methodological soundness in classroom observation research.

As BERA guidelines (e.g. BERA, 2024) have long stated, our core aim as researchers is to ensure that we do not harm participants in any way. Observational research certainly has the potential to do so, and we therefore need to be particularly cautious in looking at aspects of our research such as consent and the uses that will be made of our research.

Reflective questions

Researchers looking to use classroom observation in their education research may consider the following five reflective questions:

1 To what extent might my role influence my observations, or the way my observations are perceived by participants or others in the school?

2 Can I guarantee that data collected will not be used for purposes other than those agreed with participants in the research, with the exception of safeguarding issues?
3 If safeguarding issues are spotted, do I have a process in place to deal with this?
4 Have I ensured that I have taken measures to reduce the stress that may be put on participants due to observation in light of its common use in accountability and performance management?
5 Have I provided sufficient training to any observers in my study, and have I considered any possible biases and how to mitigate these?

Further reading

A lot of the most interesting resources about classroom observation in a research context can be found in journal articles. Authors such as Courtney Bell, Kirsti Klette, Anna-Katharina Praetorius and Charalambos Charalambous have written extensively on classroom observation and are worth checking out.

1. Bell, C. A., Dobbelaer, M. J., Klette, K. and Visscher, A. (2018). Qualities of classroom observation systems. *School Effectiveness and School Improvement*, 30(1), 3–29. https://doi.org/10.1080/09243453.2018.1539014

   This article offers a good overview of different classroom observation instruments.

   Most available books focus on classroom observation for professional development rather than research. Exceptions to this are:

2. Wragg, T. (2011). *An Introduction to Classroom Observation*. London: Routledge. https://doi.org/10.4324/9780203357279.
3. Gibson, W. and Patrick, S. (2019). *Observing Classrooms: A Guide for Researchers and Educators*. London: Sage.

Notes

1 An important consideration is the extent to which a researcher's reflective research into their own practice impinges upon others – for example, in the case of power relationships arising from the dual roles of teacher/

lecturer/manager and researcher, and their impact on students and colleagues. Dual roles may also introduce explicit tensions in areas such as confidentiality. These may be addressed appropriately by, for example, making the researcher role very explicit, involving an independent third party in the research process and seeking agreement for politically controversial research. Researchers who are researching their own practice should also consider how to address any issues arising as a result of collecting data for different purposes – for example, using data collected for evaluation purposes for research purposes, or vice versa (BERA, 2024, paragraph 19).

2   It is normally expected that participants' voluntary informed consent to be involved in a study will be obtained at the start of the study, and that researchers will remain sensitive and open to the possibility that participants may wish, for any reason and at any time, to withdraw their consent. The Association takes voluntary informed and ongoing consent to be the condition by which participants understand and agree to their participation, and the terms and practicalities of it, without any duress. It should be made clear to participants that they can withdraw at any point without needing to provide an explanation – this is detailed in paragraphs 31 and 32… Researchers should be alert to non-verbal signs that individuals who previously consented to participate may no longer wish to. In such circumstances, renewed consent should be sought (BERA, 2024, paragraph 8).

3   Anonymity may also need to be reconsidered in the context of some visual methodologies. For instance, the study of facial expressions and gestures and the increasing prevalence of video and multimodal data raise questions about whether concealing identities is always feasible or appropriate. Researchers need to discern an ethical course of action here – one that secures clear agreement about anonymity and about subsequent use of the data. Researchers need to be aware that visual material, in particular, can be misused by others, and should take steps to prevent this as far as possible (BERA, 2024, paragraph 41).

4   This case study appears in a slightly adapted form as a web case study Research Ethics Case Studies 2024 | BERA.

5   Ethical research design and implementation aim to put participants at their ease and to avoid making excessive demands on them. In advance of data collection, researchers have a responsibility to think through their duty of care in order to recognise potential harms, and to prepare for and be in a position to minimise and manage any distress or discomfort that may arise. Researchers should immediately reconsider any actions occurring during the research process that appear to cause emotional or other harm. The more vulnerable the participants, for whatever reasons, the greater

the responsibilities of the researcher for their protection (BERA, 2024, paragraph 34).

6   Researchers should do what they can to ensure that all potential participants understand, as well as they are able, what is involved in a study. They should be told why their participation is desired, what, if anything, they will be asked to do, what will happen to the data they provide and how and to whom the data will be reported. They also should be informed about the retention, sharing and any possible secondary uses of the data. Where appropriate, researchers who are BERA members may include a declaration of membership in information sheets and consent forms, to make explicit the fact that members are expected to follow BERA guidance as part of the Association's code of conduct (which contains a complaints procedure that may be helpful) (BERA, 2024, paragraph 9).

7   Researchers should recognise concerns relating to the time and effort that participation in some research can require – the long-term involvement of participants in some ethnographic studies, for example, and the repeated involvement of particular participants in survey research or in testing for research or evaluation purposes. Researchers should consider the impact of their research on the lives and workloads of participants, particularly when researching vulnerable or over-researched populations. Equally, researchers should do what they can to ensure that relevant individuals and communities are not, intentionally or otherwise, excluded from participation in their research (BERA, 2024, paragraph 37).

8   An important consideration is the extent to which a researcher's reflective research into their own practice impinges upon others – for example, in the case of power relationships arising from the dual roles of teacher/lecturer/manager and researcher, and their impact on students and colleagues. Dual roles may also introduce explicit tensions in areas such as confidentiality. These may be addressed appropriately by, for example, making the researcher role very explicit, involving an independent third party in the research process and seeking agreement for politically controversial research. Researchers who are researching their own practice should also consider how to address any issues arising as a result of collecting data for different purposes – for example, using data collected for evaluation purposes for research purposes, or vice versa (BERA, 2024, paragraph 19).

9   There are circumstances in which confidentiality may need to be broken, and information sheets and consent forms should state this. Researchers who judge that adherence to agreements they have made with participants about confidentiality is likely to result in illegal or harmful actions should carefully consider making disclosure to the appropriate authorities. In some cases, such as revelations of abuse or proposed acts of terrorism,

researchers may be under statutory duty to disclose confidential information to relevant authorities. Researchers should seek advice from a relevant responsible person before proceeding to disclosure if and when appropriate (for example, a student undertaking research should seek advice from their supervisor[s]). Insofar as it does not undermine or obviate the disclosure, or jeopardise researcher safety, researchers should inform the participants, or their guardians or responsible others, of their intentions and reasons for disclosure (BERA, 2024, paragraph 48).

10 Safeguarding the physical and psychological wellbeing of researchers is part of the ethical responsibility of employers and sponsors, as well as of researchers themselves. In general, there should be an ethics of care for researchers, including self-care. Safety can be a particular concern in certain circumstances, for example when fieldwork is undertaken in situations that are potentially risky. Researchers should be aware of the legal responsibilities as well as the moral duty of institutions towards the safety of staff and students. Institutions, sponsors and independent researchers should consider whether an in-depth risk assessment and ongoing monitoring of researcher safety is advisable, especially for those undertaking fieldwork, working in certain jurisdictions and/or investigating sensitive issues; this may be required by employers and sponsors. (BERA, 2024, paragraph 82).

11 See note 8.

12 See note 7.

13 Researchers should not undertake work in which they can be perceived to have a material conflict of interest, or in which self-interest or commercial gain might compromise the validity of the research. Any potential conflicts of interest should be declared to relevant parties at various stages of the research, including in any publications (BERA, 2024, paragraph 30).

14 In some cases, potential participants may not be in a social position vis-à-vis the researcher that enables them to give voluntary informed consent. This can occur, for example, when the researcher and potential participant are family members, or if the researcher is the participant's teacher/lecturer. Researchers need to consider carefully how to deal with such situations and, if possible, should reassure potential participants that non-participation is entirely acceptable (BERA, 2024, paragraph 20).

15 (BERA, 2024, paragraph 59) All educational researchers should aim to protect the integrity and reputation of educational research by ensuring that they conduct their research to the highest standards. Researchers should contribute to the community spirit of critical analysis and constructive criticism that generates improvement in practice and enhancement of knowledge (BERA, 2024, paragraph 59).

16 Researchers should, within the context and boundaries of their chosen methods, theories and philosophies of research, communicate the extent to which their data collection and analysis techniques, and the inferences to be drawn from their findings, are robust and can be seen to meet the criteria and markers of quality and integrity applied within different research approaches (BERA, 2024, paragraph 57).
17 See note 15.
18 Researchers must not bring research into disrepute by in any way falsifying, distorting, suppressing, selectively reporting or sensationalising their research evidence or findings, either in publications based on that material, or as part of efforts to disseminate or promote that work. When non-trivial errors or other problems are identified in published work, researchers should rectify these as best they can, typically in the form of a published correction. In some cases, a retraction may be needed (BERA, 2024, paragraph 75).

References

Bell, C. A., Dobbelaer, M. J., Klette, K. and Visscher, A. (2019). Qualities of classroom observation systems. *School Effectiveness and School Improvement*, 30(1), 3–29. https://doi.org/10.1080/09243453.2018.1539014.

BERA (2024). *Ethical Guidelines for Educational Research*. London: BERA. https://www.bera.ac.uk/publication/ethical-guidelines-for-educational-research-fifth-edition-2024

Bernhard, R., McDermott, T., Hasenhüttl, C., Burn, K. and Sammons, P. (2024). A focus on quality of teaching in schools increases students' progress of attainment. Evidence from English secondary schools. *School Effectiveness and School Improvement*, 1–25. https://doi.org/10.1080/09243453.2024.2398601.

Casabianca, J. M., Lockwood, J. R. and McCaffrey, D. F. (2015). Trends in classroom observation scores. *Educational and Psychological Measurement*, 75(2), 311–37. https://doi.org/10.1177/0013164414539163.

Chan, M. C. E. and Jazby, D. (2022). Positioning video in classroom research: Ontological and epistemic tensions. *Learning, Culture and Social Interaction*, 37, 1–12. https://doi.org/10.1016/j.lcsi.2022.100669.

Charalambous, C., Muijs, D., Londorf, A. and Steffensky, M. (2025). Conceptualizing teaching quality: Problems, prospects, and a proposal for moving forward. *Accepted for Publication in School Effectiveness and School Improvement*, 36(2), 164–91. https://doi.org/10.1080/09243453.2025.2482576.

Chi, O. L. (2023). A classroom observer like me: The effects of race-congruence and gender-congruence between teachers and raters on observation scores. *Education Finance and Policy*, 18(3), 442–66. Doi: https://doi.org/10.1162/edfp_a_00367.

Cohen, L., Manion, L. and Morrison, K. (2017). *Research Methods in Education* (8th ed.). London: Routledge.

Courtney, M. and Muijs, D. (2024). Classroom observation for 'insider' teacher-researchers. In S. W. Chong, and A. Fox (Eds.), *Research Ethics Case Studies*. British Educational Research Association (pp. 1–5). https://www.bera.ac.uk/publication/research-ethics-case-studies-2024-classroom-observation-for-insider-teacherresearchers.

Gibson, W. and Patrick, S. (2019). *Observing Classrooms: A Guide for Researchers and Educators*. London: Sage.

Good, J. and Lavigne, A. (2017). *Looking in Classrooms*. New York: Routledge.

Hofer, S., Holzberger, D. and Reiss, K. (2020). Evaluating school inspection effectiveness: A systematic research synthesis on 30 years of international research. *Studies in Educational Evaluation*, 65. https://doi.org/10.1016/j.stueduc.2020.100864.

Jentsch, A., White, M. and Klette, K. (2024). Using PLATO to assess teaching quality in Scandinavian mathematics and language arts classrooms. Paper presented at the Annual Meeting of the American Educational Research Association, Philadelphia, PA, 11/4/24. https://doi.org/10.3102/2108207.

Kane, T. J., Staiger, D. O., McCaffrey, D., Cantrell, S., Archer, J., Buhayar, S., Kerr, K., Kawakita, T. and Parker, D. (2012). *Gathering Feedback for Teaching: Combining High-Quality Observations with Student Surveys and Achievement Gains*. Seattle, WA: Bill and Melinda Gates Foundation.

Muijs, D. (2006). Measuring teacher effectiveness: Some methodological reflections. *Educational Research and Evaluation*, 12(1), 53–74. https://doi.org/https://doi.org/10.1080/13803610500392236.

Muijs, D., Kyriakides, L., van der Werf, G., Creemers, B., Timperley, H. and Earl, L. (2014). State of the art – teacher effectiveness and professional learning. *School Effectiveness and School Improvement*, 25(2), 231–56. https://doi.org/10.1080/09243453.2014.885451.

O'Leary, M. (2020). *Classroom Observation. A Guide to the Effective Observation of Teaching and Learning*. London: Routledge.

Parker, C. and Bickmore, K. (2020). Classroom peace circles: Teachers' professional learning and implementation of restorative dialogue. *Teaching and Teacher Education*, 95(1), 1–12. https://doi.org/10.1016/j.tate.2020.103129.

Pianta, R. C., Hamre, B. K. and Allen, J. P. (2012). Teacher-student relationships and engagement: Conceptualizing, measuring, and improving the capacity of classroom interactions. In S. L. Christenson, A. L. Reschly, and C. Wylie (Eds.), *Handbook of Research on Student Engagement*. Berlin: Springer Science and Business Media (pp. 365–86). https://doi.org/10.1007/978-1-4614-2018-7_17.

Pianta, R. C., Hamre, B. K. and Mintz, S. (2012). *Classroom Assessment Scoring System (CLASS) Manual, Secondary Edition*. Baltimore: Paul H. Brookes Publishing.

van de Grift, W. J. C. M., Chun, S., Lee, O. and Kim, D. (2024). Quality of teaching at secondary schools in Nicaragua, South Korea, and the Netherlands. *School Effectiveness and School Improvement*, 35(1), 73–93. https://doi.org/10.1080/09243453.2024.2319092.

Whewell, E., Garrett, B., Tiplady, H., Byles, R. and Briggs, T. (2021). A reflection of using videos of interactions between expert and novice practitioners: An in-depth exploration of the experience of expert and novice teachers. In *Learning and Teaching Conference 2021*. http://nectar.northampton.ac.uk/14741/1/LTC_IRIS_Poster.pdf.

White, M. and Klette, K. (2024). Signal, error, or bias? exploring the uses of scores from observation systems. *Educational Assessment Evaluation and Accountability*. https://doi.org/10.1007/s11092-024-09427-8.

Wragg, E. C. (2012). *An Introduction to Classroom Observation* (Classic ed.). London: Routledge.

11

Environmental Sustainability in Education Research Ethics

by *Lynda Dunlop and Lizzie Rushton*

Introduction

Anthropogenic climate change and ecological crises are the leading global challenges of our time (IPCC, 2023). As part of a researcher's ethical responsibility to contribute research which creates a societal good, the impact of such research should consider both the environmental impact and the opportunities for research to contribute to furthering environmental justice. This includes who is supported and equipped to undertake research, how that research is completed, including all phases such as fieldwork, dissemination and knowledge exchange. Crucial to these ethical responsibilities is an understanding of the ways in which research and researchers maintain or challenge inequitable and unsustainable practices and systems.

In the introduction to the fifth edition of the BERA *Ethical Guidelines for Educational Research* (BERA, 2024: 6), Vivienne Baumfield notes that 'crucially, and following BERA's wider work in this area, the updated guidelines acknowledge the role research can play in promoting environmental sustainability' and this focus on the environment is especially evident in the inclusion of the environment as part of a researcher's ethic of respect (BERA, 2024: 9),[1] as well as in paragraphs 6[2] and 54.[3] Part of BERA's work has been to commission a *Manifesto for*

Education for Environmental Sustainability (BERA, 2021), which brought together over 200 teachers, teacher educators and young people (aged 16–18 years) to explore what they understand environmental sustainability to mean and their vision for education for environmental sustainability. We draw on the shared understanding of environmental sustainability which was generated through the manifesto-making process, which understands environmental sustainability as including care for the environment, repair of social and environmental injustices and consideration of future generations. This understanding of environmental sustainability and therefore education for environmental sustainability is therefore a process of learning to live differently through collaboration, empowerment, emotional attentiveness and the creation of capabilities for dealing with spatial and temporal complexities.

These ideas and understandings are threaded across our reflections of ethical responsibilities throughout this chapter as we explore the individual responsibilities of educational researchers and the collective responsibilities to educational researchers, using the headings which structure the updated guidelines (BERA, 2024). These relationships are represented in Figure 11.1. In seeking to achieve this, we take the approach of posing questions, rather than providing a framework of fixed positions, which can imply simple solutions and minimise complexity.

The image (Figure 11.2) illustrates a key question in considering the environmental impact of educational research.

Therefore, we outline a series of questions as an invitation to iteratively come into dialogue with these issues over time. This dialogic approach can support both individual reflection, or paired or group discussion which enables researchers to situate these questions in their own contexts such that they can embrace nuance and allow for a diversity of responses focused on environmental sustainability. As well as these questions, we also provide a fictional case study to highlight some of the ways in which environmental considerations may arise during a research project and to discuss different courses of action. In this chapter, we explore the fifth edition of the BERA *Ethical Guidelines for Educational Research* (BERA, 2024) through questions which aim to prompt further thought and reflection by researchers, paying attention to the concerns and needs of environmental sustainability. We begin by considering the individual responsibilities of educational researchers.

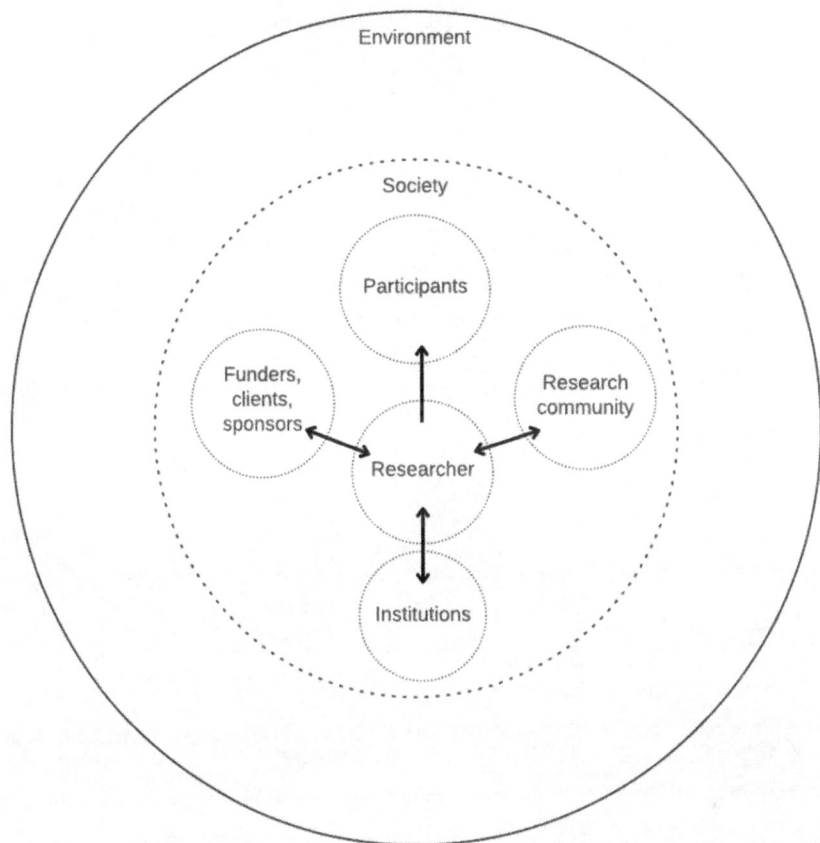

Figure 11.1 Representation of relationships of responsibilities of and to educational researchers, underpinned by responsibilities of all for society and the environment.

Source: Authors.

Responsibilities of educational researchers

The fifth edition of the BERA *Ethical Guidelines for Educational Research* (BERA, 2024) outlines the responsibilities which researchers have when seeking to develop knowledge and understanding about education through research. These responsibilities are consistent with other guidelines,

Figure 11.2 An important consideration in educational research is who speaks for nature? Image credit: Maisy Summer https://www.maisysummer.com/.

including *The Framework for Responsible Research* (UKRI, no date) which describes responsible research and innovation as generating knowledge and innovation in ways which are 'socially desirable and undertaken in the public interest … in an open, inclusive and timely way' (UKRI, n.d.). From the outset, the idea is that researchers have a responsibility towards the general public in developing research which seeks to achieve social benefits. Responsible research should move beyond foundational ideas of respect, trust, reducing risk of harm and complying with regulations and instead, through iterative phases of anticipation, reflection, engagement and action, actively influence and shape research which furthers flourishing for all.

In this section, we explore responsibilities which researchers have towards different groups, including:

- participants;
- the community of educational researchers;
- sponsors, clients, stakeholders;
- the environment.

These groups reflect the first three headings set out in the fifth edition of the BERA *Ethical Guidelines for Educational Research* (BERA, 2024: 9–10). Whilst it is helpful to use these groups and headings to reflect on the particular needs and concerns of different groups, at the same time, it is important to see these as porous groupings, which individuals and communities may move across and where there will be overlapping needs and concerns. For example, people might at the same time be participants, and also part of the wider community of educational researchers or group of stakeholders. We begin by exploring responsibilities to participants.

Responsibilities to participants

The fifth edition of the BERA *Ethical Guidelines for Educational Research* outlines different areas of concern with regard to responsibilities to participants, including consent, transparency, right to withdraw, incentives, harm arising from participating in research, privacy and data storage, and disclosure (BERA, 2024: 13–24). Here, we focus on the specific responsibilities to participants which arise in research on environmental sustainability which relate to the avoidance of harm. This includes recognising potential harms and minimising and managing any harm or discomfort which may occur (BERA, 2024, paragraphs 34–38). Harm can be understood at different scales, including immediate harm which could be visible during participants' engagement with research, and longer-term harm which could extend beyond the life of the research project. This concern for the rights of individual participants needs to be held alongside wider considerations of social benefits from research which is conducted as a public good (BERA, 2024, paragraph 36). Indeed, in a recent news article, Raffoul et al., (2021) have argued that 'do no harm' is not enough; rather, research must do good and regenerate society and ecosystems.

In the context of environmental sustainability, research which, for example, explores ideas and beliefs concerning climate change or experiences of sustainability education, researchers should pay attention to immediate emotional and/or psychological harm associated with issues of environmental sustainability. Different types of negative emotions have been described in the research literature and reported in the media as 'eco-anxiety', where negative emotions are associated with ecological crises such as species extinction, and 'climate anxiety', where negative emotions are closely linked to anthropogenic climate change (Pikhala, 2020). In a recent global study of over 10,000 young people (16–25 years), Hickmann et al. (2021) found high levels of negative emotions about climate change (e.g. anger, anxiety, guilt, helplessness, sadness) and 75 per cent of respondents reported that their future is frightening and just under half saying that negative feelings about climate change affected their daily lives. This research underlines that harms such as eco-anxiety and climate anxiety can be both an immediate harm, which is experienced on a daily basis, but also harms which could extend across a longer period of an individual's life, for example, their adolescence. This draws attention to the ethical concern researchers should have in recognising, minimising and managing discomfort or harm which could arise when asking people about issues of environmental sustainability. This includes, for example, research which asks children and young people about the climate change education they have experienced and their ideas and hopes for the future. Indeed, asking children and young people about their hopes for the future could have the potential to reinforce feelings of hopelessness and powerlessness in relation to climate and ecological crises which could extend beyond their engagement in a research project. Research suggests that planning and acting on personal climate risks could reduce climate anxiety (Fyke and Weaver, 2023) as this involves treating the cause of anxiety and reducing personal risk, rather than on coping with anxiety. Participating in research projects which include action experiences, for example the child led science and activist art to tackle dog faeces in the community around the school (Watson et al., 2021), might therefore both tackle environmental problems and reduce eco-anxiety. Questions for researchers to reflect upon further include:

- How can immediate harm to participants be recognised and minimised?
- What opportunities are there as part of the research process for participants to experience positive emotions associated with environmental sustainability, for example, active hope?

- In what ways can research findings be harnessed to act on the fundamental causes of negative emotions such as eco-anxiety and climate anxiety?
- How can research be conducted and reported which avoids making groups such as children and young people, teachers and other educators disproportionately responsible for creating and implementing solutions to environmental and sustainability issues and challenges which were not of their making?
- How can demands on participants be minimised, particularly in fields (for example, youth leadership of climate action) where participants (for example, young people) already bear a disproportionate burden of work?
- How can research be designed such that participants experience reciprocity?

Having considered the responsibilities which researchers have to participants, we now consider responsibilities towards the community of educational researchers.

Responsibilities to sponsors, clients and stakeholders in research and society

Temporal and spatial complexities are an inherent feature of both educational research and the concept of environmental sustainability. Whilst this complexity affords opportunities for environmental sustainability education and educational research to respond to be sensitive to context, the breadth and ambiguity of environmental sustainability as a concept can mean that it can mean everything and nothing.

Therefore, we highlight the key role which educational research and researchers must play in enabling stakeholders[4] (a person or body who has a direct interest in the framing and/or success of research – see BERA, 2024, paragraph 50) and society more broadly to engage with these complexities.

Educational research can provide a vital way to identify constructive solutions to environmental and sustainability challenges which have ethical, moral, social and political dimensions. From the outset, researchers have particular responsibilities to sponsors, clients and stakeholders to ensure that there is discussion of what environmental sustainability and environmental sustainability education mean. These ethical dimensions and responsibilities extend to the interests of research sponsors (see BERA, 2024, paragraph 53) – essentially, who should sponsor and fund educational research. Funding for educational research and development can be scarce, with the Royal Society and British Academy (2021) calling on the UK government to increase investment in educational research and bring it into line with other parts of the public sector.

In recent times, the influence of funding and sponsorship from industry whose wealth is generated through fossil fuel production (e.g. petroleum, oil and gas) on educational research and school-based resources has been raised as an issue of concern, especially given that we live in an age of climate and nature emergencies (Eaton and Day, 2020). For example, in the UK researchers such as Stuart Tannock (2020) have highlighted the ways in which BP (formerly British Petroleum), one of the largest fossil fuel corporations, has shaped primary and secondary school science education in the UK, funding and promoting a neoliberal model of STEM education which is, 'based on corporate and capitalist interests, poses a significant threat to our collective efforts to tackle the global climate crisis' (Tannock, 2020: 474). This includes funding of educational research, including multi-year science learning projects and education resources. British Petroleum (BP) reports that their resources are used by 'half of all UK secondary schools and over a quarter of all UK primary schools' (BP, 2022: 64). As Eaton and Day (2020) have pointed out, materials from the fossil fuel industry can promote fossil fuel industry interests, for example by advancing the idea that any learning about the environment that doesn't consider the interests of the industry is 'unbalanced and biased' and by shifting focus from the impacts of fossil fuels to local nature and wildlife, and by the prioritisation of individual consumer actions over system or political action. In addition to the shaping of narratives on climate change and environmental actions, there is also the risk that fossil fuel funding provides positive exposure to fossil fuel companies, sends the message that their actions are socially acceptable, and risks reputational damage to the organisation accepting such funding for environmental education work.

As a starting paragraph in navigating these complex issues, questions researchers might pose in relation to stakeholders, clients and stakeholders could include:

- Is it appropriate to take educational research funding from sponsors whose core business is environmentally damaging or which obstructs environmental justice?

- Is it ever possible to mitigate their interests, challenge corporate priorities or counter greenwashing tactics? (Greenwashing is where a company can appear more environmentally friendly without taking meaningful action to reduce environmental impact.)
- Can research funded by the fossil fuel industry effectively hold the same industry to account?
- How can educational researchers support different stakeholders to enhance their understanding of different conceptualisations of environmental sustainability?
- How can research design and fundings recognise and respond to issues of responsibility and justice?
- To what extent should research design ensure that opportunities to consider the voices of those stakeholders less frequently heard are prioritised?

We now consider the responsibilities which researchers and educational research have towards the environment.

Responsibilities to the environment

As we have noted in the introduction to this chapter, the updated BERA *Ethical Guidelines for Educational Research* (BERA, 2024) include paragraph 54 which foregrounds the importance of considering environmental sustainability as follows:

> Researchers should consider the implications of their research for the global community and the environment more generally, bearing in mind the interests of non-humans and broader issues to do with sustainability, climate change and biodiversity. This includes such specifics as the amount and type of travel, the nature of the food at meetings and dissemination events, and more fundamental questions about the actual research, for example, and the purposes for which it is undertaken. (BERA, 2024, paragraph 54)

This guidance underlines the ways in which researchers have a responsibility to the global community, including the more-than-human world, and should pay attention to issues concerning the environment. These issues include climate change and biodiversity and by extension, the natural world. This means individuals have a responsibility to the environment, both locally, nationally and internationally, in how they plan and undertake their research, including fieldwork, dissemination events, research collaborations and networks. As well as this immediate responsibility to consider the environment, and to reduce the risk of harm, decisions about research should also consider the potential to cause longer-term harm, for example contributing to greenhouse gas emissions (for example through air travel) which have complex temporal and spatial impacts which frequently impact communities who are least responsible for contributing to the current climate and nature crises (Sultana, 2022). Decisions about travel, computing, consumption and catering all have associated environmental impacts. The Centre for Climate Change and Social Transformations (CAST) launched a *Sustainability Charter* to embed low-carbon transformation in their research culture and practices, with associated attention to how the centre can influence others through advocacy. Their approach includes a reduction in all travel, vegetarian food as standard at events, reducing consumption and using rented, refurbished or repaired resources where possible and using low-energy heating and cooling solutions (CAST, n.d.). Some of the responsibilities outlined in paragraph 54 can be explored through the following questions:

- What steps have researchers taken to understand the environmental impact of their planned research and knowledge exchange activities?
- Have researchers considered whether the appropriate research location has the lowest possible environmental impact?
- What opportunities does the research activity have to enhance environmental sustainability at local, regional, national and international scales? How can environmental sustainability be an integral part of research and knowledge exchange activities?
- What opportunities are there to calculate and minimise the environmental impact of research data collection? For example, have researchers considered the use of online spaces or low-carbon transport options? For research sites which are geographically distant, have researchers explored local collaborations with researchers and communities which are mutually beneficial and reciprocal?
- How can the environmental impact of research meetings, partnerships and events be calculated and minimised?
- Have researchers considered whether any merchandise or gift incentives are justified and consistent with an ethic of environmental sustainability?

- How do researchers support knowledge and practice sharing across generations and geographies – and how does it do this whilst minimising the impact on the environment?

Responsibilities to the community of educational researchers

The fifth edition of the BERA *Ethical Guidelines* (BERA, 2024) outlines that researchers, as part of a community of educational researchers, have responsibilities to that community to ensure that research is undertaken with integrity (BERA, 2024, paragraph 59), and that established researchers, with the community as a whole, have a particular responsibility to support the next generation of educational researchers (BERA, 2024, paragraph 58). There is also the clear expectation that research institutions such as universities support and sustain collaborations (BERA, 2024, paragraph 60). These ideas of integrity, support and collaboration have particular resonance with the concept of environmental sustainability in the context of educational research. For example, researchers have a fundamental responsibility for the knowledge they produce and share with the educational research community. As we have noted in our discussion of the responsibilities researchers have to stakeholders, sponsors and clients, environmental sustainability challenges have complex spatial and temporal impacts which drive intersectional inequalities including in the field of education. These inequalities are underpinned and compounded by the legacies and present-day realities of colonial injustices led by Global North nations, mainly in Global South countries, including the extraction and exportation of natural resources, knowledges and peoples (Quijano, 2007; Gadotti and Torres, 2009). As educational ideas, practices and schools are central to colonial projects (e.g. Fallace, 2015), educational researchers have a responsibility to the community as a whole to contribute to the ongoing transformation of education which fosters emancipation and empowerment (see, for example, Freire, 1972; hooks, 2014) including the construction of new approaches to pedagogy and curriculum. In the context of environmental and sustainability education research, this requires the community to continue to address issues of representation. For example, much of the international literature is drawn from Anglophone contexts, including the United States, the UK and Australia, where western conceptualisations of education, human and environment relationships and sustainability dominate (Rodrigues et al., 2020). In the field of Curriculum Studies, Paraskeva (2016) highlighted the suppression and elimination of diverse epistemologies, concepts and experiences from curricula across the world, describing these processes as 'curriculum epistemicides'. The dominance of western conceptualisations of education, including the subject stories which are visible and invisible in school curricula (see Gandolfi, 2021; Nayeri and Rushton, 2022), is especially relevant to the community of education researchers, and especially those who seek to deconstruct the compounded colonial legacies and present-day realities of colonial education and environmental practices. As a starting paragraph for these vital reflections, we share the following questions:

- What opportunities can educational researchers identify, support and nurture for critical and collaborative dialogue across and within diverse Global North and South contexts from the perspective that such dialogue offers novel and varied ways to reconsider and transform environmental and sustainability education and educational research?
- Which voices and whose interests are centred or marginalised in educational research, and how can this be made explicit in the reporting and dissemination of research findings? How can research be designed to include a greater diversity of perspectives?
- How can the limits and limitations of knowledge produced by educational research be acknowledged and acted on?
- What can researchers do to rapidly develop the capacity of new educational researchers working in the field of environmental sustainability, especially those whose expertise adds to the diversity of understanding in the field?
- How can models of international collaboration be developed which minimise impact on the environment? What principles should be used to decide whether to hold an event in person or online?
- How can research findings be shared openly with those working in geographical and economic contexts, which means they cannot access research behind a paywall?
- How can educational research construct alternative futures which attend to environmental sustainability challenges?

Having considered some of the responsibilities of educational researchers to the community, we now reflect on the collective responsibilities of educational research in the context of environmental sustainability.

Responsibilities *of* educational researchers

Recognising that researchers are not solely responsible for environmental sustainability in relation to their research, there is a need to identify collective responsibilities to researchers of those hosting, funding, facilitating and leading educational research. These responsibilities relate to the research environment, culture, policies and priorities. In this section, we focus specifically on (a) how the research infrastructure (institutions, funding, publication and community) can support researchers to conduct more sustainable research and (b) the responsibilities of institutions supporting researchers engaged in climate activism.

Existing research infrastructure was not created with environmental sustainability in mind. The UK tertiary education sector is responsible for just over 2 per cent of the UK's greenhouse gas emissions (The Royal Anniversary Trust, 2023), with significant contributions from the supply chain, travel and transport, the built environment and financed emissions (e.g. pensions, investments and endowments). Indeed, academic researchers are amongst the highest emitters due to travel to conduct fieldwork, attend conferences and participate in meetings (Tyndall Centre, 2015). Environmental sustainability is not yet embedded as a key consideration when planning research, and more sustainable travel (avoiding air travel, for example) tends to be more expensive and may not fit within allocated budgets for research. International collaborations and conferences often carry prestige and are built into research expectations. It can therefore be challenging for researchers to act ethically, particularly at the beginning of a research career. Recently, many research institutions and funders have committed to action for environmental sustainability in terms of leadership, system change, infrastructure, procurement, travel, collaboration and reporting environmental impacts (UKRI/Wellcome/EAUC, 2024), but these changes involve costs at a time when the sector is facing considerable financial pressure and 'are likely to be unaffordable in the present economic environment' (OfS, 2024: 3). This creates a tension between what is possible and desirable and what is affordable. Given that there's 'no research on a dead planet' (Thierry et al., 2023: 1), it is essential that the following questions are addressed by funders and institutions:

- Does your research agenda and policy recognise environmental crises and the ways in which people are differentially affected? Does it take action to redress inequitable impacts?

- How does research on environmental sustainability inform policy-making decisions, for example, is an environmental sustainability assessment used in criteria to judge research grant applications? Is there an adequate budget to account for the current financial costs of more sustainable practices?
- In what ways do current policies promote environmentally unsustainable practices? How and when will these be updated to reflect the urgent need to bring about environmental sustainability?
- How are staff developed and resourced to take environmental sustainability into consideration when undertaking educational research?
- What opportunities are there for green travel, workspaces and infrastructure that are used in educational research, for example energy, electronic and waste contracts?

The slow pace of institutional and societal response to climate and ecological emergencies, alongside the majority of adults feeling worried amongst the general population in Great Britain (Office National Statistics (ONS), 2023) and a global majority wanting stronger climate action (United Nations Development Programme (UNDP), 2024), gives rise to tensions between institutional process and climate priorities. In the context of school climate strikers, Verlie and Flynn (2022) have noted that education may not be the solution, but rather part of the system that needs to change. Recent academic papers have focused on the question of whether there is a duty to engage in climate activism (Garcia-Gibson, 2023) and call to live in 'climate truth' (Thierry et al., 2023). There is a potential for conflict between researchers seeking to do their work in more environmentally sustainable ways and institutional or national policy, giving rise to a range of actions in response. Gardner et al. (2021) call for academics to move from publication to public action and for support to come from universities building advocacy into workload models and research leave, recognising it in appointment and promotion processes, as well as defending the right to protest. In doing so, even where cost or institutional policy prevents researchers from acting in more environmentally sustainable ways, the outlet to action can be about change: indeed, the Intergovernmental Panel on Climate Change (IPCC) has recognised the social movements have accelerated collective action on climate justice and fossil fuel extraction and supply (Denton et al., 2022).

Educational institutions, therefore, have an important role to play in bringing researchers together to share knowledge and influence policy and practice to create a better society. Questions that prompt reflection on their role in enabling or inhibiting climate action include:

- In what ways is it possible to facilitate and champion educational research which challenges existing social orders and power structures which promote unsustainable lives?
- How can staff be supported to participate in climate and environmental action?
- What specific responsibilities do British professional organisations have in relation to educational research in environmental sustainability, particularly former colonies and current overseas territories?
- How can research supervisors best support student activism?
- In what ways might professional organisations mediate between educational researchers and those responsible for making policy with implications for environmental sustainability? How can educational organisations work towards a more environmentally sustainable society? What is the approach to supporting risk-taking?
- What is the (ideal) relationship between research, advocacy and activism?

In the case study below (Dunlop and Rushton, 2024), we explore how ethical issues relating to environmental sustainability may manifest themselves in a fictional doctoral research study, touching on those associated with the environmental impact of research and addressing climate anxiety. Questions are provided to prompt reflection on the issues raised in the case study.

Case Study: Frontlines of climate change education[5]

Background

Until recently, Leila was a secondary school teacher, working in schools in the UK and Pakistan for over ten years. She was motivated to conduct research by her experiences as a teacher with a form class, struck by how her students were bringing climate change into discussions about their future careers, families and travel decisions. Her study aims to understand young people's imagined futures and identify how education can create pathways to more just and sustainable future societies. She has recently been awarded a funded doctoral scholarship including travel costs.

The proposed doctoral study will adapt climate change scenarios created by scientists, economists and modellers published in the Intergovernmental Panel on Climate Change (IPCC) Sixth Assessment Report (2023) for use with students of upper secondary school age (14–18 years). The idea is to help students envision different possible future scenarios, based on evidence linking different social and economic drivers to greenhouse gas emissions. Leila's intention is to introduce the different socio-economic pathways to young people in a series of participatory workshops. During these workshops, young people will have the opportunity to imagine their futures given a range of different emissions scenarios. Aware of the impact of colonialism, differential historical contributions to greenhouse gas emissions, and varying vulnerabilities to climate change between countries, Leila is interested in how these contexts shape young people's future thinking. Leila has a good professional network in Pakistan after teaching there, so she has designed a multisite case study, working with teachers and young people in England and Pakistan, with fieldwork planned at the start of her second year. She has discussed her plans with former teaching colleagues in both locations, and they are keen to support Leila's research. Leila has established relationships with environmental Non-Governmental Organisations (NGOs) in both locations as a result of her environmental volunteering.

The ethical dilemma

Leila is concerned about the risk of psychological pain and distress associated with climate anxiety during her data collection phase. Leila wants to ensure she is well informed about how to anticipate and mitigate climate anxiety when working with young people in the UK and Pakistan. She meets one of her peers, Beca, to discuss different approaches to addressing climate anxiety before completing her application for ethical approval.

Beca asks Leila how she justifies overseas travel, given the contribution that air travel makes to greenhouse gas emissions and the direct threat that rising sea levels pose to her potential participants. During the conversation, Beca shows Leila an online emissions calculator to paragraph out that the emissions associated with a return flight from the UK alone is just under three times Pakistan's annual per capita greenhouse gas emissions. Leila states that she is motivated to do this work in order to include perspectives of young people in geographical locations more vulnerable to climate change because they are often excluded in research and policymaking, and that she thinks it is important that she collects data in person to develop a good rapport with her participants.

The conversation moves on to the original question focused on climate anxiety. Beca and Leila agree that it is impossible to avoid this, as climate anxiety is a rational response to the nature and scale of the threat of climate change. They discuss strategies to help participants cope with climate change, such as meditation and talking, but these do not sit well with Leila because she believes it is more important to address the causes of anxiety, i.e. human activities resulting in greenhouse gas emissions. Beca suggests using positive gain framing during data collection, that is, emphasising the co-benefits to health, wealth, community and happiness through more environmentally sustainable behaviours, and concluding with messages that emphasise solutions that help the transition to a more sustainable socio-economic pathway, but Leila thinks that this is too leading in relation to her research aims. Finally, Beca suggests that Leila read a paper arguing that climate anxiety can be reduced by planning individual and collective actions that could be taken to reduce emissions and adapt to the changing climate, such as joining a climate action group. Leila can see how this would fit with her study, but she is concerned about recommending that students join climate action groups is unlikely to go down well in England, given current guidance on political impartiality in schools. Leila is also concerned that being attentive to climate anxiety is likely to be different in the UK and Pakistan, and she is worried about how she might best respond to participants who may have had more direct experience with traumatic events attributed to climate change.

After the conversation, Leila is left feeling guilty about the environmental impacts of her study, concerned about potential harms to participants, uncertain how she can provide appropriate support to her participants, and keen to find a way forward to do her research ethically.

Course of action

Leila decides that if she wants to have legitimacy in the field of climate change education, she should try to contribute to finding and testing new methods of environmentally conscious research during her doctoral study.

After meeting with her supervisor, Leila decides to arrange to speak to her contacts in the schools in Pakistan to explore an alternative approach to doing the research. Leila proposes that she remains in the UK and works with her school contacts for data collection based in Pakistan. Leila will be present virtually during data collection where possible but will otherwise work from the data produced and will have debriefing meetings online with those who did the work in person. In exchange, Leila will provide professional development on research interviewing and contribute to climate education in the schools and design resources based on the research, which she will share with all participating schools. She will request that her travel fund be repurposed and allocated to her school partners, recognising their time and support. In her written request to her funder, Leila argues that this approach will enable her to answer her research questions, test out a more environmentally conscious approach to qualitative social science research, enable her to develop more meaningful and reciprocal collaborations in both locations and develop relationships with organisations that can help ensure her work has impact. Leila intends to recognise these contributions in her thesis and any publications that result. She is encouraged by the suggestion of her supervisor that she might be able to publish her work, and in doing so she will be able to share good practice in environmentally and socially conscious research.

Leila integrates the schools into her application for ethical approval. Leila plans for the workshop to include space to reflect and share emotions, and for action planning. Leila plans to work with her partners to identify a range of responses at different scales relevant to the locations of her participants (e.g. planning to evacuate in case of flood, learning urban gardening for food production); connected to the work of environmental NGOs she knows that can act as a paragraph of contact with place-based knowledge and experience should participants want to take action.

Alternative courses of action

Leila could have decided to examine climate futures in different parts of the UK more and less vulnerable to the impacts of climate change such as extreme heat, floods, forest fires and sea level rise; however, this would have excluded perspectives from the Global South and would not have allowed her to explore the impact of place and context on imagined futures informed by evidence, which is a key research aim.

Alternatively, Leila could have conducted the fieldwork as intended, on the basis that the potential social benefits of the work in terms of incorporating underrepresented perspectives into her study outweigh the potential harms. However, this approach perpetuates existing environmentally harmful practices and does not contribute to finding new, less harmful ways to do research which have potential co-benefits. She could have considered making the most of her visit by working in her partner schools or volunteering with the NGO. This course of action does not respond to Beca's challenge about emissions due to air travel, although it does allow Leila to make more of her time in Pakistan and contribute to the education system.

With respect to climate anxiety, Leila could provide an editable list of 'further support' resources to teachers so that they can decide which organisations and resources to include before sharing with students. However, these might not be shared with students who do not express their anxiety, and it risks placing an additional burden of responsibility on teachers.

Case Study – concluding section

Whilst research has an important role to play in creating knowledge to help societies respond to climate change, academic researchers are amongst the highest greenhouse gas emitters in society as a result of travel by air to conferences, project meetings and fieldwork. The environmental impact of research must be considered at all stages of research, and efforts made to reduce any negative impacts and address existing environmental injustices. Where these are not currently incorporated into systems, for example, for gaining ethical approval or assessing funding applications, questions about the environmental impacts should be included. This applies to all topics, not only research focusing on climate change. This may require flexibility and creativity on the part of funders and institutions, as well as the research community.

Researchers can pay attention to climate anxiety by ensuring that the research process allows space for empathy and emotions and includes discussions about actions in response to climate change at different scales, including opportunities to influence others and connect with individuals and groups with similar concerns.

The case study draws attention to both the responsibilities of educational researchers (specifically, risk of harm, authorship, reciprocity and attention to participants' wellbeing) and responsibilities to educational researchers in terms of flexibility with funding to reduce environmental impacts. There are many possible alternative courses of action, each with strengths and limitations, and it is important that the environment features in the weighing of alternative research strategies – not just by individual researchers but by funders, ethical reviewers, risk assessors and peer reviewers. Research supervisors have an important role here in mediating between the researcher, the institution and the broader field of educational research. Key considerations for Leila as a researcher include how best to nurture meaningful relationships with participants at a distance and authorship and anonymity, confidentiality and data sharing resulting from the collaborative approach with teachers. Exploring the questions throughout this chapter through research supervision meetings can potentially help researchers to identify more just ways of conducting research.

Final thoughts

Environmental sustainability in educational research is an ethical issue that needs to be given greater prominence in educational research, whether or not the focus of the research is on environmental issues. In this chapter, we have attempted to identify where environmental considerations may intersect with research processes and to draw out questions that researchers can use to explore ethical dilemmas. The questions are by no means exhaustive, but rather a starting paragraph on a journey which requires all researchers to change their practices if we are to prevent the bleakest future scenarios of climate change. There is a need to uphold responsibilities to people and the planet whilst enabling the production of educational research. It is important to consider the means by which knowledge is created, and question how educational research can be conducted in a more environmentally sustainable way – and to share and disseminate practices which show promise. The means by which this can be achieved are not well established, particularly given the cultural context in which educational research is carried out, which often frames environmental challenges in ways that fit prevailing social orders. Questions – to researchers, research supervisors, research leaders and funders – serve as requests for information and also as interruptions of the status quo, and can draw attention to the need for accelerated climate action and new ways of doing research which foreground environmental justice.

Further reading

1. Concordat for the Environmental Sustainability of Research and Innovation Practice (n.d.). https://www.ukri.org/news/ukri-welcomes-cross-sector-environmental-sustainability-concordat/.

   This cross-sector commitment to embedding sustainability in research, signed by many higher education institutions, outlines ways in which institutions can embed more environmentally sustainable practices across leadership, procurement, travel, infrastructure, partnerships and reporting.

2. Hoolohan, C., McLachlan, C., Jones, C., Larkin, A., Birch, C., Mander, S. and Broderick, J. (2021). Responding to the climate emergency: How are UK universities establishing sustainable workplace routines for flying and food? *Climate Policy*, 21(7), 853–67. https://www.tandfonline.com/doi/full/10.1080/14693062.2021.1881426.

   This paper examines the environmental impact of routine workplace practices in universities. Reflecting on the environmental impact of these choices using tools like TR2AIL, as well as sharing and reporting on more sustainable practices, can help reshape professional practices.

3. Le Quéré, C., Capstick, S., Corner, A., Cutting, D., Johnson, M., Minns, A., Schroeder, H., Walker-Springett, K., Whitmarsh, L. and Wood, R. (2015). *Towards a Culture of Low-Carbon Research for the 21st Century*. Norwich: Tyndall Centre for Climate Change Research. https://tyndall.ac.uk/wp-content/uploads/2021/09/TWP-161.pdf.

   Based on the recognition that academics are amongst the highest emitters, this working paper examines the practicalities of reducing emissions for travel, suggests a way of weighing the importance of different activities and proposes alternatives to air travel for developing collaborations.

4. Wilkens, J. and Datchoua-Tirvaudey, A.R.C. (2022). Researching climate justice: A decolonial approach to global climate governance. *International Affairs*, 98(1), 125–43. https://academic.oup.com/ia/article/98/1/125/6484828.

   This paper centres on justice as it plays out in coloniality of knowledge production, time and solutions and considers how research relationships can be decolonised to bring about more mutually beneficial research relationships across different locations.

5. Wyatt, T. D., Gardner, C. J. and Thierry, A. (2024). Actions speak louder than words: The case for responsible scientific activism in an era of planetary emergency. *Royal Society Open Science*, 11(7), 240411. https://royalsocietypublishing.org/doi/full/10.1098/rsos.240411.

   The authors of this perspective argue that it is ethical for scientists to both work through their institutions and participate in social movements calling for climate action and call for more activist researchers in order to bring about change at the scale needed to address the planetary emergency.

Notes

1 'Responsibilities to sponsors, clients, stakeholders and the environment'.
2 'Researchers also have a responsibility to put in place ways of maximising the benefits and minimising the likelihood of any potential harms to participants, sponsors, the community of educational researchers and educational professionals and the environment more widely (BERA, 2024, paragraph 6).'
3 'Researchers should consider the implications of their research for the global community and the environment more generally, bearing in mind the interests of non-humans and broader issues to do with sustainability, climate change and biodiversity. This includes such specifics as the amount and type of travel, the nature of the food at meetings and dissemination events, and more fundamental questions about the actual research, for example, and the purposes for which it is undertaken (BERA, 2024, paragraph 54).'
4 Whilst we note the continued use of the term 'stakeholder' in the fifth edition of the BERA *Ethical Guidelines for Educational Research*, we also note research which highlights that the term continues to have problematic colonial linkages and connotations (Reed et al., 2024) and guidance from the United States which provides alternative terms such as 'working partners' and 'community collaborators' (CDC, 2022).

5   This case study appears in a slightly adapted form as a web case study. Research Ethics Case Studies 2024 | BERA. https://www.bera.ac.uk/publication/research-ethics-case-studies-2024-frontlines-of-climate-change-education

References

British Educational Research Association (BERA) (2018). *2018 Public Engagement and Impact Award Winners.* https://www.bera.ac.uk/bera-in-the-news/2018-public-engagement-impact-award-winners. Accessed on 23 July 2024.

BERA (2021). *Manifesto for Education for Environmental Sustainability.* (EfES). BERA Research Commission 2021/2022. https://www.bera.ac.uk/publication/bera-research-commission-2019-2020-manifesto-for-education-for-environmental-sustainability-efes. Accessed on 24 July 2024.

British Educational Research Association (BERA) (2024). *Ethical Guidelines for Educational Research* (5th ed.). London: BERA. www.bera.ac.uk/publication/ethical_guidelines-for-educational-research-2024

British Petroleum (bp) (2022). *Our Impact on the Economy 2022.* Available at: https://www.bp.com/content/dam/bp/country-sites/en_gb/united-kingdom/home/images/economic-impact-report/pdf/Our-impact-on-the-UK-economy-2022.pdf.

Centre for Climate Change and Social Transformations (CAST) (n.d.). *The CAST Sustainability Charter.* https://cast.ac.uk/sustainability/.

Centers for Control Disease and Prevention (CDC) (2022). *Preferred Terms.* https://www.cdc.gov/healthcommunication/Preferred_Terms.html. Accessed on 6 December 2024.

Denton, F., Halsnæs, K., Akimoto, K., Burch, S., Morejon, C. Diaz, Farias, F., Jupesta, J., Shareef, A., Schweizer-Ries, P., Teng, F. and Zusman, E. (2022). Accelerating the Transition in the Context of Sustainable Development. In *IPCC, 2022: Climate Change 2022: Mitigation of Climate Change. Contribution of Working Group III to the Sixth Assessment Report of the Intergovernmental Panel on Climate Change* [P. R. Shukla, J. Skea, R. Slade, A. Al Khourdajie, R. van Diemen, D. McCollum, M. Pathak, S. Some, P. Vyas, R. Fradera, M. Belkacemi, A. Hasija, G. Lisboa, S. Luz, J. Malley (Eds.)], Cambridge, UK and New York: Cambridge University Press. Doi: 10.1017/9781009157926.019.

Dunlop, L. and Rushton, E. (2024). Frontlines of climate change education. In S. W. Chong, and A. Fox (Eds.), *Research Ethics Case Studies,* British

Educational Research Association (pp. 1–5). https://www.bera.ac.uk/publication/research-ethics-case-studies-2024-frontlines-of-climate-change-education.

Eaton, E. M. and Day, N. A. (2020). Petro-pedagogy: Fossil fuel interests and the obstruction of climate justice in public education. *Environmental Education Research*, 26(4), 457–73.

Fallace, T. D. (2015). The savage origins of child-centered pedagogy, 1871–1913. *American Educational Research Journal*, 52(1), 73–103.

Freire, P. (1972). *Pedagogy of the Oppressed*. London: Penguin Press.

Fyke, J., and Weaver, A. (2023). Reducing personal climate risk to reduce personal climate anxiety. *Nature Climate Change*, 13(3), 209–10.

Gadotti, M. and Torres, C. A. (2009). Paulo Freire: Education for development. *Development and Change*, 40(6), 1255–67.

Gandolfi, H. E. (2021). Decolonising the science curriculum in England: Bringing decolonial science and technology studies to secondary education. *The Curriculum Journal*, 32(3), 510–32.

Garcia-Gibson, F. (2023). The ethics of climate activism. *Wiley Interdisciplinary Reviews: Climate Change*, 14(4), e831. https://doi.org/10.1002/wcc.831.

Gardner, C. J., Thierry, A., Rowlandson, W. and Steinberger, J. K. (2021). From publications to public actions: The role of universities in facilitating academic advocacy and activism in the climate and ecological emergency. *Frontiers in Sustainability*, 2, 679019. https://www.frontiersin.org/journals/sustainability/articles/10.3389/frsus.2021.679019/full.

Hickman, C., Marks, E., Pihkala, P., Clayton, S., Lewandowski, R. E., Mayall, E. E. and Van Susteren, L. (2021). Climate anxiety in children and young people and their beliefs about government responses to climate change: A global survey. *The Lancet Planetary Health*, 5(12), e863–e73.

hooks, b. (2014). *Teaching to Transgress*. London: Routledge.

Intergovernmental Panel on Climate Change (IPCC) (2023). *Climate Change 2023 Synthesis Report Summary for Policymakers*. https://www.ipcc.ch/report/ar6/syr/downloads/report/IPCC_AR6_SYR_SPM.pdf.

Nayeri, C. and Rushton, E. A. C. (2022). Methodologies for decolonising geography curricula in the secondary school and in initial teacher education. *London Review of Education*, 20(1), 4. https://doi.org/10.14324/LRE.20.1.04.

Office for National Statistics (ONS) (2023). *Climate Change Insights, Families and Households*. UK: August. https://www.ons.gov.uk/economy/environmentalaccounts/articles/climatechangeinsightsuk/august2023.

Office for Students (OfS) (2024). *Navigating Financial Challenges in Higher Education*. https://www.officeforstudents.org.uk/media/kegazm0o/insight-brief-21-financial-challeges.pdf.

Paraskeva, J. M. (2016). *Curriculum Epistemicide: Towards an Itinerant Curriculum Theory* (1st ed.). London: Routledge.

Pihkala, P. (2020). Anxiety and the ecological crisis: An analysis of eco-anxiety and climate anxiety. *Sustainability*, 12(19), 7836.

Quijano, A. (2007). Coloniality and modernity/rationality. *Cultural Studies*, 21(2–3), 168–78. https://doi.org/10.1080/09502380601164353.

Raffoul, A. W., Fopp, D., Elfversson, E., Avery, H. and Carolan, R. (2021). *The Climate Crisis Gives Science a New Role. Here's How Research Ethics Must Change Too*. https://theconversation.com/the-climate-crisis-gives-science-a-new-role-heres-how-research-ethics-must-change-too-171201.

Reed, M. S., Merkle, B. G., Cook, E. J., Hafferty, C., Hejnowicz, A. P., Holliman, R. and Stroobant, M. (2024). Reimagining the language of engagement in a post-stakeholder world. *Sustainability Science*, 19, 1481–90. https://doi.org/10.1007/s11625-024-01496-.

Rodrigues, C., Payne, P. G., Grange, L. L., Carvalho, I. C. M., Steil, C. A., Lotz-Sisitka, H. and Linde-Loubser, H. (2020). Introduction: 'New' theory, 'post' North-South representations, praxis. *The Journal of Environmental Education*, 51(2), 97–112. https://doi.org/10.1080/00958964.2020.1726265.

Sultana, F. (2022). Critical climate justice. *The Geographical Journal*, 188(1), 118–24.

Tannock, S. (2020). The oil industry in our schools: From Petro Pete to science capital in the age of climate crisis. *Environmental Education Research*, 26(4), 474–90. https://doi.org/10.1080/13504622.2020.1724891.

The Royal Anniversary Trust (2023). *Accelerating the UK Tertiary Education Sector towards Net Zero*. https://www.queensanniversaryprizes.org.uk/wp-content/uploads/2023/01/Accelerating-towards-Net-Zero.pdf.

The Royal Society and The British Academy (2024). *Investing in a 21st-Century Educational Research System*. https://royalsociety.org/-/media/policy/projects/education-research/investing-in-a-21st-century-educational-research-system.pdf.

Thierry, A., Horn, L., von Hellerman, P. and Gardner, C. J. (2023). 'No research on a dead planet': Preserving the socio-ecological conditions for academia. *Frontiers in Education*, 8, 1237076. https://doi.org/10.3389/feduc.2023.1237076.

Tyndall Centre (2015). *Travel Strategy – Towards a Culture of Low Carbon Research for the 21st Century*. Tyndall Working Paper 161. https://tyndall.ac.uk/about/travel-strategy/.

UCL (no date). *Enterprising Science*. https://www.ucl.ac.uk/ioe/departments-and-centres/departments/education-practice-and-society/stem-participation-social-justice-research/enterprising-science. Accessed on 23 July 2024.

UKRI/Wellcome/EAUC (2024). *Concordat for the Environmental Sustainability of Research and Innovation Practice.* https://wellcome.org/who-we-are/positions-and-statements/environmental-sustainability-concordat.

UKRI (no date). *Framework for Responsible Research and Innovation.* https://www.ukri.org/who-we-are/epsrc/our-policies-and-standards/framework-for-responsible-innovation/. Accessed on 22 July 2024.

UNDP (2024). *Peoples' Climate Vote.* https://peoplesclimate.vote/.

Verlie, B. and Flynn, A. (2022). School strike for climate: A reckoning for education. *Australian Journal of Environmental Education*, 38(1), 1–12.

Watson, D., Morgan, E. and Bull, K. (2021). Child-dog faeces assemblages and children's engagements in activist art. *Children's Geographies*, 19(6), 735–53. https://doi.org/10.1080/14733285.2021.1893276.

Section 2

Case Studies

Section 2-3 Foreword – Responsibilities to the Community of Educational Researchers and for Researchers' Wellbeing and Development

by *Sally Baker*

In this sub-section of the book, attention is turned from focusing on the responsibilities of researchers to others to our responsibilities *to* ourselves and other researchers when it comes to ethical practice. The contributions that follow ask important questions about the deontic dimensions of ethical practice, prompting us to consider the dynamic and multidirectional elements of engaging in research. In particular, this sub-section considers researchers' responsibilities to reflexivity, self-care and wellbeing in the context of new researchers and more experienced colleagues. The sub-section of the book takes as its starting point guidelines 58–69 and 82–3 of the BERA ethical guidance (BERA, 2024).

The aim of Sections 2–3 is to examine the micro-ethical dilemmas and decisions that researchers negotiate before entering, while in, and leaving 'the field'. In the three chapters in this sub-section, ethical dilemmas relating to both new doctoral researchers and supervisors (Chapters 13 and 14), and more established researchers (Chapter 12) are included, covering ethical issues relating to affect, gender, relationality and researching/working within the constraints of neoliberal institutions. The chapters explore the ethical tensions that emerge in relationships between individuals, colleagues and institutions, focusing particularly on how power influences researchers' engagement with and capacity to take ethical responsibility. In Chapters 13 and 14, you can hear the voices of doctoral researchers in frank conversation with their doctoral supervisors. In Chapter 13, Sin-Wang Chong, Qi Liu, Natalie Tegama and Grace Anna Baby explore through two case studies of systematic literature review generation the exercising of power. Emily Dowdeswell, Carolyn Cooke, Petra Vackova, Donata Puntil and Lucy Caton, a collective of emerging and experienced researchers, set the scene in academia for the need to care for one another, taking a post-humanist perspective to illustrate their mutual support. Returning to the doctoral research arena, Anna Xavier, Carly Hawkins and Sally Baker pick up on the responsibilities of supervisors working with doctoral researchers of modelling this caring, illustrated through the particular demands of studies in fragile research settings.

Through care-full consideration of relational dynamics, these chapters prompt us to consider how and where our responsibilities lie with regard to our participants, our disciplines, our institutions, the project of research and ourselves. These chapters highlight the challenges of marking clear and transparent boundaries when it comes to the messiness of human interaction in research contexts, even when the interaction is a review of the literature. As such, this sub-section allows us to examine how researchers respond to the imperative to take responsibility following an ethical dilemma and offers lessons for researchers to engage in more proactive self-care and protective practices, such as collective writing, journaling and debriefing with supervisors.

12

Tackling Undercare: Towards Wellbeing and Care in Academia through Collaborative Writing

by *Emily Dowdeswell, Carolyn Cooke, Petra Vackova, Donata Puntil and Lucy Caton*

Introduction

Intensified workloads, uncertain career prospects and the hyper-competitive landscape of higher education are impacting the wellbeing of students and academics. Scholars have reported on a climate of stress and anxiety (Barry et al., 2018; Nicholls et al., 2022), growing inequality in access to resources and opportunities (Oliver and Morris, 2022) and increases in burnout (Stoten, 2023). While the safeguarding of wellbeing has been a core principle of national guidance (BERA, 2018, 2024), institutional actions to mitigate harm are falling short, with minoritised scholars disproportionately affected (Lahiri-Roy and Martinussen, 2024). Despite the latest updates to national guidance encouraging universities and other sponsors to employ ethics of care for researchers, researcher wellbeing is mostly constrained to a remit of protection from physical and psychological harm in the course of fieldwork (BERA, 2024, paragraph 82).[1]

Yet academics grapple with a wide range of challenges that impact their safety and wellbeing without institutional support (Elmgren et al., 2016) (BERA, 2024, paragraph 83).[2] Although, *a*midst a climate of massification, marketisation and managerialism, a 'hurried, mechanical, assembly-line' (Ulmer, 2017: 201) approach to academic writing has become a norm in higher education. This *production* of academic writing is now a source of unprecedented pressure, especially for students and academics early in their career and on precarious contracts (Read and Leathwood, 2021). In the environment of *publish or perish*, Nygaard writes, 'there seems to be more perishing than publishing for the majority of researching academics' (2017: 519) as scholarly writing alienates academics, and individualises academic labour and knowledge production (Campbell et al., 2024). These tensions around scholarly writing highlight the *endemic undercare* in academia and the need for 'more *care-full* institutional cultures' (Baker and Burke, 2023: 231).

In this chapter, we write as the Posthumanist Collective – an interdisciplinary research group formed in 2020 at a large public university in the UK by doctoral students and early career researchers – to collectively address a set of ethical dilemmas related to scholarly writing. We explore how writing together can challenge normative institutional practices of care and illustrate the possibilities and tensions of caring otherwise when writing. Enacting care otherwise through, in and around collaborative scholarly writing, we argue here, is an important step towards 'becoming well' (McPhie, 2019: 300) as a community in academia.

Ethical guidelines and courses of action

Current institutionalised ethical guidelines that safeguard the wellbeing of researchers are rooted in humanist philosophies which promote the notion of the autonomous subject (Mauthner, 2019), positioning students and academics as competitive entrepreneurs with individual responsibility for their own wellbeing (Burton, 2021), and moving 'academic life towards the authority of the market' (Harland et al., 2010: 86). However, applying an ethic of respect reveals tensions, prompting decisions to balance research aspirations, societal concerns, institutional expectations and individual rights. Reducing practices of care to a performative check-box approach towards 'mood maintenance' (Burton, 2021: 28) and individual resilience extracts wellbeing from the dynamic reality of lived experience.

To reclaim the possibilities of/for care in higher education, we engage and think with posthumanist and new materialist scholarships (Haraway, 2016; Puig de la Bellacasa, 2017) which reframe care and wellbeing as relational and dynamic socio-material phenomena. Starting with the proposition that ethical practice cannot be reduced to autonomous actions of a rational human enables different ways of thinking about ethical frameworks (Sidebottom, 2024), reframing scholarly writing as a social practice that interweaves ideas and conversations across different spaces and times.

While the marketisation of higher education labour impacts our ability to connect, collaborate and care for one another, belonging to the Posthumanist Collective has helped us to engage our personal experiences to 'stay with the trouble' (Haraway, 2016: 31) of being and staying well in academia. Committed to doing *academia otherwise*, we experiment with collaborative writing as a restorative, communal practice of becoming well (BERA, 2024, paragraph 58).[3] We embrace the tensions within our work to recognise the connectedness of our digital and physical spaces (Vackova et al., 2023) and attend to 'neglected things' (Puig de la Bellacasa, 2011: 100) in our daily environments, framing disregarded objects, stories, sounds and voices as important writing partners.

Drawing on our experience of writing together, we explore in the following three case studies a set of ethical dilemmas that prompt questions of wellbeing and care within collaborative writing. Firstly, we interrogate practices of writing that reify the trope that writing can be 'produced'. Secondly, we explore the ethical challenges of working collaboratively online. We thirdly turn our attention to the possibilities and pitfalls of writing creatively. Each ethical dilemma sets the scene for illustrative courses of action. Together, these examples offer a window into our experimentations rather than a manual or template to follow. We hope the questions they pose elicit a space for others to reflect *with* their own settings and practices and interrogate the too often unaddressed complexities of writing and care in academia.

Case Study One: The challenges of writing as production

The fast-paced production of publications, books, grants and reports sustains the marketised environment of academia as knowledge becomes commodified and privately owned behind paywalls. An extensive publication profile is now a critical element of academic work. It is essential for career progression, and perhaps even more importantly for securing employment in the first place (Laudel and Glaser, 2008). Writing has become a *high-stakes activity* (e.g. Nygaard, 2015). The 'prevailing publish-or-perish culture that has symbiotically developed alongside contemporary institutional performance expectations' (Receveur et al., 2024: 1), paired with job insecurities, creates existential pressures for early career academics, making them a particularly vulnerable group in the academic system (Laudel and Glaser, 2008). This is especially true for women and minoritised scholars, who face greater barriers to the publishing process (Araneda-Guirriman, 2023; Liu, 2023).

Our experiences of writing in academia

The pressure to write, produce and publish at early stages of our research careers, while balancing precarious employment circumstances, was a key concern when we began meeting as a Collective. Individually, we feel the pressure to publish quickly, whether through doctorate processes to 'ready' us for academia, or to meet institutional expectations. Fast production secures our place within institutions as 'active' and therefore able to access further support (both financial and material). These pressures are focused on individual production, what we as individuals complete within certain timeframes, and evidence of individual progress forms. This individualisation of effort and production, amidst precarious and ever-changing workload pressures, creates a momentum of 'hurriedness' (Ulmer, 2017: 201), where conversations with colleagues require working on the margins of our time to complete complex and intricate writing tasks.

> Kindly send us your proofread manuscript by email by 31 May 2023, and do confirm you are aware that no major changes can be applied to the text after this stage. (Publisher via email)

This hurriedness is exacerbated for early career researchers, where the feeling of time (and therefore opportunity) passing to 'prove' oneself in order to gain employment, or progression, adds additional pressure to produce.

Alongside this momentum to write and publish are issues of time. As a group of students and early career researchers, we all face the challenge of creating time and space to write, particularly to do deep-thinking and creative work. We work in the margins of the workday – evenings, early mornings and weekends – lacking the time for research at this stage in our careers (Laudel and Glaser, 2008). In doing so, we can often feel isolated and lacking in support (i.e. the understanding of more established colleagues, financial recompense for our extended work time or material support with writing processes).

These feelings of isolation are further exacerbated for us as we work with less mainstream theories. Posthumanist and feminist new materialist theories are less well known to reviewers and audiences, can be difficult to communicate in conventionally structured academic formats and critique traditional knowledge-making and dissemination practices. The struggle to work with these theories that challenge the status quo around publication requirements can come at a significant personal cost in both time and resilience.

Precarious work contracts, an associated lack of access to financial support for publication fees or travel expenses, create additional financial barriers to meeting the institutional expectations.

> at present we are not in the position of writing the paper due to the costs of the publication. Originally, when we sent the abstract, we thought we could have some funding from our own universities, but this unfortunately is not the case any longer. (DP email)

The sense of isolation from not being able to attend events with researchers exploring similar issues or working with similar methodologies, or to publish in spaces that would increase our personal visibility, further amplifies the struggle to produce at pace.

Course of action: Writing as Collective

Coming together as a Collective has created a relational space in which we can support each other to mitigate the challenges of knowledge making.

First, to address the pressures to produce writing at a fast pace, we learned to assemble our texts across different times and spaces. By each contributing the fragments of time we have, we collectively write and publish more than we could by ourselves. Working in this asynchronous way – adding notes and partial thoughts in online documents and sending WhatsApp messages and emails to keep everyone on track – we have managed to meet tight publishing timescales without any one of us feeling that a deadline is their sole responsibility. Writing within the precarious yet flexible spaces in the margins of our time, we collectively manage the tensions between research as production (with the tight writing deadlines, the pressure to produce for contractual or job application purposes) and our collective approach to supporting one another (offering spaces for us to think and create together while exchanging and developing care). However, we struggle to create spaces that are relaxed, generative, positive and creative, amongst the production pressures to 'complete' and 'move on' at speed.

> *"Sorry I haven't done as much as expected today – tired and body not up to being creative just now, but I'll try and do a big stint on Mon*/Tues" (CC WhatsApp)*
> **note Monday was a holiday.*

We write asynchronously to put less pressure on each other to perform at a certain time and place. We write when we have the energy and time, respecting and responding to each other's availability and ability to contribute. By sharing writing responsibility, the individualised responsibility to complete writing tasks is lessened. The sharing of responsibility is not straightforward nor is it easy, and must be continuously discussed and negotiated, but it allows us to divide tasks and attend to each other's needs, support each other's writing, and create a better work-writing-life balance while also meeting institutional expectations.

Second, to address our need for alternative spaces and paces to write, we draw from Springgay's notion of 'writing as "felt"' (2019) to reframe what we see as 'productive'. For us, engagement with the materiality of our writing – taking time to move, touch, feel, see, smell, hear with our environment as we write – is an important part of the process. Our collaborative writing draws our attention to mundane virtual and physical entanglements to centre a slowness of attention to disregarded senses and material partners in writing, extending our relationships beyond 'production', while protecting our wellbeing and the wellbeing of others.

Third, our increasing concern with the accessibility of academic publishing has encouraged us to diversify the modalities through which we write. We explore digital spaces where we can share, self-publish and broaden our discussions with others. In doing so, we recorded a podcast (Vackova et al., 2021), exchange thoughts on social media (#PosthumanistCollective) and published an e-zine (Vackova et al., 2024). By broadening our engagements across diverse media, we experiment playfully with relationships between ourselves, texts, images, conventions, senses and audiences.

Within these alternative spaces, we create time differently. Co-creating writing collaboratively through heightened attention to our entanglement with words, places, images, sounds, absences and presences moves us away from the rapid writing of production towards creative experimenting with/in human and material relations. In doing so, our writing becomes *differently authored* from other tasks that consume our working lives. These spaces *act with us* and change how we feel, what we think, how we write and how we engage as we create together. Many of these spaces reduce the pressure for creating long texts, instead focusing on small, and meaningful, ways to communicate. By reducing the pressures to type fast, get words on a page and fill the word count, *we can linger*. We can slowly edit. We can deeply consider our collective additions to the space and let us ourselves be affected in return.

Case Study Two: The challenges of writing in the digital

The increasing digitalisation of higher education, driven by the dominant view that digital technologies aid academic practices and production (Ifenthaler et al., 2022), is presented as more inclusive and transformative, overcoming barriers to participation and supporting new modes of communication (Swartz et al., 2020). However, these claims are being problematised across different fields of scholarship, in particular encouraging critical reflection on the limitations and pitfalls in discourses of inclusion (see, for example, Tyler, 2019 and Shaw et al., 2024). In developing this fifth edition of ethical guidelines, the editors have reflected on issues of inclusion, acknowledged the Equality Act 2010, and underlined the impact of structural inequalities throughout research, emphasising the particular responsibility on researchers to guard against inadvertently compounding marginalisation (BERA, 2024, paragraph 54).[4] With the increasing role of technology in education, knowledge production has accelerated exponentially, making information and ideas more readily available yet not always easily accessible (Arostegui, 2020).

Our experiences of writing online

As a group of dispersed academics with different responsibilities, affiliations and relationships to time, space and place, we regularly encounter the possibilities and the limitations of writing together online, attentive to the exclusions that are created even within seemingly inclusive ways of working. The tension between embracing digital practices to increase our productivity, while attending to how technology creates hidden barriers, is ever-present in our work as a Collective.

> *Recording. By attending this meeting, you consent to being included. (Microsoft Teams)*

While collaborative online spaces present shared access as merely a question of a click of a button, we often struggle to simply share our document with one another. Permissions are affected by the commercial competition between digital platforms that rival for subscriptions amongst academic institutions at the expense of researcher collaboration. Access to institutional software is problematic for those of us with part-time or precarious employment. The experience of hectic switching between multiple institutional accounts in Microsoft Teams before an event or the seeming impossibility of accessing a document without an institutional email delineates how academia remains a silo for hegemonic knowledge production. Working with these limitations leads us to repeatedly search through emails for links to different platforms, losing valuable time and causing frustration.

> *I was not able to access our Microsoft Team's shared folder, so if you could send me some of the paper you mentioned about collaborative writing, that would be great, thanks. (DP email)*

Our broadband coverage and digital hardware act more often as a chasm than a bridge, as the failure of our systems to synchronise in real time while we work on the same sections leads us to leave the document so that one of us can work uninterrupted by error messages and disappearing text. *Conflict* takes on a new meaning in these digital contexts, slowing down our progress and hindering our ability to work with one another, reinforcing individualised approaches to research. Paradoxically, here, the platforms we depend upon for working together demand that we work alone.

This paragraph is locked, another user is currently editing it. (Word in Sharepoint)
I can leave you in the doc if you want to work on it for a bit? (ED WhatsApp)

Digital platforms reduce our experience of each other's presence to a flickering cursor, intensifying the disembodiment of scholarship from our bodies, our rooms and our wider communities, and reinforcing the erasure of the multimodal effects and ethics of collaborative writing (Taylor, 2014). Not satisfied with such disembodied togetherness, we seek and sustain alternative communications to connect while separated within digital writing spaces.

Hello! Lovely to see you in here too. (CC WhatsApp)

However, there is also the associated pressure of seeing comment responses 'ping' into our email spaces while working on other urgent tasks, signalling that others are actively engaging with the documents when we are unable to, and the knowledge that our initials next to our cursor arrow or our initialled coloured circle at the top of the document is absent for them.

Sorry I can't be in there with you. Having to deal with an urgent tutor issue. (CC email)

Working often outside of traditional work hours and sometimes on-the-go – reading and writing on mobile devices as we travel to and from conferences or between hospital appointments and other family commitments – we are mindful that flexible ways of working can also be harmful and disruptive. Emailing with colleagues via small screens of mobile phones while attending to other tasks breaks down communication into smaller chunks, generating interrupted and interrupting conversation flows that disrupt time and space for rest, relaxation and family.

Ping ... ping ... ping. (Microsoft Outlook)
Sorry for falling off the radar. I just managed to catch up. (LC email)

Research choices in digital contexts are material configurations that raise ethical concerns. We reflect on our responsibility to safeguard our mental wellbeing [paragraph 82] and are anxious about the stress caused by barriers to connectivity and the reductive experience of digital platforms

(BERA, 2024, paragraph 82).[5] We take seriously emerging hierarchies of access and how they manifest for colleagues on temporary contracts and working across institutions (BERA, 2024, paragraph 83).[6]

Course of action: Writing as material

By attending to how writing integrates physical and digital encounters and framing writing as material, we disrupt narratives of writing as a contained, individualised and cognitive-only pursuit. We playfully entangle writing materiality, experimenting with collaging words and images, walking around our spaces and environments and inviting surrounding soundscapes into our writing.

In attending to our entanglement with digital platforms, we interrupt the divide between our online presence (often as a cursor or with a blurred-out background to a video call) and our daily lives. While flickering cursors can act as a reminder of our digitally separated lives, we also take comfort and care in 'being with' and 'caring with' each other in that moment, as a reminder of the potential for collective enactments of 'becoming well' together in any given moment.

> DP: *It was so lovely to 'see' you all in the document, all of us working together, seeing what began to appear in the writing as I was typing above or below. (Email)*

In this way, and via synchronous messaging, we celebrate our commitment and perseverance, acknowledging how our 'beyond screen' lives leak into how we sit/write/message at any particular moment. Equally, emails showing someone has commented or edited the shared document, although arriving whilst our focus is often elsewhere, entangle our writing with our everyday lives, percolating our writing practices with everyday moments.

> *I'm thinking about a thing I did with my kids during lockdown using yeast – it almost became a pet. I was going to talk about that in relation to materials as a 'doing' if that fits ok (CC Teams meeting).*

> *I've just finished a conversation with a colleague about a student issue. It made me think about how A.I. is fundamentally changing the nature of our communications and how that links to our discussions of disrupting space-time when we write collaboratively. I've added something about that to our document (LC email).*

This generative entanglement of people-materials-places-spaces-time, as always in motion, requires us to acknowledge the speculative nature of what will arrive into, and write with, us. This speculative openness to the socio-material creates a more responsive space where precarious voices, marginalised materialities and overlooked kinships are taken seriously and responded to. Indeed, by attending to the tensions of working asynchronously across different time zones, juggling conflicting responsibilities and navigating technological issues that impact our ability to consistently contribute at times, our voices are woven together with their contingent context without prioritising any one *author*.

Case Study Three: The challenges of writing creatively

The current emphasis on public, business or sector engagement with research, and a dissatisfaction among some academics with current publishing practices, has led to a significant rise in interest in 'non-traditional', more creative ways to share research (Leavy, 2020; Koro and Tanggard, 2022). However, there are many cases where such texts are 'systematically pushed back and mis-read as non-academic' (Beauchamps, 2021: 392) or not seen to fit institutional rubrics of 'what counts' as academic research (Norton, 2012).

While pragmatic challenges frame debates about creative writing in academia, broader questions about the *role of creativity* are less explored (Colyar, 2009). To shift attention to creative writing in academia not only as a product-focused discussion but also as a form of *academic practice* is to consider the ethical dilemma of how the 'habitual canon' (Beauchamp, 2021: 394) of academic writing – that is 'predominantly white ... male ... quantitative' – represses voices and writing practices to a fraction of what they could be (Beauchamp, 2021: 394). To re-see writing, not only as a *writing up* phase (e.g. Yoo, 2017) that happens after thinking and doing have been completed, but as a form of creating together, re-frames writing as a collective and creative practice in which we are ethically bound and where both the possibilities and tensions of wellbeing and care in and around writing can both be explored and enacted otherwise.

Our experiences of writing creatively

Working collaboratively across digital and physical spaces highlights the ethical dilemmas we face in our abilities to be creative together. As a Collective, how we write and what we write is shaped by the digital platforms we use, the conference set-ups we engage in, and the publication conventions surrounding academia. In ensuring we, as a group of early career researchers, meet the expectations regarding academic publishing, we must grapple with how our chosen profession views these activities.

> *While I know this is likely to be in tension with posthumanist theory, we do need to have an identified data, discussion and conclusion section for our publication format. Could you find a way to make these sections explicit? (Editor comment on early draft of article)*

Digital platforms, with their helpful inbuilt grammar checks and heading formats, also push us into linear sequences of writing. While these software architectures align with academic conventions, promoting linear arguments, establishing a coherence of formatting and embedding a levelled structure using the heading settings, they are less consistent with our Collective's aims. Inbuilt grammar and automated spelling checks interfere with playful experiments with word conjunctions, bracketing, and hyphens to emphasise new meanings and relationalities.

> *I'm assuming that the hyphen here is deliberate, but could you please confirm? (Editor's comment)*

As a result, while our collaborative practices often involve images, videos, sketches and materials, our writing often does not, or cannot communicate the intricacies of these material relationships in traditional publishing. Turning towards the multimodality of our practices, against the scripted demands of digital platforms, initiates a tidal effect as we move towards multimodal practices only to return to the medium of the blank page. Where we do experiment with modality, we are conscious of alienating some of the community we are seeking to involve in developing discussions. We hear stories of experimental articles that are rejected due to their challenge to conventions. While reaching towards multimodality means expanding who and what we work with, there is a risk involved in venturing away from the well-worn grounds of our disciplines.

> *We can't include that image because I don't have copyright and it is going to be difficult to get, and we can't include the YouTube clip of the washing machine*

sound, so will the text provocation be enough for readers to understand what we did? (CC comment)

We continually grapple with how to collaborate in creative ways that challenge our thinking, disrupt normative ways of working and allow for new possibilities to unlearn writing together.

Course of action: Writing as experiment

Non-linear, multimodal and collaborative ways of writing that are expansive, generous and include diverse colleagues, places and environments are difficult to achieve without experimentation and ample time. Springgay (2019) writes that we must first *defamiliarise* ourselves with what is normally understood as writing in order to find and 'amplify' creativity in writing. Through all our experiments in collaborative writing, we deliberately play with images, video and sound. While other forms of writing may 'use' such 'tools', as an illustrative point, or to generate texts, we reframe such artefacts as 'doings' (Murris, 2016). As active participants within our writing processes, it becomes troubling to create texts without embedding multimodal elements.

The question arises: what does it mean to *defamiliarise* conventional writing practices? To *defamiliarise* entails critically interrogating the socially constructed and often unexamined norms that govern the act of writing. As a Collective, we therefore aim to create spaces for experimentation by challenging these conventions through both individual and collaborative engagements with video, sound and images via diverse collaborative writing platforms. Our multimodal explorations are integrated into a tapestry of diverse forms, designed to stimulate further reflection and open new avenues of thought. In our recent self-published e-zine, we play with layering various voices, texts, imaginaries and materialities to explore the agentic *doings* of our more-than-word texts.

We experiment with writing differently to develop new affective landscapes where we feel cared for and well. In several writing experiments, we have, for example, reframed our written contributions as *gifts*, forms of relation rooted in reciprocity, participation and collaboration (Sansi, 2020). The most notable example was our quilted poetry writing, where we organised a process for sharing lines of poems, to which we then added our next line. We deliberately chose not to use a shared document, where the writing of the four poems was revealed to all as it was developed, but instead to use emails, where the cumulative writing *revealed* itself line by line until the final poem was shared.

> *It was the first time I was excited to hear the ding sound of the emails coming into my inbox (PV email).*

Using emails in this way meant our collective communications intersected with our *normal* work emails, interrupting everyday stresses and problem-filled emails. Reframing writing as a gift creates a different space for writing within our lives, eliciting a different emotional response, of excitement, appreciation and anticipation.

To write differently, we resist the pressure to pursue a desired outcome moulded to professional conventions. This is imperative to us as academic writing limits both who and what is included in writing, as well as who and what gets published and who can access it. Experimenting with arts-based research approaches (Cahnmann-Taylor and Siegesmund, 2017; Leavy, 2018, 2020) reduces the pressure of academic production, brings joy into our practice and re-frames writing as an affective assemblage. We expand words by acknowledging our multisensory entanglements and introduce art-full activities to disrupt formal, sedimented ways of working. The affective dimension of the arts offers a particular transformative agency that increases our power and desire to act, to disrupt and to do things differently. Art-full writing interactions (Hofsess and Hanawalt, 2018; Mitchell et al., 2018; Snooks, 2022) enable us to enact writing differently. Rather than the expected *confident writer* and a *lead author* with cognitive authority, we developed a situated, distributed practice where we became an interconnected, vulnerable and responsive collective.

Alternatives

As we continue to experiment with our collaborative writing, we are constantly in conversation with alternative approaches that push against the boundaries of convention. We are in particular interested in collaborative academic writing that addresses the ethical dilemmas we face around writing as production, writing in the digital and writing creatively. In this section, we therefore introduce and highlight alternative pathways to writing collaboratively that inspire and challenge us.

As we continue to develop strategies that mitigate the pressure to produce conventional scholarly writing, we are inspired by hydrofeminist scholarship (e.g. Gumbs, 2021; Osgood and Bozalek, 2024) that invites researchers to slow down, notice forms of reciprocal knowledge produced through de-individualised, embodied, affective writing practices and 'disrupt and displace neoliberal imperatives that determine what educational research *should* be' (Osgood and Bozalek, 2024: 2). We find the concept of *becoming-wit(h)ness* valuable to scholarly writing because it calls on researchers to pause and examine what is made visible and erased in research practices and pay closer attention to our ongoing involvement in the violence of colonialism and extractivism (Osgood and Bozalek, 2024).

The coming together, or co-mingling, of different more-than-human partners in and around writing is a rich terrain for the exploration of academic writing. For example, Springgay examines how to 'generate a practice of writing that engenders bodily difference that is affective, moving, and woolly' (2019: 58). Touch and felt are foregrounded as analytical lenses that attend to how bodies and matter connect and are separated. This focus on research creation (Truman, 2021) as an ecology of practices at the interstices of thinking and making (Manning, 2016; Romano, 2023) fosters transdisciplinary approaches to text-based projects. These experimentations can spark different ways of thinking about the ethical dilemmas involved in the materiality of textual modalities and computer-generated scripts, including aspects of reciprocity, relationality, stewardship and ethics of care (Springgay, 2021).

Finally, with regard to the dilemmas raised by creative collaboration and our desire to share our reflections widely, we continue to think with our ethical concerns surrounding reliance on text-based mediums to communicate. We are encouraged by an array of emerging innovative collaborative 'writing' practices and spaces for publication which challenge academia to move beyond professional texts (for example, see Diaz, 2020; Harkin, 2020; Love and Fillerup, 2022; Wardle et al., 2022; Mackinlay and Madden, 2023; Smolicki, 2023). We find such practices both within and beyond academia, in art, zine publishing, collage techniques, quilting, poetry, videography and other material interactions. Of particular interest is non-text research in the performing arts and other 'making' disciplines (Springgay, 2005; Back and Puwar, 2012; Jungnickle, 2018). By exploring writing (and non-writing) as a performative act (MacLure, 2013), where the emphasis is not on 'representing' an idea, argument or findings but on the performative quality of what is created, the question is not *What does a text or non-text say?*, but *What does it do?* (Barad, 2007).

Final thoughts

In educational research, collaborative writing is commonly understood as the process of writing together to produce an academic text. However, this meaning minimises the ethical complexities sparked when writing together. In this chapter, we suggest that attending to ethical dilemmas in and around writing can inspire new practices of care to support wellbeing in academia. Sharing concrete examples developed when writing together online, we problematise the notion of 'researcher wellbeing' and reimagine ethical responsibility for wellbeing in academia. We illustrate how creative, experimental and collaborative approaches to writing have helped us to highlight the ethical dilemmas around care and wellbeing in academia and move towards enacting care differently. We argue that collaborative writing, as an act central to academic practices that is constantly under pressure from a range of factors, is a space in which care in academia can be reframed.

Working towards more responsive and interactive practices of collaborative writing may help decentre expertise and individual authorship, thereby destabilising traditional power hierarchies in academic writing while encouraging a more supportive writing environment (BERA, 2024, paragraph 83).[7] Moreover, inviting unexpected partners and entangling neglected objects, places and spaces of academic life with scholarly writing materialises more embodied, affective and care-full elements of academic discourse. Such writing makes the bonds that shape bodies, thinking, choices and the past-present-future lives of researchers matter within academia.

Caring, and safeguarding wellbeing, in and around writing, we found, also entails addressing accessibility as a community-wide concern, the poorly understood effects of digital isolation, the barriers to fostering a sense of belonging within academia, and the technology-enabled intensification of labour, all of which impact negatively on students' and researchers' mental health (BERA, 2024, paragraph 82).[8] Although the guidelines highlight that special training might be needed in certain contexts, it should not be assumed that researcher safety is exclusively a concern for researchers entering conflict or post-conflict settings, or areas with high levels of infection or other risks. The uncritical acceptance of digital technologies may inadvertently stifle discussions on access, inclusion and more just ways of working and the development of more care-full and response-able communities in higher education. There is an ethical cost to digital contexts that remains under theorised and misunderstood, partly because the complexity of collaboration and creativity is underestimated.

Finally, writing creatively together entangles multiple voices and theoretical positions without underplaying their differences. Creative, collaborative writing disrupts the linear, disembodied and universalising voice of academic convention. This plurivocal way of being produces a textured narrative that moves, diverges, converges and splinters (Small, 2017; Hernandez et al., 2021; Koutropoulos, 2023), challenging how we write in academia. We propose it is important to pay attention to *how* writing comes to be, *how* entanglements (with others, work, life, environment) infuse what is written and open up what writing together involves to challenge ongoing exclusions, hierarchies and inequities.

In this chapter, we have examined how collaborative writing spaces can encourage a structural shift from neoliberal, 'productivity' focused practices of individualised care towards more dynamic, entangled, constantly shifting and composite practices of care. Practices of care that are produced through diverse interactions with the neglected and marginalised bodies and stories of academia. Continuing to explore alternative, art-full, care-full modalities of collaboration will further offer valuable insights into fostering more dynamic and healthy working environments amidst technological constraints and affordances. Such practices must be part of our next step towards institutional justice and thus towards becoming well in academia.

Reflective questions

In thinking with BERA's guidance on keeping individual researchers' safe and protecting them from harm, we have proposed an expanded consideration of who and what is considered during collaborative writing:

1 Take a moment to reflect on the writing practices you enact in your collaborations with others. What care-full writing strategies do you already do?

In this chapter, we connect our lived experiences of scholarly writing with a posthumanist attention to the cracks and the liveliness of research processes. By this, we mean acknowledging the gaps, uncertainties and unexpected developments ('cracks') that arise during research, as well as the vibrant and evolving nature ('liveliness') of how knowledge is produced.

2 Reflecting on the cracks and liveliness you identify in your own research projects, how might you attend to ethical dilemmas differently?

In case study one, we address production and precarity in academia.

3 Drawing on the call to explore alternative ways of working, how do you, or could you, enact knowledge production to promote more care-full research practices?

In case study two, we address the practices of exclusion that arise with/in purportedly inclusive digital technologies. There is a growing coalition of interdisciplinary researchers problematising these new technologies.

4 Beginning with sticky moments (Moxnes and Osgood, 2018) in your research practices, how have digital technologies intersected with possibilities of care? And of harm?

In case study three, we address the ethical implications of our collaborative writing by considering questions of affect as part of writing.

5 Reflecting on the relationships involved in your everyday settings, slow down and attend to the affective dimensions with/in your writing practices. What might understanding writing as affective offer?

Further reading

1. Peers, D., Joseph, J., McGuire-Adams, T., Eales, L., Fawaz, N. V., Chen, C. and Kingsley, B. (2023). We become gardens: Intersectional methodologies for mutual flourishing. *Leisure/Loisir*, 47(1), 27–47. https://www.tandfonline.com/doi/full/10.1080/14927713.2022.2141836.

   This article explores collective writing practices as 'nourishing'. This involves deep visiting, revisiting notions of accessibility and accountability and intersectional praxis to resist overlapping systems of oppression.

2. Rauber-Baio, H. J., Ung Loh, J. and Kim, K. (2024). Collaborative collaging. *Feminist Review*, 136(1), 161–8. https://doi.org/10.1177/01417789241237516.

This article explores how collage allows a collective sense-making act. The resulting collages act as an invitation to read, think and make with the articles within one journal edition in attentive ways.

3. Vackova, P., Puntil, D., Dowdeswell, E., Cooke, C. and Caton, L. (2023). Collaborative writing as bio-digital quilting: A relational, feminist practice towards 'academia otherwise'. *Social Inclusion*, 11(3), 65–76. https://www.cogitatiopress.com/socialinclusion/article/view/6616/3293.

Our own article shares our experimental methodology of quilted poetry. Quilted poetry makes precarious kinships (with each other, our environments, materials and bodies) tangible. In writing quilted poetry, we argue for new ways of becoming and living in academia.

Notes

1. Paragraph 82 (BERA, 2024) advises that safeguarding the physical and psychological wellbeing of researchers is part of the employers and sponsors, as well as of researchers themselves.
2. Paragraph 83 (BERA, 2024) emphasises that employers are also responsible for supporting researchers' personal and professional career development.
3. Paragraph 58 (BERA, 2024), which explains that the 'community of educational researchers' is considered to mean all those engaged in educational research.
4. Paragraph 54 (BERA, 2024) emphasises that researchers should consider the implications of their research for the global community and the environment more generally, bearing in mind the interests of non-humans and broader issues to do with sustainability, climate change and biodiversity.
5. Paragraph 82 (BERA, 2024) advises that safeguarding the physical and psychological wellbeing of researchers is part of the employers and sponsors, as well as of researchers themselves.
6. Paragraph 83 (BERA, 2024) reflects on the need to avoid exploiting differences in the conditions of work and roles of other researchers, including student researchers and those on time-limited contracts.
7. Paragraph 83 (BERA, 2024) underlines that researchers employed in higher education institutions in the UK are covered by the Concordat to

Support the Career Development of Researchers, which aims to create the healthy and supportive culture needed to ensure researchers are given every opportunity to thrive and realise their potential, ensuring a consistency of experience.

8 Paragraph 82 (BERA, 2024) states that principal investigators, other researchers, students undertaking research and their supervisors should ideally be offered training on researcher safety.

References

Alaimo, S. (2016). *Exposed: Environmental Politics and Pleasures in Posthuman Times*. Minneapolis, MN: University of Minnesota Press.

Araneda-Guirriman, C., Sepúlveda-Páez, G., Pedraja-Rejas, L. and San Martín, J. (2023). Women in academia: An analysis through a scoping review. *Frontiers of Education*, 8, 1137866. https://doi.org/10.3389/feduc.2023.1137866.

Aróstegui, J. L. (2020). Implications of neoliberalism and knowledge economy for music education. *Music Education Research*, 22(1), 42–53. https://doi.org/10.1080/14613808.2019.1703923.

Back, L. and Puwar, N. (2012). A manifesto for live methods: Provocations and capacities. *The Sociological Review*, 60(1_suppl), 6–17. https://doi.org/10.1111/j.1467-954X.2012.02114.x.

Baker, S. and Burke, R. (2023). Rethinking Institutional Care in Higher Education. In S. Baker, and R. Burke (Eds.), *Questioning Care in Higher Education*, Cham: Palgrave Macmillan (pp. 231–53). https://doi.org/10.1007/978-3-031-41829-7_8.

Barad, K. (2007). *Meeting the Universe Halfway: Quantum Physics and the Entanglement of Matter and Meaning*. Durham, NC, and London: Duke University Press.

Barry, K. M., Woods, M., Warnecke, E., Stirling, C. and Martin, A. (2018). Psychological health of doctoral candidates, study related challenges and perceived performance. *Higher Education Research & Development*, 37(3), 468–83. https://doi.org/10.1080/07294360.2018.1425979.

Beauchamps, M. (2021). Doing academia differently: Loosening the boundaries of our disciplining writing practices. *Millennium*, 49(2), 392–416. https://doi.org/10.1177/03058298211031994.

British Educational Research Association (BERA) (2018). *Ethical Guidelines for Educational Research* (4th ed.). London: BERA.

British Educational Research Association (BERA) (2024). *Ethical Guidelines for Educational Research* (5th ed.). London: BERA. https://www.bera.

ac.uk/publication/ethical-guidelines-for-educational-research-fifth-edition-2024.
Bleyer, J. (2004). Cut-and-Paste Revolution: Notes from the Girl Zine Explosion. In V. Labaton, and D. Martin (Eds.), *The Fire This Time: Young Activists and the New Feminism*, New York: Anchor Books (pp. 42–60).
Braidotti, R. (2019). A theoretical framework for the critical posthumanities. *Theory, Culture & Society*, 36(6), 31–61. https://doi.org/10.1177/0263276418771486.
Brown, C., Spiro, J. and Quinton, S. (2020). The role of research ethics committees: Friend or foe in educational research? An exploratory study. *British Educational Research Journal*, 46 (4), 747–69. https://doi.org/10.1002/berj.3654.
Burton, S. (2021). Solidarity, now! Care, collegiality, and comprehending the power relations of 'Academic Kindness' in the Neoliberal Academy. *Performance Paradigm*, 16, 20–39.
Cahnmann-Taylor, M. and Siegesmund, R. (Eds.) (2017). *Arts-Based Research in Education: Foundations for Practice* (2nd ed.). New York: Routledge. https://doi.org/10.4324/9781315305073.
Campbell, S., Floristán Millán, E., Wolf, O., Thornton, R. and Riva, S. (2024). Collective writing as survival tool: Mechanisms of reflexivity against neoliberal academia. *Emotion, Space and Society*, 50(101007), 1–8. https://doi.org/10.1016/j.emospa.2024.101007.
Clark, A. (2022). *Slow Knowledge and the Unhurried Child: Time for Slow Pedagogies in Early Childhood Education* (1st ed.). London: Routledge. https://doi.org/10.4324/9781003051626.
Colyar, J. (2009). Becoming writing, becoming writers. *Qualitative Inquiry*, 15(2), 421–36. https://doi.org/10.1177/1077800408318280.
Diaz, N. (2020). *Postcolonial Love Poem*. Chicago, IL: Faber & Faber.
Elmgren, M., Forsberg, E. and Geschwind, L. (2016). Life and work in academia. *Nordic Journal of Studies in Educational Policy*, 2016(2–3), 1–4. https://doi.org/10.3402/nstep.v2.34001.
Gale, K. and Wyatt, J. (2023). Between-ing: Collaborative writing and the unfoldings of relational space. *Qualitative Inquiry*, 31(1), 70–6. https://doi.org/10.1177/10778004231207130.
Gumbs, A. P. (2021). Undrowned: Black feminist lessons from marine animals. *Soundings*, 78(Summer), 20–37. http://doi.org/10.3898/SOUN.78.01.2021.
Haraway, D. J. (2016). *Staying with the Trouble: Making Kin in the Chthulucene*. London: Duke University Press. https://doi.org/10.1515/9780822373780.
Harkin, N. (2020). Weaving the colonial archive: A basket to lighten the load. *Journal of Australian Studies*, 44(2), 154–66. https://doi.org/10.1080/14443058.2020.1754276.

Harland, T., Tidswell, T., Everett, D., Hale, L. and Pickering, N. (2010). Neoliberalism and the academic as critic and conscience of society. *Teaching in Higher Education*, 15(1), 85–96. https://doi.org/10.1080/13562510903487917.

Hernández, K. J., Rubis, J. M., Theriault, N., Todd, Z., Mitchell, A., Country, B. and Wright, S. (2021). The creatures collective: Manifestings. *Environment and Planning E: Nature and Space*, 4(3), 838–63. https://doi.org/10.1177/2514848620938316.

Hofsess, B. A. and Hanawalt, C. (2018). Art (full) gifts: Material disruptions and conceptual proddings as creative acts of mentoring for early career art teachers. *Visual Inquiry: Learning & Teaching Art*, 7(3), 183–96. https://doi.org/10.1386/vi.7.3.183_1.

Ifenthaler, D., Isaías, P. and Sampson, D., D. G. (Eds.) (2022). *Orchestration of Learning Environments in the Digital World*. Cham: Springer. https://doi.org/10.1007/978-3-030-90944-4.

Jungnickle, K. (2018). Making Things to Make Sense of Things: DIY as Research and Practice. In J. Sayers (Ed.), *The Routledge Companion to Media Studies and Digital Humanities*, London: Routledge (pp. 492–502). https://doi.org/10.4324/9781315730479.

Koro, M. and Tanggaard, L. (2022). Creative methods for creativity research(ers)? Speculations. *Review of Research in Education*, 46(1), 324–44. https://doi.org/10.3102/0091732X221090510.

Koutropoulos, A. (2023). Enabling Rhizomatic Collaborations: Social and Technical Factors That Impact Agile Thinking and Learning. In *New Directions in Rhizomatic Learning*, London: Routledge (pp. 158–78).

Lahiri-Roy, R. and Martinussen, M. (2024). 'Do our diversities count?' Collaborative reflections on dwelling in academe's intersectional shadowlands. *International Journal of Qualitative Studies in Education*, 37(4), 975–89. https://doi.org/10.1080/09518398.2023.2178037.

Laudel, G. and Gläser, J. (2008). From apprentice to colleague: The metamorphosis of early career researchers. *Higher Education*, 55, 387–406. https://doi.org/10.1007/s10734-007-9063-7.

Leavy, P. (2018). Introduction to arts-based research. In P. Leavy (Ed.), *Handbook of Arts-Based Research*, New York: Guilford Press (pp. 3–21).

Leavy, P. (2020). *Method Meets Art: Arts-Based Research Practice*. New York: Guilford Press.

Liu, F., Rahwan, T. and AlShebli, B. (2023). Non-white scientists appear on fewer editorial boards, spend more time under review, and receive fewer citations. *Proceedings of the National Academy of Sciences*, 120(13), 1–10. https://doi.org/10.1073/pnas.2215324120.

Love, J. and Fillerup, J. (Eds.) (2022). *Sonic Identity at the Margins*. Santa Barbara, CA: Bloomsbury Publishing USA.

Mackinlay, E. and Madden, K. (Eds.) (2023). *Departing Radically in Academic Writing: Alternative Approaches to Writing and Methods in Qualitative Research* (1st ed.). London: Routledge. https://doi.org/10.4324/9781003360766.

MacLure, M. (2013). Researching without representation? Language and materiality in post-qualitative methodology. *International Journal of Qualitative Studies in Education*, 26(6), 658–67. https://doi.org/10.1080/09518398.2013.788755.

Manning, E. (2016). *The Minor Gesture*. Durham, NC: Duke University Press. https://doi.org/10.1215/9780822374411.

Mauthner, N. S. (2019). Toward a posthumanist ethics of qualitative research in a big data era. *American Behavioral Scientist*, 63(6), 669–98. https://doi.org/10.1177/0002764218792701.

McPhie, J. (2019). *Mental Health and Wellbeing in the Anthropocene: A Posthuman Inquiry*. London: Palgrave Macmillan.

Mitchell, G. J., Rice, C. and Pileggi, V. (2018). Co-emergence: An art-full dance of inquiry into artists' experiences of making art. *Research in Drama Education: The Journal of Applied Theatre and Performance*, 23(4), 563–81.

Moxnes, A. R. and Osgood, J. (2018). Sticky stories from the classroom: From reflection to diffraction in early childhood teacher education. *Contemporary Issues in Early Childhood*, 19(3), 297–309. https://doi.org/10.1177/1463949118766662.

Murris, K. (2016). *The Posthuman Child: Educational Transformation through Philosophy with Picturebooks* (1st ed.). London: Routledge. https://doi.org/10.4324/9781315718002.

Nicholls, H., Nicholls, M., Tekin, S., Lamb, D. and Billings, J. (2022). The impact of working in academia on researchers' mental health and well-being: A systematic review and qualitative meta-synthesis. *PloS One*, 17(5), e0268890. https://doi.org/10.1371/journal.pone.0268890.

Norton, S. (2012). Betwixt and between: Creative writing and scholarly expectations. *New Writing*, 10(1), 68–76. https://doi.org/10.1080/14790726.2012.694451.

Nygaard, L. P. (2017). Publishing and perishing: An academic literacies framework for investigating research productivity. *Studies in Higher Education*, 42(3), 519–32. https://doi.org/10.1080/03075079.2015.1058351.

Oliver, C. and Morris, A. (2022). Resisting the 'academic circle jerk': Precarity and friendship at academic conferences in UK higher education. *British Journal of Sociology of Education*, 43(4), 603–22. https://doi.org/10.1080/01425692.2022.2042193.

Osgood, J. and Bozalek, V. (2024). 'This thing that we do': In pursuit of hope-full renewals through hydrofeminist scholarly praxis. *Gender and Education*, 36(8), 1013–32. https://doi.org/10.1080/09540253.2024.2325407.

Peers, D., Joseph, J., McGuire-Adams, T., Eales, L., Fawaz, N. V., Chen, C. and Kingsley, B. (2022). We become gardens: Intersectional methodologies for mutual flourishing. *Leisure/Loisir*, 47(1), 27–47. https://doi.org/10.1080/14927713.2022.2141836.

Puig de la Bellacasa, M. (2011). Matters of care in technoscience: Assembling neglected things. *Social Studies of Science*, 41(1), 85–106. https://doi.org/10.1177/0306312710380301.

Puig de la Bellacasa, M. (2017). *Matters of Care: Speculative Ethics in More than Human Worlds* (Vol. 41). London: University of Minnesota Press.

Read, B. and Leathwood, C. (2021). Gender and the Politics of Knowledge in the Academy. In A. Ross (Ed.), *Educational Research for Social Justice: Evidence and Practice from the UK. Series: Education Science, Evidence, and the Public Good (1)*. Cham: Springer Nature (pp. 205–22).

Receveur, A., Bonfanti, J., d'Agata, S., Helmstetter, A. J., Moore, N. A., Oliveira, B. F., Petit-Cailleux, C., Rievrs Borges, E., Schultz, M., Sexton, A. N. and Veytia, D. (2024). David versus Goliath: Early career researchers in an unethical publishing system. *Ecology Letters*, 27(3), e14395. https://doi.org/10.1111/ele.14395.

Romano, N. (2023). Touching text: Feeling my way through research-creation. *Qualitative Inquiry*, 29(1), 69–81. https://doi.org/10.1177/10778004221099565.

Rose, D. B. (2017). Connectivity thinking, animism, and the pursuit of liveliness. *Educational Theory*, 67(4), 491–508. https://doi.org/10.1111/edth.12260.

Sansi, R. (2020). *Art, Anthropology and the Gift*. London: Routledge.

Sidebottom, K. (2024). Why Posthumanism? And Why Now? Ethics and Method for Complex Times. Blog post, BERA blog. May. Retrieved from https://www.bera.ac.uk/blog/why-posthumanism-and-why-now-ethics-and-method-for-complex-times.

Shaw, M., Toliver, S. R. and Tanksley, T. (2024). The internet doesn't exist in the sky: Literacy, AI, and the digital middle passage. *International Literacy Association. Research Quarterly*. https://t.co/vxFmgDaPtA.

Small, N. (2017). (Re) kindle: On the value of storytelling to technical communication. *Journal of Technical Writing and Communication*, 47(2), 234–53. https://doi.org/10.1177/0047281617692069.

Smolicki, J. (Ed.) (2023). *Soundwalking: Through Time, Space, and Technologies* (1st ed.). Waltham, MA: Focal Press. https://doi.org/10.4324/9781003193135.

Snooks, G. (2022). Care-filled classrooms: Heart (art) full life writing pedagogy. a/b. *Auto/Biography Studies*, 37(3), 445–52. https://doi.org/10.1080/08989575.2022.2154444.

Springgay, S. (2005). A/r/tography as living inquiry through art and text. *Qualitative Inquiry*, 11(6), 897–912. https://doi.org/10.1177/1077800405280696.

Springgay, S. (2019). 'How to write as felt': Touching transmaterialities and more-than-human intimacies. *Study of the Philosophy of Education*, 38, 57–69. https://doi.org/10.1007/s11217-018-9624-5.

Springgay, S. (2021). Feltness: On how to practice intimacy. *Qualitative Inquiry*, 27(2), 210–14. https://doi.org/10.1177/1077800420932610.

Swartz, S., Barbosa, B. and Crawford, I. (2020). Building intercultural competence through virtual team collaboration across global classrooms. *Business and Professional Communication Quarterly*, 83(1), 57–79. https://doi.org/10.1177/2329490619878834.

Stoten, D. W. (2023). 'I've been in a box too long and I didn't even realise that I was'. How can we conceptualise the subjective well-being of students undertaking a part-time DBA? The IICC Model. *The Journal of Continuing Higher Education*, 71(3), 241–58. https://doi.org/10.1080/07377363.2022.2037067.

Taylor, C. A. (2014). Telling transitions: Space, materiality, and ethical practices in a collaborative writing workshop. *Cultural Studies? Critical Methodologies*, 14(4), 396–406. https://doi.org/10.1177/1532708614530312.

Truman, S. E. (2021). *Feminist Speculations and the Practice of Research-Creation: Writing Pedagogies and Intertextual Affects* (1st ed.). London: Routledge. https://doi.org/10.4324/9781003104889.

Tuck, J. (2018). 'I'm nobody's Mum in this university': The gendering of work around student writing in UK higher education. *Journal of English for Academic Purposes*, 32, 32–41. https://doi.org/10.1016/j.jeap.2018.03.006.

Tyler, M. (2019). Reassembling difference? Rethinking inclusion through/as embodied ethics. *Human Relations*, 72(1), 48–68. https://doi.org/10.1177/0018726718764264.

Ulmer, J. B. (2017). Writing slow ontology. *Qualitative Inquiry*, 23(3), 201–11. https://doi.org/10.1177/1077800416643994.

Ulmer, J. B. (2018). Composing techniques: Choreographing a post qualitative writing practice. *Qualitative Inquiry*, 24(9), 728–36. https://doi.org/10.1177/1077800417732091.

Vackova, P., Puntil, D., Cooke, C. and Dowdeswell, E. (2021). The posthuman collective research group [Audio podcast episode]. *Research @ the OU*. Soundcloud. https://soundcloud.com/user-629453123/posthuman-collective-research-group-at-the-ou.

Vackova, P., Puntil, D., Dowdeswell, E., Cooke, C. and Caton, L. (2023). Collaborative writing as bio-digital quilting: A relational, feminist practice towards 'Academia Otherwise'. *Social Inclusion*, 11(3), 65–76. https://www.cogitatiopress.com/socialinclusion/article/view/6616/3293.

Vackova, P., Cooke, C., Dowdeswell, E., Puntil, D. and Caton, L. (2024). *Care in Academia*. https://issuu.com/posthuman_collective/docs/phc_care_zine_final

Wardle, D., van Loon, J., Taylor, J. S., Rendle-Short, F., Murray, P. and Carlin, D. (Eds.) (2022). *A-Z of Creative Writing Methods*. London: Bloomsbury.

Yoo, J. (2017). Writing out on a limb: Integrating the creative and academic writing identity. *New Writing*, 14(3), 444–54. https://doi.org/10.1080/14790726.2017.1317274.

13

Power Inequalities and Quality of Supervised Evidence Syntheses: Ethical Use of Reflexive Practices

by *Sin-Wang Chong, Qi Liu, Natalie Tegama and Grace Anna Baby*

Introduction

This chapter reports and discusses two in-depth case studies of conducting evidence synthesis in postgraduate supervision in the UK. Evidence synthesis is a type of literature review that employs a transparent, systematic, reproducible and often pre-registered methodology to identifying, screening, extracting and synthesising information from published research (Chong et al., 2022). Evidence synthesis is regarded as a rigorous form of research because of the systematicity and replicability of its methodology. At the heart of a rigorous evidence synthesis is the collaborative effort by a team of researchers in every stage of the process, including developing research questions, designing a search strategy (e.g. keywords or search strings, databases), appraising the suitability and quality of publications by piloting and developing inclusion and/or exclusion criteria, piloting and designing a data extraction form and synthesising the extracted data.

To appraise the quality of evidence (BERA, 2024, paragraph 68),[1] it is commonly accepted that high-quality evidence syntheses embrace the notion of *reliability*, especially in the stages of data extraction and data synthesis, where inter-coder reliability is calculated as an indicator of objectivity. However, in this chapter, we argue that *reliability* may not be the most suitable to gauge the quality of evidence syntheses conducted in the context of postgraduate research supervision, from an ethical perspective, due to the unequal professional status between the supervisors and the supervised (Pizzolato et al., 2024). The decision to focus on research supervision is encouraged by the inclusion of 'students following research-based programmes of study' as part of the 'community of educational researchers' in the latest BERA Ethical Guidelines (BERA, 2024, paragraph 58[2]; also see Chapters 12 and 16 on discussions on how to work ethically with early career researchers). Evidence syntheses are increasingly preferred in postgraduate supervision due to easy access to online publications for master's students and their usefulness in identifying research opportunities for doctoral students.

In this chapter, we consider an alternative notion called *reflexivity* and illustrate how it can serve as a useful lens to tackle power imbalance between supervisors and supervisees in evidence syntheses. The first case study is between a supervisor and a supervisee in a Master of Science in Teaching English to Speakers of Other Languages (TESOL) programme at a university in Northern Ireland, where the supervisee completed a qualitative synthesis of research as her dissertation (Liu and Chong, 2023). The second case study is between a postgraduate medical student on an intercalated Master of Public Health programme at a university in England and a postdoctoral researcher at the same university, working on a large global health cancer research programme led by the student's supervisor. The postdoctoral researcher worked on various aspects of the systematic review (a type of evidence synthesis), together with the student, including reviewing work and offering guidance at different stages of the review. As the student's research project would serve as a pilot for a larger-scale systematic review for publication that would be led by the postdoctoral researcher, the postdoctoral researcher played a supervisory role in her collaboration with the student.

In each case study, we share background information related to the supervision contexts, the ethical issues that we experienced, how we responded to the ethical issues, and alternative courses of action and their implications related to the quality of evidence synthesis and supervision experience. The two case studies are connected and complementary to each other in that the supervisors and supervisees faced challenges related to the traditional notion of inter-coder reliability in the review process. Inter-coder reliability is commonly used in certain stages of evidence synthesis, where more than one researcher is involved, such as for screening, extracting and synthesising data. Inter-coder reliability is 'a numerical measure of the agreement between different coders regarding how the same data should be coded' (O'Connor and Joffe, 2020: 2). There are numerous ways to calculate inter-coder reliability; for example, calculating the number of agreement scores divided by the total number of scores and presenting it as a percentage. Some criticised that per cent agreement is inadequate because it does not take chance agreement into consideration and thus advocated for using correlation statistics like kappa (McHugh, 2012).

The implemented and suggested actions in this chapter exemplify how *reflexivity*, which is defined as 'the process of a continual internal dialogue and critical self-evaluation of researcher's positionality as well as active acknowledgement and explicit recognition that this position may affect the research process and outcome' (Berger, 2015: 220), can be operationalised to address the ethical concern of power imbalance when it comes to supervising students to conduct evidence synthesis at postgraduate levels. Drawing on insights from the two case studies, we discuss the roles of supervisors and supervisees in an evidence synthesis project as well as resources and support that can be provided to both supervisors and supervisees to foster reflexive and ethical evidence synthesis practice.

Case Study One

Background

The first case study focuses on the supervision experience between Sin-Wang and Qi at Queen's University of Belfast in 2021. At that time, Sin-Wang was a lecturer, and Qi was a master's student in the TESOL programme at the School of Social Science, Education and Social Work. In the UK, master's students are usually given four to five months to complete their dissertation, a kind of capstone project. Master's students at the school completed a dissertation proposal form that details initial ideas of their research project. Students were then paired with supervisors who had the relevant expertise by the school. At the time when Sin-Wang and Qi were at the university, there was no specific requirement regarding the number of meetings to be had, but it was Sin-Wang's practice to hold fortnightly meetings with his students. These meetings were a combination of online discussions on Microsoft Teams and in-person meetings because it was during Covid.

Following an initial meeting between Sin-Wang and Qi, Qi expressed her interest in conducting an evidence synthesis. Qi was interested in synthesising the relevant literature qualitatively because it made the scope of the search more manageable, and she was more familiar with qualitative data analysis methods such as thematic analysis. It was agreed that Qi would conduct a qualitative synthesis of research, which refers to the use of qualitative data analysis to synthesise qualitative and quantitative findings in published research (Chong, Bond and Chalmers, 2023). The topic of the qualitative synthesis of research is bilingual education in China. Qi was interested in this topic because it is relevant to her educational context and her experience as an English teacher in China. Since evidence synthesis methodology was not included in the methodology module of the master's programme, Sin-Wang decided to introduce additional methodological texts and resources to guide Qi through the process of conducting a high-quality review. These resources included a methodological framework for conducting evidence syntheses in TESOL (Chong and Plonsky, 2021) as well as other published evidence syntheses in the area of TESOL as exemplars for the student. Qi completed her dissertation and was awarded a distinction. She was encouraged to turn her dissertation into a journal article, which was published in an SSCI-indexed journal, *Applied Linguistics Review* (Liu and Chong, 2023).

The ethical dilemma – case study one

Despite the enthusiasm of Qi to embark on an evidence synthesis project for her master's dissertation and Sin-Wang's commitment and expertise to support her in the process, several ethical issues need to be acknowledged. From a supervisor's perspective, Sin-Wang faced the questions about the extent to which he could be involved in the research process and how rigour could be demonstrated in an evidence synthesis conducted as part of a master's degree (BERA, 2024, paragraph 68).[3] Evidence syntheses are usually conducted by a team of researchers who share different expertise, which may include both substantive and methodological specialists, and at times, non-academic members such as librarians, who advise on search strategy. Obviously, within the context of a master's dissertation, it is impossible for the student to collaborate with other researchers to complete her dissertation because it is an important assessment component of her degree. As her supervisor, it is Sin-Wang's responsibility to provide relevant advice and feedback, but he is unsure where the line is drawn, as it is his first time supervising an evidence synthesis project in a master's programme although he has conducted and published numerous evidence syntheses. For instance, given the methodological expectation and tradition to have literature screened, extracted, and synthesised by more than one researcher in evidence syntheses, is it acceptable, in a supervision context, for Sin-Wang to be the other researcher who contributes to these stages? If this is acceptable, there is a further question related to whether the support is ethical and fair to other students because it may result in an impression that the supervisor provides substantial aid to a student's research project, which may be deemed inappropriate when the research project is assessed as part of a taught programme. If a supervisor's participation in co-screening, co-extraction and co-synthesis is not allowed, how can the methodological rigour of this evidence synthesis be demonstrated, for example, through inter-coder reliability?

In the process of supervision, the concern of demonstrating methodological rigour in the evidence synthesis became more eminent (BERA, 2024, paragraph 68).[4] Sin-Wang had decided that he should not provide direct assistance to Qi in the synthesis process, as it would be perceived as inappropriate in a postgraduate supervision context. Sin-Wang made clear to Qi that he would not be able to serve as a second reviewer. Sin-Wang proposed that when Qi worked on the three stages where an additional researcher is required, namely screening, data extraction and data synthesis, she did a pilot on a small sample of the included literature. For example, during screening, instead of screening all the search results on her own, Qi was advised to screen 10 per cent of the search results against the inclusion criteria she developed and discussed her decisions with Sin-Wang in the next supervision meeting. Similarly, in the data extraction and synthesis stages, Qi would chart the information from 10 per cent of the included literature and thematically code the extracted information, which would then be discussed with Sin-Wang in their upcoming meeting. Although Qi was appreciative of the fact that she received timely feedback from her supervisor at every stage, it became apparent to Sin-Wang that there was an issue of power imbalance between them, which rendered the voice and opinions of Qi ignored or discarded. When Sin-Wang reviewed the piloted work that Qi completed and offered a different view, Qi would almost always be convinced to adopt Sin-Wang's view. For example, Sin-Wang suggested excluding a study that Qi originally decided to include due to their different interpretations of an inclusion criterion. Instead of making a case for her inclusion and defending her decision, Qi agreed with Sin-Wang's decision because Sin-Wang was perceived as the more knowledgeable other. To Sin-Wang, this was not ideal because he wanted to develop Qi's critical thinking skills, and there were in fact times when Sin-Wang's opinion was erroneous as he was not as close to the literature as Qi. However, due to the hierarchical relationship between Sin-Wang and Qi and the fact that Sin-Wang was the first marker of the dissertation, Qi found it important to respect and agree with Sin-Wang's opinions.

From a student's point of view, Qi also experienced numerous ethical dilemmas, mostly because she was placed in a vulnerable position (BERA, 2024, paragraph 58).[5] First, as evidence synthesis was not covered as part of the research methodology module in the master's programme, she did not have any experience in and knowledge about how to conduct one. It was Qi's expectation to receive some methodological input and support from her supervisor. At the same time, through interacting with her peers and reading the dissertation handbook, Qi understood that the role of her supervisor was to advise and provide feedback on her work, instead of giving her lecture-style input on a methodology unfamiliar to her. Having had a few meetings with Sin-Wang and reading up on evidence synthesis methodology, Qi realised that she needed help from another researcher in certain stages of the project. This posed a great challenge to her as she was unsure whom she could approach. She was hesitant to ask one of her classmates in the TESOL programme for help because she knew that all students were busy completing their own dissertations. Moreover, at the time when the dissertation started, many of the international students had returned to their home countries. It made it even more challenging to seek help from peers. Qi wondered if she could ask Sin-Wang for help or recommend a researcher to assist her. Nevertheless, after conversing with Sin-Wang, the former was perceived as inappropriate in the supervision context because the dissertation is an assessed piece of work, and it would be too time-consuming and complicated to invite another researcher.

Courses of action

A researcher logbook was developed to record the actions taken in different stages, issues to be solved and reflections. The researcher logbook idea evolved from Qi's habit of taking notes. In general, Qi's initial notes, which were written in both her first language (Chinese) and English, included three elements: (a) tasks to be done before next meeting; (b) actions that Qi has done and newly obtained knowledge (e.g. methodology) about her research; (c) questions to be answered by Sin-Wang. Specifically, in every supervision meeting, Qi took notes in her notebook about the tasks that she needed to finish before the next meeting. The notebook helped Qi to ensure that all previously discussed work had been done. At the same time, Qi understood that the supervisor plays the role of giving feedback and advice, and the supervisee should be the person to make decisions, so Qi read a few articles recommended by Sin-Wang. To check her own understanding of the new knowledge, Qi wrote a few keywords about her comprehension and discussed them with Sin-Wang in the supervision meetings. Also, Qi recorded her actions in her notebook, which were usually written together with reasons. For example, when screening articles, Qi wrote down the reasons to exclude articles (see Figure 13.1).

Moreover, Qi understood the supervisor's workload, so instead of asking Sin-Wang questions whenever she was confused, she preferred to put all the questions down in her notebook in advance of each meeting and provided her own answers, to be compared with those by Sin-Wang (see Figure 13.2).

Making notes in a notebook enabled Qi to keep a record of the actions that she had taken and ensured that all the actions were based on the discussions with her supervisor. Sin-Wang was impressed by Qi's initiative to document her research process and suggested she organise the original notes using a more systematic electronic researcher logbook (see Figure 13.3). This first version of Qi's researcher logbook was dominated by objective descriptions and only a small proportion of the supervisee's reflections were mentioned. Although the researcher logbook can provide a more systematic and accessible record of the research process compared with the notes Qi initially took, it did not cover all communication details (e.g. disagreements). For example, the following quote shows that Qi presented the search results to Sin-Wang, and, after discussing with Sin-Wang, Qi needed to conduct the search again. However, the disagreement in the discussion was not mentioned and the process of reaching agreement was also omitted. Thus,

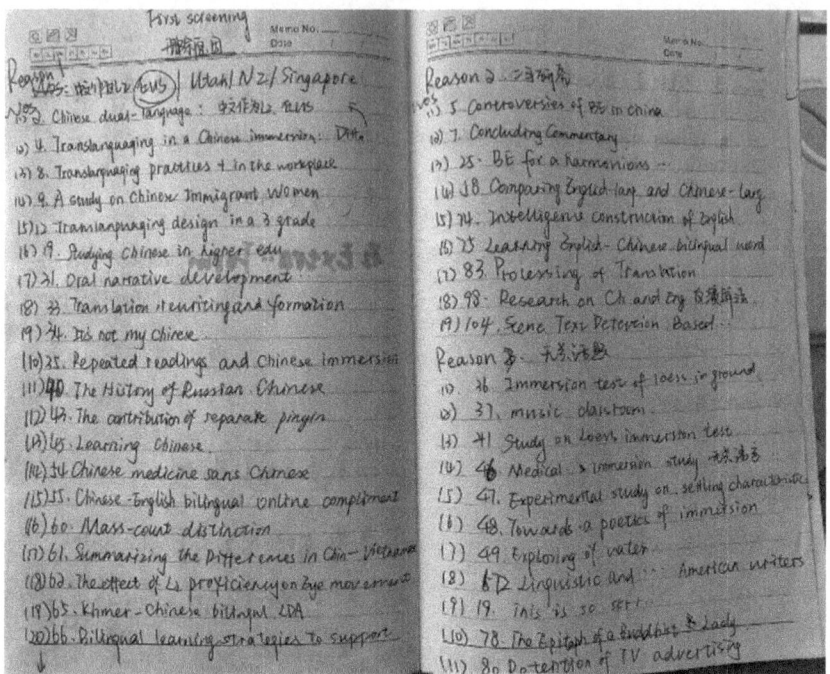

Figure 13.1 Excluded articles with reasons.

Source: Author.

Qi and Sin-Wang realised that the researcher logbook can be further revised by adding a reflection section.

> The first meeting on data extraction and literature search was on March 25th 2022. I (Qi) raised a list of questions in the photo below and we discussed them together. The photo below shows not only the questions but also the solutions to fix them. Sin-Wang viewed the search results and had a discussion about the results and the inclusion criteria with me. The result was to conduct the search again and to design an extraction form based on the three research questions.

When thinking about how to further improve the researcher logbook design, Qi and Sin-Wang discussed extensively on the limitations of inter-coder reliability. Inter-coder reliability emphasises more on the rate of agreement that the supervisor and supervisee reach. However, the reasons that the supervisor and supervisee reach agreements can vary (e.g. power imbalance between them). Thus, Qi and Sin-Wang agreed that reflexivity

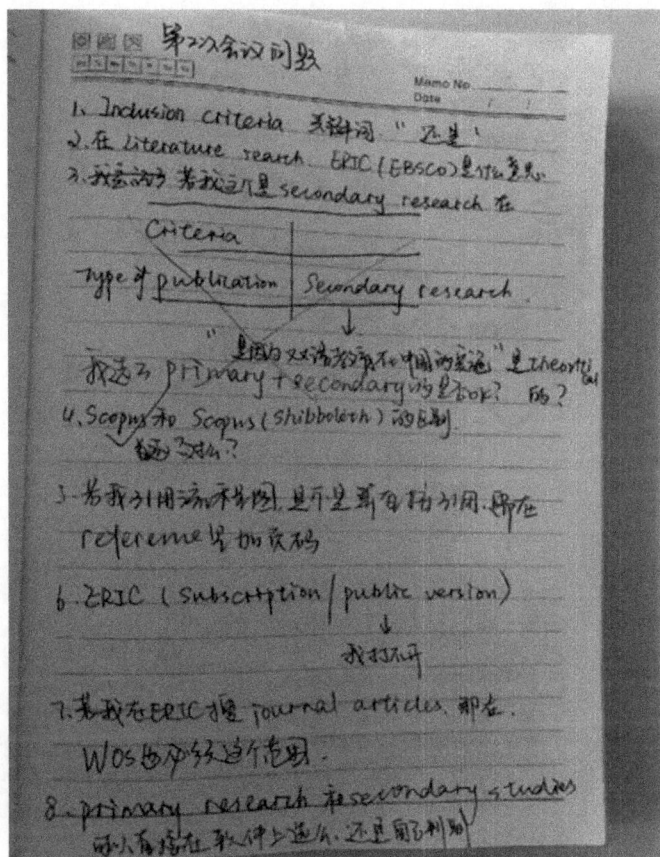

Figure 13.2 Questions for the next supervision meeting.

Source: Author.

needs to be taken into consideration to focus more on not only the outcome of discussion (i.e. agreement vs. disagreement) but also the process through which agreements are reached (e.g. interpretating data from different perspectives). The revised researcher logbook was developed and applied when Qi was involved with another evidence synthesis project led by Sin-Wang . It mainly includes two parts: (a) the first part is to record discussions among researchers and actions that need to be done; (b) the second part is to record researchers' reflections (see Figure 13.4). The former provides a summary of the meeting and follow-up actions. The latter involves the process of reaching agreements, expressing feelings and summarising experience and miscellaneous thoughts (BERA, 2024, paragraph 59).

The literature search started on March 20th 2022 and I asked two questions on Teams about the literature search. Additionally, I had an overall understanding of the methodology, which incorporates seven steps (e.g. searching, extraction) (see the picture below).

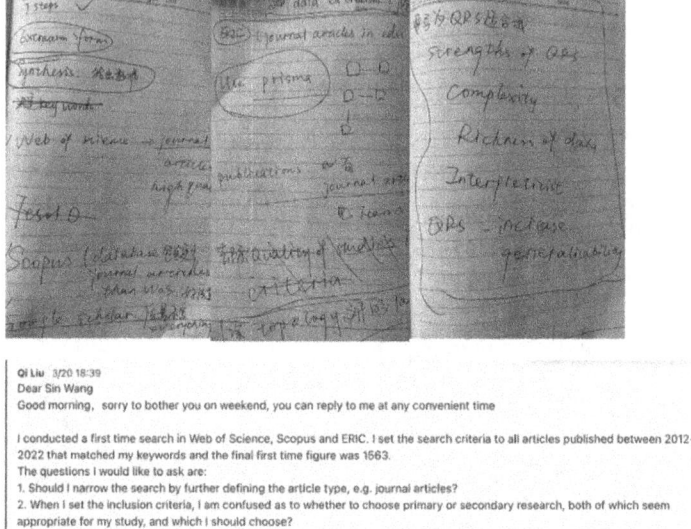

Figure 13.3 Initial researcher logbook.

Source: Author.

Alternative courses of action

As mentioned earlier, reflexivity is a process whereby researchers critically reflect on their own experience, backgrounds, viewpoints, strengths and weaknesses in the research process, and acknowledge how these personal traits influence the analysis and interpretation of data. If reflexivity is a process, there needs to be mechanisms in place to document such a reflective and self-appraisal process as well as to encourage such processess. While the researcher logbook idea in the previous section provides a means for postgraduate students to document their thinking process, dialogues and discussion outcomes, another way to promote reflexivity in the evidence

Agenda item	Action points/minutes
Reflection	

Figure 13.4 The revised researcher logbook.
Source: Author.

synthesis process is to establish a system, at a policy level, that encourages postgraduate students, peers and supervisors to collaborate with each other in the evidence synthesis process, drawing on each other's experience and expertise while making sure that both voices of the supervisors and supervisees are equally heard and acknowledged. This alternative course of action is based on the current practice at the International Education and Lifelong Learning Institute at the University of St Andrews, where Sin-Wang works. In his capacity as Director of Research and Director of Impact and Innovation, Sin-Wang promotes supervisor-supervisee/student-student partnership when it comes to conducting evidence syntheses. While policy is in place for both master's and doctoral students to engage in reflexive and ethical evidence synthesis practice, this section focuses only on that for doctoral students.

A guideline document, entitled *Frequently Asked Questions on Conducting Research Syntheses for PGR Students at the International Education and Lifelong Learning Institute* for doctoral students, was created by Sin-Wang. This school-level policy was circulated to all doctoral students, and an online event was held by Sin-Wang for supervisors and students to develop a better understanding of the document and ask questions. The impetus for creating this document is the growing number of doctoral students at the institute who are interested in conducting evidence syntheses, and there is a lack of publications on evidence synthesis methodologies for postgraduate supervision. The document is written in a question-answer format based on inquiries from doctoral students and their supervisors, providing straightforward and accessible answers. The questions include:

> What is a research synthesis?
> What types of research synthesis are suitable for my research portfolio?
> Why would I want to conduct a research synthesis?
> Why would I NOT want to conduct a research synthesis?
> How to conduct a research synthesis?
> What are the roles of students, peers and supervisors in a research synthesis?
> Where can I locate some examples of research syntheses?

Of relevance to the focus of this chapter on promoting reflexive and ethical evidence synthesis practice is the question: *What are the roles of students, peers, and supervisors in a research synthesis?* This question prompts students to consider the need to collaborate with other researchers in various stages of conducting an evidence synthesis. As part of the reflexive research process, students are reminded that it is crucial to make clear their role and responsibilities as it is a piece of research that will be assessed for the award of a degree:

> You should be the main researcher in the project and the first author of any publication that stems from the research synthesis. This means that you should be involved in all stages of the research synthesis, from conceptualisation, writing up of the protocol, conducting screening, extraction, and synthesis, to writing up of the results.

It is clearly set out in the guidelines that doctoral students are encouraged to work with their supervisors and/or peers when conducting an evidence synthesis because this enables students to draw on and collectively reflect on diverse research and professional experiences from peers and supervisors when conducting evidence syntheses. Apart from sending a clear message to the students about the institute's support to cultivate a collaborative research culture that promotes reflexivity in research, the guideline remarks issues that students need to consider, such as how authorship order is determined and how support can be acknowledged in publications (BERA, 2024, paragraph 76–77).[6] Doctoral students are also asked to make use of the Contributor Roles Taxonomy (CRediT) to document specific contributions made by the research team. These issues are especially relevant to the 'by-publication' nature of the doctoral programme offered at the institute, where students develop a research portfolio of published research in lieu of a thesis:

You can invite a fellow student and your supervisor to be a co-researcher ... Since the research synthesis will be published, authorship needs to be discussed and agreed prior to undertaking any work. The student who leads the research synthesis should be the first author and the co-researchers should be second or third author depending on the amount of work that they are involved in. Normally, a supervisor will be the last author if they are only involved in giving comments and revising the manuscript. Co-researchers reserve the right to indicate that they do not want to be listed as a co-author. Regardless, an acknowledgement section should be added in the manuscript (usually before the references section) to document the support that the student received from their peer or supervisor.

The production of the guideline is an important step to striking a balance between fairness in assessment in a postgraduate degree and fostering a collaborative research culture among doctoral students that supports reflexive and ethical research practice. It is explicitly stated in the guideline that doctoral students are encouraged to seek help from their supervisors and peers to ensure methodological rigour of their evidence syntheses. At the same time, there are clear recommendations in the document to ensure students are the main contributors of publications submitted for degree-awarding assessment. Furthermore, to address the ethical dilemmas stated earlier regarding power imbalance between supervisors and supervisees, and supervisees being in a vulnerable position due to lack of support, the guideline makes explicit that doctoral students at the institute can not only work collaboratively with their supervisors but also their peers, and students are empowered to approach collaborators based on their needs. Moreover, a dialogic approach is encouraged in the guideline document to facilitate reflexive and ethical evidence synthesis practice; for example, co-researchers are encouraged to set up a Teams channel to facilitate discussions on various issues related to conducting an evidence synthesis, combining the researcher logbook idea mentioned in the section before.

Case Study One – concluding section

This case study documents the shift from reliability-centric to reflexive methodological practice as a means to overcome ethical challenges associated with conducting evidence synthesis as a supervised form of research. The impetus for this alternative view lies in the constraints presented in postgraduate supervision in the UK, where the supervisor is not able to provide direct support to students when it comes to completing the dissertation. In the UK and elsewhere, postgraduate students are expected to work on their own to complete their research, which proves to be quite challenging, especially when they opt to conduct an evidence synthesis. An evidence synthesis is a complex and labour-intensive piece of research that usually requires the collaborative effort of a team of researchers with different expertise, including subject experts, methodologists, librarians and practitioners. Nevertheless, in postgraduate supervision, this is impossible. Another challenge presented was the power imbalance between the supervisor and the supervisee. Both authors of the first case study reflected that there were moments when decisions were dominated by the supervisor, who was perceived as more knowledgeable and experienced; even when the supervisee was encouraged to share her own thoughts, she did not feel empowered to do so. Such a power imbalance compromised the 'inter-coder reliability' in the synthesis process. Even though the reliability was high, it was likely due to the student showing agreement with what the supervisor said while suppressing her view. Despite the differences in policies and practices of postgraduate supervision, supervisors and supervisees in other countries are expected to face such an ethical challenge; in fact, the issue of power inequality is likely to be more serious given the authoritative role of teachers in some countries in the Global South.

The notion of *reflexivity* was introduced, not to replace but as an addition to *reliability* in supervised evidence synthesis. Reflexivity originates from qualitative research that recognises the positionality, experiences, backgrounds, expertise and views of researchers as a strength and integral part of research. In evidence syntheses, especially those conducted using qualitative methods, it is a limitation that only reliability measures are considered when it comes to minimising biases and upholding objectivity. The use of reliability measures only provides information about the tip of the iceberg, that is, the outcome that two researchers strongly (dis)agree with each other when it comes to searching, extracting, and synthesising, but it offers no representation of the process through which such (dis)agreement is reached. Ultimately, in addition to the ethical conundrum of power disparity between supervisors and supervisees, it is unethical to use incompatible tools or concepts (i.e. those with a quantitative and positivist influence) to appraise the quality of studies that are from another research paradigm (i.e. the qualitative, interpretivist paradigm).

In practical terms, we shared two examples of how reflexivity can be captured when conducting supervised evidence syntheses. The process of developing a researcher logbook that documents not only outcomes and action points of supervision meetings but also paragraphs of reflections on how outcomes or decisions were reached was introduced. As an alternative course of action, we suggested that much can be done at a departmental or school level where there are explicit and centralised guidelines that encourage collaboration among postgraduate students and between supervisors and supervisees.

Case Study Two

Background

The second case study focuses on the co-working and supervisory experience between Natalie and Grace at Queen Mary University of London in 2023. At that time, Grace was an intercalated fourth-year medical student undertaking a Master's in Public Health and conducting a dissertation focusing on global health cancer research. Natalie was a postdoctoral researcher in global health cancer research, working on a large, National Institute for Health and Care Research (NIHR)-funded global health cancer research programme (BERA, 2024, paragraph 58).[7] One of the project co-PIs served as Natalie's line manager and Grace's supervisor. Similar to the case described by Sin-Wang and Qi, Grace's Master's programme required her to complete a dissertation over a period of four months. Grace was paired with a supervisor based on her interest in global health, cancer research and digital health. Whilst Natalie worked in no official supervisory capacity, rather both were expected to work together, Natalie, in part ensuring that Grace's work would be up to par for use as preliminary work to contribute to the larger systematic review, offered guidance and acted as the first point of contact for queries in case anything arose in between the two-week supervisory meetings, of which Natalie attended most of as these were largely subsumed into the research team meetings at Queen Mary University of London. Over the course of the research period, Grace and Natalie met for weekly discussions in person and online on Microsoft Teams; it is worth noting that meetings per week between the two increased after screening, initially to discuss disagreements between the two and then to cross-reference and check for agreement after full extraction. Grace was introduced to the global health cancer project team as a student with interests in conducting research in digital health along the cancer pathway in Sub-Saharan Africa. The potential of Grace's work was introduced in terms of its relevance to the larger project, with relevance to the projected outputs and the deliverables of systematic reviews in line with commitments made to donors. The initial goal was therefore to consider whether Grace's and the team's interests could be synthesised, adding a collaborative element at an early stage of Grace's work that is still largely unusual within the context of a Master's project but one that raises important questions in terms of ways of working and ways of collaborative thinking within a higher education context where research and donor funding are now prevalent in the academy, especially within the sphere of emergent research where there exists evidence gaps. These can be exciting spheres where innovative methods abound and their abundance is commensurate with the research gaps, the kind of gaps that budding researchers may be interested in engaging in the context of their studies, much like within the scope of digital health for the cancer pathway in sub-Saharan Africa. Having worked within this specific context, Natalie and Grace argue for the place of reflexivity in evidence synthesis. Due to challenges with conducting evidence synthesis in emergent fields, including the limited scope of available data and literature, it was impossible to employ quantitative synthetic methods such as meta-analyses; instead, it required a reliance on narrative synthesis.

The ethical dilemma – case study two

For both Grace and Natalie, the primary ethical concerns were similar to sentiments discussed in the first case study. From Natalie's perspective, tension was evident between commitment to support a student in conducting rigorous research and gaining training and experience in conducting a systematic review as part of a team and balancing this with the fact that the project was an assessed piece of work within a master's programme where a student was required to demonstrate aptitude to undertake research independently. Whilst there is the question of how much support is too much support for a systematic review based on published guidelines, there is the challenge of meeting the rigour requirement of evidence syntheses with the master's student working mostly independently (BERA, 2024, paragraph 68).[8] Unlike the first case study, where tools were developed proactively to meet the standard, it was difficult for Grace to adequately engage reflexively over the course of her research project, in part because it was a first for both Natalie and Grace. We were therefore not anticipatory in our approach, in part because there remains limited literature and guidance within the university on guiding postgraduate research students through systematic reviews. We therefore write this chapter to add to the literature that may help supervisors and supervisees adopt a more anticipatory approach. Our approach is therefore to, in the first instance, outline our course of action we undertook and, in the second instance, to outline alternative courses of action based on reflexive work, done largely retrospectively to consider how we could have reshaped the process to better meet the challenges in rigour, reliability and fairness that we encountered.

From Grace's perspective, working closely with Natalie was invaluable in refining the research question and defining the scope of the evidence synthesis using PICO (Population, Intervention, Comparison and Outcome). Following initially defining the PICO and search string, Grace and Natalie met with an information specialist to further develop the search string and receive guidance on ensuring they covered different synonyms to ensure they did not miss some literature within the search. Guidance from the information specialist included guidance on database searches, especially discussing databases that researchers were unfamiliar with. Natalie, being more familiar with the literature, was able to recognise the papers that Grace's search string should have been able to capture. Grace then piloted the search string across all relevant databases to ensure that the search string was fit for purpose. Grace encountered multiple challenges in piloting, including not having access to certain databases. The information specialist was able to assist in navigating Grace towards ways of gaining access. Throughout this, Grace had Natalie as a regular point of contact, where she was able to leverage Natalie's research expertise and ongoing experience of a similar systematic review to Grace's. Whilst the readiness with which Grace could contact Natalie brought a sense of comfort to her, it also created an ethical dilemma of the appropriateness of receiving what she felt like a high level of assistance for a master's dissertation that other students may not have received. Grace therefore recognised the importance of transparency within her work; she was therefore in her writing transparent about having another researcher working alongside her during conception, screening and later extraction, and the university accepted this. However, Grace felt that she was unable to seek help from within her peer group because systematic reviews largely remain an uncommon choice among students due to time constraints and a lack of transparency about how one would conduct a review within the scope of a master's dissertation. Thus, in terms of reviews, Grace found that where her peers had opted for conducting an evidence synthesis, they had largely opted for traditional literature reviews. However, evidence synthesis methodologies had been taught in the master's programme, and she could therefore receive support from lecturers if she had any doubts.

Courses of action

The initial stage of developing research questions and designing a search strategy highlighted the inherent tension between the rigour demanded by an evidence synthesis and the limitations imposed by working without a larger team (BERA, 2024, paragraph 68).[9] Unlike traditional team-based approaches where diverse perspectives inform search strategies, Grace grappled with ensuring comprehensiveness and precision in developing search terms and presenting them to the larger research team which consisted of two professors and Natalie, one of the former being her supervisor. In presenting her search strategy, Grace was effectively able to gain peer review; however, she also grappled with the pressure of wanting to present good work, coming from a tradition of presenting finished work rather than engaging in progressive peer review. Peer review is a crucial aspect of ensuring the quality and credibility of research; in a team-based synthesis, peer review occurs naturally as team members review each other's work, provide feedback and engage in discussions to refine interpretations, largely without great power differentials. Whilst there were aspects of peer review within the scope of the systematic, these were limited. The notion of supervisory capacity placed limitations on the traditional engagement of peer reviewing, as there were clear power differentials both within the larger research group and where the supervisor and supervisee relationship was concerned. Further, it was not possible for Grace to benefit from a readily available research team, as in the case of systematic reviews conducted, and thus she faced the challenge of wanting to demonstrate independence across the different parts of the research, including in engaging the health science librarians throughout the process of creating and refining the search strategy.

Whilst Grace found working closely with Natalie helpful, she remained aware that approach limited the diverse perspectives derived from working in a team and potentially influenced her independent thinking as Natalie appeared more knowledgeable from Grace's perspective. Whilst Natalie was listed as a second reviewer, only 10 per cent of the abstracts were double screened, which was in part associated with the challenge to meet the deadline. Natalie's role as a second reviewer therefore enhanced Grace's efficiency, effectively splitting the screening in half. Screening was conducted using the Rayyan software to facilitate remote collaboration and streamline the screening process, with precautions like the 'blind' option to minimise bias. However, ensuring consistency and reliability within this stage was difficult without the checks and balances of a team-based approach, heightening the argument for reflexivity, as each decision carried weight in shaping the synthesis outcomes. In the data-extraction phase, Grace and Natalie cross-referenced their spreadsheets, ensuring extracted data was the same and that they had reached the same include/exclude decisions for full review and data extraction. Following extraction, Grace and Natalie conducted a quality assessment, which initially required looking for appropriate tools to assess risk of bias. Grace's supervisor was able to provide guidance on a risk of bias tool that may be appropriate for the papers they had included, which were largely Mixed Methods. After looking at several tools, the team arrived at the decision to use the Mixed Methods Appraisal Tool (MMAT) (Hong et al., 2018).

Alternative courses of action

In terms of the ethical dilemma pertaining to fairness, the primary concern was with the level of support that would be received by Grace as a master's student within the context of an assessed piece of work that would be a major component of her attaining a master's degree. The proposed alternative courses of action could focus on carving out space for independent, reflexive thinking and writing by adopting the use of a project log similar to the first case study; we advocate for the continuous use of a project log to review and reflect on contributions and engage in reflexive thinking. Furthermore, we advocate that at the end of a project, students use the project log alongside the contributor roles taxonomy (CRedIT, 2025) to map contributions made by various actors including information specialists and supervisors (BERA, 2024, paragraph 76–77).[10]

The contributor taxonomy is a high-level taxonomy that describes the fourteen roles that are typically played by contributors in research outputs. It is typically used to assign authorship in a large research team. Using the contributor roles taxonomy as guidance would allow postgraduate students to systematically reflect on their contributions and decision making. It would allow them to discuss how interactions with other researcher influenced or shaped their thinking, including discussions on positionality and decision making. The use of a contributor taxonomy is good practice for researchers because it gives postgraduate students the opportunity to understand collaborative work and the crediting processes. Project logs could also be used within the context of the university as an auditing tool in assessments for postgraduate students who engage in evidence synthesis projects within the context of research teams (BERA, 2024, paragraph 59).[11] This would benefit both students and research teams, by facilitating real-life research experience for students whilst providing research teams with greater scope for collaborative work with students, including in emergent and interdisciplinary fields, where these types of evidence synthesis could contribute to piloting work as in the context of the second case study with Natalie and Grace, where the student's work was used as a pilot for a larger systematic review for publication, allowing the student the opportunity to gain both experience and a publication.

Another alternative course of action we would have taken comes primarily from Grace's reflections, where she found difficulty in adeptly maintaining critical autonomy across various stages of the research. For example, while Grace created her own notes for the meetings with her main supervisor, Natalie was present at meetings and created official meeting notes, of which Grace would often be reliant on because Natalie's note-taking as an experienced researcher was more comprehensive. The use of logbooks for students, as discussed, can be structured and targeted towards being more reflexive throughout the research process, but also for teaching and instructing postgraduate students in note-taking within collaborative team meetings, a useful skill for working across an evidence synthesis team. We believe a systematic use of logbooks will foster a more robust and nuanced approach to evidence synthesis within the context of postgraduate supervision, where students (especially doctoral students) can emerge not merely as passive recipients of knowledge but as active agents capable of navigating the complexities of evidence synthesis with intellectual rigour and integrity.

Final thoughts

The two case studies in this chapter demonstrated the constraints of conducting evidence synthesis projects within the context of supervised research. While Sin-Wang and Qi focused on challenges within the context of one-to-one supervision, Natalie and Grace presented challenges that arose within the context of a larger research team with a focus on the relationship between the postgraduate student and a postdoctoral researcher who worked in a collaborative and supervisory capacity. Both illustrations recognised the traditional approach to evidence synthesis as a key ethical challenge. Typically, a research team is comprised of subject matter experts, methodologists, librarians and researchers who act as second reviewers and provide ongoing peer review. Both examples were marked by two ethical predicaments centred on the question of how much supervisory support is appropriate within the supervision context and how qualities of rigour could be met without multiple team members who would traditionally take part in secondary screening, extracting and analysing with the view to, for example, calculating agreement using inter-coder reliability. Sin-Wang and Qi adopted an anticipatory approach, developing the use of a researcher logbook to keep accurate records of decision making and developments within the project to add a reflexive component to research that could be complementary to the quality of reliability, especially in the context of qualitative methods. This would further a more transparent documenting of the research process. Dissimilarly, Natalie and Grace did not adopt an anticipatory approach or immediately add reflexivity to the process of conducting a systematic review. In part because the postgraduate researcher acting in both a collaborative and supervisory capacity for the student was also an early career researcher. Natalie and Grace, therefore, retrospectively reflected on possible alternative courses of action to meet the quality of demonstrating rigour and reliability, concluding that actions taken by Sin-Wang and Qi in developing a researcher logbook would be a welcome alternative course of action that would facilitate a reflexive approach. In addition to the logbook, Natalie and Grace advocate for the use of a contributor role taxonomy in developing a reflexive piece that maps out actions taken, decisions made by all actors involved in the process, which could then be used in assessing students, auditing to ensure independence and providing a fair way of marking a student based on their independent work and, where applicable, collaborative work. In practical terms, this chapter, which focuses on ethical dilemmas related to the methodology for conducting evidence syntheses in postgraduate supervision settings, exemplifies how reflexivity can be a panacea for redressing power inequalities between supervisors and supervisees, and providing guidelines for assessing students who conduct evidence synthesis within larger research teams. The issues and solutions discussed in the chapter are applicable to broader ethical discussions related to social justice and inclusion when it comes to research supervision of (international) postgraduate students, who need to be viewed as an integral part of the educational researcher community (BERA, 2024, paragraph 58).[12]

Reflective questions

1. How can reflexive practices and reliability measures (e.g. inter-coder reliability) be incorporated into evidence syntheses when conducted in postgraduate research settings?
2. What activities and practices can be used to encourage supervisees or junior researchers to share their views in the synthesis process?
3. What support can be provided to postgraduate students when conducting an evidence synthesis as (part of) their dissertation without compromising the rigour of the assessment?
4. At a departmental or school level, what can be done to encourage reflexive and ethical research practices when conducting evidence synthesis as part of a master's or doctoral degree?
5. How can social and cultural practices of international students be considered during postgraduate supervision?

Further reading

1. Chong, S. W., Lin, T. J. and Chen, Y. (2022). A methodological review of systematic literature reviews in higher education: Heterogeneity and homogeneity. *Educational Research Review*, 35, 100426. https://doi.org/10.1016/j.edurev.2021.100426.

This methodological review analyses systematic reviews published in higher education journals to develop a bottom-up methodological framework. It is accompanied with a checklist that shows the different methodological steps and how frequently reported those steps are in published reviews.

2. Page, M. J., McKenzie, J. E., Bossuyt, P. M., Boutron, I., Hoffmann, T. C. and Mulrow, C. D., Shamseer, L., Tetzlaff, J. M., Akl, E. A., Brennan, S. E., Chou, R., Glanville, J., Grimshaw, J. M., Hróbjartsson, A., Lalu, M. M., Li, T., Loder, E. W., Mayo-Wilson, E., McDonald, S., McGuinness, L. A., Stewart, L. A., Thomas, J., Tricco, A. C. Welch, V. A., Whiting, P. and Moher, D. (2021). The PRISMA 2020 statement: An updated guideline for reporting systematic reviews. *British Medical Journal*, 372, n71. https://doi.org/10.1136/bmj.n71.

The statement includes a checklist with items for each section of an evidence synthesis and a flow diagram that serves as a template to guide the search process of literature. This is one of the most widely used tools in conducting evidence synthesis in Education and beyond.

3. The Campbell Collaboration (2020). *Campbell Systematic Reviews: Policies and Guidelines.* https://doi.org/10.4073/cpg.2016.1.

The Campbell Collaboration is one of the leading organisations that champions the use of evidence syntheses to inform policies and practices in education and social development. This document outlines the steps for conducting an evidence synthesis and the information needed for each section of a synthesis.

4. Okorocha, E. (2007). *Supervising International Research Students.* Society for Research into Higher Education. https://srhe.ac.uk/wp-content/uploads/2022/07/S2Iss4-Supervising-International-Research-Students.pdf.

This concise guide provides concrete examples for supervisors to consider issues such as prejudice and discrimination in research supervision as well as practical advice for supporting international students in the supervision process, including language barriers and religious beliefs.

5. Wilson, A. B., McCallum, C. M. and Shupp, M. R. (2020). *Inclusive Supervision in Student Affairs: A Model for Professional Practice.* London: Routledge.

This book addresses the broader ethical issue of this chapter, which is, ethical and inclusive practices in student supervision. Although the book focuses on supervision conducted by student affairs professionals, the focus on social justice and vulnerability of students is equally applicable to academic supervision.

Notes

1. Paragraph 68, (BERA, 2024): Assessment of the quality of the evidence supporting any inferences is an especially important feature of any research, and should be open to scrutiny. Where sponsors initiate a request for scrutiny, and disclosure of aspects of the data may be injurious to participants or not previously agreed by them, researchers should with sponsors consider appointing a mutually acceptable third party to undertake such a scrutiny, who would also be bound by any existing non-disclosure agreements.
2. Paragraph 58, (BERA, 2024): The 'community of educational researchers' is considered to mean all those engaged in educational research – including, for example, students following research-based programmes of study, independent researchers and practitioners who undertake research, as well as staff who conduct educational research in their employment within organisations such as universities, schools, local and national government, charities and commercial bodies. Established educational researchers, and the community as a whole, have a responsibility to support the next generation of educational researchers, including independent and practitioner researchers. The Association is supportive of the Researcher Development Concordat in this respect.
3. See note 1.
4. See note 1.
5. See note 2.
6. Paragraph 76, (BERA, 2024): The authorship of publications normally comprises a list of everyone who has made a substantive and identifiable contribution to the research being reported. Examples of this include: contributing generative ideas, conceptual schema or analytic categories; writing first drafts or substantial portions of text; significant rewriting or editing; contributing significantly to relevant literature reviewing; and contributing substantially to data collection and analysis, and to judgments and interpretations made in relation to it. Where research has involved collaboration across different roles or professions – for example, between education researchers who are academics and those who are teachers or other practitioners – then anyone who has made a substantive contribution should be credited as a co-author. Less substantive contributions should be acknowledged; Paragraph 77, (BERA, 2024): Academic status or any other indicator of seniority does not determine first authorship. Rather, the order of authorship should reflect relative leadership and contributions made. Alternatively, co-authors may agree to a simple alphabetic listing of their names. Consensual agreement on authorship should be gained as early as

possible in the writing process. An increasing number of publishers now require author contribution statements.
7   See note 2.
8   See note 1.
9   See note 1.
10 See note 6.
11 Paragraph 59, (BERA, 2024): All educational researchers should aim to protect the integrity and reputation of educational research by ensuring that they conduct their research to the highest standards. Researchers should contribute to the community spirit of critical analysis and constructive criticism that generates improvement in practice and enhancement of knowledge.
12 see note 2.

References

BERA (2024). *Ethical Guidelines for Educational Research* (5th ed.). London: BERA. https://www.bera.ac.uk/publication/ethical-guidelines-for-educational-research-fifth-edition-2024

Berger, R. (2015). Now I see it, now I don't: Researcher's position and reflexivity in qualitative research. *Qualitative Research*, 15(2), 219–34. https://doi.org/10.1177/1468794112468475.

Chong, S. W. and Plonsky, L. (2021). A primer on qualitative research synthesis in TESOL. *TESOL Quarterly*, 55(3), 1024–34. https://doi.org/10.1002/tesq.3030.

Chong, S. W., Bond, M. and Chalmers, H. (2023). Opening the methodological black box of research synthesis in language education: Where are we now and where are we heading? *Applied Linguistics Review*, 15(4), 1557–68. https://doi.org/10.1515/applirev-2022-0193.

Chong, S. W., Lin, T. J. and Chen, Y. (2022). A methodological review of systematic literature reviews in higher education: Heterogeneity and homogeneity. *Educational Research Review*, 35, 100426. https://doi.org/10.1016/j.edurev.2021.100426.

CRedIT (2025). *Contributor Role Taxonomy*. Baltimore, MD: National Information Standards Organisation (NISO). https://credit.niso.org/

Hong, Q. N., Gonzalez-Reyes, A. and Pluye, P. (2018). Improving the usefulness of a tool for appraising the quality of qualitative, quantitative and mixed methods studies, the Mixed Methods Appraisal Tool (MMAT). *Journal of Evaluation in Clinical Practice*, 24(3), 459–67. https://doi.org/10.1111/jep.12884.

Liu, Q. and Chong, S. W. (2023). Bilingual education in China: A qualitative synthesis of research on models and perceptions. *Applied Linguistics Review*, 15(4), 1671–93. https://doi.org/10.1515/applirev-2022-0194.

McHugh, M. L. (2012). Interrater reliability: The kappa statistic. *Biochemia Medica*, 22(3), 276–82.

O'Connor, C. and Joffe, H. (2020). Intercoder reliability in qualitative research: Debates and practical guidelines. *International Journal of Qualitative Methods*, 19, 1–13. https://doi.org/10.1177/1609406919899220.

Pizzolato, D., Labib, K., Skoulikaris, N., Evans, N., Roje, R., Kavouras, P., Bonn, N. A., Dierickx, K. and Tijdink, J. (2024). How can research institutions support responsible supervision and leadership. *Accountability in Research: Ethics, Integrity and Policy*, 31(3), 173–95. https://doi.org/10.1080/08989621.2022.2112033.

14

The Ethics of Doctoral Researcher Care: Learning to Research in Fragile Contexts

by *Anna Xavier, Carly Hawkins and Sally Baker*

Introduction

Researching in fragile contexts is often complex and challenging, as they are characterised by situational vulnerability, trauma, sociopolitical precarity and marginalisation (Burke et al., 2023: 2), and where fragility can be characterised by 'power imbalances, distrust of authority and trauma' (Baker et al., 2023: 1). These complexities require careful and ongoing thinking about participant wellbeing to uphold the ethos of 'do no harm' in ethical research e.g. Australian Association of Research in Education (AARE, 1993); British Educational Research Association (BERA, 2024). However, while participant protection is paramount, this emphasis often undermines the researcher's obligation to care for self (Baker et al., 2023). The literature highlights the multiple risks researchers in fragile contexts encounter, including intense emotional labour, isolation, burnout and vicarious trauma (Astill, 2018; Ratnam, 2019; Butler-Rees and Robinson, 2020; Moran and Asquith, 2020; Baker et al., 2023). Care for self is therefore highlighted as fundamental when undertaking research in fragile contexts (Ratnam, 2019; Butler-Rees and Robinson, 2020; Baker et al., 2023). This aligns with BERA's *Ethical Guidelines for Educational Research*, which highlights the ethical responsibility of researchers in safeguarding their psychological wellbeing, as 'there should be an ethics of care for researchers, including self-care' (2024: 33).

However, researcher care often remains unaddressed in institutional ethics protocols (Baker et al., 2023) and is not a consistent feature of researcher training (Burke et al., 2024). While there is a growing body of literature on researcher self-care in fragile contexts, arguing for 'putting your own oxygen mask first' (Baker et al., 2023: 3), there has been limited attention paid to thinking about creating spaces and strategies to support doctoral students (and their supervisors) to develop ethical approaches to working around fragility and situational vulnerability (albeit see Ratnam, 2019; Butler-Rees and Robinson, 2020; Burke et al., 2024).

The doctoral journey, while exciting and rewarding, can be fraught with difficulties. It is somewhat a solitary endeavour, and doctoral students are often 'figuring things out' as they move along their research trajectory (Sverdlik et al., 2020; Golding, 2023). This includes navigating the nexus between being a student and an expert and undertaking fieldwork with little training (Schwartz and Cronin-Furman, 2023). Exploring fragile contexts, marked by heightened sensitivity, compounds the challenges researchers meet (Schwartz and Cronin-Furman, 2023; Burke et al., 2024). This terrain is fraught with potential volatility and participant retraumatisation, demanding increased emotional resilience from doctoral students. The pressure of higher degree research further exacerbates these stressors, fostering an environment where doctoral students grapple with uncertainty and self-doubt, often referred to as 'imposter syndrome' (Sverdlik et al., 2020; Wilkinson, 2020). As students progress through the doctoral journey, they are expected to evolve into experts in their field (Lantsoght, 2018). This transition, however, is filled with self-questioning and critical scrutiny.

In what follows, we offer as case studies two ethical dilemmas from Anna and Carly's experiences of undertaking doctoral research, with Sally offering commentary from a supervisor's perspective at the end of each case.

Case Study One: Anna's ethnographic fieldwork during Covid-19

This case study explores the challenges of the unidirectional notions of maleficence in procedural ethics and their impact on researcher self-care. My thesis focused on the role of education in integration for refugee-background students in regional Australia, and a significant part of my study was conducted during the Covid-19 global pandemic, which intensified the already fragile context in which refugee-background students live, adding layers of complexity to their experiences and my research. My doctoral journey, therefore, included many unanticipated challenges and uncertainties, which significantly impacted my mental and emotional wellbeing, especially during fieldwork in Rolling Hills, a regional town eight hours away from where I lived. Through my experience of undertaking ethnographic fieldwork in a fragile context during the ongoing COVID-19 pandemic, I explore my struggles in balancing my responsibilities as a researcher and ensuring my wellbeing, and the impact of an absence of self-care as a novice researcher.

Like many researchers operating within fragile contexts (Astill, 2018; Ratnam, 2019; Butler-Rees and Robinson, 2020; Baker et al., 2023), I entered the field wanting to make a difference to the refugee community I was researching, specifically in the educational experiences of the refugee-background students in this regional town. Receiving approval from the institutional ethics board led me to believe that I had sufficiently addressed the ethical and methodological concerns surrounding my research, including obtaining access to participants,[1] managing participant wellbeing, and ensuring reciprocity of research. However, upon entering the field, I faced challenges that significantly affected my emotional and mental state. Firstly, I encountered numerous unanticipated obstacles in gaining access to my potential participants. The state-wide lockdown due to the Covid-19 pandemic had restricted my travel to the field for almost a year, resulting in significant delays to my data collection. While the travel restrictions were finally lifted, I arrived during the height of the Omicron virus outbreak in the field, hindering my ability to engage with the community and establish rapport. Many individuals from the refugee community were Covid positive and remained in isolation, resulting in the temporary suspension of their community activities.

Additionally, despite two months of communication, the cultural broker[2] I had employed from the refugee community to assist me with participant recruitment quit due to personal matters. I was already in the field at this point and was relying on this person to introduce me to key gatekeepers. As I attempted to mitigate the constant 'closed doors' during my fieldwork, I felt disappointed, anxious and discouraged. These emotions reflect findings from previous studies that highlight the emotional reactions that researchers in fragile contexts are susceptible to (Astill, 2018; Moran and

Asquith, 2020; Baker et al., 2023). As I truly wanted to make a difference through my research, my high emotional investment compounded by the constant challenges I experienced eventually led to burnout, aligning with Baker et al.'s caution of such harm when there is 'high research investment' (2023: 4). Hence, while disappointment, anxiety and discouragement are possible emotional reactions in all fieldwork contexts, these reactions can often be exacerbated for researchers in fragile contexts due to the guilt of *letting down the participants* when things do not go according to plan.

Furthermore, the access-related challenges I experienced were exacerbated by the challenges of regionality. A significant yet unanticipated challenge that I encountered was isolation, as I was researching in a regional town for six months with a very limited social network. I did not anticipate the difficulties of entering a town with long-established close-knit communities, which hindered the development of new friendships. While people were friendly and welcoming, I struggled to develop a sense of belonging. This significantly impacted my mental wellbeing, especially on days when the fieldwork felt challenging, as I struggled to find someone that I could speak with to process my experiences and receive emotional support. Based on their experiences in the field, Irgil et al. (2021) highlight how fieldwork could impact negatively on a researcher's mental health and wellbeing as they leave their support networks and enter unfamiliar areas, often experiencing social isolation (Hummel and El Kurd, 2021; Irgil et al., 2021). Hummel and El Kurd (2021) therefore highlight the importance of a fieldwork support network, including local friends for a researcher's mental and emotional wellbeing during fieldwork. Additionally, I also experienced vicarious trauma through my interactions with individuals from refugee backgrounds during my fieldwork. As I volunteered with one of the local educational institutions to provide conversational English classes for adults from refugee backgrounds, I often had conversations that involved the disclosure of sensitive and painful information. One significant incident involved a woman sharing about how devastated she was that her husband had been kidnapped by the ISIS two years ago, and she does not even know if he is still alive. That conversation deeply affected me, and I struggled to respond to the woman.

Although these challenges and disappointments deeply impacted my emotional and mental wellbeing in the field, I struggled to pause and respond to my emotions as I was focused on ensuring the timely completion of my fieldwork. As Baker et al. (2023) and Ratnam (2019) reflect, while researchers in fragile contexts are often empathetic towards their research participants, they often struggle to offer that empathy to themselves and respond to their needs. Additionally, as the emotional challenges of conducting fieldwork in fragile contexts are not addressed in institutional ethics protocols, I perceived admitting my struggles and seeking support as a sign of my failure as a researcher. As Burke et al. highlight, doctoral students are often hesitant to admit the struggles they experience in the field, as these challenges are 'so rarely acknowledged in the wider community' (2023: 785). My inability and unwillingness to respond to my emotions (or depression) led me to almost quit the fieldwork, as I reached a point where I could no longer see a way forward.

Course of action: Addressing the burnout

Following the burnout I experienced, I eventually decided to inform my supervisors regarding my challenges during our monthly supervision meeting and explained that I was considering a three-month program leave. My supervisors emphasised that my mental and emotional health is paramount and advised me to leave the field immediately. I felt the burden of my responsibilities as a researcher, so I was determined to complete my fieldwork; nevertheless, I realised that I needed to take a proactive approach to the challenges I was experiencing. Hence, following their advice, I scheduled more regular mental health visits back to my city to manage my isolation, although I was worried that my research funds would not cover these additional trips. However, with a supportive letter from my supervisors, these visits were approved by the university research funding board because they were fundamental to improving my emotional and mental wellbeing. The visits played a critical role in supporting my mental and emotional wellbeing as I could connect with my friends and loved ones.[3]

I also gained the realisation that depending solely on my supervisors, one of whom is also a researcher working in the fragile context of forced migration, would be insufficient in managing my emotional and mental wellbeing (Baker et al., 2023). I therefore accessed professional counselling to support me with the vicarious trauma I was experiencing. Additionally, the counselling sessions also provided opportunities to debrief following the challenges that I was experiencing in the field, as I reviewed, reflected on and discussed my experiences while engaging in fieldwork. Debriefing is particularly important for researchers in fragile contexts, as they face various risks of harm relating to emotional labour, vicarious trauma, but where often a focus on participant protection masks the need to protect the researcher (Baker et al., 2023). These opportunities to debrief and gain advice on the challenges I was facing provided ongoing psychological support for me for the remaining duration of my fieldwork.

Alternative course of action: Pausing the fieldwork/altering research methods

For my ethnographic fieldwork, an alternative course of action would entail leaving the field and returning later to complete my study, once my mental and emotional wellbeing had improved. However, due to financial and time constraints in my doctoral candidature, this would not be a feasible option. Another alternative course of action involves conducting digital ethnography, which would allow me to connect with potential research participants and collect data online. However, I decided to retain the ethnographic component of being in the field, as I believe that it contributes significantly to gaining an understanding of the regional context for my study, as well as developing rapport with my potential research participants and the community.

As Garcia and Barclay argue in a study exploring the adaptation of research methodologies during the Covid-19 pandemic, while it provides some assistance in collecting data for ethnographic research, technology is not an 'adequate substitute' (2020: 31) for developing relationships and understanding the context of one's study. Similarly, Abdul Rahman et al. (2021) reflect on how the challenges of establishing rapport with the interviewees affected the quality of online interviews conducted for their research project. The significance of developing relationships and building rapport is particularly relevant in fragile contexts, as participants often struggle with developing trust towards researchers (Clark-Kazak, 2017). Being in the field for a duration of six months provided me with valuable opportunities to observe and experience the social and cultural norms in the field and develop relationships that significantly aided in the process of data collection. Hence, while digital fieldwork has demonstrated its validity in specific research contexts, it is not a 'one size fits all solution' (Paupini et al., 2022: 212). Fieldwork methodologies originally designed for in-person settings do not always seamlessly adapt to digital formats, often impacting data collection (Konken and Howlett, 2023), particularly in fragile contexts.

Therefore, I decided the best course of action was to undertake the research in the field.

Lessons learned: Importance of empathy and establishing support systems

Reflecting on my experiences in the field strongly suggests the importance of establishing avenues of support to debrief, as well as proactively developing strategies to manage isolation, which I experienced throughout the six months of my fieldwork in Rolling Hills.[4] As argued by Baker et al., it is essential for forced migration researchers to develop 'proactive psychological supports' (2023: 8) during their fieldwork, as challenging emotions are inevitable in this context. My mental health visits were critical in managing my emotional and mental wellbeing during my fieldwork, as I gained emotional support from close family and friends and felt less isolated.

I also learned that while my supervisors played a key role in offering opportunities for debriefing, accessing other forms of emotional support via professional counselling and communication with other colleagues was fundamental in regulating my emotions and successfully completing my data collection. As argued by Baker et al., a 'communal caring space' (2023: 8) is critical for researcher wellbeing in fragile contexts. In addition, a reflection of my experiences reiterates the importance of listening to my own needs as a researcher to mitigate the risk of burnout when researching in a challenging time and space. As Ratnam (2019) reflects, while researchers in forced migration are empathetic listeners to their research participants, they often struggle to be empathetic with themselves and respond to their own needs.

Additionally, my experience indicates a critical gap in the university's approach to preparing doctoral researchers for fieldwork in fragile contexts, particularly in researcher self-care and establishing avenues of support. In fragile contexts, researchers often face unique challenges that demand more than the traditional preparation for fieldwork. Yet, it appears that institutions often fall short in equipping researchers with the tools and strategies necessary for effective researcher self-care in such high-stress environments (Ratnam, 2019; Hummel and El Kurd, 2021). This gap underscores a broader issue regarding the responsibility of duty bearers – such as university administrators, research coordinators and ethics committees – to uphold a duty of care for doctoral researchers (Baker et al., 2023). A comprehensive analysis is needed to assess how these stakeholders can better support researchers in fragile contexts, thereby fostering a more resilient and prepared research community capable of thriving in complex and challenging environments.

Reflections from a supervisor

As Anna's primary supervisor and an experienced educational/forced migration researcher, I was fully aware of the challenges that Anna might face in her studies, especially given her ambition to do ethnographic fieldwork that necessitated a move to an unfamiliar area. However, several factors contributed to the pressure and emotional discomfort that Anna experienced. Firstly, navigating public health orders, such as lockdowns and travel restrictions, during the pandemic was tricky, meaning by the time Anna went to do fieldwork, she was effectively on 'plan E'. A perhaps predictable consequence of such uncertainty was heightened feelings of precarity, which left Anna open to ill health (physical and emotional) and left her vulnerable to self-doubt and less able to react positively to setbacks.

Secondly, ethical reflexivity is paramount to taking an ethics-in-practice approach (Guillemin and Gillam, 2004; Block et al., 2013) and this requires the researcher to know the field/context and themselves well. There is little in established research training that encourages the researcher to get to know themselves well enough to respond in situ and know their limits; this is not something that is assessed when a student applies for a doctorate. Likewise, there is little advice for supervisors on how to support students in crisis; it felt clichéd to tell Anna to speak to an expert and somewhat ineffectual advice when the limited availability of mental health experts is considered (Newton et al., 2021; LaMontagne et al., 2023). This also pushed responsibility and the cost for Anna's mental health onto her at a time of profound difficulty. There was no opportunity for professional debriefing, as would be the case for other professions (social worker, counsellor). The responsibility demonstrated by universities – as employers and as institutions that profit from doctoral students' timely completions[5] – is underwhelming (Litalien and Guay, 2020; Torka, 2020; Baker et al., 2023).

Ultimately, Anna was able to move through the inertia and depression that accompanied her burnout and complete her fieldwork. This is not a story of trial against adversity; it's true that Anna was resilient and has learnt a lot that will be useful for when she next enters the field. However, the broader point is that responsibility for researcher care is distributed between many stakeholders, including the individual, supervisors, graduate research staff, university senior executives, funding bodies (see Baker et al., 2023), and this needs to be better valued and resourced.[6] This is especially crucial in the forced migration contexts which are characterised by situational vulnerability, trauma, sociopolitical precarity and marginalisation (Burke et al., 2023: 2).

Case Study Two: Carly's experience of managing imposter syndrome and learning to trust in her expertise/decisions

This case study reflects on my doctoral journey and highlights the dual role I navigated: being both a novice researcher and an expert at the same time. My research focuses on the impact of immigration detention on asylum seeker and refugee children, and specifically their experience of education and schooling. I came to this research because of my personal experience working in immigration detention as a teacher. For three years, I worked alongside imprisoned children and watched the effect of detention on their wellbeing, motivation and day-to-day lives. There was very little research on this politically charged and highly sensitive topic, as the detention centres were almost impossible to gain access to. I found myself in a unique position; I had the contacts, the relationships, and the knowledge to conduct much-needed research on the impact of Australian refugee policy. Completing my research in this fragile context meant talking to participants with deep trauma and who still lived in precarious situations. I knew these people well, and many participants stated they agreed to be interviewed *because* they knew me. The relationship between participants and myself engendered trust and resulted in open and honest conversations (Hugman et al., 2011). I cared for my participants. They trusted me. I knew their stories. I had witnessed their experiences in detention. Yet I struggled to trust in my own decisions and expertise as I continued along the doctoral path.

Navigating the transition from novice to expert

As I traversed the unknown territory of my doctoral journey, one of the most significant ethical dilemmas was rooted in the transition from a novice researcher to an emerging expert. This transition was difficult, exacerbated by the dearth of clear guidance on how to navigate the evolving landscape of academia as a doctoral student (Siltanen et al., 2019; Wilkinson, 2020). Doctoral students, including myself, often find themselves thrust into the spotlight of dissemination long before they feel fully equipped to do so. Expected to share their research findings through conference presentations and publications, doctoral students face the daunting task of presenting themselves as experts while still in the nascent stages of comprehending their own data and methodologies (Petre and Petre, 2010). The tension between presenting oneself as an expert and experiencing feelings of inadequacy is a conundrum faced by doctoral students. Despite dedicating significant time and effort to their research endeavours, doctoral students often find themselves as the most junior individuals in academic circles, leading to internal conflicts and ethical quandaries (Amran and Ibrahim, 2012). Navigating this precarious balance proved to be a formidable barrier to my self-confidence, particularly as I contended with the unwelcome presence of impostor syndrome – a pervasive phenomenon in academia where high-achievers believe their success is not based on merit and often feel like frauds (Bothello and Roulet, 2019). The pressure to present myself as an authority figure in my field while filled with self-doubt only served to exacerbate the ethical complexities inherent in my doctoral journey.

The culmination of these challenges came to a head during a pivotal moment in my academic trajectory – a conference presentation three and a half years into my doctorate. It was during this presentation that I encountered an unforeseen obstacle: harsh (and hurtful) criticism from an audience member questioning the very essence of my research, the validity of my methodologies and even the stylistic choices of my presentation slides.[7] In that moment, I felt paralysed by self-doubt in the face of this unexpected scrutiny. Despite intimately knowing my work, the rigour of my methods and having a strong relationship with my participants, the exposure of presenting as an 'expert' left me feeling vulnerable and ill-prepared to defend my research effectively. The audience member had said my research presented 'nothing new', even though I knew my research contained the only qualitative data gathered with (not on) children who had been detained under this particular policy. I knew that this was the only research on a global level that delved into education and schooling in immigration detention. The audience member also accused me of 'Googling the word refugee and using whatever images appeared' for my presentation. This criticism hurt the most, as I was very careful and purposeful about the images I selected. The image in question was a photo of two refugee girls in detention. The refugees were Shay and Melanie,[8] girls whom I knew extremely well and had participated in the research. The photo was one they requested I use to show people the conditions in which they were detained. It was a publicly available photo from a 2016 Australian Broadcasting Corporation (ABC) news article about the children held in detention in Nauru. In the ABC article, both Shay and Melanie were interviewed using their real identities and provided video interviews to the ABC to accompany the written article.[9] Instead of responding to the audience member with confidence in my research design and choices, I froze and said nothing. Even being near the end of my thesis, I felt like a complete novice in that moment and presumed the audience member knew more than me. After the presentation, other audience members approached me immediately and assured me I was doing necessary and important research. I could hear some refugee lawyers, who were also in the audience, refuting this particular audience member's claims and explaining that their comments were incorrect. A human rights lawyer sought me out to confirm that they needed my research in compiling evidence for claims against the Australian government. Despite the affirmation from academics and practitioners, I felt like a failure. The way academics behave with one another is an ethical concern, in this example, when offering feedback, and is especially crucial for doctoral students who are on a learning journey and are particularly reliant on guidance from the academic community (Sverdlik et al., 2020).

The aftermath of the conference presentation further underscored the ethical complexities of the academic journey. The negative feedback not only shook my confidence but also made me hesitant about presenting at future conferences, of which one was occurring the following week. The experience raised doubts about subjecting myself to similar criticism, prompting introspection and questioning of the balance between projecting authority and acknowledging limitations. The significant impact of the negative remarks Carly received emphasises paragraph 61 of the BERA (2024) ethical guidelines.

Course of action: Navigating the aftermath

In the aftermath of the challenging conference presentation, I found myself grappling with overwhelming self-doubt and embarrassment. Initially, I attempted to brush off the incident, suppressing my feelings of inadequacy and pretending to be unaffected. However, the shock and inappropriateness of the audience member's comments prompted senior academics to reach out to me after the conference, expressing concern and offering support. The chair of the panel called me the following day to apologise for not intervening and explained that it was her responsibility to do so as the session chair. Despite my reluctance to discuss the incident due to awkwardness, I gradually recognised the importance of processing what had transpired.[10] Acknowledging the benefits of belonging to an academic community (Siltanen et al., 2019; Golding, 2023), I began to open up about my experience, allowing peers and mentors to provide reassurance regarding the validity of my research. The discussions were helpful in not only affirming my research but knowing I was not alone in the shock of the comments.

As I contemplated my future conference presentations, I faced a pivotal decision. I had a strong temptation to withdraw from further academic engagements, fuelled by lingering doubts about my expertise and the potential for further criticism. However, with the encouragement and guidance of my doctoral peers, I ultimately chose to press forward, recognising the value of continuing to share my research findings despite the unpleasant experience I had faced. Speaking at another conference the following week, *imposter syndrome* loomed, acutely aware of my perceived inadequacies. Yet, as I recounted my experience and defended the merits of my research, I underwent a profound realisation. Despite my self-perceived shortcomings, I possessed a deep understanding of my research that surpassed that of any external critic. This newfound self-assurance empowered me to reclaim my expertise and confidently assert the validity of my work. The conversations that had occurred between myself, my doctoral colleagues and senior academics during that week gave me a wealth of encouraging words to draw upon which boosted my confidence.

In navigating through the difficult presentation, I demonstrated resilience and growth. By confronting my feelings of self-doubt and seeking support from peers and mentors, I emerged with a renewed sense of confidence in my abilities as a researcher. This experience underscored the importance of open dialogue and validation within academic communities, reinforcing the significance of researcher care in fragile contexts.

Alternative courses of action: Navigating responses to criticism

Amidst the difficult encounter with the critical audience member at the conference, alternative courses of action were available to address the situation. Although I internally had responses to the audience member's criticisms, I chose not to voice them in the moment. An alternative course of action could have been to address them directly. This proactive approach would have allowed me to assert my expertise and defend the integrity of my research. By responding assertively to the audience member's criticisms, I could have bolstered my confidence in my capabilities as a researcher and asserted my right to be considered an expert in my topic. Moreover, addressing the criticism head-on may have contributed to an improvement in my emotional wellbeing, as I would have felt empowered to advocate for myself and my research.

However, it is important to consider the potential consequences of this alternative course of action. While pushing back against the audience member's comments may have improved my emotional wellbeing in the short term, it could have also escalated the situation and led to further conflict. Additionally, engaging in a confrontational exchange may have diverted attention away from the substantive aspects of my research, potentially undermining the focus and impact of my presentation. Ultimately, although I chose not to respond directly to the audience member's criticisms, the experience served to reinforce my confidence in the strength of my research. Through the process of navigating the criticism and reflecting on my responses, I gained a deeper understanding of the value of my work and my capabilities as a researcher.

Lessons learned: Nurturing researcher wellbeing

In conclusion, my journey through the challenges of presenting research in fragile contexts has underscored several key lessons. Firstly, the imperative of a supportive community during the doctoral journey cannot be overstated (Sverdlik et al., 2020). Having peers and mentors who understand the rigours of academic research and can provide validation and encouragement is essential for maintaining emotional wellbeing.[11] Moreover, the experience highlighted the importance of sharing research findings, even in the face of pushback and criticism. While facing scepticism and doubts is inevitable, having a community of individuals who are familiar with and supportive of one's research can help counteract feelings of impostor syndrome and bolster confidence (Kis et al., 2022). Ultimately, the experience reaffirmed the notion that as researchers, we are the experts in our own fields. Embracing this identity and trusting in our capabilities is crucial for navigating the trajectory of academia with resilience and integrity. By fostering supportive communities, sharing our research and embracing our expertise, we can navigate the complexities of academic research in fragile contexts with confidence and purpose.

Reflections of a supervisor

I was one of the more experienced academics in the audience for Carly's presentation, and the (vitriolic?) comments that she received were wildly inappropriate. There was a sense of slowly unfolding but palpable shock in the room; I remember being so taken aback by the comments that I scanned the faces in the room to check for signs of similar disbelief that this was unfolding in real time. To my shame, I did not call out the speaker when they were 'schooling' Carly on the use of images, nor did I speak up when they essentially questioned the premise and warrant for Carly's inquiry. I have long been a champion for Carly's research, recognising – as others did (see above) – that it offers a unique and timely examination of the educational (and broader) impacts of detention on children and young people. Carly's warrant for undertaking this study is robustly and (in my view) irrefutably grounded in her lived experience as a teacher in detention contexts, having previously taught many of the young people included in her study. It is an extremely important account of the terrible outcomes of an inhumane policy and a case of what Foucault (1983/2001) called parrhesia (or 'fearless speech') by speaking truth to the power of governments to detain and harm people seeking asylum.

I later reflected on my silence while the audience member was speaking. Firstly, there is a latent etiquette here – I was not chairing the session (and I wonder whether I would have spoken up if I had been) – so it was 'not my place' to admonish, query or silence the speaker. Secondly, there is an (erroneous) assumption that understandings about ethical conduct are shared and that the audience will be supportive, curious and critical – these are tacit *rules of engagement* rather than explicitly stated, and clearly left a space for criticism rather than a welcome critique. Thirdly, and perhaps most pernicious, is the notion of academic freedom; in such spaces as symposia and academic conferences, there are unstated levels of expertise, knowledge and lived experience. Questioning another person's credentials in such colloquia is not a common practice, especially not in public or in the moment.

The moments that Carly has reflected on in her dilemma passed quickly – perhaps no more than two minutes. She held herself well, avoided the kind of defensive snappiness that I would quickly jump to, and respectfully acknowledged the contributions. But I could also see she was wounded and was understandably tearful afterwards when I checked to see how she was. I spoke to the chair of the session during the lunch break, and it was agreed that she would check in with Carly the following day and would also send a message to the audience member to advise them of the impact of their harsh comments. However, all of this remains unsatisfactory – the teachable moment somewhat being lost for all of those present, and a lingering sense of unease about how easy it is to thoughtlessly cause harm and how difficult it is to speak out. This is clearly an area for further education and training of all academics, but especially in fragile contexts, where sensitivity and politics are heightened.

Discussion: What can we learn about the ethics of doctoral care?

The experiences of Anna and Carly illustrate the plurality of challenges experienced by novice researchers in fragile contexts and the consequent ethical dilemmas. Anna's struggles with protecting her psychological wellbeing while balancing her responsibilities as a researcher, and Carly's challenges with the imposter syndrome as she abruptly transitions from a novice to an expert in her field, particularly when faced with harsh criticisms emphasise two key areas of BERA's *Ethical Guidelines for Educational Research* (5th, 2024): responsibilities to the communities of researchers and responsibilities for researchers' wellbeing and development.

Responsibilities to the community of educational researchers

As highlighted in the guidelines, the responsibilities of the educational research community extend far beyond the pursuit of knowledge – established researchers have a duty to guide emerging researchers even as they navigate the complex field of forced migration. This guidance should be characterised by constructive feedback and encouragement that promotes growth, develops confidence and fosters resilience in the face of the complex challenges faced when researching in fragile contexts. Carly's experience indicates the absence of shared understandings within the academic research community on providing appropriate feedback towards peers. This is especially important for emerging researchers who are developing their confidence. It is paramount to explicitly support and cultivate a culture of respect and professionalism in academic discourse, as articulated in paragraph 61 of the Guidelines. Articulating this explicitly would help to communicate such respectful discourse to people outside of academia, such as a lay audience attending a public lecture, who are likely less familiar with the guidelines.

The two case studies also highlight the importance of having an academic support network. Both Anna's and Carly's reflections emphasise the role of academic communities in providing both psychological and professional support, helping them build resilience and overcome the challenges encountered during their doctoral research. The significance of a communal caring space therefore cannot be overstated in supporting emerging researchers in fragile contexts. As stipulated in the BERA Guidelines, 'Established educational researchers and the community as a whole, have a responsibility to support the next generation of educational researchers, including independent and practitioner researchers' (paragraph 58, BERA, 2024).

Responsibility for researchers' wellbeing and development

Reflections from the experiences of Anna and Carly also highlight how working in fragile contexts heightens risks to researchers' psychological wellbeing, emphasising the importance of practicing an ethics of care. As articulated in paragraph 81 of the guidelines, the ethical responsibility to safeguard researchers' wellbeing in fragile contexts extends to all levels of the academic hierarchy. Employers and sponsors, including institutional ethics committees, must recognise the toll of fragile research environments on researchers' wellbeing and take the necessary measures to mitigate their adverse effects. This includes addressing the challenges of fragile context research in institutional ethics protocols and providing support for researchers at institutional levels. These include ensuring researchers have considered strategies to ensure their wellbeing during research and providing training for fieldwork in fragile contexts.

It is also important to note that researchers are also responsible for their own wellbeing, as self-care is especially crucial when researching in fragile contexts. As Anna discovered, developing self-care strategies was critical in managing stress and preventing burnout, especially in high-pressure or crisis contexts. Anna's experience with isolation and vicarious trauma while researching during a global pandemic underscores the importance of having access to psychological support and a network of peers that could provide emotional and professional guidance. Additionally, Carly's struggle with imposter syndrome illustrates the importance of accessing ongoing support as researchers transition from novice to expert roles.

Final thoughts

The takeaway is clear: institutions and researchers must practice an ethics of care, as mandated in Paragraph 81 of the guidelines. Institutions need to go beyond procedural ethics to ensure the wellbeing and development of researchers in fragile contexts. Researcher self-care should be emphasised in institutional ethics reviews, and researchers should practise proactive strategies to ensure their emotional and mental wellbeing. Finally, there is a pressing need for education in the academic community on providing feedback to peers, especially in public platforms such as conferences, to ensure that it is both constructive and respectful, as articulated in Paragraph 61 of the guidelines. Ultimately, a concerted effort is required to build a supportive academic environment that not only advances the field of educational research in fragile contexts, but also nurtures the researchers that contribute to its growth.

Reflective questions

In relation to the issues raised in Case Study One, Anna would like to ask:

1. How can institutional ethics boards implement measures to address researcher self-care in ethics protocols?
2. What forms of ongoing support can institutional ethics boards provide for researchers operating within fragile contexts?

In relation to Case Study Two, Carly asks us all to consider:

1. How can universities better support doctoral students in developing and defending expertise in their field?
2. What protective guidelines should be established for audience members at conferences to ensure respectful academic discourse?
3. How can academic communities foster an environment of affirmation and support for doctoral students?

Further reading

1. Baker, S., Bellemore, P. and Morgan, S. (2023). Researching in fragile contexts: Exploring and responding to layered responsibility for researcher care. *Women's Studies International Forum*, 98(May–June), article 102700, 1–12. https://doi.org/10.1016/j.wsif.2023.102700.

    This article reflects on the lived experiences of three forced migration scholars researching in fragile contexts and explores strategies to mitigate risks of harm to researchers.

2. Burke, R., Baker, S., Molla, T., Cabiles, B. and Fox, A. (2023). How do higher degree research students and supervisors navigate ethics-in-practice for educational research in sensitive or 'fragile' contexts? *British Educational Research Journal*, 50(2), 837–54. https://doi.org/10.1002/berj.3945.

This paper draws on interviews with doctoral students and supervisors researching in the fragile context of forced migration to explore their experiences with micro-ethical complexities in fieldwork. In exploring the gaps in extant support, the paper examines the collective and institutional responsibility regarding the duty of care for novice researchers working in fragile or sensitive contexts.

3. Ratnam, C. (2019). Listening to difficult stories: Listening as a research methodology. *Emotion, Space and Society*, 31, 18–25. https://doi.org/10.1016/j.emospa.2019.03.003.

This article offers a critical reflection on the author's experiences of their ethnographic study with Sri Lankan refugees and asylum-seekers, including attention to issues of using interpreters and care for self-as-researcher. This article also advances a worked example of listening as methodology.

4. Sverdlik, A., Hall, N. C. and McAlpine, L. (2020). Doctoral imposter syndrome: Exploring antecedents, consequences, and implications for doctoral well-being. *International Journal of Doctoral Studies*, 15, 737–58. https://doi.org/https://doi.org/10.28945/4670.

This article examines the mediating role of a sense of belonging in mitigating imposter syndrome among doctoral students and explores how imposter syndrome contributes to mental distress in doctoral students. The researchers advocate for universities to adopt strategies that better integrate doctoral students into academic communities, thereby fostering a stronger sense of belonging.

5. Wilkinson, C. (2020). Imposter syndrome and the accidental academic: An autoethnographic account. *International Journal for Academic Development*, 25(4), 363–74. https://doi.org/10.1080/1360144X.2020.1762087.

This article explores the personal narrative of an academic reflecting on how imposter syndrome affected her early career, particularly in questioning her legitimacy as a lecturer. The author offers valuable insights into navigating the initial stages of an academic career and emphasises the need for universities to provide more practical support for early career academics.

Notes

1   I established contact with the local cultural broker from the refugee community in Rolling Hills, who agreed to connect me with the other refugees for participant recruitment.

2   A cultural broker is an individual who acts as an intermediary between the researcher and the community being studied. Their role is to facilitate communication, understanding and interaction across cultural boundaries, helping the researcher navigate the complexities of the local culture, norms and social dynamics.
3   These actions align with **Responsibilities for Researchers' Wellbeing and Development:** *Safeguarding the physical and psychological wellbeing of researchers is part of the ethical responsibility of the employers and sponsors, as well as the researchers themselves. In general, there should be an ethics of care for researchers, including self-care* (BERA, 2024, paragraph 81).
4   This lesson aligns with paragraph 81 (BERA, 2024) – see note 3.
5   Timely completion refers to the successful completion of the thesis within a period that aligns with the normative time-to-degree guidelines decided by the academic institution or funding agency. This period typically ranges from three to four years for full-time study in Australia, depending on the field of study, the nature of the research and institutional policies. Timely completion is often used as a benchmark for academic efficiency and the effectiveness of institutional support structures.
6   This aligns with **Responsibilities to The Community of Educational Researchers:** *Established educational researchers, and the community as a whole, have a responsibility to support the next generation of educational researchers, including independent and practitioner researchers* (BERA, 2024, paragraph 58).
7   This aligns with **Responsibilities to The Community of Educational Researchers:** *Educational researchers should not criticise their peers in a defamatory or unprofessional manner, in any medium* (BERA, 2024, paragraph 61).
8   Names have been changed.
9   The article can be accessed here: https://www.abc.net.au/news/2016-10-17/meet-the-forgotten-refugee-children-of-nauru/7935674.
10 These actions align with paragraph 81 (BERA, 2024) – see note 3.
11 This aligns with paragraph 58 (BERA, 2024) – see note 6.

References

Amran, N. N. and Ibrahim, R. (2012). Academic rites of passage: Reflection on a doctoral journey. *Procedia – Social and Behavioral Sciences*, 59, 528–34. https://doi.org/https://doi.org/10.1016/j.sbspro.2012.09.310.

Astill, S. (2018). The importance of supervisory and organisational awareness of the risks for an early career natural hazard researcher with personal past-disaster experience. *Emotion, Space and Society*, 28, 46–52. https://doi.org/10.1016/j.emospa.2018.06.009.

Australian Association for Research in Education (AARE) (1993). *AARE Code of Ethics*. https://www.aare.edu.au/research-and-advocacy/research-ethics/.

Baker, S., Bellemore, P. and Morgan, S. (2023). Researching in fragile contexts: Exploring and responding to layered responsibility for researcher care. *Women's Studies International Forum*, 98(May–June), article 102700, 1–12. https://doi.org/10.1016/j.wsif.2023.102700.

Block, K., Warr, D., Gibbs, L. and Riggs, E. (2013). Addressing ethical and methodological challenges in research with refugee-background young people: Reflections from the field. *Journal of Refugee Studies*, 26(1), 69–87. https://doi.org/10.1093/jrs/fes002

Bothello, J. and Roulet, T. J. (2019). The imposter syndrome, or the misrepresentation of self in academic life. *Journal of Management Studies*, 56(4), 854–61. https://doi.org/https://doi.org/10.1111/joms.12344.

British Educational Research Association (BERA) (2024). *Ethical Guidelines for Educational Research* (5th ed.). London: BERA. https://www.bera.ac.uk/publication/ethical-guidelines-for-educational-research-2018-online#harm.

Burke, R., Baker, S., Molla, T., Cabiles, B. and Fox, A. (2024). How do higher degree research students and supervisors navigate ethics-in-practice for educational research in sensitive or 'fragile' contexts? *British Educational Research Journal*, 50(2), 837–54. https://doi.org/https://doi.org/10.1002/berj.3945.

Butler-Rees, A. and Robinson, N. (2020). Encountering precarity, uncertainty and everyday anxiety as part of the postgraduate research journey. *Emotion, Space and Society*, 37, article 100743, 1–12. https://doi.org/10.1016/j.emospa.2020.100743.

Clark-Kazak, C. (2017). Ethical considerations: Research with people in situations of forced migration. *Refuge: Canada's Journal on Refugees*, 33(2), 11–17. https://doi.org/10.7202/1043059ar.

Foucault, M. (1983). Afterword: The Subject and Power. In H. L. Dreyfus, and P. Rabinow (Eds.), *Michel Foucault: Beyond Structuralism and Hermeneutics* (2nd ed.), Chicago, IL: University of Chicago Press (pp. 208–26).

Foucault, M. (2001). *Fearless Speech* (J. Pearson, Ed.). Los Angeles, CA: Semiotext(e).

Garcia, S. G. and Barclay, K. (2020). *Adapting Researching Methodologies in the COVID 19 Pandemic: Resources for Researchers*. Nippon Foundation Ocean Nexus Centre: University of Washington. https://www.uts.edu.au/sites/default/files/2020-06/uts-adapting-research-methodologies-covid-19-pandemic-resources-researchers.pdf.

Golding, J. (2023). Supporting doctoral students in crisis. *Encyclopedia*, 3(4), 1197. https://doi.org/https://doi.org/10.3390/encyclopedia3040087.

Guillemin, M. and Gillam, L. (2004). Ethics, reflexivity, and 'ethically important moments' in research. *Qualitative Inquiry*, 10(2), 261–80. https://doi.org/10.1177/1077800403262360.

Hugman, R., Bartolomei, L. and Pittaway, E. (2011). Human agency and the meaning of informed consent: Reflections on research with refugees. *Journal of Refugee Studies*, 24(4), 655–71. https://doi.org/10.1093/jrs/fer024.

Hummel, C. and El Kurd, D. (2021). Mental health and fieldwork. *PS: Political Science and Politics*, 54(1), 121–5. https://doi.org/10.1017/S1049096520001055.

Irgil, E., Kreft, A.-K., Lee, M., Willis, C. N. and Zvobgo, K. (2021). Field research: A graduate student's guide. *International Studies Review*, 23(4), 1643–69. https://doi.org/10.1093/isr/viab046.

Konken, L. C. and Howlett, M. (2023). When 'home' becomes the 'field': Ethical considerations in digital and remote fieldwork. *Perspectives on Politics*, 21(3), 849–62. https://doi.org/10.1017/S1537592722002572.

Kis, A., Tur, E. M., Lakens, D., Vaesen, K. and Houkes, W. (2022). Leaving academia: Doctoral attrition and unhealthy research environments. *PLoS One*, 17(10), e0274976. https://doi.org/10.1371/journal.pone.0274976.

LaMontagne, A. D., Shann, C., Lolicato, E., Newton, D., Owen, P. J., Tomyn, A. J. and Reavley, N. J. (2023). Mental health-related knowledge, attitudes and behaviours in a cross-sectional sample of australian university students: A comparison of domestic and international students. *BMC Public Health*, 23(170), 1–12. https://doi.org/10.1186/s12889-023-15123-x.

Lantsoght, E. O. L. (2018). *The A-Z of the Doctoral Trajectory: A Practical Guide for a Successful Journey*. Chamonix: Springer International Publishing. https://doi.org/10.1007/978-3-319-77425-1.

Litalien, D. and Guay, F. (2020). Improving doctoral completion rates: Where should we start? *Wiley Network*. https://www.wiley.com/en-us/Improving+doctoral+completion+rates%3A+where+should+we+start-p-9781119520156.

Moran, A. and Asquith, N. L. (2020). Understanding the vicarious trauma and emotional labour of criminological research. *Methodological Innovations*, 13(2), 1–11. https://doi.org/10.1177/2059799120926085.

Newton, D. C., Tomyn, A. J. and LaMontagne, A. D. (2021). Exploring the challenges and opportunities for improving the health and wellbeing of international students: Perspectives of international students. *JANZSSA: Journal of the Australian and New Zealand Student Services Association*, 29(1), 18–34.

Paupini, C., Teigen, H. F. and Habib, L. (2022). A change of space: Implications of digital fieldwork in connected homes during the COVID-19 pandemic.

Digital Creativity, 33(3), 204–18. https://doi.org/10.1080/14626268.2022.21 30943.

Petre, M. and Petre, M. (2010). *Unwritten Rules of Doctoral Research*. Maidenhead: McGraw-Hill Education. http://ebookcentral.proquest.com/lib/unsw/detail.action?docID=557105.

Rahman, S. A., Tuckerman, L., Vorley, T. and Gherhes, C. (2021). Resilient research in the field: Insights and lessons from adapting qualitative research projects during the COVID-19 pandemic. *International Journal of Qualitative Methods*, 20, 1–16. https://doi.org/10.1177/16094069211016106.

Ratnam, C. (2019). Listening to difficult stories: Listening as a research methodology. *Emotion, Space and Society*, 31, 18–25. https://doi.org/10.1016/j.emospa.2019.03.003.

Schwartz, S. and Cronin-Furman, K. (2023). Ill-prepare: International field research methods training. *Qualitative and Multi-Method Research*, 21(1), 20–7. https://doi.org/10.5281/zenodo.7921273

Siltanen, J., Chen, X., Doyle, A. and Shotwell, A. (2019). Teaching, supervising, and supporting doctoral students: Identifying issues, addressing challenges, sharing strategies. *Canadian Review of Sociology/Revue canadienne de sociologie*, 56(2), 274–91. https://doi.org/https://doi.org/10.1111/cars.12239.

Sverdlik, A., Hall, N. C. and McAlpine, L. (2020). Doctoral imposter syndrome: Exploring antecedents, consequences, and implications for doctoral well-being. *International Journal of Doctoral Studies*, 15, 737–58. https://doi.org/https://doi.org/10.28945/4670.

Torka, M. (2020). Change and continuity in Australian doctoral education: Doctoral completion rates and times (2005–2018). *Australian Universities' Review*, 62(2), 69–82. https://eric.ed.gov/?id=EJ1267338.

Wilkinson, C. (2020). Imposter syndrome and the accidental academic: An autoethnographic account. *International Journal for Academic Development*, 25(4), 363–74. https://doi.org/10.1080/1360144X.2020.1762087.

Section 2

Case Studies

Section 2-4 Foreword – Responsibilities for Publication and Dissemination

by *Alison Fox and Nicole Brown*

In this sub-section of the book, two chapters cover the ways researchers can, and should, think about knowledge generation as an ethical endeavour. Rather than conducting researching and 'pushing' it out into academic and practice fields, seeking to engage audiences for the research once findings become apparent, researchers can build a 'pull' for research at the outset. However, the model of pushing out research through peer-reviewed journals remains the bedrock of academic knowledge generation, and so working within this normative landscape is also interrogated through an ethical lens. The section of the book takes as its starting point guidelines 70–81 of the BERA ethical guidance (BERA, 2024).

These chapters raise questions as to who should be involved in the authoring of new knowledge (particularly Chapter 15) and evaluating it as of quality (particularly Chapter 16). The politics of dissemination and publication are highlighted as being under-addressed, and as readers, you will hear from those early in their careers of their calls to action. These chapters contribute to a wider manifesto for ethical assessment of research publication quality, captured in the San Francisco Declaration on Research Assessment (an active space for publication reform, which can be accessed at: https://sfdora.org/).

In Chapter 15, Amber Fensham-Smith, Alison Twiner and Fadoua Govaerts reflect on how research needs to reach out to those in under-researched environments to empower marginalised groups to participate in the generation of knowledge. This involves academic researchers overcoming the traditional expectations of many Western universities on them to publish as an academic and seeking to build knowledge with and for communities in ways which will see them disseminating other than peer-reviewed journals or books, such as this one. The first case study examines dissemination from school-based research, which embraced online opportunities to educate as an outcome, and the second examines the care needed when supporting children and young people as researchers to present their findings. Sin-Wang Chong and Natalie Tegama pick up on this 'publish or perish' culture to examine ethical approaches to introducing and empowering early career researchers to publish, through engagement with the sector's currently necessary peer review processes. The tensions associated with peer review are voiced, both related to (dis)empowerment and maintaining the quality of publications. That this remains unpaid labour is a challenge to the whole sector in recognising and celebrating the time spent as reviewers in encouraging authors into the academe alongside striving for original, significant and rigorous research being available for others to access. As many of these peer-reviewed journals, as outlined in Chapter 16, are behind a subscription paywall, other contributions in this sub-section might then have taken on the open science/access agenda.

Together, these chapters offer not only provocation but inspiration, providing a roadmap for building an academy that values participation over prestige, collaboration over competition, and care over compliance. This is not just a conversation about publishing. It is a call to build a more just academic future – one manuscript, one peer review, and one community at a time.

15

Publish, Perish, or Build Community? Towards Alternative Ethical Publication and Dissemination Practices

by *Amber Fensham-Smith, Alison Twiner and Fadoua Govaerts*

Introduction

Being an ethical researcher doesn't start and end with data collection and analysis (BERA, 2024: 7). Educational researchers have an ethical, social and moral responsibility to their participants, co-researchers and other stakeholders in publishing and disseminating knowledge made by, with and for them. At the core of putting into practice ethical and inclusive publication and dissemination practices lie essential questions and, often, dilemmas surrounding how to maximise benefits from the 'fruits' (outputs) of the research process and the role and responsibilities of educational researchers to create and extend opportunities to communicate, share and exchange knowledge across excluded groups.

A *publish or perish* neoliberal culture that dominates traditional modes of academic publication within Western universities has historically marginalised and excluded the representation of communities and researchers in locations and community spaces outside of academia (Madikizela-Madiya, 2023a). The privileging of narrow research impact metrics has exacerbated inequities in access to high-quality, subscription-only research outputs (Aprile et al., 2021). As a product of formal ethical regulatory frameworks and legal obligations, community and practitioner researchers' authentic and applied knowledge is subsequently sometimes misrepresented or hidden from public and policy discourses about education (Bolton-King et al., 2020).

To address these gaps, this chapter explores the activities of communities and stakeholders seeking to widen the social and public benefit of their educational research projects through alternative, ethical modes of publication and community dissemination practices. Case One illustrates the practical, moral and theoretical opportunities and challenges of establishing alternative mechanisms and space for publishing open-access practitioner research for the social benefit of practitioners working across educational settings. Case Two explores alternative community dissemination practices through a hybrid community event with young co-researchers and the opportunities and ethical dilemmas encountered through this medium to disseminate research with young people. It discusses power, representation, dissent, data ownership and safeguarding issues through a moral, procedural and social justice lens.

Through our collective learning across both cases, the authors offer tangible ideas and solutions for planning and implementing more inclusive, accessible and diverse modes of community dissemination in the early stages of research design. In so doing, we draw attention to utilising opportunities for publication and community dissemination to democratise educational research and to build and broker authentic and inclusive relationships for the social, moral and ethical benefit of the wider public.

Case Study One: Establishing ethical publication for practitioner research – Camtree

Background

Established educational researchers and the wider community have a responsibility to support the next generation of educational researchers, including independent and practitioner-researchers (BERA, 2024, paragraph 58).[1] However, community inclusion is not always mirrored in published or valued expertise, nor by some practitioners who feel academic benchmarks are inappropriate for practitioner research (e.g. Parsons, 2021). Historically, debates surrounding *quality* and *rigour* and how to assess this within practitioner research have attracted critical interest and debate from a range of stakeholders (Wyse et al., 2021).

To address some of these complex issues, this case study reports on the collaborative work to offer a more tailored outlet for publishing practitioner research through the Cambridge Teacher Research Exchange (Camtree[2]) – a global platform for practitioner research in education.

Camtree was initiated by university-based academics at Hughes Hall, University of Cambridge, with input from many practitioners. Established in 2021, it seeks to raise the profile of practitioner research and respond to a problem: the research knowledge base about education and policy on which this is based is largely uninformed by the expertise and experience of education practitioners. This suggests there are barriers to practitioner researchers, as members of the educational community, in meeting paragraph 70 of the BERA 2024 guidelines: 'researchers have a responsibility to make the results of their research public for the benefit of educational professionals, policymakers and the wider public'. This reflects a vast gulf in social justice, representation, and responsibility to practitioner communities; much of the research wisdom informing education policy and practice is conducted by academic researchers. Academic researchers, of course, benefit from distance and access to tools and methodologies. However, they often lack lived and local understandings and the impact of implementing findings in an educational context to meet the needs of learners around which a problem of practice was identified.

Founding members of the Camtree team had worked with practitioners using research to change their practice for many years before the network and platform were established. The team's experiences reinforced that those practitioners often wanted, but could not locate, examples of pedagogic practices and strategies of interest piloted by other educators. Additionally, there is a long history of practitioner research in professional development and teacher education, but the learning from these local contexts is rarely shared beyond local contexts. Camtree wanted to establish mechanisms, opportunities and collaborative ways of working to facilitate an alternative way to publish ethical practitioner research.

The ethical dilemma

There are ethical considerations inherent in practitioner research that largely do not feature in academic research, mainly when there is an intention to share findings from research into practice, including:

1 the need for clear articulation of what is practice and what is research;
2 relatedly, what participants are expected to engage with and what is optional; and
3 whether participants genuinely feel they could opt out or withdraw from the research without repercussions for their learning or professional relationships. (Fancourt et al., 2022)

For university-based research, the standard procedure generally involves applying for and receiving ethical approval following the scrutiny of an ethical review committee at a very early stage, before contacting participants or collecting data. Practices are shifting slightly in this regard, acknowledging that for practitioners and wider participants truly to have a stake in research agendas and findings, they need to be involved in setting the remit of research and so in crafting the submission to an ethics committee (Madikizela-Madiya, 2023b). This arguably represents a welcome move, but such opportunities and infrastructures tend to be hidden or absent for practitioners conducting inquiries into their practice, who are otherwise not affiliated with a university. This creates additional barriers to the ethical publication of practitioner research and impinges on the social benefit of sharing learning from research into practice among practitioners.

Early in the formation of Camtree, the team, therefore, had to consider how to effectively design an alternative visible and explicit framework that potential practitioner authors (and peer reviewers) could use to support the peer-review process and ethical publication of inquiries. This raised further difficult considerations for defining *markers of quality* and whether these should be aligned with benchmarks used to *assess quality* and rigour for university-based research or alternative criteria.

Additionally, the Camtree team was mindful that they could not just ask practitioners to share research that had already been conducted in context (BERA, 2024, paragraph 19),[3] if it was not done with a view or with permission for wider sharing (BERA, 2024, paragraph 9).[4] The team were also not naïve to the fact that inviting practitioners to write up an inquiry after they had gained the benefit to their own practice was an extra task for already-busy people (BERA, 2024, paragraph 34).[5] It was important, therefore, to be clear in terms of the team's own ethical practice, whether this invitation was mutually beneficial for individual practitioners and the wider community of practice. As one group lead working with Camtree articulated, the benefits needed to be visible to practitioners:

> the moment that made it, though was when I shared with the two groups, who hadn't completed their work, ... the three completed pieces of work. And I said, ... 'Look at how cool these three are. Look at ... the high standard that they're published. Look at how amazing they look'. That then galvanised those other two groups once they could see that kind of quality of outcome, I guess. (UK group lead, reflective interview)

The ethical dilemma facing Camtree was, therefore, broken down into three primary considerations and actions, recognising the team's role as broker and potential outsider across these areas:

1. how to encourage practitioners to engage intentionally with ethical considerations of conducting and sharing their inquiries, to share from the outset (BERA, 2024, paragraph 3);[6]
2. how to give confidence to the practitioner, university-based researcher and policymaker that practitioner research can be shared ethically;
3. how to offer structure and support to practitioners regarding ethical practice-based inquiry that they could implement towards publishing their findings without adding undue burdens to already-busy practitioners. This arguably relates to a more general principle of ethical research – maximising benefits and reducing risk or harm.

Having worked with teachers, schools and school networks over previous decades in using practitioner research to inform pedagogic change, but noticing that the learning from such contextualised inquiry was repeatedly ring-fenced to local connections, the creators of Camtree sought to address this balance.

Course of action

The following course of action outlines the steps taken by Camtree to develop a platform and open-access digital library for the publication solely of practitioner research, with embedded peer-review mechanisms and to ensure the transparency, implementation focus and rigour of work published.

Firstly, it is important to note that despite years of experience across practice and supporting practitioner co-inquiry, the Camtree team – as white, Western academics and Higher Education Institution practitioners – were setting the benchmarks of quality and rigour against which reports of practitioner research would be judged worthy of publication, as relative outsiders. Recognising this, regular meetings were held with a development group. The development group is comprised of academics and practitioners based in a range of sectors, settings, and countries of different races, ethnicities and ages. Through regular meetings, the development group ensures the core team is held accountable for making informed decisions and offering resources that are genuinely wanted, useful for, and evaluated by practitioners in a range of educational settings – with feedback implemented in revisions. In parallel, a more formal advisory group comprising leaders in practitioner organisations offers further space to check strategic decisions on where and how to develop existing and new resources. Thus, in seeking to balance demands on practitioner time with building a platform of resources useful to practitioners, the involvement of both the development and advisory groups ensured that practitioner voice and experience offer a regular checkpoint, feeding into and funnelling directions, decisions and developed material.

One essential element in the formation of Camtree was that the library, the individual reports within it, and aligned resources were useful for practice and practitioners. If an author wrote about an intervention and its results, fellow practitioners needed to be able to understand through the report what the intervention involved so they could try it or adapt it to their contexts (BERA, 2024, paragraph 70).[7] To support the process of peer-review, Camtree developed eight criteria (see Table 15.1) for authors and reviewers to use, which are published on the website: https://camtree.org/about/values-and-principles/

Authors are asked to engage with these criteria when writing a report for peer review. For transparency, the website provides annotated examples of accepted reports indicating how and where criteria were met.

To support this collaborative peer process, Camtree offers training for potential reviewers (via a self-paced online short course) to implement these criteria in a way that enables publication and is consistent across multiple reviewers. As Camtree grows and more reports are submitted, the aim is to expand and diversify the network of Camtree peer reviewers – with the eight criteria as a point of consistency – but with a global pool of locally situated reviewers able to give appropriate feedback on practitioner research reports. Thus far, the team has worked with schools and groups in the UK, UAE, India and Kazakhstan to train practitioners in peer-reviewing reports

Table 15.1 Camtree quality criteria.

1. Is there a **clear outline** or analysis of the focus, issue or challenge that the inquiry addresses?
2. Is some appropriate **prior research evidence/literature used to ground the inquiry** or interpret the outcomes? (If relevant)
3. Are **clear aims or inquiry questions given**, that relate to the challenge faced?
4. Is it clear **what the author did to address their challenge**? This would include details such as data collection activities (e.g. interviews, surveys, observations), who participated (e.g. learners, teachers, lecturers, parents), how many participated, how chosen, or detailing an intervention.
5. Does the author state how they followed **good research practice** throughout their inquiry, such as addressing any ethical issues, safeguarding concerns, gaining informed consent for participation and use of data, anonymisation of presented data?
6. Are **findings reported clearly** (with some analytic commentary of what this means in response to the challenge or inquiry questions, not just presenting data)?
7. Does the **evidence presented match the strength of claims** made?
8. Are **implications of findings** suggested, even if tentative or small scale? Does the author identify what other education practitioners might find useful from their study?

Source: With thanks to Camtree, https://camtree.org/lessons/what-makes-a-good-report/

from fellow practitioners in their contexts. This afforded an increasingly authentic *peer* element to the review process, potentially enabling authors receiving feedback to feel it is more relational and sympathetically given, with an understanding of contextual and curricular frames and constraints. This was mutually beneficial for both authors and reviewers themselves, as the following illustrates:

> [B]eing trained as a peer reviewer was really good for me, being able to support and advise the writing process ... So I felt like by learning what the examples were I could help the people through that process. (UK group lead, reflective interview)

To support accessibility and sharing, Camtree hosts an online open-access digital library of peer-reviewed practitioner research reports. As of June 2024, just over 300 reports have been published, by 309 authors, reporting on practices in eighteen countries. However, the creation of this large open-access repository created new ethical risks regarding participants' anonymity and confidentiality. A fundamental issue that needed to be addressed, by the nature of authors being named and traceable to their institutions, is that participants, colleagues and other related people are difficult (if not impossible) to anonymise (BERA, 2024, paragraph 21).[8] Encouraging practitioners to publish their research-in-context may include references to and data from colleagues and learners who are rendered identifiable through connection. To address this challenge, Camtree created a self-paced online course, *Ethics in Close-to-Practice Research*, to serve as a reference point and scaffold for authors and reviewers on key considerations and mechanisms (e.g. safeguarding, data protection, etc.) relevant to ethical, open-access dissemination. The content, duration and framing of this course was developed and refined in response to practitioner feedback before being made public.

Alternative courses of action

One alternative course of action was to maintain the status quo: that practitioners largely do not have time to write reports of their practice-based inquiries; that ethical considerations of publishing practitioner inquiry are too risky; and that the educational knowledge base remains largely uninformed by the understandings and expertise of education practitioners (BERA, 2024, paragraph 81).[9] This would avoid difficult conversations and questions of ethics, protect participants involved in inquiries of practitioners who do explore their practice locally and avoid the potentially time-consuming investment of individual settings or networks establishing their own interpretations of research ethics review.

However, this assumes that practitioner communities are disconnected and largely disinterested in learning from each other. It also assumes that those working *outside* or on the periphery of practitioner communities of practice are disinterested and unwilling to support the sharing of practitioner research and knowledge and, in turn, learn from it, which is problematic. It could also be argued that risk and ethics, as a process of checking conformity performed by an ethics committee in the university, undermines opportunities and spaces for alternative forms of dissemination and the social benefit of good-quality research being made available to different communities and the public.[10] Such a stance and risk aversion risks reinforcing an insider/outsider dichotomy and hierarchies of so-called *pure* versus applied knowledge that Camtree aims to challenge.

If the position is taken that practitioners individually and as a community are interested in conducting and sharing research, a second alternative course of action was not just to be informed and held to account by practitioner members of development and advisory groups, but for the initiative itself to have been created and fully led by practitioners. Taking this path, the team would be (and arguably be seen by other practitioners) as agentic insiders to the work and stance they are trying to promote, potentially reducing fears regarding misrepresentation or misunderstanding discussed earlier. It might also enable the metrics of quality and systems of judgement to be set by practitioners, for practitioners. There is much appeal in this alternative approach, and many schools and other settings do have their own sharing processes – for internal and external access. However, many of the ethical and practical dilemmas raised through this case study would still require considerable attention. For instance, creating such a platform, developing resources and peer reviewing submissions on top of a practitioner workload would be very time-consuming, unless the teaching load was light, which necessitates a parallel move further from a practice-based role to be viable.

Secondly, maintaining such a space for global open access is a long-term and resource-intensive commitment, often not possible under ring-fenced and annually set local budgets. For members of the Camtree team, this would have required a stance of inaction amidst awareness of need. The approach taken by the Camtree team was, therefore, to raise rather than replace practitioner voice and expertise, working with and informed by practitioners in a range of settings and sectors.

Case Study One – concluding section

Brokering and extending opportunities to publish many forms and kinds of educational research including those made by practitioners, community and independent researchers are important and worthwhile pursuits. To understand how to teach and learn to suit our context and needs, we must ask questions, try things and change what we do based on what we find.

Unlike many domains, educational research has been largely polarised between research conducted by academics and that conducted by practitioners, with different values, principles and processes implicitly and sometimes explicitly applied – leading to barriers in sharing and a sense of misrepresentation. However, in terms of research ethics, considerations around sharing findings from practitioner research are fundamentally different to research conducted outside of one's own context of practice in many ways. There are profound benefits to sharing and synthesising the learning from research into education across approaches and methodologies – for learners, practitioners, researchers and policymakers. To do this, however, it is likely that different processes and judgements of what is locally appropriate are needed to share research findings, albeit with clear articulation about the basis on which judgements are made.

As reviewed in this case study, the Camtree team therefore took on the challenge of misrepresentation and imbalance in the expertise within the education knowledge base – creating a space dedicated to publishing research conducted by practitioners, authored by practitioners and written with practitioners in mind. Aware that this is not ethically straightforward, they developed peer-review mechanisms and criteria around processes that support practitioner-researchers to articulate how their work is ethically conducted and reported, through information and examples. In creating this open-access space for practitioners as authors and with access to a body of practitioner knowledge, the team also sought to support practitioners in unpacking the tacit knowledge embedded in *good examples of practice* (Richardson, 2022), through the process of sharing their work for audiences and communities within and outside their immediate contexts of practice. As a point of reference, content in the digital library would also be informative for relatively 'distanced-from-practice' academic researchers, policymakers and the wider public.

Case Study Two: Negotiating power, representation and dissent with young-researchers in active community dissemination

Background

Beyond publishing or perishing via peer-reviewed journal articles, educational researchers have a number of alternative and dynamic ways to authentically co-create (with participants), share and disseminate educational research to the wider public, including blogs, vlogs, social media and various avenues and means to extend the reach of work with the public around the world.

Drawing on the theme of community building through ethical publication considered in Case Study One, this case study considers a grassroots example of co-production through community dissemination. Importantly, while practitioner knowledge is sometimes hidden or misrepresented, as discussed in Case Study One, educational research dissemination with children and young people and opportunities to extend the social benefits of research with and for them seldom feature in public discourses.

Researchers following the United Nations Convention on the Rights of the Child (UNICEF, 1989) must ensure a child's or young person's right to participate meaningfully in all research processes that concern them. This extends to identifying ways to facilitate participation in dissemination practices. Yet, participatory research with young people often ends at the point of data collection, with few opportunities for young co-researchers to actively shape how their lived experiences are told and retold by adult researchers/community educators speaking 'for' them. With the proliferation of online platforms, tools and technologies come new opportunities, risks and dilemmas, including power and dissent. The following anonymised case study explores the ethical opportunities and challenges of a community-educator and doctoral researcher whom we have called 'Nadine'.[11]

Nadine is a practising home educator who spent the last three years pursuing a doctorate in alternative education. Following the principles of the UNCRC (UNICEF, 1989),[12] Nadine supported four young people (aged 13–16 years) as co-researchers to jointly plan, co-design and conduct their own personalised qualitative research projects on their lived experiences of being home-educated. The young-researchers collected their data using interviews and multiple visual and creative methods, including vlogs, blogs and visual committees. To foster high levels of autonomy, participation and inclusion, Nadine facilitated several training workshops for the young-researchers. Topics covered include research design principles, qualitative interviewing, thematic analysis, research ethics and community dissemination. As the young-researchers' individualised data generation neared completion, an opportunity arose to co-plan and disseminate their research findings to an influential community of stakeholders, including policymakers, practitioners and academic researchers, via a large cross-university hybrid event (paragraphs 70, 72 and 81,[13] BERA, 2024).

Nadine discussed this opportunity verbally with the young-researchers, their parents, her supervisors and the event organisers (paragraph 6, BERA, 2024).[14] She followed the ethical protocols and risk-assessment procedures stipulated by her institution. To ensure informed consent (paragraph 28, BERA, 2024)[15] before the hybrid event, Nadine facilitated multiple meetings with the young-researchers and their parents on privacy and the ownership of their data, their preferences for anonymity, and the risks and benefits of a recorded hybrid event for the group's digital footprint. Nadine's explanation to the parents and young people about the risks involved in leaving a digital footprint aligns with ethical principles of transparency, duty of care, minimising harm and balancing individual rights with the public good (paragraphs 35 and 36, BERA, 2024).[16] Over the next eight weeks, Nadine and the young-researchers met regularly to plan and practise their personalised presentations. Group workshops cover online audience engagement, the young-researchers' preferred medium and mode of presentation communication, and anonymisation procedures. Nadine facilitated mock presentations and provided ongoing one-to-one and group support to each young-researcher (paragraphs 9 and 10, BERA, 2024).[17] Throughout the preparation, Nadine upheld participatory research principles (Mann et al., 2014) and children's rights, prioritising the young-researchers' voices and agency in disseminating their findings effectively and safely. She co-ordinated communication between the group, event host institutions and the young-researchers' parents, ensuring all parties had a shared understanding and consent to their participation.

The group of four young-researchers prepared and intended to deliver their individual presentations alongside digital artefacts, including two slideshow presentations, a digital storytelling application presentation and a digital research poster. By allocating time for informal conversations and light refreshments before and after the presentations, Nadine provided a supportive environment for the young-researchers. The informal approach was an opportunity for participants to alleviate their pre-presentation nerves and to address any last-minute questions. Nadine also arranged for a nominated 'responsible other' to be present outside the teaching room should any young-researcher need to take a break or withdraw from the event. She followed her university's safeguarding policy (paragraph 11, BERA, 2024)[18] and the young-researchers agreed to present their research synchronously with Nadine in a teaching room on a university campus (paragraph 81, BERA, 2024).[19] She also invested in a 360-degree camera and delegated parts of the technical management of the online meeting space (as agreed with the university information security team) to an event host institution (a research centre at another university). The host institution for the online meeting space had met with the young people online, prior to the event and had put into place a process to manage and safeguard the young people online, in the unanticipated event of unforeseen audience responses. Though the online space was open to members of the public, access was permitted by registration only (paragraph 34, BERA, 2024).[20] The young-researchers were excited, well-prepared and looking forward to the event.

The ethical dilemma

The hybrid event commenced, as planned, with the group sitting around a table, with Nadine positioned at the centre and managing the camera. The young-researchers were well-prepared, their notes at the ready and drinks placed on the table. They had rehearsed their presentations together, ensuring a smooth flow for the event. Nadine was in control of the laptop, equipped with a clicker that would give the young presenters control over their slides, as well as a wireless mouse for other presentation modes if needed. The young-researchers could see a large screen on the wall displaying their presentation and the names of attendees, but they could not see the video feed of the eighty people in attendance online. This setup provided them with essential information about their presentation and audience while minimising potential distractions or nervousness that might arise from seeing the faces of such a large online audience. The participants could also view their presentations on the laptop screen in front of them, offering a more immediate reference point. This dual-screen arrangement allowed the presenters to navigate their content confidently, maintaining eye contact with the in-person audience while staying aware of their progress through the presentation. The setup struck a balance between providing necessary information and maintaining a focused environment for the young presenters.

Two young-researchers delivered their presentations to the live audience as planned, adhering to the agreed-upon order and format. However, when the third young-researcher, Ali, was about to begin, Nadine noticed that he suddenly seemed uncomfortable (paragraphs 8 and 34, BERA, 2024).[21] She quickly realised that Ali had just seen his parents' name appear on the large display screen on the wall. Before the event, it was discussed and agreed that Ali's preference for his parent not to attend the event online or in person would be upheld. The 360-degree rotating camera was poised to capture Ali's presentation, heightening tension.

Although withdrawal before the event was discussed in their planning, Nadine did not anticipate this unintended risk. Additionally, as the online event lobby was managed by the event organiser, Nadine had no forewarning of Ali's parents' entry into the online meeting space (paragraphs 43 and 44, BERA, 2024).[22] Nadine did not have a backup plan. She felt this young-researcher had important findings to share that would give a unique insight into this rare opportunity with an influential audience, including a Department for Education (England) representative (paragraphs 36 and 70, BERA, 2024).[23] If Ali did not present, Nadine worried that he would feel disappointed, having invested so much time and energy in preparing for this moment. Nadine recognised that she needed to respond promptly to maintain the ethical integrity of the participatory principles of her co-researcher positionality (paragraph 59, BERA, 2024).[24]

Course of action

In response to his non-verbal cues of dissent, Nadine immediately redirected the camera away from Ali's presentation slides to focus on her face, announcing technical difficulties to the online audience. Nadine then turned off the camera and muted the microphone to speak to Ali. She felt it would be unethical to compel Ali to narrate his presentation verbally, as initially planned, and to respect his non-verbal cues of dissent irrespective of his reasons (paragraph 31, BERA, 2024).[25] In this moment, Nadine was also very aware of the material space and group environment they shared. She was concerned that this young-researcher might feel compelled socially to conform and present (paragraph 20, BERA, 2024).[26]

She was also aware of Ali's distinctive way of engaging with learning material and his preference for alternative learning methods. Home education approaches, which Nadine is familiar with as a home-educator herself, also influenced her thinking. Home education often involves personalised learning experiences that cater to learners' individual needs and preferences. When working through the research project and preparing for this event, Nadine learned that Ali sometimes finds it difficult to engage with traditional text-based learning methods and lacks confidence in public speaking. Although it seems that the preparation sessions helped him to overcome this, she believed it may also be a factor in Ali's reaction. In this context, Nadine recognised Ali's unique engagement with learning material and their preference for alternative methods. As a home educator, Nadine was familiar with the role of an adult in a young person's learning journey, where adults are seen as support and facilitators who can be flexible and value all learning approaches. Nadine was aware that even adults can become nervous before a presentation, in person or online, therefore the feeling of anxiousness to a certain level may be normal and understood that for a young person who is still developing these skills, she needed to be supportive rather than assertive or dismissive. Therefore, Nadine's reflexivity and awareness of participatory principles and home education approaches guided her to handle the situation with sensitivity and respect. She understood that compelling Ali to conform to a traditional presentation format would not only be unethical but also counterproductive to his learning experience. Instead, she aimed to create a supportive and inclusive environment where his voice could still be heard without forcing him into an uncomfortable situation.

Nadine considered these thoughts and possibilities rapidly and judged that Ali's dissent is rooted in nerves triggered by his parents' unexpected online presence, indicating a need for her support rather than being silenced. Verbally, she reassured Ali of the quality, impact and significance of his presentation. She then offered Ali a range of choices for what he could do next, including moving to the next item on the programme, taking a break or a complete withdrawal (paragraph 31, BERA, 2024).[27] Ali verbally asked Nadine to present his digital research artefacts on his behalf and to use his chosen pseudonym while doing so (paragraph 39, BERA, 2024).[28] Nadine interpreted this verbal exchange as a renewal of his consent (paragraph 23, BERA, 2024).[29] She turned the camera and microphone back on and verbally narrated Ali's research findings and conclusions to the online audience, thereby aiming to honour his contribution while respecting his autonomy and preferences.

Alternative course of action

The unanticipated situation illustrates how rigid ethical committee approvals can fail to account for the dynamic nature of community-based research, especially when working with young-researchers. This connects to the *publish or perish* mentality, where academic success is often measured by publications rather than meaningful community engagement. Nadine's capacity to respond effectively to Ali's non-verbal cues of dissent was predicated on the robust rapport and trust she had cultivated with the young-researchers over an extended period. This relationship was developed through two key phases: first, during the weeks of their research projects, and subsequently, through the preparatory period leading up to the dissemination event. As a participatory researcher, Nadine had established a nuanced understanding of Ali's individual communication patterns, preferences and potential vulnerabilities.

Nadine was sensitive and attuned to this young-researcher's non-verbal expression of dissent. This was predicated on the trust and rapport she had established with the group in the months preceding the event. In this temporary and relationally situated context between the physical space of a university classroom and an online meeting room, group communication and participation evolved dynamically, impacting the researcher–participant relationship and the planned and 'unintended' dissemination process. On the one hand, the hybrid and asynchronous medium from within which the group chose to co-present offered a valuable opportunity to extend the reach and audience for their community dissemination.

Nadine might have interpreted Ali's cues of dissent as rooted in pressures to conform to social expectations and the asymmetric power relationship between the adult co-researcher and the audience. In this context, Ali's verbal consent renewal could have been considered impossible to give (paragraph 20, BERA, 2024).[30] Instead, Nadine could have proceeded to manage an active withdrawal from the dissemination of any artefacts belonging to this young-researcher, either directly or narrated on his behalf. In their brief verbal exchange, Nadine could therefore have further emphasised the option to abstain amidst the other options that she provided. However, managing a full withdrawal in this context would have created new risks and other potential harms within an intra-group dynamic of non-participating and participating young-researchers. This includes the risk of the non-presenting young-researcher experiencing feelings of inferiority, heightened anxiety and diminished self-confidence compared to his presenting young-researcher peers. Managing a full withdrawal while potentially mitigating these individual risks could have introduced new challenges, such as perceived exclusion or reinforcement of the non-presenting researcher's sense of inadequacy. This scenario underscores the complex interplay between individual participant wellbeing and group cohesion in participatory research with young people, highlighting the need for nuanced and context-sensitive approaches to ethical decision-making.

Nadine thought that she had prepared for every ethical risk, but her fluid participatory research approach reconfigured a multilayered context for unanticipated risks to surface. Participant consent, dissent and assent are not absolutes but a continuum of communication expressed in diverse ways.

The opportunities and benefits of disseminating participatory research to reach wider community audiences (paragraph 54, BERA, 2024)[31] across online and offline spaces, where the young-researchers were given high levels of autonomy, created complex ethical issues. In this case, Nadine pivoted to low levels of participation to protect Ali by presenting on his behalf. Reflecting on her role and actions, Nadine realised that this decision making was heavily influenced by her insider position (paragraph 19, BERA, 2024).[32] This led to an inclination to advocate for the representation of knowledge and experiences of the young-researchers, who she felt were frequently excluded from broader public discourses about education (paragraph 37, BERA, 2024).[33] While this positioning reinforced her belief in supporting young-researcher autonomy, it simultaneously brought into tension balancing this with her duty to protect the young-researchers from a wide array of incidental and unanticipated risks and harms in this hybrid community dissemination context.

Case Study Two – concluding section

This case study highlights the nuanced nature of participation preferences and the ethical considerations surrounding autonomy, consent and dissent in community research dissemination with young-researchers. Importantly, dissent, assent and consent are non-binary continuums that must be reflexively considered across all stages of research, including community dissemination.

It underscores the necessity to adapt modes and levels of participation both before and during live dissemination events to accommodate unforeseen circumstances. This adaptive approach must respond to the power dynamics at play and the complexities of the shifting nature of non-verbal and verbal communication.

This case study demonstrates the importance and the need for researchers to engage in open dialogue with participants and institutions, to respect their autonomy and to carefully consider the implications of consent and dissent, considering participants' individual preferences and the broader ethical principles of UNCRC (UNICEF, 1989) guiding research practice with children and young people.

It reinforces the need for researchers to see and enact consent as a relational and ongoing process through all phases of a research project and to maintain ethical reflexivity and flexibility in community dissemination practices, ultimately ensuring the ethical integrity and meaningful social benefit of all stakeholders.

Final thoughts

Case studies One and Two surfaced the opportunities, dilemmas and reconfigured practices for new and established educational researchers aligned to democratising traditional academic publication and dissemination practices. While Case Study One focused on the collective efforts of university-based researchers to broker and extend new mechanisms and tools for the representation, visibility and public benefit of practitioner communities over a period of years, Case Study Two concentrated on a smaller, localised and grassroots valuing of young-researcher voices and experiences, suggesting an alternative to traditional academic practices. Crucially, across both distinctive contexts and stakeholders represented, both case studies illustrated a commitment and responsibility to utilise and value research publication and dissemination to strengthen and extend the skills, knowledge and exchange of *expertise* within and across the formal boundaries of a university.

The value of authentic collaboration and partnership working in this process, where authors, participants and co-researchers have a genuine stake in shaping what and how knowledge (with, about and for them) is made and shared, is worthwhile for all educational researchers to consider in their own research inquiries (or inquiries into practice). Importantly, as highlighted in Chapters 1 and 21, this underscores the importance of acknowledging the diversity and contributions that all stakeholders may bring to an artefact or event that is collaboratively developed.[34] Both case studies surface the challenges and limitations of sharing research artefacts online both asynchronously and synchronously, and the newly reconfigured ethical tensions that accompany access, resources, for example, internet speed and consent to share. This inferred the time-consuming and resource-intensive nature (e.g. Camtree) of building and facilitating opportunities to do things differently.

Evidently, the barriers that practitioners and independent and community researchers face in accessing opportunities for engagement with formal ethical review committees, as shown in Case Study One, surface the need for alternative ways of seeing, valuing and measuring quality and rigour, as part of a more flexible, context-sensitive ethical frameworks.

To do so would be to work towards and promote more inclusive and equitable modes and mediums of publication.

While wider resource constraints create additional pressures which makes the pursuit of community building through dissemination and publication challenging at scale, new and experienced educational researchers alike might consider ways and means to broker and forge new partnerships to extend the value, benefit and social impact of their research outputs.

Reflective questions

In response to Case Study One in particular, questions for reflection include:

1. How else might the research team support the sharing of ethical and rigorous practitioner research?
2. Is it appropriate for a mainly academic group to host a digital library of practitioner research?
3. How can practitioner research be shared ethically, effectively balancing participant anonymity with a desire and responsibility to share findings?
4. Should practitioner research and non-practitioner research be judged against the same metrics, in terms of ethics and publication?

Thinking about the issues raised by the chapter more broadly:

5. How can the insider knowledge of practitioners and community members about their setting be integrated with academic expertise to enhance the quality and relevance of research involving communities or young people?
6. How can the principles of community-based participatory research be applied to bridge the gap between academic and practitioner knowledge in studies involving young-researchers?
7. How can researchers develop flexible ethical frameworks that accommodate both the protective needs of young-researchers and their right to participate meaningfully in research that affects them?
8. What alternative and open-access publication and/or dissemination opportunities suit the needs of different stakeholders within your own research context?
9. How might open-access dissemination extend the impact and value of your educational research?

Further reading

1. Alderson, P. and Morrow, V. (2011) *The Ethics of Research with Children and Young People: A Practical Handbook* (2nd ed.) [Online]. London: SAGE Publications.

   A seminal resource, comprehensively covering key processes and practical ethical questions when researching with children and young people, from planning and research design to funding dissemination and impact on policy.

2. Billett, P., Hart, M. and Martin, D. (Eds.) (2020) *Complexities of Researching with Young People: Youth, Young Adulthood and Society*. London: Routledge.

   This resource provides practical examples and guidance for engaging with young people in diverse contexts, including digital research challenges, informed consent in vulnerable populations and the complexities of power dynamics.

3. Groundwater-Smith, S., Dockett, S. and Bottrell, D. (2015). Ethical Questions in Relation to Participatory Research with Children and Young People. In S. Groundwater-Smith, S. Dockett and D. Bottrell (Eds.), *Participatory Research with Children and Young People*, Thousand Oaks, CA: SAGE Publications (pp. 37–54), https://doi.org/10.4135/9781473910751.

   This chapter addresses the complex ethical considerations of the relationship between the researcher and child and youth participants, exploring power dynamics and practical strategies while offering guidance on empowering participants' voices.

4. Mann, A., Liley, J. and Kellett, M. (2014). Engaging Children and Young People in Research. In A. Clark, M. Robb, M. Hammersley and R. Flewitt (Eds.), *Understanding Research with Children and Young People*, London: SAGE Publications(pp. 285–304).

   Through an example of an original research project by an eleven-year-old, the authors illustrate the processes and challenges of involving young people as researchers, highlighting the unique insights and impact that emerge from the dissemination of child-led research.

5. The Centre for Resilient and Inclusive Societies (2022). *Youth Co-research Toolkit*. https://childethics.com/reflexive-tool/#1638255390841-abef32af-6648

   An essential resource for novice and experienced researchers, providing a comprehensive toolkit that prompts reflection throughout the research cycle, offering ethical strategies, practical tools and frameworks grounded in the UNCRC, along with best practice tips and FAQs to support meaningful youth participation in research.

Notes

1. Paragraph 58, (BERA, 2024) states that the community of 'educational researchers' is considered to mean all those engaged in educational research, including students, independent researchers and practitioners, charities and independent bodies. In support of Researcher Development Concordat, (BERA, 2024) contextualises that established educational researchers and the whole community hold a responsibility to support these groups. We use the term practitioner research and practitioner research broadly and to include and refer to a variety of forms and types of independent and community researchers across a range of settings and practices.
2. Information about Camtree is available here: https://camtree.org/about/.
3. This point is aligned to paragraph 19 (BERA, 2024), in terms of dual roles and collecting data for different purposes: 'An important consideration is the extent to which a researcher's reflective research into their own practice impinges upon others – for example, in the case of power relationships arising from the dual roles of teacher/lecturer/manager and researcher, and their impact on students and colleagues. Dual roles may also introduce explicit tensions in areas such as confidentiality. These may be addressed appropriately by, for example, making the researcher role very explicit, involving an independent third party in the research process and seeking agreement for politically controversial research. Researchers who are researching their own practice should also consider how to address any issues arising as a result of collecting data for different purposes – for example, using data collected for evaluation purposes for research purposes, or vice versa.'
4. This aligns with paragraph 9 (BERA, 2024): 'Researchers should do what they can to ensure that all potential participants understand, as well as they are able, what is involved in a study. They should be told why their participation is desired, what, if anything, they will be asked to do, what will happen to the data they provide and how and to whom the data will be reported. They also should be informed about the retention, sharing and any possible secondary uses of the data.'
5. Mindful of our own role and practice in terms of not putting undue demands on practitioners in the pursuit of sharing research, related to paragraph 34 (BERA, 2024): 'Ethical research design and implementation aim to put participants at their ease and to avoid making excessive demands on them.'
6. This aligns with paragraph 3 (BERA, 2024), though noting that those in the context of practitioner research may be part of the context, or

they may indeed be 'active' participants: 'Participants in research may be actively or passively involved in such processes as observation, experiment, auto/biographical reflection, survey or test. They may be collaborators or colleagues in the research process, or they may simply be implicated in the context in which a research project takes place. (For example, in a teacher or lecturer's research into their own professional practice, students or colleagues will be part of the context, but will not themselves be the focus of that research.) It is important for researchers to take account of the rights and interests of those indirectly affected by their research, and to consider whether action is appropriate – for example, they should consider whether it is necessary to provide information or obtain informed consent.'

7   This is aligned to mechanisms that support sharing and accessing research, in paragraph 70 (BERA, 2024): 'Educational researchers should communicate their findings, and the practical significance of their research, in a clear, straightforward fashion, and in language judged appropriate to the intended audience(s).'

8   This particularly aligns with paragraph 21 (BERA, 2024): 'Researchers using auto/biographical approaches and autoethnography need to consider how their work implicates other people, and what the consequences may be for individuals who, although not directly involved in a study, may be identifiable through their relationship with the researcher or other participants; consent may need to be sought from these individuals in some cases.'

9   It is worth noting, however, that such a position would potentially undermine guidance in paragraph 36 (BERA, 2024): 'The rights of individuals should be borne in mind along with any potential social benefits of the research, and the researcher's right to conduct research in the service of public understanding. The researcher's obligations to the wider research community and to the public good may, in some circumstances, outweigh the researcher's obligations to act in accordance with the wishes of those in positions of economic, legal or political authority over the participants (such as employers, headteachers or government officials).'

10 This aligns with paragraph 81 (BERA, 2024): 'The format(s) in which research is published, and the means by which those publications are disseminated, should take into account the needs and interests of the communities that were involved in the research. Researchers have a responsibility to share their findings with participants and their wider social groups as fully as possible, while maintaining confidentiality.'

11 This case study appears in a slightly adapted form as a web case study. Research Ethics Case Studies 2024 | BERA.

12 Article 12 of the UNCRC grants children the right to express their views freely in matters affecting them, with due consideration given to their age and maturity. They should also have the opportunity to be heard in legal proceedings. Article 13 of the UNCRC guarantees children the freedom of expression, allowing them to seek, receive and share information and ideas without restriction, regardless of borders or media (UNICEF, 1989).
13 Aligns with paragraph 70 (BERA, 2024) – See note 7. 'To assist researchers in making the results of their research accessible, consideration should be given to providing open access, as is increasingly required by sponsors and some other bodies. Mindful of the potential impact of research findings outside of academia or specific educational institutions and organisations, researchers should think carefully about the implications of publishing in outlets that restrict public access to their findings' (paragraph 72, BERA, 2024); and paragraph 81 (BERA, 2024) – see note 9.
14 Aligns with paragraph 9 (BERA, 2024) – see note 4.
15 'Principles of consent also apply to possible reuse of data. There are two relevant categories of such reuse: secondary data analysis by the same research team to address new research questions; or the sharing of the dataset for use by other researchers' (paragraph 28, BERA, 2024).
16 Additionally, '[r]esearchers should make known to the participants (or their guardians or responsible others) any predictable disadvantage or harm potentially arising from the process or reporting of the research' (paragraph 35, BERA, 2024) and '[t]he rights of individuals should be borne in mind along with any potential social benefits of the research' (paragraph 36, BERA, 2024).
17 Aligns with paragraph 9 (BERA, 2024) – see note 4 and 'Participants may be willing to take part in research even though they are unable to be fully informed about the implications of their participation' (paragraph 10, BERA, 2024).
18 'The institutions and settings within which the research is set also have an interest in the research, and ought to be considered in the process of gaining consent. Researchers should think about … whether they should adopt an institution's own … safeguarding procedures; this is usually a requirement' (paragraph 11, BERA, 2024).
19 Aligns with paragraph 81 (BERA, 2024) – see note 9.
20 Aligns with paragraph 34 (BERA, 2024) – see note 5.
21 'Researchers should be alert to non-verbal signs that individuals who previously consented to participate may no longer wish to. In such circumstances, renewed consent should be sought' (paragraph 8, BERA, 2024) and paragraph 34, (BERA 2024) - see note 5.

22 'In cases where participants are anonymised, researchers should be aware of the possible consequences to participants should it prove possible for them to be identified by association or inference' (paragraph 43, BERA, 2024) and 'Researchers need to be aware that participants' understandings of their level of privacy in a particular place, especially in online spaces, may be inaccurate' (paragraph 44, BERA, 2024).

23 Aligns with paragraph 36 (BERA, 2024) – see note 16 and paragraph 70 (BERA, 2024) – see note 7.

24 'All educational researchers should aim to protect the integrity and reputation of educational research by ensuring that they conduct their research to the highest standards. Researchers should contribute to the community spirit of critical analysis and constructive criticism that generates improvement in practice and enhancement of knowledge' (paragraph 59, BERA, 2024).

25 'Researchers should recognise the right of all participants to withdraw from the research for any or no reason, and participants should be informed of this right' (paragraph 31, BERA, 2024).

26 'In some cases, potential participants may not be in a social position vis-à-vis the researcher that enables them to give voluntary informed consent' (paragraph 20, BERA, 2024).

27 Aligns with paragraphs 31 and 33 – see note 25.

28 'Appropriate treatment of participants' data is required for the conduct of ethical research. Researchers should recognise the entitlement of both institutions and individual participants to privacy. This could involve anonymisation, pseudonymisation or employing "fictionalising" approaches when reporting; when using such approaches researchers should fully explain how and why they have done so. However, in some circumstances individual participants, or their guardians or responsible others, may willingly waive their right to confidentiality and anonymity. Researchers should recognise the right of participants to be identified as the originator of their own work if they so wish' (paragraph 39, BERA, 2024).

29 'Principles of consent apply to children and young people as well as to adults. This is termed assent for those under the age of legal consent in the setting/culture. However, children of different ages vary in their capacity to make informed decisions. BERA endorses the United Nations Convention on the Rights of the Child (UNCRC) the best interests of the child are the primary consideration, and children who are capable of forming their own views should be granted the right to express those views freely, and have them taken into consideration, in all matters affecting them, commensurate with their age and maturity. Information sheets and consent forms should be appropriately designed for participants who may differ in such factors as age, reading ability and attention span. Researchers

should be aware of issues to do with neurodiversity, as referenced in paragraph 2' (paragraph 23, BERA, 2024).
30 Aligns with paragraph 20 (BERA, 2024) – see note 26.
31 'Researchers should consider the implications of their research for the global community and the environment … This includes such specifics as the amount and type of travel, the nature of the food at meetings and dissemination events, and more fundamental questions about the actual research, for example, and the purposes for which it is undertaken' (paragraph 54, BERA, 2024).
32 Aligns with paragraph 19 (BERA, 2024) – see note 3.
33 '[R]esearchers should do what they can to ensure that relevant individuals and communities are not, intentionally or otherwise, excluded from participation in their research' (paragraph 37, BERA, 2024).
34 As outlined in Contributor Role Taxonomy (NISO, 2025), source: https://credit.niso.org/.

References

Aprile, K. T., Ellem, P. and Lole, L. (2021). Publish, perish, or pursue? Early career academics' perspectives on demands for research productivity in regional universities. *Higher Education Research and Development*, 40(6), 1131–45. https://doi.org/10.1080/07294360.2020.1804334.

British Educational Research Association (BERA). (2024). *Ethical Guidelines for Educational Research* (5th ed.). London: BERA. https://www.bera.ac.uk/publication/ethical-guidelines-for-educational-research-fifthedition-2024.

Bolton-King, R. S., Kara, H., Cassella, J. P., Rankin, B. W. J., Morgan, R. M., Burke, S., Fripp, D. and Kaye, J. P. (2020). Increasing the accessibility and impact of justice-related student and practitioner research. *Forensic Science International: Synergy*, 2, 60–71. https://doi.org/https://doi.org/10.1016/j.fsisyn.2019.09.009.

Fancourt, N., Foreman-Peck, L. and Oancea, A. (2022). Addressing ethical quandaries in practitioner research: A philosophical and exploratory study of responsible improvisation through hermeneutical conversation. *Teaching and Teacher Education*, 116, article 103760, 1–12. https://doi.org/https://doi.org/10.1016/j.tate.2022.103760.

Madikizela-Madiya, N. (2023a). Transforming higher education spaces through ethical research publication: A critique of the publish or perish aphorism. *Higher Education Research and Development*, 42(1), 186–99. https://doi.org/10.1080/07294360.2022.2048634.

Madikizela-Madiya, N. (2023b). Transforming higher education spaces through ethical research publication: A critique of the publish or perish aphorism. *Higher Education Research and Development*, 42(1), 186–99. https://doi.org/10.1080/07294360.2022.2048634.

NISO (2025). *Contributor Role Taxonomy*. CRedIT. 4 April. Retrieved 1 August 2025, from https://credit.niso.org/.

Parsons, S. (2021). The importance of collaboration for knowledge co-construction in 'close-to-practice' research. *British Educational Research Journal*, 47(6), 1490–9. https://doi.org/https://doi.org/10.1002/berj.3714.

Richardson, A. (2022). Introduction: Close-to-practice research in Holocaust Education. *Holocaust Studies*, 29(2), 167–80. https://doi.org/10.1080/17504902.2022.2058724

UNICEF (1989). *United Nations Convention of Rights for the Child*. https://www.unicef.org.uk/what-we-do/un-convention-child-rights/.

Wyse, D., Brown, C., Oliver, S. and Poblete, X. (2021). Education research and educational practice: The qualities of a close relationship. *British Educational Research Journal*, 47(6), 1466–89. https://doi.org/10.1002/berj.3626.

16

Openness, Inclusivity and Diversity: Supporting Early Career Researchers as Ethical Practice of Journal Peer Review

by *Sin-Wang Chong and Natalie Tegama*

Background

The prevalent 'publish-or-perish' culture in academia presented as the context to the previous chapter contributes to the exponential growth of academic publications, particularly journal articles, which are viewed as a more prestigious type of scholarly output in some disciplines such as the social sciences. In this chapter, we consider the role of Early Careers Researchers (ECRs) in journal peer review as an ethical imperative for cultivating a more inclusive and sustainable academic publishing ecosystem. We contend that the exclusion of ECRs based on perceived inexperience is misguided and that, with proper training and support, ECRs offer fresh insights and methodological awareness that enrich peer review and offer a practical response to reviewer shortages. We further demonstrate that creating structures, such as mentorship opportunities and the 'living' repository of ECR reviewers, advances equity and aligns with ethical standards that prioritise care, diversity and transparency in scholarly review practices. It is estimated that there are over 46,000 academic journals internationally, publishing over five million journal articles each year, and the number of articles published continues to increase every year (Curcic, 2023). Academic publishing relies on peer reviewers; academics who voluntarily devote their time and effort to contribute to the scientific community and provide expert feedback to journal manuscripts. Journal peer review has always been operating on a voluntary basis with little or no tangible reward, relying mostly on the goodwill of academics. While most universities acknowledge such contribution as part of an academic's citizenship or service, peer reviewing for journals is not always regarded as the most rewarding activity in academia. Academic publishers rely on the free labour of academics when it comes to reviewing for journals, although some sort of recognition is offered to reviewers. The most common form of recognition is an email from the publisher or journal, normally automatically generated by the system, showing appreciation to the reviewers' effort; some journals publish the names of peer reviewers at the end of each year and others offer the chance to add contributions to a researcher's Open Researcher and Contributor ID (ORCID). More recently, there have been discussions on whether peer reviewers need to be paid for the work that they do (Cheah and Piasecki, 2022), and if so, what forms of remuneration would be the most appropriate. However, it seems that monetary rewards for peer reviewers are not a viable option at present due to the additional expenses for publishers and resources needed to appraise peer-review reports to ensure that high-quality comments are provided.

Many have commented that journal peer review is not a sustainable system due to some of the reasons discussed above. Journal editors, for example, find it increasingly challenging to identify peer reviewers who have the relevant expertise and are willing to review for them. It is not uncommon to have manuscripts sitting in the system for months without being sent out for peer review despite the numerous invitations sent to reviewers. The crux of the problem with journal peer review can be illustrated with a basic economics principle: there is more demand than supply, with academics prioritising publishing over peer reviewing. The result of this is not only the scarcity of journal peer reviewers but the subpar quality of feedback received at times, leading to unnecessary tardiness in the review process because editors have to invite additional reviewers to make an informed editorial decision, or editors may end up reviewing the papers themselves. Advocates for responsible use of the peer-review system have suggested that, for every manuscript that academics submit to journals, they should expect to review at least one manuscript, if not more. We believe this is a good reminder, but it still will not solve the problem at hand because it is impossible to increase the base of active peer reviewers exponentially in a short period of time. In our view, the long-term solution should be to diversify the pool of peer reviewers and strengthen the quality of reviews by involving early career researchers (ECRs).

While we recognise that the definition of ECRs varies across countries, contexts and funders, in this chapter, we refer to ECRs as researchers who are currently reading for a doctorate or those who have recently been appointed to a fixed-term or permanent academic position, such as a research fellow or a lecturer in the UK context. To ECRs, journal peer review is a mystified process because they have little or no experience submitting to a journal, let alone reviewing. In a traditional doctoral programme within the UK context and other higher education systems that follow similar processes, students are expected to submit a thesis at the end of their study, and students rarely think about publishing parts of the thesis before graduation. Besides, ECRs may feel that they are not qualified to review manuscripts for journals because, in their view, peer reviewers should be senior academics. While it is necessary for peer reviewers to have some experience in academic publishing, and preferably with a record of publications, we believe that ECRs can be competent reviewers for journals provided that appropriate training, mentoring and support are in place. In addition, we argue that it is necessary to provide training, mentoring and support in the earlier stages of academic careers to develop the necessary competencies for good reviewership.

We do not see the involvement of ECRs to peer review for journals as a quick fix to the issue of having inadequate peer reviewers, but ECRs are crucial for developing an inclusive and sustainable academic publishing ecology. Based on a review of ethical guidelines for conducting research in Education and Social Sciences (Chong, 2022), we would even argue that opening up peer review to ECRs should be seen as an ethical practice in journal peer review. This chapter, which is written by an experienced journal editor and an ECR, offers complementary view towards ethical peer-review practices by suggesting ways to involve and support ECRs. Sin-Wang is an experienced journal editor who edits three international journals and an encyclopaedia for Elsevier at the time of writing, serves on the editorial board of a number of journals, and has reviewed for over thirty journals and academic publishers. With an aim to make the journal peer-review process more transparent and accessible for ECRs, Sin-Wang co-founded and co-directs the Scholarly Peers (https://scholarlypeers.substack.com/) platform, which includes a Twitter/X account, a blog and a podcast. In the twenty episodes of podcast, Sin-Wang interviewed ECRs and established scholars about how they navigate the peer-review process. Natalie is an ECR with limited experience of reviewing for journals. At the time of writing, she has reviewed for five international journals. However, she has worked in a capacity-building role, supporting other ECRs with developing both their writing and reviewing capacities.

The ethical dilemma

Ethical issues associated with journal peer review have always been around its objectivity and the broader implications of that on scholars and scholarship. While there are various models of journal peer review such as open peer review (identities of authors and peer reviewers are known to each other, and often the reviewers' comments will be published alongside the accepted manuscript), single-blind review (identity of author is known to the peer reviewer), double-blind review (identities of both authors and reviewers are hidden), collaborative review (two or a group of peer reviewers review a manuscript together), and post-publication review (peer review takes place after the manuscript is published in a journal), the one that is most adopted in educational research is double-blind peer review. In double-blind peer review, the identities of both the authors and peer reviewers are only known by the editor who handles the manuscript but not to each other. This is achieved by asking authors to submit a manuscript with all identifiable information about the authors removed (e.g. names, affiliations, references of work by the authors). The premise is that peer reviewers can assess the manuscript with less bias when they do not have the knowledge of who the authors are. Equally, without the identity of the peer reviewers revealed in the process, reviewers can be more vocal in their comments, without the fear of damaging professional relationships or even retaliation. For instance, if a manuscript is submitted by a leading scholar in the field and the identities of both the author and the reviewers are known, reviewers may find it uncomfortable to provide constructive criticism about the paper due to power imbalance.

Maintaining the blindness of the review

Even with double-blinding peer review, reviewing is not hassle-free. Ethical issues noted in double-blind peer review include instances where an author's identity becomes known and/or when unprofessional peer review comments are made (BERA, 2024, paragraph 59)[1]. Even when authors are asked to remove all information from the manuscript that would potentially reveal their identities, there is still a chance that an author's identity can be revealed to peer reviewers. This is possible when the author has published extensively in a niche or new area of research, and they refer to their work (albeit blinded) frequently in the manuscript. It is not difficult for peer reviewers to infer who the author is if they work in the same area, especially when the author directly quotes their work in the manuscript or when a preprint of the manuscript is made available online. When the identity of the author is no longer blinded, the objectivity of peer review is at risk. This is something that Sin-Wang, as editor of a journal, has experienced. After a reviewer accepted his invitation to review a manuscript, the reviewer came to realise that the manuscript was submitted by their colleague, with whom they had a conflict. Instead of notifying the editor, the reviewer completed the review and notified their colleague (the author of the manuscript) that they had submitted a review. This was brought to Sin-Wang's attention as handling editor, and it was decided that the comments of the peer reviewer should be removed, and another peer reviewer was sought. Furthermore, the double-blind nature of peer review may be taken advantage of by some, resulting in unprofessional peer reviewer comments in the form of personal attacks and unnecessarily harsh criticisms (Chong and Lin, 2024). These unhelpful comments are detrimental to the quality of peer review, and it is especially so when ECRs, who are still finding their feet in navigating journal peer review, receive such feedback. This may lead to ECRs becoming less willing to submit their work to academic journals to avoid such traumatic experience or they are mistakenly led to believe that their work has no value and place in academia.

Recruitment of reviewers

Regardless of the model of peer review that a journal adopts, it is increasingly difficult to find suitable peer reviewers who are willing to accept an invitation. It is not unheard of that an editor's invitation to review is declined by a dozen peer reviewers. This results in not only delays in the peer-review process but also additional workload for journal editors, with some editors needing to review the manuscripts themselves.

There are a number of reasons leading to the challenge of eliciting peer reviewers' support. First, as pointed out at the outset of the chapter, to survive (let alone thrive) in the 'publish-or-perish' culture in academia, researchers prioritise publishing their research in top-tiered international journals rather than reviewing for journals. In some contexts, research excellence of academics is measured quantitatively by universities; for example, academics are expected to publish a certain number of first-authored articles every year. Academics working in some universities are required to publish in high-ranking journals, typically indexed in the Social Sciences Citation Index for educational researchers, in order for them to be qualified for tenure and promotion applications. Although peer reviewing for journals is acknowledged by universities as contributions, they usually carry much less weight when compared to publications in high-ranking journals and successful grant applications. Second, the motivation of academics to serve as peer reviewers is dampened by the fact that it is unpaid labour. After a peer reviewer spends hours, if not days, reading a manuscript and providing constructive feedback, the only recognition they receive is an automatically generated email from the publisher thanking them for their contributions, justifying their unpaid work as service to the common good of academia. Lately, there has been slight improvement in the situation where we have started to see tangible rewards or mechanisms in place to explicitly acknowledge the contributions of peer reviewers. One example of tangible reward is that some publishers provide complimentary access to the journal or book content to peer reviewers for a fixed period of time. Platforms such as Publons work in partnership with major publishers to provide a space for academics to display their track record of peer review openly, including the number of reviews they have completed and the journals that they have reviewed for. Some journals (e.g. *Higher Education Research & Development*) offer an annual peer reviewer award to publicly recognise the exemplary performance of peer reviewers.

The potential for embracing ECRs

The root of the problem in journal peer review remains: there are more manuscripts to be reviewed than peer reviewers who are available to do so. At the beginning of the chapter, we made a case for inviting ECRs to review for journals. At the same time, we acknowledge that ECRs are not 'cheap labour' or a 'low-cost remedy' to the peer-reviewer shortage problem. However, excluding ECRs from journal peer review under the banner that they are inexperienced is at best misguided. Equally, we would argue that asking ECRs to review for journals without providing adequate training and support is unethical (BERA, 2024, paragraph 83).[2] ECRs have a lot to offer in journal peer review. Apart from the obvious fact that they may be more likely to accept an invitation from journal editors, ECRs provide fresh perspectives to reviewing a piece of research as they are normally highly acquainted with the latest literature or innovative research methodologies due to their doctoral or post-doctoral research. Nonetheless, from our experience, there are challenges associated with ECRs acting as peer reviewers for journals. Without stating the obvious, ECRs may not have a lot of experience in reviewing for journals and therefore would benefit from training. In the context of doctoral researchers or recent postgraduates, they may not have the chance to submit parts of their thesis to journals, let alone reviewing for journals. In some universities, there are school-run or student-led journals that provide doctoral researchers with the experience to review. However, the process and rigour of peer review are likely to differ from that in an international-refereed journal. In terms of peer review training, it is our understanding that such training is rarely provided as an integral part of doctoral programmes, at least in the UK. We find this surprising as other forms of researcher development training such as academic or research writing are integral. Chong (2021) commented that peer review training is mostly provided by publishers in the form of online workshops or online resources. These training opportunities focus on developing the knowledge of ECRs about the journal peer-review process, yet there is often a lack of support where skills- and community-based training are concerned. We understand skills-based training as focused on developing the skills of ECRs to give constructive and specific feedback, and community-based training as building communities of practice where ECRs share both experiences and good writing practices.

ECR access and capacity issues

An additional challenge for ECRs to get involved in peer reviewing is that there is a lack of opportunities for them to review for journals. Peer reviewers are selected based on their research areas, which are usually demonstrated through their track record of publications. This is also how some peer-review systems such as ScholarOne recommend peer reviewers to journal editors. ECRs, especially those who are new to academic publishing, may not be known by editors. We have heard stories from ECRs about how their supervisors, who serve on editorial boards or as editors, invite them to review for their journals. In other cases, the supervisor may receive an invitation to review but is not available. Instead of declining the invitation, the supervisor suggests their doctoral student as a potential reviewer or they co-review the manuscript with their student. Even though opportunities to peer review are made available to ECRs, not all ECRs might appreciate the invitation because of workload. Some doctoral researchers may perceive peer reviewing as less important and urgent when compared to completing their thesis and graduating on time. Doctoral researchers these days have multiple roles, especially those who are on scholarships; in addition to completing their research, they serve as teaching or research assistants to their supervisors. Peer reviewing sounds even less appealing with these additional teaching, marking and research activities. For ECRs who have recently graduated from their doctoral programme, their focus is usually on finding a job in academia, in the industry or in the third sector. For those who have started their first academic position, their priority may be to get familiar with the new work environment and requirements. All these are valid reasons for ECRs to turn down peer-review invitations.

Maximising ECR peer-review participation

To encourage ECRs to participate in journal peer review, a three-pronged approach is needed. First, there is a clear need to focus on knowledge and skills development for ECRs, which may include developing repositories to compile resources on peer reviewing for ECRs, making them easier to access. Second, to facilitate greater levels of support in the peer-review process, there is scope to develop more opportunities for joint peer-review experiences, coupling ECRs with senior academics, leveraging the opportunity for both mentorship and experiential learning. Journal editors and publishers need to be encouraged to invite ECRs with the relevant experience to review for journals.

The case study: Platform development for supporting ECR peer review

The case study we present describes the development of *Scholarly Peers*, a platform that is co-founded and co-directed by Sin-Wang and his colleague, Shannon Mason (Nagasaki University, Japan) and similarly encapsulates this three-pronged approach. In particular, the focus of the section will be on the latest endeavour of *Scholarly Peers*, that is, the development of a 'living' repository of ECR peer reviewers in the fields of Education and Applied Linguistics.

Courses of action

Scholarly Peers (https://scholarlypeers.substack.com/) was founded in 2021. At the time, Sin-Wang and Shannon were higher education ECR researchers with relatively limited experience and new to the publishing process as peer reviewers and editors. After winning the Higher Education Research and Development Society of Australasia (HERDSA) Routledge Reviewer of the Year Award in 2020, Sin-Wang and Shannon decided to join forces to work on several projects about journal peer review. These included publishing a collaborative autoethnography on the development of their 'feedback literacy' (Chong, 2021) as journal peer reviewers, a genre analysis of their peer-review reports, recording podcasts for the British Educational Research Association on the topic and delivering a workshop series for the British Association for Applied Linguistics. With the support of Sin-Wang's institutional funding, they also embarked on a new initiative to create a community of practice for ECRs in all disciplines to share experiences and find resources about journal peer review, which led to the establishment of *Scholarly Peers*. On its inception, it included a Twitter/X account that Sin-Wang and Shannon manage and, at the time of writing, continue to use to repost information or resources about journal peer review and provide tips and suggestions for ECRs who are reviewing for the first time. Users are encouraged to tag the account when sharing their peer-review experiences. At the time of writing, *Scholarly Peers* has over 900 followers, who are ECRs from disciplines in humanities, social sciences and natural sciences. In addition to this, scholars are provided with a website where peer review-related content and resources are curated across a number of topics, including but not limited to an overview of the peer reviewing process, opting in and out of reviewing, navigating peer review, including developing key competencies for reviewing and understanding ethics in review discourse. Other topics include guidance on responding to reviewers and dealing with rejection and resubmission. These are coupled with personal narratives on review processes from either side of the review process.

Additionally, the website hosts various video-audio visuals, including symposium recordings on journal peer review; these are coupled with a blog on which peers are encouraged to share their peer-review experiences, and a podcast, which at the time of writing has produced twenty episodes, with the first ten focusing on experiences of ECRs and the subsequent ten on reflections from senior academics (e.g. journal editors). Beyond the website, the podcast is also accessible from other podcasting platforms. Each podcast episode is approximately thirty minutes, and the host discusses the following questions with the guest:

- Can you briefly introduce yourself and your experience in journal peer review?
- Can you share with us some unforgettable peer-review experiences as an author?
- Can you share with us some unforgettable peer-review experiences as a peer reviewer/journal editor?
- How do you learn to navigate the peer-review process?
- What are the challenges that you face in the peer-review process?
- What do you think can be done to support early career researchers/doctoral researchers in the peer-review process?
- What advice will you give to early career researchers/doctoral researchers who are going to submit their first-ever manuscript to a journal?

With regard to the latest projects of *Scholarly Peers*, Sin-Wang has co-edited a book on developing feedback literacy for journal peer reviewers with a doctoral researcher (Chong and Gao, 2025). The focus of the book is on academics' reflections on becoming more skilled at providing useful and constructive feedback as peer reviewers. Another initiative, which is the focus this chapter, is the development of an online repository of ECR peer reviewers in Education and Applied Linguistics.[3] This endeavour is a milestone for *Scholarly Peers* as it aims to change the culture of journal peer review to be more inclusive by providing a 'living' database that hosts information about ECRs who have expressed an interest in reviewing for journals. From his experience as an author, peer reviewer and journal editor, Sin-Wang understands that there are many ECRs who are interested in gaining experience in journal peer review, but they do not know where to look for opportunities. Even though ECRs are encouraged to approach journal editors directly, some may not feel this is appropriate. At the same time, Sin-Wang understands that journal editors are also desperately seeking committed reviewers who share the relevant experience and expertise. However, it is not easy for them to identify ECRs apart from their own doctoral researchers or junior colleagues. Sin-Wang also believes that there needs to be a way to formally recognise and document the wealth of experience that ECRs have in journal peer review to repel the impression that ECRs are not qualified to review for journals.

This 'living' database invites ECRs who are interested in serving as a peer reviewer to register on the database. The idea was inspired by the 'Volunteers in the Librarian Peer Reviewers Database'[4] that Sin-Wang came across on Twitter/X. To make the project manageable, Sin-Wang decided to focus on two disciplines that he works in: Education and Applied Linguistics in the current phase. A registration form was created using Google Form.[5] On the form, the purpose of the 'Repository of Early Career Researcher Peer Reviewers' is clearly stated, and a definition of ECRs is provided. Other information included in the registration form includes how information in the repository will be shared and used, and to obtain consent from registrants to use the information they supplied:

> Please note that this form is a public document and all the information can be accessible by anyone. By completing this form, you give consent to having your information shared with the public. Your information will be stored in a **fully identifiable** form. Your information will be stored in a Google Drive that is password-protected. For more details about how your information is handled, please refer to the 'privacy policy' of Google at the end of the page.

On the form, it is made clear that this 'living' repository is a *Scholarly Peers* initiative, and there is no agreement between *Scholarly Peers* and journal editors or academic publishers that ECRs in the repository will be invited to serve as peer reviewers. ECRs, who have registered on the database, are given an option to update their information anytime by completing the change request form. In the registration form, ECRs are asked to provide the following information, which will be shown on the 'living' repository:

- Name (last, first)
- Current affiliation
- Current position
- Example publication 1 (including DOI)
- Example publication 2 (including DOI)
- Areas of expertise
- Journals they have reviewed for
- Website (e.g. Google Scholar, personal/institutional website, ResearchGate)
- ORCID ID
- Degree(s)
- Other information about them

As can be seen from the information above, the aim of this repository is to provide journal editors with a comprehensive list of ECRs who are willing to review for journals. Although the information provided by the ECRs is not verified, the inclusion of some items could hopefully provide journal editors with some evidence that the ECRs in this database have some experience in academic publishing and reviewing for journals. For instance, ECRs are asked to include two of their example publications as well as the names of the journals that they have reviewed for. ECRs are also required to include their academic profiles, which can provide additional information about the researcher for journal editors. At the time this chapter was being written, the repository had 205 ECRs registered. Although they are primarily based in the UK, others are based in universities more widely, in Australia, Austria, China, Finland, Germany, Ireland, Italy, Malaysia, Norway, Spain, South Africa and Tunisia. Positions that these ECRs hold can be broadly categorised into three types academic positions, teaching positions and administrative and managerial positions. Academic positions include Associate Lecturer, Assistant Professor, Associate Professor, Associate Social Researcher, Associate Tutor, Sessional Academic, Lecturer, Doctoral Candidate, Doctoral Researcher, Doctoral Student, Postdoctoral Fellow, Research Assistant, Research Associate, Research Fellow and Senior Lecturer. Teaching positions include Instructor, Teacher, Teaching Assistant and Teaching Fellow. ECRs who are currently holding administrative and managerial positions are also interested in reviewing for journals; these positions are Dean Assistant for Administrative & Financial Affairs, Director of English Department, Education Manager, Initial Teacher Education Quality and Compliance Manager, Principal and Senior Technical Analyst. It is both welcoming and concerning to see that ECRs with a wide range of professional and academic backgrounds are interested in serving as peer reviewers for journals. On the one hand, it is encouraging that the list is growing and there are more ECRs than we originally anticipated, who are interested in reviewing for journals; from a research-practice partnership perspective, we are especially pleased to see ECRs who hold teaching and administrative/managerial positions expressing an interest in peer reviewing. On the other hand, we notice there are diverse needs among the ECRs that need to be addressed. The list provides insights into how we often perceive ECRs as a unitary group rather than acknowledging that there are individual needs and different motivations for them to review for journals. To make ECR-inclusive peer review a reality in the long run, there needs to be a more fine-grained and bottom-up understanding of who ECRs are and the diversity they represent.

Alternative courses of action

We find that initiatives such as the 'living' repository are important in nurturing the type of inclusivity and diversity that is recommended within the British Education Research Association Guidelines (BERA, 2024). While BERA recognises the diversity and multidisciplinary of the education research community and positions itself as open to diversity of approaches and philosophical positions, prizing respect and 'an ethic of care for all involved in educational research by and for researchers' (BERA, 2024: 9), there remains a clear need for developing activities that nurture and create an environment of care amongst researchers.

Embracing diversity towards decolonisation

Specific to reviews, the BERA guidelines advocate for an open-minded and inclusive approach to reviewing that maintains plurality in the interpretation of concepts such as 'reliability, validity, credibility, trustworthiness, subjectivity and objectivity' (BERA, 2024: 9). These are concepts that, for example, are routinely in question within scholarship that advocates for greater inclusivity for previously and presently oppressed groups of people, including scholars of decolonial thought. Within these groups, for example, there are emergent ideas that may sit outside the dominant ideas, associated with hegemony, which should be heard and embraced within a more inclusive academy. Decolonial scholars usefully refer to the relationship between previously colonised and colonised peoples as a centre-periphery relationship (Mignolo and Walsh, 2018), with those who sit in the periphery typically being scholars from previously colonised places whose past and present-day attempts to resist and decolonise fields such as education have been met with resistance. We therefore contend that taking seriously BERA guidelines on the 'ethics of care for all involved' (BERA, 2024: 9) and reinterpreting openness as inclusivity and diversity specific to ECR participation requires multiplicity in the consideration and uptake of alternative courses of action.

Explicitly opening the doors

Firstly, journals engaging seriously with the question of ethics around the gatekeeping practices of reviewers would be powerful. An approach may be to include audits and aggregated publication of reviewers' profiles, to, for example, make more apparent where reviewers are geographically located and whether they are ECRs or otherwise. This transparency may encourage a shift in how the community of practice engages with ECRs in terms of participation, particularly those from previously or presently disadvantaged groups. This type of action may work to benefit the diversity of perspectives being brought to assessing what counts as quality through the peer-review process.

Workshopping as ECR invitations to the academy

Secondly, it is essential to draw lessons from other fields where there are efforts to build greater inclusivity and plurality of voices by nurturing ECRs who are disadvantaged in various ways, such as working within financially less-privileged institutions, including through initiatives such as the bioethics workshops. These seek to develop researcher capacity across the entire writing-to-publishing pipeline. These workshops include writing skills development for publication, teaching how to engage with and respond to reviewers' comments in contexts where there is disagreement. We find this to be particularly important for enriching the field of education research as it serves to bolster the confidence of scholars whose work may sit in the periphery. The workshops also engage ECRs in developing their capacity as reviewers. This presents the opportunity for more experienced scholars who are committed to creating an environment of care for all involved in education research with an opportunity to teach an ethic of care, paying forward to the educational community of practitioners as part of practising good academic citizenship. In some contexts, these workshops can be conducted in collaboration with journals that can then invite ECRs to submit to their journal as authors and special editors. Overall, we believe this approach to be not only in keeping with BERA guidelines but also an opportunity to embed BERA's ethics early on in the career journeys of ECRs, ensuring not only an ethic of care but also that the commitment that 'educational researchers should not criticise their peers in a defamatory or unprofessional manner' (BERA, 2024, paragraph 61).[6]

Institutional responsibility for researcher resilience-building

Thirdly, the BERA guideline section on 'Responsibilities for researchers' wellbeing and development' (BERA, 2024, paragraphs 82 and 83)[7,8] brings to attention the legal and moral obligation of institutions towards the academic community of practice broadly. This includes physical and psychosocial wellbeing. BERA specifically addresses the institution and its obligations to safeguard researchers as well as promote their personal and professional growth. We understand institutional culture to be primarily experienced through interactions with not only the rules, explicit or implicit, but also the relationships between employees within the institution. According to AdvanceHE, researcher culture across UK institutions is often scored lowly by ECRs (Neves and Stephenson, 2023). It is therefore important that both institutions and senior academics create opportunities for professional and personal growth for ECRs, including through resilience-building within the context of developing feedback literacy (Chong, 2021). Resilience-building within this context will reduce the likelihood of traumatic experiences from receiving peer-review feedback, such that it leaves them reluctant to either write or submit their work to academic journals and feel displacement within academia. Resilience-building is an invitation for institutions and senior academics to commit to developing ECRs' capacities in feedback literacy from an early stage of the doctoral process using opportunities within the doctoral process as opportunities for critical and caring engagement. This would enable ECRs to develop feedback literacy, including the understanding of how to identify and reject undue, unkind criticism in the review process. This is important as ECRs' relationship with the academy and sense of belonging or unbelonging can be established during these foundational years. For some doctoral researchers, fraught relationships with supervisors and undue criticism contribute to feelings of unbelonging. This is particularly important given some of the data arising on ECRs' experiences. For example, the Neves and Stephenson (2023) Advance HE report on postgraduate research experience found that nearly half (43 per cent) of over 10,000 ECRs did not feel part of the research community. For racialised and minoritised groups, this can be compounded with the intersection of other negative experiences within the academy and can lead to their leaving the academy with broader implication retention and potentially a less diverse academy (Islam et al., 2024).

Rewarding reviewers with accruing fee waivers

Taking into account disparities within the wider, global educational community for example, colleagues from low- and middle-income countries (LMICs) may work within institutions that cannot afford the often-exuberant publishing fees required by journals to publish their work. This in turn puts many 'high impact-factor' journals outside the realm of possibility for many, and most certainly for ECRs. Where some journals now charge reduced fees for LMIC scholars, this is not uniform across the journals, nor does it make the reduced fees affordable. We therefore propose a fourth cluster of alternative action, for example, including further reductions of publishing fees for these scholars who demonstrate academic citizenship through reviews, etc. This is already happening within some open access publications that are offering a credit system to reviewers towards future full or partial waiver of their article-processing charges. As discussed above, we hold contention with the review process's reliance on the free labour of academics. The ethical issues with this are ever more pronounced in the context of scholars from LMICs whose institutions may not be able to afford the publishing fees of the very journals in which they are publishing.

Conclusion

We started off this chapter with a question of whether supporting ECRs should be perceived as one of the essential criteria for ethical practice of journal peer review. We highlighted several areas in the review process that raise ethical concerns. These include the labour intensiveness, the question of free labour, not only for ECRs, but for academics more broadly, alongside other challenges such as limited opportunities to review for ECRs. In the wider context of ECRs hoping to publish, challenges associated with reviewers not exercising an ethic of care in their engagement with the review process can lead to potentially traumatic experiences that may see ECRs growing reluctant to engage not only with submitting papers for publication but significant implications for their confidence in academic writing more generally and a marginalisation in their sense of belonging within the academy. We highlighted that, whilst these present ethical challenges in the immediate and personal sense, they also contribute to a lack of diversity in the academy, as these experiences may compound and intersect with other negative experiences for minoritised scholars. We presented an example of a course of action led by Sin-Wang in the form of a 'living' repository of ECR scholars. We then looked further afield to the field of bioethics, where there have been demonstrable efforts to develop ECRs' capacity across the research to publication pipeline. There remains a clear need for further engagement with alterity, to consider other courses of action. We therefore provide some reflective questions below for readers' engagement.

Reflective questions

1 What support mechanism does your institution provide to build ECR capacity in reviewing? Are there ways this can be improved at the institutional level?

2   In what ways do you think senior academics can demonstrate an ethic of care in their engagement with the work of ECRs?
3   Reflecting on your own experience, have you given or received an ethic of care? What impact has this had on your own practice?

Reflecting on the above questions, how can an ethic of care be implemented or improved at your institution and in your own practice.

Further reading

1. Chong, S. W. (2021). **Improving peer-review by developing reviewers' feedback literacy.** *Learned Publishing*, 34(3), 461–7. https://doi.org/10.1002/leap.1378.

    This article introduces and discusses the concept of feedback literacy in the realm of journal peer review and suggests three approaches to developing authors' and reviewers' feedback literacy: a knowledge-based, skills-based, and community-based approaches.

2. Chong, S. W. and Mason, S. (2021). **Demystifying the process of scholarly peer-review: An autoethnographic investigation of feedback literacy of two award-winning peer reviewers.** *Humanities and Social Sciences Communications*, 8, 266. https://doi.org/10.1057/s41599-021-00951-2.

    This is a collaborative reflection of two early career educational researchers on how they developed their resilience for responding to critical feedback and skills to provide constructive feedback as peer reviewers.

3. Mason, S. and Chong, S. W. (2022). **Bringing light to a hidden genre: The peer review report.** *Higher Education Research & Development*, 42(3), 664–78. https://doi.org/10.1080/07294360.2022.2073976.

    Using genre analysis, the authors analysed their own peer review reports and developed an organisational framework for journal peer reviewers to develop their comments.

Notes

1   Paragraph 59, (BERA, 2024): All educational researchers should aim to protect the integrity and reputation of educational research by ensuring that they conduct their research to the highest standards.

Researchers should contribute to the community spirit of critical analysis and constructive criticism that generates improvement in practice and enhancement of knowledge.

2   Paragraph 83, (BERA, 2024): Employers and sponsors need to avoid exploiting differences in the conditions of work and roles of other researchers, including student researchers and those on time-limited contracts. Employers are also responsible for supporting researchers' personal and professional career development. The BERA Charter for Research Staff in Education provides guidance on these issues. Researchers employed in higher education institutions in the UK are covered by the Concordat to Support the Career Development of Researchers, which stipulates the standards that research staff can expect from the institution, as well as their responsibilities as researchers.

3   https://docs.google.com/spreadsheets/d/1z0-CYseAP_nQBv0YCr-T1_aQAZAm2-CzLLGEj7Obipc/edit?usp=sharing.

4   https://docs.google.com/spreadsheets/d/1r0_LhQUM8bkXV0-SFCNF954Ebl8yljrRS5qmrC0yL1U/edit#gid=1340033345.

5   https://forms.gle/GsicRaUefR8GHjAHA.

6   Paragraph 61, (BERA, 2024): Educational researchers should not criticise their peers in a defamatory or unprofessional manner, in any medium.

7   Paragraph 82, (BERA, 2024): Safeguarding the physical and psychological wellbeing of researchers is part of the ethical responsibility of employers and sponsors, as well as of researchers themselves. In general, there should be an ethics of care for researchers, including self-care. Safety can be a particular concern in certain circumstances, for example when fieldwork is undertaken in situations that are potentially risky. Researchers should be aware of the legal responsibilities as well as the moral duty of institutions towards the safety of staff and students. Institutions, sponsors and independent researchers should consider whether an in-depth risk assessment and ongoing monitoring of researcher safety is advisable, especially for those undertaking fieldwork, working in certain jurisdictions and/or investigating sensitive issues; this may be required by employers and sponsors. Principal investigators, other researchers, students undertaking research and their supervisors should ideally be offered training on researcher safety. Specialist training should be made available to researchers entering conflict or post-conflict settings, or areas with high levels of infection or other risks.

8   Paragraph 83, (BERA, 2024): Employers and sponsors need to avoid exploiting differences in the conditions of work and roles of other researchers, including student researchers and those on time-limited contracts. Employers are also responsible for supporting researchers' personal and professional career development. The BERA Charter for

Research Staff in Education provides guidance on these issues. Researchers employed in higher education institutions in the UK are covered by the Concordat to Support the Career Development of Researchers, which stipulates the standards that research staff can expect from the institution, as well as their responsibilities as researchers.

References

BERA (2024). *Ethical Guidelines for Educational Research* (5th ed.). London: BERA. https://www.bera.ac.uk/publication/ethical-guidelines-for-educational-research-fifth-edition-2024

Cheah, P. Y. and Piasecki, J. (2022). Should peer reviewers be paid to review academic papers? *The Lancet*, 399(10335), 1601. https://doi.org/10.1016/S0140-6736(21)02804-X.

Chong, S. W. (2021). Improving peer-review by developing reviewers' feedback literacy. *Learned Publishing*, 34(3), 461–7. https://doi.org/10.1002/leap.1378.

Chong, S. W. (2022). *Researcher's Report for BERA Ethical Guidelines Review* [unpublished report]. United Kingdom: British Educational Research Association.

Chong, S. W. and Gao, A. L. (Eds.) (2025). *Developing Feedback Literacy for Academic Journal Peer Review: Narratives from Researchers in Education and Applied Linguistics*. London: Routledge.

Chong, S. W. and Lin, T. (2024). Feedback practices in journal peer-review: A systematic literature review. *Assessment & Evaluation in Higher Education*, 49(1), 1–12. https://doi.org/10.1080/02602938.2022.2164757.

Curcic, D. (2023). Number of academic papers published per year. *WordsRated*. June. https://wordsrated.com/number-of-academic-papers-published-per-year/.

Islam, M., Das, N. and Odaro, L. (2024). *Understanding and exploring the experiences of Black and Asian Postgraduate Research (PGR) students*. University of Southampton. https://doi.org/10.5258/SOTON/P1131.

Mignolo, W. D., and Walsh, C. E. (2018). *On Decoloniality: Concepts, Analytics, Praxis*. Durham, NC: Duke University Press. https://doi.org/10.1215/9780822371779.

Neves, J. and Stephenson, R. (2023). *Student Academic Experience Survey 2023*. https://www.hepi.ac.uk/wp-content/uploads/2023/06/Student-Academic-Experience-Survey-2023.pdf.

Section 3

Situating Ethical Guidance

Section 3 Foreword
by *Nicole Brown*

Section 3, of what the book editors hope is proving an enlightening book for readers, stands apart by delving deeply into the ethical dimensions of educational research. Unlike previous sections that may have focused on case studies and practical applications, Section 3 aims to problematise and theorise ethical guidelines, questioning their relevance and adaptability in diverse research contexts. As Section 3 shows, not every research context and research relationship fit neatly into conventional categories. Rather, individual settings and circumstances mean that ethical guidelines may require more radical rethinking. As such, Section 3 is a must-read for anyone involved in educational research, offering profound insights and practical guidance on navigating the complex ethical landscape of our field.

All chapters in Section 3 deal with aspects of research that lie somewhat outside what is considered conventional, traditional, 'normal' within educational research. Here, we explore what it means to be so closely involved with and in the field of study that a research project may have begun before it is even recognised as such. In Chapter 17, Sara Young presents 'I'm going to be in a book' as to the negotiation of research with adolescents. Lisa-Maria Müller and Victoria Cook take you, as a reader outside academia, to explore in Chapter 18 the establishment of The Chartered College of Teaching Research Ethics Panel and what it means to be independent as researchers, thus not having academic affiliations and not belonging to higher education institutions. Chapter 19 is set across Ukrainian Universities, where Oksana Zabolotna and Iryna Kushnir reflect on research about ethical guidance awareness at a time when the fourth edition of the BERA *Ethical Guidelines for Educational Research* (BERA, 2018) was translated into the Ukrainian language as a basis for developing national guidelines. This explores how cultural and linguistic influences and specificities may impact ethics and ethical thinking in research, and then what this all means for ethics approval processes and the negotiation of ethics in the research process. Barbara Skinner, Ronan Kelly and Maria Stewart pick up on the importance of attention to multilingualism in education and education research in Chapter 20, focusing on decisions to use interpreters through two vignettes, also with reference to the fourth edition of the guidelines (BERA, 2018) in place at the time.

By drawing on specific research experiences, the chapters engage critically rather than descriptively with ethics. It is a vital resource that equips you with the knowledge and tools to conduct ethical research in education.

17

'I'm Going to Be in a Book': Negotiating Research with Adolescents in Accordance with Ethical Guidelines

by *Sara Young*

Introduction

This chapter examines the ethical implications of working in a participatory way with children, and how far the revised British Educational Research Association (BERA, 2024) guidelines speak to the issues raised. It presents as an illustration the use of ethical guidelines that underpinned a doctoral study investigating the experiences of Polish-born adolescents living in the UK, including the anti-migrant hostility they had encountered. Undertaken between 2014 and 2018, it focused on a group of 11–16-year-olds who had migrated from Poland with their families. While the participants and their exact location were pseudonymised, this did not necessarily align with the children's perception of the project. This chapter considers their participation in the study in relation to the revised guidelines. I first highlight the new emphasis on requesting assent from child participants; I then unpack the potential disparity between ethical guidelines that advise anonymity for participants and participants' expectations. A discussion of how these elements were negotiated leads to a reflection on changes that could have been adopted to make the study more participant-led. I consider how these amendments in research design might be navigated differently, with particular reference to the revised BERA 2024 (5th ed.) guidelines, and in comparison with those of 2011 (3rd ed.), which underpinned the study.

Context

Poland's ascension to the European Union (EU) in 2004 prompted a wave of migration to the UK, often families with children (Ryan et al., 2009; White, 2017). However, this took place within a UK context that was increasingly hostile to EU migration, especially that from Eastern Europe (Spigelman, 2013), culminating in the Brexit referendum where the UK voted to leave the EU. In examining the experiences of Polish-born teenagers who had migrated to the UK since 2004, the study explored how the adolescents negotiated their sense of identity as they attempted to build their lives in the UK in the face of the anti-EU immigrant discourse which characterised the period (Young, 2018).

The project was designed as a narrative inquiry, which foregrounds the 'positionality and subjectivity' of the individual narrator (Riessman, 2002: 696). Participants were recruited from two settings: a Polish complementary (Saturday) school and an after-school Polish General Certificate in Secondary Education (GCSE)[1] class at a state secondary school. They were initially interviewed as a full group to foster an openness about the types of issues that might be discussed; this was followed by pair and individual interviews during three blocks of interviews held in February, March and May 2016. The scheduling was dictated by the school timetable and student availability (see Young, 2018). A conscious decision was taken not to involve parents in the research, so that children felt their voices were being heard independently. They were enthusiastic about the project, but it quickly became apparent that they were unclear about the nature of a doctoral project.

As the project was designed in 2014–15, the guidelines followed were the third edition of BERA's *Ethical Guidelines for Educational Research* (BERA, 2011). These strike a careful balance between responsible protection and adherence to the rights of the child to be heard, in accordance with Article 12 of the *United Nations Convention on the Rights of the Child*[2] (UNCRC). As per the guidelines, before the children were recruited for the study, it was necessary to negotiate several layers of gatekeeping. The first was the university; as a novice researcher, I was required to negotiate an ethical process with which I was not yet wholly familiar. The next stage involved requesting consent from the children's parents/guardians. To minimise the risk of linguistic misunderstanding (Koulouriotis, 2011), letters sent to parents were in Polish and English. Consent was also sought from the heads of the schools attended by the children, where the interviews would be conducted, and from the Polish teacher facilitating the research in the state secondary school. The adolescents were given age-appropriate information sheets and asked for their assent before participating. This aligns with Dockett et al. (2013: 803), who argue for a rights-based approach to children, 'whereby children have opportunities to make informed decisions about research participation'.

The earlier BERA guidelines are clear on the need for participant consent (BERA, 2011 *Voluntary Informed Consent*); however, they remain vague on the way that those under the age of eighteen should be regarded. While recognising the rights of children to be heard, neither the 2011 guidelines, nor the 2018 revisions, mention explicitly the notion of assent. Where *consent* denotes an agreement given by a 'competent' adult, which has 'both legal and moral/ethical implications', in contrast *assent* 'is not a legal term but rather a concept concerned with gaining children's agreement' (McPherson et al., 2020: 730). The inclusion of assent in the 2024 guidelines, making a lucid distinction between asking legal consent from gatekeepers and assent from children, is therefore a welcome addition. This recognises not only the value of children's right to participate in research that affects them, but also to ask their permission as individuals separate from their parents or other gatekeepers. The emphasis thereby shifts from research that is done *to* or *on* children, to research that engages *with* children (Dockett et al., 2013: 803; Facca et al., 2020: 1). Equally, it respects the rights of children to demonstrate *dissent* and refuse their participation independently from their gatekeepers (Huser et al., 2022).

Anonymisation/Pseudonymisation

The question remains of how to acknowledge the contribution made by young participants, thereby speaking to guidelines on the use of anonymisation/pseudonymisation. The BERA 2011 guidelines state that: 'The confidential and anonymous treatment of participants' data is considered the norm for the conduct of research' (BERA, 2011: paragraph 25).

Mindful of the sensitive nature of my study, I included on the forms sent to gatekeepers and children an assurance that names of participants, their schools and anyone or anywhere mentioned would be pseudonymised. Since the participants in the study were from a small Polish community, and there were fairly few Polish children in the state school where I conducted the research, this could make them more easily identifiable, not only within their schools and communities but also beyond. Moreover, following Baker and Plows (2015: 197), I considered the participants in this study as vulnerable in that they belonged to a minority group which was facing particular hostility and discrimination at the time (Young, 2017).

Yet when I went to talk to the children about the project, I realised that the notion of pseudonymisation was not something which had been understood, when one of the boys exclaimed excitedly, 'I'm going to be in a book!' His reaction seemed to indicate that he envisaged becoming a visibly acknowledged part of the project and the final output: that he equated participating in a doctoral study with appearing in a published book where people would read about his story. Yet this felt far removed from the reality of working on a doctoral study and the outcome of such a project. Unsure how to navigate this, I rather clumsily explained that it was not exactly a book, and in any case, I would not be using his real name. Yet, I was uncertain whether the clarification I attempted to provide allowed him to understand that, and if he was therefore participating in the project with false expectations of the outcome. Had he fully understood the limitations of the output, I wondered, would he have participated so willingly? This led me to question two elements of the study: my automatic decision to pseudonymise the data, and a research design which in retrospect appeared to sideline the participants. This chimes with Dockett et al. (2013), who asked young children about their involvement in participatory research on improving their towns. The researchers found the children were confused by the need for pseudonymisation; rather, they took pride in participating, and felt their views should be credited accordingly (Dockett et al., 2013: 818).

While the BERA (2011) guidelines are fairly clear on the need for anonymisation, they are quite vague about any deviation from this. They argue that, in accordance with Article 12 of the UNCRC:

> children who are capable of forming their own views should be granted the right to express their views freely in all matters affecting them, commensurate with their age and maturity. (BERA, 2011: 6, paragraph 16)

However, the guidelines also instruct researchers to follow participants' wishes on waiving anonymity, advising researchers to 'recognise participants' rights to be identified with any publication of their original works or other inputs, if they so wish' (BERA, 2011: 7, paragraph 25), a phrase repeated in the 2018 guidelines (BERA, 2018: 21, paragraph 40). The revised 2024 guidelines are slightly more nuanced, urging: 'Researchers should recognise the right of participants to be identified as the originator of their own work if they so wish' (BERA, 2024: 22, paragraph 39). Yet they do not offer any guidance on how this might be negotiated. In my own case, the 2011 guidance did not sit comfortably with my feeling that pseudonymisation should be used. If one child asked to be revealed, this would result in the other participants being identified, echoing the concern that 'when real names are used, the persons directly connected to the participant are also known' (Lahman et al., 2015: 450). A similar caution is not included in the BERA guidelines of 2011 or 2024.

I also chose the pseudonyms myself, aware that young people may inadvertently select a name by which they may be identified (Delamont, 2002; Dockett et al., 2013). Yet it was important to remain conscious of the care required when creating pseudonyms (Morrow, 2008). I therefore endeavoured to select pseudonyms which reflected names that the participants had already created for themselves, including whether they had elected to anglicise their names, such as through an abbreviation (e.g. 'Greg', for 'Grzegorz') or whether they had chosen to retain the original Polish (e.g. 'Tomasz'). Others, like 'Richard', used the English version of their name when speaking in English, but the Polish version of their name ('Ryszard') when speaking Polish. In some cases, pseudonyms mirrored the way a participant's name was spelt identically in English and Polish (e.g. 'Anna').

However, the boy's comment made me reflect on my decision and recognise how the problem of anonymisation/pseudonymisation is more complex than ethical guidelines might indicate. As Guenther (2009: 412) argues, '[t]he act of naming is an act of power' (cf. Heaton, 2022), which takes on increased pertinence when there are already heavily imbalanced power relations between an adult researcher and school children. Lahman et al. (2015: 446) argue that assigning a pseudonym removes a participant's autonomy; this reflects the contradiction of giving voice to participants whilst maintaining appropriate levels of confidentiality (Guenther, 2009). How could I then have reconciled my need to adhere to ethical guidelines which gave little room for negotiation with the participant's wish to be more present in the research?

The 2024 guidelines expand on those of 2011, in the implication that participants may be acknowledged as 'the originator of their work' (BERA, 2024: 22, paragraph 39). However, further guidance on how this could be steered ethically would be welcomed. This is particularly relevant to participatory research where children are seen as co-creators of knowledge. Even young children have a greater understanding of their rights than is sometimes acknowledged, demonstrating awareness that they are entitled to have their ideas openly acknowledged (Dockett et al., 2013), while also showing an awareness of privacy (Huser et al., 2022) which should be respected. The revised guidelines make clear the expectation that researchers should:

> consult more specialist literature relevant to the tradition of research or specific methods as needed, so as to ensure that their research is undertaken in a way that is both valid and ethically appropriate. (BERA, 2024: 6, Letter from the President)

However, further indication on how this might align with the specific BERA framework would help novice researchers to unpick the ethical issues in balancing respect for the rights of the child with a recognition of the responsibility of the researcher who may be aware of wider concerns relating to anonymity.

Beyond the questions of anonymity and pseudonymisation, the project also raised the issue of the role of the participants in contributing to the research and being more actively involved in the dissemination of the findings. Once my doctorate had been awarded, I sent a hard copy of a condensed report on the findings to the schools whose students I had interviewed. Unfortunately, the Polish teacher with whom I had liaised at the state school had returned to Poland. The headteacher simply agreed to pass the report on, and there was no further engagement with the students who had participated so warmly and enthusiastically. To date, I am unsure whether they ever saw the result of their participation. This unsatisfactory way of finishing the project bothered me personally and ethically: I felt as though I had let the participants down, and not produced the output they might have anticipated.

Reflections on potential changes to the design

The outcome of the project led me to contemplate several dilemmas: How to square the ethical circle of feeling that students' experiences had been used and then discarded? How to reconcile the requirements of my research project and adherence to ethical obligations which had been signed off at the start of my research, with the participants' request to be more involved? These questions made me reflect on what other methods could have been used which protected participants' identities, but that would have allowed them greater ownership of the study.

Access to more detailed ethical guidelines might have encouraged me to consider several changes to the research design, including the use of more participatory methods. While I might still have insisted on pseudonymisation, a more active involvement in the creation of the research would have given greater agency to the participants. This would then have spoken more directly to their idea of being 'in a book' and have acknowledged them as co-creators of knowledge, rather than subjects of a thesis which ultimately offered them little value in terms of output. Even if the research still needed to take place within school premises, a more creative approach could have allowed the participants to step out of their institutional contexts (Groundwater-Smith et al., 2014). This would have reflected the positioning of children and young people as agentive in research projects, allowing for a fuller interpretation of the rights of children to be heard, aligning with Article 12 of the UNCRC, and echoed in the BERA 2024 guidelines through the emphasis on assent.

Such changes would have been possible even within the constraints of a doctoral project. Questions exist around what constitutes a doctoral project with all the 'strain and stress' and the limitations of working as a sole researcher on a project to prove your credentials as a researcher (Naveed et al., 2017: 3). More comprehensive guidelines on participatory research, especially studies involving children, would have allowed me to navigate the questions that arise in such work and provided me with stronger support in redesigning my research to allow the participants more agency within it. I might have felt more empowered to talk with the children about the nature of the study. I could then have broached more openly how their involvement within the project could take different forms, and how their contributions could be acknowledged, feeling secure that I was adhering to robust ethical practices.

While I may still have been hesitant to divulge the names of the children, supported by more detailed guidelines, I might have offered them an opportunity to choose their own pseudonyms, or create an avatar through whom to express their experiences. Pinter (2014: 174) highlights how, as 'social actors', children have increasingly 'become active participants in the events and institutions, which affect their lives'. Reflecting this, I could have used more imaginative research methodologies, such as diaries or artwork, in a way that was more negotiated and less researcher-dominated, giving the children more agency in co-constructing their narratives, and in disseminating the findings. More nuanced guidance would have helped me navigate such a research design more confidently and to balance the need to protect the identities of children with their right to be heard. Even if the children may still have been pseudonymised in the final report, they might have felt themselves better represented.

Final thoughts

My doctoral project raised issues of anonymity and participant involvement which were not addressed directly in the ethical guidance available at the time, thereby constraining what I felt was available in terms of research design. Comparing BERA 2024 with the 2011 version, through the explicit clarification of the notion of assent in relation to children and other vulnerable groups, the revised guidelines allow for the voices of such individuals to warrant attention in their own right rather than their participation being decided by parents or other gatekeepers. This recognises their active role in a research project, underlining that it should be agreed to and undertaken of their own volition, and as a separate agreement from that of the consent given by adults. This is an important clarification and in keeping with the view that the agency of children and other vulnerable participants should be recognised and acknowledged.

Where the guidelines perhaps do not go far enough is in tackling some of the attendant queries that children may raise about a project. The issue of pseudonymisation, for example, which researchers often assume is in the best interests of their participants, is one which children do not necessarily accept. Moreover, given the contemporary emphasis on children as co-creators of knowledge who may expect recognition for their participation in research studies, it would be helpful for future guidelines to address ethical issues that arise in participatory research with children. While these questions are addressed in research methodology literature, it is not always clear how such projects might sit with BERA expectations. Greater specificity would help to offer more robust support to educational and social science research involving children, and allow researchers to tackle with greater confidence the ambiguities of ethical practices in new participatory methods. This would facilitate a more imaginative approach to designing research projects, while maintaining high standards of ethical rigour and protection for research participants.

Reflective questions

1 From a supervisory perspective, how could support be given to a doctoral researcher embarking on such a project?
2 How far can children give 'fully informed consent' and how can issues relating to this be navigated?
3 How can a researcher reconcile notions of anonymity with the ethical responsibility to offer a voice to younger participants?
4 How can questions of anonymity and confidentiality be broached between gatekeepers and participants deemed vulnerable?
5 What responsibility does the researcher have towards vulnerable participants? How is vulnerability defined?

Further reading

1. Alderson, P. and Morrow, V. (2020). *The Ethics of Research with Children and Young People: A Practical Handbook* (2nd ed.). Los Angeles, CA: Sage.

   A revised edition of an earlier work, providing comprehensive and practical guidance for those working with young people and children, compiled by two leading experts in the field.

2. Block, K., Warr, D., Gibbs, L. and Riggs, E. (2013). Addressing ethical and methodological challenges in research with refugee-background young people: Reflections from the field. *Journal of Refugee Studies*, 26(1), 69–87. Doi: 10.1093/jrs/fes002.

   The authors discuss their work with vulnerable child participants, focusing in particular on negotiating informed consent and how to engage participants with research in a meaningful way.

3. Cuevas-Parra, P. (2023). **Multi-dimensional lens to article 12 of the UNCRC: A model to enhance children's participation**. *Children's Geographies*, 21(3), 363–77. Doi: 10.1080/14733285.2022.2071598.

Looking at participatory research with children and discussing how this might be navigated ethically, the author addresses the tension between adhering to guidelines and also allowing children's voices to be heard.

Notes

1 GCSE examinations are taken in England and Wales usually at the age of 15–16.
2 https://www.ohchr.org/en/instruments-mechanisms/instruments/convention-rights-child.

References

Baker, A. and Plows, V. (2015). Re-Presenting or Representing Young Lives?, In K. Riele, and R. Gorur (Eds.), *Interrogating Conceptions of 'Vulnerable Youth' in Theory, Policy and Practice* (3rd ed.), Rotterdam: Sense Publishers, (pp. 197–211). doi.org/10.1007/978-94-6300-121-2_13.

British Educational Research Association (BERA) (2011). *Ethical Guidelines for Educational Research*. (3rd ed.). London: BERA. Retrieved from: www.bera.ac.uk. Accessed 10 June 2016.

British Educational Research Association (BERA) (2018). *Ethical Guidelines for Educational Research* (4th ed.). London: BERA. https://www.bera.ac.uk/researchers-resources/publications/ethical-guidelines-for-educational-research-2018.

British Educational Research Association (BERA) (2024). *Ethical Guidelines for Educational Research* (5th ed.). London: BERA. www.bera.ac.uk/publication/ethicalguidelines-for-educational-research-2024.

Delamont, S. (2002). *Fieldwork in Educational Settings: Methods, Pitfalls and Perspectives* (2nd ed.). London & New York: Routledge.

Dockett, S., Perry, B. and Kearney, E. (2013). Promoting children's informed assent in research participation. *International Journal of Qualitative Studies in Education*, 26(7), 802–28. Doi: 10.1080/09518398.2012.666289.

Facca, D., Gladstone, B. and Teachman, G. (2020). Working the limits of 'giving voice' to children: A critical conceptual review. *International Journal of Qualitative Methods*, 19, 1–10.

Groundwater-Smith, S., Dockett, S. and Bottrell, D. (2014). *Participatory Research with Children and Young People*. London: Sage.

Guenther, K. M. (2009). The politics of names: rethinking the methodological and ethical significance of naming people, organizations, and places. *Qualitative Research*, 9(4), 411–21.

Heaton, J. (2022). 'Pseudonyms are used throughout': A footnote, unpacked. *Qualitative Inquiry*, 28(1), 123–32.

Huser, C., Dockett, S. and Perry, B. (2022). Young children's assent and dissent in research: Agency, privacy and relationships within ethical research spaces. *European Early Childhood Education Research Journal*, 30(1), 48–62. Doi: 10.1080/1350293X.2022.2026432.

Koulouriotis, J. (2011). Ethical considerations in conducting research with non-native speakers of english. *TESL Canada Journal*, Special Issue 5, 1–15. doi.org/10.18806/tesl.v28i0.1078.

Lahman, M. K., Rodriguez, K. L., Moses, L., Griffin, K. M., Mendoza, B. M. and Yacoub, W. (2015). A rose by any other name is still a rose? Problematizing pseudonyms in research. *Qualitative Inquiry*, 21(5), 445–53.

McPherson, A., Saltmarsh, S. and Tomkins, S. (2020). Reconsidering assent for randomised control trials in education: Ethical and procedural concerns. *British Educational Research Journal*, 46(4), 728–46.

Morrow, V. (2008). Ethical dilemmas in research with children and young people about their social environments. *Children's Geographies*, 6(1), 49–61. Doi: 10.1080/14733280701791918.

Naveed, A., Sakata, S., Kefallinou, A., Young, S. and Anand, K. (2017). Understanding, embracing and reflecting upon the messiness of doctoral fieldwork. *Compare: A Journal of Comparative and International Education*, 47(5), 773–92. Doi: 10.1080/03057925.2017.1344031.

Pinter, A. (2014). Child participant roles in applied linguistics research. *Applied Linguistics*, 35(2), 168–83. Doi: 10.1093/applin/amt008.

Riessman, C. K. (2002) Analysis of Personal Narratives, In J. F. Gubium, and J. A. Holstein (Eds.), *Handbook of Interview Research: Context and Method*, Thousand Oaks, CA: Sage (pp. 695–710).

Ryan, L., Sales, R., Tilki, M. and Siara, B. (2009). Family strategies and transnational migration: Recent polish migrants in London. *Journal of Ethnic and Migration Studies*, 35(1), 61–77. Doi: 10.1080/13691830802489176.

Spigelman, A. (2013). The depiction of Polish migrants in the United Kingdom by the British press after Poland's accession to the European Union. *International Journal of Sociology and Social Policy*, 33(1/2), 98–113.

White, A. (2017). *Polish Families and Migration since EU Accession* (updated ed.). Bristol: Policy Press.

Young, S. (2017). Experiences of Polish-born adolescents in Britain during the run-up to Brexit. In M. Fleming (Ed.), *Brexit and Polonia: Challenges Facing the Polish Community during the Process of Britain Leaving the European Union*, London: PUNO Press (pp. 63–82). http://puno.edu.pl/puno-press/brexit-and-polonia/.

Young, S. (2018). The construction of ethno-linguistic identity amongst Polish-born adolescents living in the UK. Doctoral Thesis. UCL (University College London).

18

The Chartered College of Teaching Research Ethics Panel: Exploring Practical Relevance, Workload Implications and Representativeness of Research

by *Lisa-Maria Müller and Victoria Cook*

Introduction and context

The Chartered College of Teaching is the professional body for teachers in England. We are dedicated to bridging the gap between practice and research and equipping teachers with the knowledge and confidence to make the best decisions for their pupils. Evidence-informed practice has the potential to improve the quality of teaching and learning (Burns and Schulle, 2007; Mincu, 2014) but top-down approaches often fail to recognise the importance of context-specific implementation of research findings and thus the crucial role of teacher expertise (Scutt, 2019).

The aim of the research department at the college is to capture and share teachers' views, which are based on their daily experiences in their classrooms, to complement findings from more controlled experiments and trials. This can help to democratise the research process, which continues to be dominated by findings emerging from more traditional research institutions that tend to be further removed from day-to-day practice in schools. Recent research projects conducted at the college include a report series outlining teacher's views on school closures and effective approaches to distance learning (Müller and Goldenberg, 2020a, 2020b; 2021a, 2021b) and a cognitive science research priority setting activity outlining teachers' priorities for applied cognitive science research (Müller & Cook, 2023; 2024). This work highlights how teachers' daily classroom practice and their resulting expertise can complement findings from controlled experiments and the need for two-way communication between practitioners and researchers.

As our research portfolio has grown, and given the important societal implications that educational research entails (Govil, 2013), it was deemed necessary to set up a research ethics panel to ensure that research follows ethical guidelines, that it does not represent any risks to participants and that all persons involved in or affected by the research are treated fairly and respectfully. This chapter outlines the strategic and pragmatic decisions that were central to establishing and running a new research ethics panel at the college. We offer a series of questions that are important to consider when researching with teachers, focusing on the ethical dilemmas of practical relevance, workload implications and the inclusivity and accessibility of research.

Ethical dilemmas

Following the fourth edition of the BERA *Ethical Guidelines for Educational Research* (2018) and guidelines by the Council of Europe (2012), a research ethics panel was established that was informed by the following overarching principles:

- autonomy
- beneficence and non-maleficence
- justice

Acknowledging that the applicability of biomedical ethical models to educational research is far from straightforward (Sikes and Piper, 2010), the BERA guidelines were used to navigate the multifaceted and dynamic nature of educational research.

As suggested by the guidelines, it is important to consider ethical dilemmas and as 'few ethical dilemmas have obvious or singular solutions, researchers will take different approaches to resolving them' (BERA, 2024: 7). The guidelines highlight that 'all educational research should be conducted within *an ethic of respect* for: people; knowledge; the quality of educational research; the environment; and academic freedom' ((BERA, 2024: 9) emphasis in original). Furthermore, '[a]pplying an ethic of respect may reveal tensions or challenges. For example, there will usually be a need to make decisions about how best to balance research aspirations, societal concerns, institutional expectations and individual rights' (BERA, 2024: 9).

The three main ethical dilemmas we have tried to address through our research ethics panel and processes in addition to those named above are:

- practical validity
- concerns around teacher workload
- under-representation of individuals with protected characteristics.

We will discuss these different principles and how they relate to the BERA *Ethical Guidelines for Educational Research* below after diving deeper into the practical issues relating to the establishment of a new research ethics panel.

Establishing a research ethics panel

Expressions of interest were sought from members of the college via an open call to join the research ethics panel in 2022. The expression of interest form included questions about participants' background and their past experience of assessing ethics applications and/or conducting their own (action) research. From a total of fifty-one applications, twenty-five individuals were appointed across the following categories:

- Academics
- Fellows
- Chartered Teachers
- Individuals representing typically under-represented groups (ethnicity, LGBTQ+, disability)
- Chartered College central team members

An application is submitted to the panel for review for new projects undertaken by the research department at the college. Applications submitted for review by the panel are assessed by a rotating combination of members, with seven forming a quorum. For Chartered Teachers, attention is paid to a balance between science and humanities. As outlined by Kohn and Shore (2017), university ethics panels can lack the necessary expertise to accurately understand and assess research methods that lie outside each individual's and/or the committee's collective expertise. To avoid that, we aim to have every application assessed by representatives from different research and teaching traditions to ensure that the application is understood and assessed appropriately.

As a professional body, the college also sits at the intersection of theory and practice and therefore has a responsibility to produce research that is both theoretically and practically valid. The college thus applies a broader, complex understanding of 'validity' that goes beyond construct validity and takes potential social and practical consequences of research into consideration (Messick, 1989; Wolming and Wikström, 2010). By combining academics' and teachers' expertise on the panel, the aim is to have projects assessed according to their academic rigour as well as their practical relevance.

Finally, four rotating members of the panel represent the interests of individuals who are typically under-represented in research to make the college's research more inclusive and representative. They represent the views of the ethnic minority, disabled, LGBTQ+ and economically disadvantaged individuals. While all panel members are required to assess applications in terms of accessibility and representation, these four panel members use their lived experiences and/or expertise to scrutinise applications even further.

Ethics application process

When relevant, research ethics panel members are contacted to check their availability to assess an application, and the whole assessment process takes place entirely online. Following their confirmation, they are sent a project description and/or a funding application, depending on whether the project was internally or externally funded, a data management plan, a consent form and links to any data-collection tools (e.g. surveys, focus group questions) where relevant. Members then have two weeks to assess the application by completing an online checklist. Where issues arise, meetings are called either individually or involving the whole committee to resolve them through dialogue.

Autonomy

> It is normally expected that participants' voluntary informed consent to be involved in a study will be obtained at the start of the study, and that researchers will remain sensitive and open to the possibility that participants may wish, for any reason and at any time, to withdraw their consent. (BERA, 2024, paragraph 8)

> The following questions assess the concept of *autonomy* within the college's *Research Ethics Checklist*, which reflects the context of UK data protection (Data Protection Act, 2018):
> - Does the project require informed consent from participants?
> - Does the consent form inform participants about the purpose of the study?
> - Does the consent form inform participation about research methods?
> - Does the consent form inform participants about data protection, storage and sharing?
> - Does the consent form inform participants about their right to withdraw their data at any point without any negative consequences for them?
> - Does the consent form inform participants that participation is voluntary?
> - Is there any reason to believe that participants have been coerced or unduly influenced to participate in the research project?

These questions are intended to help panel members assess whether participation in the study is voluntary and whether participants have been fully informed and given the opportunity to withdraw their participation. Panel members use the consent form and information sheet to assess and answer these questions.

Beneficence and non-maleficence

Researchers also have a responsibility to put in place ways of maximising the benefits and minimising the likelihood of any potential harms to participants, sponsors, the community of educational researchers and educational professionals and the environment more widely. (BERA, 2024, paragraph 6)

Researchers should not undertake work for which they are not competent. (BERA, 2024, paragraph 7)

- Do the benefits of the research project outweigh its risks?
- Does the research aim to make a relevant contribution to our understanding of teaching and learning or teacher development?
- Is the design of the research project appropriate for the research question?
- I judge the researchers to have the necessary qualifications to conduct this project in a sound manner and without putting participants at risk.
- Are there any notable risks for research participants? If so, what risks?

The questions in this section aim to capture whether the benefits of the research outweigh its risks, whether any risks to participants are to be expected and to what extent the selected research methods are appropriate to answer the question. It is also in this section that a connection to relevance and thus validity is drawn. As outlined above, given the college's role as a professional body, it is important that all of our research is guided by the principles of both theoretical and practical validity. Finally, the research team's competence to conduct a specific type of research is assessed as part of the questions in this section.

Justice

All educational researchers should aim to protect the integrity and reputation of educational research by ensuring that they conduct their research to the highest standards. Researchers should contribute to the community spirit of critical analysis and constructive criticism that generates improvement in practice and enhancement of knowledge. (BERA, 2024, paragraph 59)

- Have research participants been recruited fairly?
- Have research participants been recruited with the research purpose in mind?

The aim of these two questions is to ensure that research is conducted to the highest possible standards and that participants have been recruited fairly and appropriately as per the first principle outlined in the guidelines.

Workload

> Researchers should recognise concerns relating to the time and effort that participation in some research can require – the long-term involvement of participants in ethnographic studies, for example, and the repeated involvement of particular participants in survey research or in testing for research or evaluation purposes. Researchers should consider the impact of their research on the lives and workloads of participants, particularly when researching vulnerable or over-researched populations. (BERA, 2024, paragraph 37)

I judge the project to have acceptable workload implications for participants. Despite recent government initiatives (DfE, 2022), high teacher workload continues to be a major concern in UK schools that negatively affects teacher retention (McLean et al., 2024). Given the current teacher shortages, which show no signs of subsiding, we therefore consider it a significant ethical concern and responsibility not to add unnecessarily to teachers' busy schedules as this would likely further negatively affect their job satisfaction and, ultimately, their retention. Workload concerns are thus an important ethical dilemma to be considered as part of ethics applications and panel members are asked to consider whether workload implications are judged to be acceptable. Of course, any research project will always have workload implications beyond teachers' day-to-day roles, but the aim of this question is to explore to what extent any additional work associated with the project is deemed reasonable when balanced against the potential positive outcomes of the project.

Inclusion

> The Association reminds researchers of the protected characteristics as defined by the Equality Act 2010 – age, gender reassignment, being married or in a civil partnership, being pregnant or on maternity leave, disability, race

including colour, nationality, ethnic or national origin, religion or belief, sex and sexual orientation. Beyond this, the Association expects researchers to be mindful of the ways in which structural inequalities – including those listed above but also socio-economic status, parental status and neurodiversity – affect all social relationships, including those that are formed in the course of research. (BERA, 2024, paragraph 2)

- Are the needs of individuals with protected characteristics considered and protected?
- Have attempts been made to recruit research participants representative of the wider teaching population?

Despite some progress, much educational research continues not to be inclusive to all (Nind, 2014). Too often, individuals with disabilities and marginalised groups continue to be excluded, whether deliberately or inadvertently. Inclusion is an important consideration at every stage of the research process (research design, data collection, analysis and reporting) to ensure that the voices of underrepresented groups in particular are heard. Different research approaches have different advantages and disadvantages in relation to inclusion. The long-held view that quantitative research, with its emphasis on measurement and empirical data, is more rigorous and robust than qualitative research is starting to be challenged (Santoro, 2023). Statistical practices such as eliminating outliers when cleaning the data (where data points that lie outside of the normal distribution are deleted) perpetuate structural inequity by silencing voices from the research (Arellano, 2022). In comparison, qualitative research, with its focus on lived experiences, can deepen our understanding of the educational experiences of historically marginalised groups. This is not to say that one method should be favoured over another but rather that we ought to consider how different research methods risk to emphasise or silence the voices of certain groups of individuals.

We therefore consider it paramount to focus on the ethical dilemma of inclusion as part of assessing research applications and to hold ourselves accountable for how accessible and inclusive our research methods are.

However, despite our best intentions, we have already met obstacles in the application of this principle, which the following example illustrates.

Applying the principle of inclusion – a Vignette

As part of our efforts to improve the representation of under-represented voices in our research, we recently aimed to develop a background questionnaire to capture information on participants' protected characteristics. The purpose was to help us understand which groups are currently under – and over-represented, so we could address any gaps in future research and understand how representative our research samples are of the wider teaching population. We first explored the option of simply having open text boxes for participants to self-identify instead of asking them to select from existing categories. However, it quickly became clear that while arguably the most inclusive approach, it may (a) be alienating for participants as it is more time-consuming to complete than tick boxes, which is suboptimal in the context of a voluntary additional questionnaire and (b) analysis would be significantly more time-consuming, adding an additional burden to the research team's limited resources. We thus sought advice from organisations representing typically underrepresented groups such as DiverseEd and attempted to develop an inclusive list of categories that participants could choose from. While this approach addressed concerns around time spent on the survey for participants and workload for the research team, it quickly became clear that it did not allow us to draw conclusions regarding the representativeness of our samples when compared to the wider teaching population. In order to do so, we would need to use categories from the DfE's School Workforce survey despite its many shortcomings and omissions. After long deliberations with the college's council, its research ethics panel and colleagues, we decided on a mid-way point which combined categories from the census with an option for participants to self-identify, should they not feel represented by the proposed categories. While far from perfect, this has allowed us to create an instrument that meets our requirements, does not represent an unacceptable burden on participants and still attempts to be more inclusive than traditional methods. This development process illustrates the ethical dilemmas in which we continuously operate as researchers.

Informing participants about research outcomes

> Researchers have a responsibility to determine the most relevant and useful ways of informing participants about the outcomes of research in which they are or were involved. (BERA, 2024, paragraph 6)

Research conducted at the college typically culminates in an open-access report, which is shared with members of the college and its networks, ensuring that participants can access the final results of the research they have contributed to. For focus group participants and interviewees, a copy of the final report is usually shared with them directly. Furthermore, research findings tend to be summarised and shared as research summaries, policy briefs or articles for the peer-reviewed practitioner journal 'Impact'. To ensure accessibility beyond the written word, findings are also typically shared via webinars and contributions to the college's podcast.

Conclusions

This chapter has outlined the approach taken at the Chartered College of Teaching to establish a research ethics panel and the principles underlying its development. In addition to the traditional principles of autonomy, beneficence and justice, the panel aims to focus especially on ethical dilemmas relating to the practical relevance, workload implications and inclusivity and accessibility of research. It does so through a combination of the panel's membership and the categories against which applications are assessed. As a professional body, the college sits at the intersection of research and practice and thus considers it paramount that its research is considered both in terms of its academic rigour and its practical validity. Applications are therefore assessed by a combination of academics and practitioners from a range of subject specialisms. Furthermore, dedicated members represent the interests of typically underrepresented groups to make research more inclusive. However, ethical dilemmas continue to persist, which need to be resolved through professional, respectful dialogue, sometimes accepting that a perfect solution cannot be found.

Overall, the BERA guidelines (BERA, 2024) provide a suitable level of specificity for the practice context within which we work at the college, enabling us to take a reflexive and situated approach to the concept of validity. As the redevelopment of our background questionnaire demonstrates, ethical decision-making is an ongoing, iterative process, which is supported by the deliberative approach taken to the language of the guidelines. Reflecting on the changes to the latest edition of the BERA guidelines, we welcome the responsibility placed on researchers to guard against inadvertently compounding marginalisation whilst also promoting participants' rights to participation. The additional detail provided through reference to protected characteristics as defined by the Equality Act 2010 and the inclusion of parental status and neurodiversity is important in this respect. We are also supportive of paragraph 37 of the new guidelines, which states that 'researchers should do what they can to ensure that relevant individuals and communities are not, intentionally or otherwise, excluded from participation in their research' (BERA, 2024: 21). At the college, where the issue of workload implications is at the forefront of our minds, we are continually reflecting on how this may be reduced for participants in our research. We also welcome the recognition that educational research should be conducted within an ethic of respect for the environment. Whilst our research has been conducted remotely to date, should this change in the future, it will be important to consider issues such as the amount and type of travel. Finally, the emphasis placed on the duty of care towards supporting the next generation of researchers will be an important consideration for our research ethics panel in the future as we seek to grow our research portfolio and, by association, our research team.

Reflective questions

1 Why is it important to problematise ethical guidelines when establishing a new research ethics panel?
2 How is a focus on ethical dilemmas beneficial for educational research?
3 What creative approaches may researchers take to resolving ethical dilemmas?
4 What is the value of taking a reflexive and situated approach to the concept of validity?
5 Why is it important to view ethical decision-making as an ongoing, iterative process?

Further reading

1. Scutt, C. (2018). *Building a culture of evidence and research use: Selected reading*. Chartered College of Teaching. https://my.chartered.college/research-hub/building-a-culture-of-evidence-and-research-use-selected-reading/.

   A collection of articles, blog posts, tools and resources to help you embed research in your school.

2. Wolming, S. and Wikström, C. (2010). The concept of validity in theory and practice. *Assessment in Education: Principles, Policy & Practice,* 17(2), 117–32.

   This article charts the evolution of the concept of validity in the literature as a broad and complex issue.

3. Brown, R. (2020). Ethical Dilemmas in Education Research. In R. Iphofen (Ed.), *Handbook of Research Ethics and Scientific Integrity,* Cham: Springer (pp. 675–91). https://doi.org/10.1007/978-3-030-16759-2_47.

   This chapter reflects on the ethical complexity of education research, highlighting some of the distinctive features of education research that require special consideration.

References

Arellano, L. (2022). Questioning the science: How quantitative methodologies perpetuate inequity in higher education. *Education Science,* 12(116), 675–91. https://www.mdpi.com/2227-7102/12/2/116. Accessed 29 March 2024.

British Educational Research Association (BERA) (2018). *Ethical Guidelines for Educational Research* (4th ed.). London: BERA.

British Educational Research Association (BERA) (2024). *Ethical Guidelines for Educational Research* (5th ed.). London: BERA. Ethical-Guidelines-for-Educational-Research-5th-edition.pdf. Accessed 20 September 2024.

Burns, T. and Schuller, T. (2007). The evidence agenda. In T. Burns and T. Schuller (Eds.), *Evidence in Education: Linking Research and Policy,* Paris: OECD (pp. 15–32). https://www.oecd.org/en/publications/evidence-in-education_9789264033672-en.html.

Council of Europe (2012). *Guide for Research Ethics Committee Members.* https://www.coe.int/t/dg3/healthbioethic/activities/02_biomedical_research_en/Guide/Guide_EN.pdf. Accessed 29 March 2024.

Data Protection Act (2018). c. 12. https://www.legislation.gov.uk/ukpga/2018/12/contents/enacted. Accessed 20 September 2024.

Department for Education (DfE) (2022). *Education staff wellbeing charter*. https://www.gov.uk/guidance/education-staff-wellbeing-charter. Accessed 22 March 2024.

Equality Act (2010). c39. https://www.legislation.gov.uk/ukpga/2010/15/contents. Accessed 20 September 2024.

Govil, P. (2013). Ethical considerations in educational research. *International Journal of Advancement in Education and Social Sciences*, 1(2), 17–22.

Kohn, T. and Shore, C. (2017). The ethics of university ethics committees. *Risk Management and the Research Imagination, in Death of the Public University*, 22(1), 229–49.

McLean, D., Worth, J. and Smith, A. (2024). *Teacher labour market in England annual report 2024*. https://www.nfer.ac.uk/publications/teacher-labour-market-in-england-annual-report-2024/. Accessed 21 March 2024.

Messick, S. (1989). Validity. In R. L. Linn (Ed.), *Educational Measurement*, vol. 3, New York: American Council on Education, MacMillan (pp. 13–103).

Mincu, M. (2014). Inquiry Paper 6: Teacher Quality and School Improvement – What Is the Role of Research? In British Educational Research Association/the Royal Society for the Encouragement of Arts, Manufactures and Commerce (Eds.), *The Role of Research in Teacher Education: Reviewing the Evidence Edited*. https://www.bera.ac.uk/wp-content/uploads/2014/02/BERA-RSA-Interim-Report.pdf. Accessed 22 March 2024.

Müller, L. M. and Cook, V. (2023). Cognitive science in education. Chartered College of Teaching. https://my.chartered.college/wp-content/uploads/2023/05/Cognitive-Science-in-Education-Teachers-priorities-for-research.pdf. Accessed 29 March 2024.

Müller, L. M. and Cook, V. (2024). Setting research priorities for applied cognitive sciences—What do teachers want from research? *British Educational Research Journal*. 50(3), 1471–1494.

Müller, L-M. and Goldenberg, G. (2020a). *Education in times of crisis: The potential implications of school closures for teachers and students: A review of research evidence on school closures and international approaches to education during the Covid-19 pandemic*. Chartered College of Teaching. https://my.chartered.college/wp-content/uploads/2020/05/CCTReport150520_FINAL.pdf. Accessed 5 October 2021.

Müller, L-M. and Goldenberg, G. (2020b). *Education in times of crisis: Teachers' views on distance learning and school reopening plans during COVID-19: Analysis of responses from an online survey and focus groups*. Chartered College of Teaching. https://my.chartered.college/resources/publications/. Accessed 29 March 2024.

Müller, L-M. and Goldenberg, G. (2021a). *Education in times of crisis: Effective approaches to distance learning: A review of research evidence on supporting all students' learning, wellbeing and engagement.* Chartered College of Teaching. https://115Referencesmy.chartered.college/wp-content/uploads/2021/02/MullerGoldenbergFEB21_FINAL-1.pdf. Accessed 29 March 2024.

Müller, L-M. and Goldenberg, G. (2021b). *Education in times of crisis: Effective approaches to distance learning. Sharing teachers' views and experiences.* Chartered College of Teaching: London, UK. https://my.chartered.college/wp-content/uploads/2022/01/MullerGoldenberg_FULL_NOV21.pdf. Accessed 29 March 2024.

Nind, M. (2014). Summary and Where Next? The Pursuit of Quality in Inclusive Research. In *What Is Inclusive Research?* London: Bloomsbury Academic (pp. 83–92).

Santoro, H. (2023). *The push for more equitable research is changing the field. 2023 Trends report.* American Psychological Association, 1 January 2023. https://www.apa.org/monitor/2023/01/trends-inclusivity-psychological-research. Accessed 29 March 2024.

Scutt, C. (2019). Is Engaging with and in Research a Worthwhile Investment for Teachers? In C. Carden (Ed.), *Primary Teaching*, London: SAGE Publishing (pp. 595–610).

Sikes, P. and Piper, H. (2010). Ethical research, academic freedom and the role of ethics committees and review procedures in educational research. *International Journal of Research and Method in Education,* 33(3), 205–13. https://doi.org/10.1080/1743727x.2010.511838.

Wolming, S. and Wikström, C. (2010). The concept of validity in theory and practice. *Assessment in Education: Principles, Policy & Practice,* 17(2), 117–32.

19

Research Ethics: Issues and Solutions in Education Research in Ukrainian Universities

by *Oksana Zabolotna and Iryna Kushnir*

Introduction

This chapter explores how members of the Ukrainian higher education (HE) community pursue ethical research in education. This area, arguably, plays a central role in societal development, and therefore, deserves special attention due to its long-reaching effects (Annan-Diab and Molinari, 2017; Fim'yar et al., 2019; Oleksiyenko, 2021). Existing scholarship on research ethics in Ukraine is limited and fragmented. There are a handful of studies available on this topic (e.g. Basarab and Anderson, 2022; Shykhnenko and Sbruieva, 2022; Sulaieva et al., 2023). However, research ethics practices specifically in the area of education – particularly in the war context (Howlett and Lazarenko, 2023), while the Ukrainian Higher Education (HE) community are also dealing, at the same time, with a range of persisting post-Soviet legacies in research – is unploughed terrain in the scholarship.

Relying on the analysis of a survey of and semi-structured interviews with members of the Ukrainian HE community, this chapter problematises research practice in Ukraine and raises persisting issues. The chapter argues that ethical research has become a complex challenge, exacerbated by the war, but also a symbolic tool for scholars striving to align their work with international standards.

Ukrainian educational research and BERA Research Ethical Guidelines

The Ukrainian translation of BERA's *Ethical Guidelines for Educational Research* (4th ed., 2018) was initiated by colleagues at Nottingham Trent University (UK), including Dr. Iryna Kushnir, one of the authors of this chapter, and Dr. Gareth Williams. On its website, BERA acknowledges that 'these guidelines may not always be fully applicable in an international context, but they are intended to provide guidance and support to researchers' (BERA Guidelines, 2018). Thus, the key takeaway is that the translated version has made these internationally recognised ethical principles accessible to Ukrainian researchers, providing them with guidance in conducting ethically sound research. It should be mentioned that this Ukrainian version, published by BERA and the Ukrainian Educational Research Association (UERA), is a direct translation of the original guidelines and has not been adapted for the Ukrainian context yet. The translation process was carried out by professional translators, with further proofreading conducted by another expert to ensure accuracy.

Since their publication in January 2023, the guidelines have been referenced in various presentations and roundtable discussions organised by the UERA (April 2023; June 2023; September 2023). However, they have yet to spark in-depth, detailed or thought-provoking debates. Instead, the focus has often shifted towards issues like plagiarism. The study, portions of which we present in this chapter, helps explain why the adaptation of the guidelines in Ukraine may require additional time and effort. Are there challenges specific to the local research environment, or are broader systemic issues at play? These are the foci that guide our study in the following sections.

Adapting BERA Ethical Guidelines: Where do issues come from?

Challenges in establishing ethical oversight in educational research

We seek to uncover the challenges that rise when attempting to adapt the BERA Ethical Guidelines to the Ukrainian context. The approach involves identifying evidence-based contradictions, inconsistencies or tensions, which signal areas where ethical principles may diverge from or challenge local practices, expectations or institutional frameworks.

This gap between the necessity to establish ethical oversight in educational research and the absence of relevant services in Ukraine complicated the process of aligning the study with international ethical standards and necessitated alternative solutions. Following a favourable ethics decision from the Schools of Business, Law and Social Sciences Research Ethics Committee at Nottingham Trent University (UK), the project's mixed-method research design involved two phases: a quantitative phase followed by a qualitative phase. The research design rested on data generation from two sources, both having taken place in 2024: (1) an online survey with the members of the UERA and (2) in-depth semi-structured interviews with emerging researchers and experts in the field. The survey received

Table 19.1 Contradictions between local practices and BERA guidelines – issue 1.

Local practices	BERA guidelines
The absence of an ethical commission authorised to approve research tools for studies in the field of education. Some institutions in Ukraine have ethics boards that focus primarily on medical or bioethical research while education researchers do not have a clear institutional pathway for obtaining formal ethical approval.	Researchers should think about whether they should approach gatekeepers before directly approaching participants, and about whether they should adopt an institution's own ethical approval and safeguarding procedures; this is usually a requirement (BERA 2018: 10).

Source: Authors.

120 responses, which is 30 per cent of the total UERA membership. An opportunistic/snowball sample of ten members of the HE community in Ukraine was recruited (five doctoral candidates and five experts, i.e., members of academic staff or senior leadership) for the interviews. The qualitative data helped explain and contextualise the quantitative findings, offering deeper insights into specific areas of awareness and application ethics research principles identified in the first phase.

The received evidence provided further nuance to the issue associated with ethics committees, contrasting with the provisions outlined in the BERA guidelines (BERA, 2018). See Table 19.1.

Doctoral candidates have struggled with answering the questions about ethical approval as they had never engaged in such practices:

> the only thing we sign at admission is about academic integrity, and I can't even say anything else. (Expert 1)
> I would only go for it if we had such a commission; I just don't know about it. (Expert 1)

They are unsure about the specific requirements for ethical approval in their institutions, indicating a need for clearer guidelines and education on this topic. Experts generally view the absence of a requirement for ethics committee approval similarly. They do not consider it essential in the context of education research.

> I don't think it [ethics committee approval requirement] should be endorsed, although perhaps for some types of research it might be appropriate. (Expert 1)
> Specifically ... medical research, maybe psychological. That is, where it may affect the people being investigated. (Expert 1)
> I think that one thing is research ethics, for example, in medical sciences, and the other thing is where a person as a social being is concerned. (Expert 2)
> In our university, for example, there is a different code of research conducted by medical doctors and biologists, which concerns ethics in behaviour with animals. (Expert 3)
> It is connected with the fact that the environment today does not really feel the need to turn to such commissions and, accordingly, to additional workload. (Expert 1)

The experts acknowledge that, while each university has committees or boards addressing ethical issues, these bodies do not always operate actively.

Such issues in the work of ethics committees seem to be a trend in Ukraine spanning over a few decades and crossing multiple fields, not just existing in the area of bioethics which is exactly what Pustovit (2006) analysed. When these committees do convene, their primary focus tends to be on cases of plagiarism reported externally.

Even according to documents, these are primarily commissions that if there is an appeal against plagiarism they consider. (Expert 1)

Ethics commissions are everywhere, in every faculty at our university. As for checking the quality of research tools, this is terra incognita, and everything depends on the researchers' ethics. (Expert 2)

They (ethics commissions) rely on post-factum things. (Expert 4)

All in all, the interviewed experts acknowledged that while universities have committees or boards addressing ethical issues, these bodies are not always active and their primary focus tends to be on addressing plagiarism cases. This is an important finding on its own as it demonstrates a limited understanding of the breads of what research ethics entails. The main focus on avoiding plagiarism in research outputs perhaps has its roots in the issues that Ukrainian universities dealt a while ago, concerning the lack of student academic integrity in research (Yukhymenko-Lescroart, 2014). The experts pointed out that these commissions primarily function post-factum, dealing mainly with issues of academic dishonesty after they have been reported, rather than proactively ensuring the ethical quality of research tools and practices. This highlights a gap in the current system in Ukraine where the ethical oversight is often reactive rather than preventative.

This trend appears to stem from a longstanding historical context in Ukraine, where the emphasis on academic integrity has often been formal and overshadowed a comprehensive understanding of research ethics. As one expert pointed out, *'in most establishments where they should be, they don't actually work'* (Expert 1), suggesting that the issue is systemic and has persisted for decades. Furthermore, the focus of committees on post-factum evaluations of plagiarism, as opposed to proactive measures to ensure ethical quality, underscores the challenges Ukrainian educational researchers face in adapting to modern ethical standards. As noted by another expert, *this is only a commission on the issue of academic dishonesty, which, already based on the results of the discovered facts, continues work regarding responsibility* (Expert 5).

Struggling to create the culture of respect for any persons involved in or touched by the research

The BERA Ethical Guidelines are structured around multiple areas of responsibility: to participants, sponsors, clients and stakeholders; to the educational research community; for the publication, dissemination and use of findings; and for researchers' wellbeing and professional development. All these domains are important parts of the complex ethical landscape in which educational research operates. Our survey focused mainly on responsibilities to participants and researchers' wellbeing. The rationale behind it is that these are particularly relevant as, in the war context, ensuring participants' rights and safety is of great importance, and researchers are under significant personal and professional pressure. The topics covered in the survey included: awareness and adherence to ethical principles in research; institutional support and availability of resources for ethical decision-making; frequency and types of ethical dilemmas encountered in educational research; informed consent and data confidentiality practices; integration of BERA *Ethical Guidelines for Educational Research* into Ukrainian research practices. In the survey responses, we found data that might point to some issues based on contradictions and inconsistencies that require delving deeper into the issues. See Table 19.2. As a result, we identified some areas that prompted focuses for questions for the in-depth interviews.

The respondents' awareness of the importance of conducting ethical research is evident in their statements:

> Ethical research is research that does not harm anyone and that does not violate any norms. (Expert 1)

Table 19.2 Contradictions between local practices and BERA guidelines – issue 2.

Local practices	BERA guidelines
There is insufficient awareness of current data protection regulations: 68.33% claim they apply strong data protection measures, yet 60.83% are unfamiliar with relevant laws.	Any changes to the degree of anonymity afforded to participants should be considered in the light of potential harm that may be caused by doing so and, in particular, the rights to confidentiality of other individual participants or institutions. (BERA 2018: 22)

Source: Authors.

> *I consider it [research ethics] fundamental because I work with people and write about people. (Expert 4)*
> However, the phrasing also demonstrates a somewhat general or intuitive interpretation of ethics, rather than referencing specific frameworks or formal guidelines like the BERA standards.

When the questions went deeper into specific areas, such as awareness of current data protection regulations, some researchers admitted practical challenges of navigating legal frameworks and struggled to demonstrate familiarity with the relevant laws. For example, one respondent noted: *'These issues are agreed upon with the research supervisor'* (Expert 4), showing that decisions on data protection are not always based on personal knowledge but rather depend on the supervisor's input. Another shared: *' ... in communication with the scientific supervisor, such a check is constantly passed ... '* (Expert 5), indicating that compliance is often ensured through interactions with supervisors, rather than through independent understanding of legal or institutional frameworks. These responses demonstrate a reliance on hierarchical support rather than on personal knowledge or formal institutional mechanisms.

The experts who work for the National Agency for HE Quality Assurance and/or for different commissions dealing with academic integrity issues also focused on the absence of a national legal framework for research ethics. A national framework spelled out in the national legislature for research ethics seems to be an expectation by the participants, perhaps because of the centralised HE governing system in Ukraine inherited from the Soviet times (Kushnir, 2021; Huisman, 2023; Oleksiyenko, 2023). The current situation with producing a national framework in the form of legislature in the field of education can be illustrated by the following quotations:

> The work on Academic Integrity Law started in 2020 ... now four years have passed; it has only reached the first stage of the procedural process.
> *The committee recommended its adoption as a basis for the first reading. (Expert 1)*
> *There is a ministerial document ... all university documents were created based on it ... (Expert 2)*

The experts admit that although there is no national law on governing research ethics in the area of education in Ukraine, each university has a set of regulations of different kinds that predominantly deal with problems caused by violating academic integrity rules. And the brightest examples of it are the cases when the highest Ukrainian educational officials had to refuse their doctorate after plagiarism had been detected in their research work (NGL Media, 2024).

This reflects a challenge in aligning individual research practices with international standards like BERA, where ethical responsibilities are expected to be understood and autonomously implemented by all researchers. Furthermore, this situation can be traced back to the Soviet legacy with top-down governance and reliance on authority for guidance. This path-dependency mindset hinders the development of a culture of ethical research autonomy, where researchers engage with ethical standards independently thus complicating efforts to foster a culture of ethical awareness within the Ukrainian HE system.

This lack of recognition further results in the fact that safeguarding mental and emotional health of researchers is not integrated into the broader ethical framework guiding research practices. Consequently, only 52 per cent of the respondents agreed that there is minimal institutional support or structured initiatives to address the pressures and challenges that researchers face, such as ethical dilemmas, emotional strain or burnout. This gap contrasts with the emphasis on researcher wellbeing outlined in the BERA guidelines see Table 19.3, thus drawing attention to institutional oversight in prioritising the holistic care of individuals engaged in academic work.

The above findings about challenges and gaps in research ethics practices in Ukrainian universities cannot be separated from the discussion of path dependency (Cairney, 2011) in the wider context in which Ukrainian HE works. This is because both are still influenced by the path dependency linked to the Soviet past (Kushnir, 2021). Expecting a national framework for research ethics is, arguably, rooted in the legacy of top-down policy-making (Huisman, 2023; Oleksiyenko, 2023), and the absence of which

Table 19.3 Contradictions between local practices and BERA guidelines – issue 3.

Local practices	BERA guidelines
Neither researchers nor institutions perceive researchers' wellbeing as a core ethical responsibility.	Safeguarding the physical and psychological wellbeing of researchers is part of the ethical responsibility of employing institutions and sponsors, as well as of researchers themselves. (BERA, 2018: 35)

Source: Authors

equated to the absence of expected censorship (Malle, 2009) gave way to such practices as not obtaining a favourable ethics opinion for research in many cases discussed by the interviewees.

An important milestone in advancing ethics foundations has been the translation into Ukrainian and adoption of the 2018 edition of the *Ethical Guidelines for Educational Research* from BERA in 2023 (BERA, 2018; UERA, 2023). However, a more comprehensive explanation and dissemination is needed. The translated guidelines have not featured in the responses as the go-to framework, perhaps because it has not come from the 'top' – the government. Additionally, as it turned out, the barrier to understanding, and, consequently, accepting and putting into practice, is not in the language but in the approach. The ideas above demonstrate the conceptual differences between the Ukrainian so-called 'what should NOT be done approach' and the UK 'what should be done', between the Ukrainian 'how to threaten researchers' strategy' and the UK strategy of 'how to care for researchers and research participants'. While acknowledging the general understanding of academic ethics in Ukraine as primarily focusing on plagiarism, we should highlight the importance of broadening this understanding to include a wider range of ethical considerations with the focus on responsibilities to participants, sponsors, clients, stakeholders and researchers.

Recommendations and future directions

Given that the translated BERA guidelines are currently the only framework for education researchers in Ukraine, its review and further adaptation to the Ukrainian context, perhaps also considering the updates from the fifth edition of BERA guidelines (BERA, 2024), may be helpful. Following this, UERA could continue its research ethics awareness-raising work through liaising with the senior leadership teams from Ukrainian HEIs and organising train-the-trainer events which would equip individuals within each HEI to spread the knowledge about the framework and build on it. Not taking the route of liaising with the Ministry of Education and Science of Ukraine to exercise its top-down implementation would, arguably, be a 'window of opportunity' (Steiner-Khamsi, 2006: 670) to make a step-in response to Shchepetylnykova and Oleksiyenko's (2024: 1) call for the 'de-Sovietisation in higher education and research' in Ukraine.

Conclusions

Existing scholarship on research ethics in Ukraine is scarce and fragmented, focusing predominantly on the lack of research integrity in the work of students and academics (Yukhymenko-Lescroart, 2014; Fimyar et al., 2019; Shykhnenko and Sbruieva, 2022) and issues in bioethics (Pustovit, 2006; Basarab and Anderson, 2022; Sulaieva et al., 2023). This chapter has made a contribution to this literature by exploring a new niche – how members of the Ukrainian HE community pursue ethical research in the area of education. The chapter has demonstrated that research ethics has become a quest for the members of the Ukrainian HE community. This quest has been complicated by the legacies of the past and the current war context; it has also emerged as a symbolic tool for the members of the Ukrainian HE community to pursue their work while seeking the alignment of their research practice with international practices abroad, such as those following BERA *Ethical Guidelines for Educational Research*.

The analysis in this chapter has been informed by the path-dependency approach and the analysis of a survey of and semi-structured interviews with members of the Ukrainian HE community. In doing so, this chapter has problematised research practice in Ukraine and proposed solutions to the persisting issues, primarily through developing further the current working version of the translated BERA *Ethical Guidelines for Educational Research* by adapting them to the Ukrainian context and furthering their application.

Reflective questions

1 How can and should we advance our ethical considerations in doing research in the area of education in war-torn settings?
2 How can we ensure positive practical impact generation by such research for the communities impacted by wars, so that this research

goes beyond the production of scholarly publications and building their authors' careers?

These questions are inspired by Howlett and Lazarenko's (2023: 722) powerful claim informed by their reflections on how scholars have handled the war in Ukraine, 'We conclude that the production of knowledge about the war requires an elevation of ethics above research outputs to protect our participants, ourselves, and the larger communities affected by the conflict. At its core, this paper thus underscores that ethical knowledge production sometimes requires scholars to remain silent.'

Further reading

1. Howlett, M. and Lazarenko, V. (2023). How and when should we (not) speak?: Ethical knowledge production about the Russia–Ukraine war. *Journal of International Relations and Development*, 26(4), 722–32.
2. Malejacq, R. and Mukhopadhyay, D. (2016). The 'tribal politics' of field research: A reflection on power and partiality in 21st-century warzones. *Perspectives on Politics*, 14(4), 1011–28.
3. Olson, R. E. (2023). Emotions in human research ethics guidelines: Beyond risk, harm and pathology. *Qualitative Research*, 23(3), 526–44.

Data access

The dataset with the English version of the interview transcripts, generated and analysed during the current study, is available in the Research Data Archive of Nottingham Trent University, at TBC.

Acknowledgements

We would like to express our gratitude to the members of the Ukrainian Educational Research Association for participating in the interviews and survey to inform this chapter. Producing this chapter would not have been possible without their time and effort invested in the midst of the very difficult circumstances of living in a war zone.

References

Annan-Diab, F. and Molinari, C. (2017). Interdisciplinarity: Practical approach to advancing education for sustainability and for the Sustainable Development Goals. *The International Journal of Management Education*, 15(2), 73–83.

Basarab, M. and Anderson, E. E. (2022). Research during wartime—Ethical challenges faced by oncology researchers in Ukraine. *JAMA Oncology*, 8(9), 1254–5.

British Educational Research Association (BERA) (2018). *Ethical Guidelines for Educational Research* (in Ukrainian). https://www.bera.ac.uk/publication/ethical-guidelines-for-educational-research-2018-ukrainian-translation. Accessed 30 May 2024.

BERA (2024). *Ethical Guidelines for Educational Research* (5th ed.). London: BERA. https://www.bera.ac.uk/publication/ethical-guidelines-for-educational-research-fifth-edition-2024. Accessed 30 May 2024. Ukrainian version, https://www.bera.ac.uk/publication/ethical-guidelines-for-educational-research-2018-ukrainian-translation. Accessed 1 October 2025.

Cairney, P. (2011). The new British policy style: From a British to a Scottish political tradition? The new British policy style. *Political Studies Review*, 9(2), 208–20.

Fim'yar, O., Kushnir, I. and Vitrukh, M. (2019). Understanding Ukrainian pedagogical sciences through textbook analysis of four 'Pedagogy' textbooks. *European Educational Research Journal*, 18(5), 576–95.

Howlett, M. and Lazarenko, V. (2023). How and when should we (not) speak?: Ethical knowledge production about the Russia–Ukraine war. *Journal of International Relations and Development*, 26(4), 722–32.

Huisman, J. (2023). The Bologna process in European and post-Soviet higher education: Institutional legacies and policy adoption. In C. Dienel (Ed.), *Globalizing Higher Education and Strengthening the European Spirit*, London: Routledge (pp. 63–78).

Kushnir, I. (2021). *The Bologna Reform in Ukraine: Learning Europeanisation in the Post-Soviet Context*. Bingley: Emerald.

Malle, S. (2009). Soviet legacies in post-Soviet Russia: Insights from crisis management. *Post-Communist Economies*, 21(3), 249–82.

NGL Media (2024). Only two people in Ukraine stepped away from their scientific titles. 28 May. https://ngl.media/2024/05/28/lishe-dvoye-lyudej-v-ukrayini-dobrovilno-vidmovilis-vid-naukovih-stupeniv/. Accessed 30 May 2024.

Oleksiyenko, A. V. (2021). Is academic freedom feasible in the post-Soviet space of higher education?. *Educational Philosophy and Theory*, 53(11), 1116–26.

Oleksiyenko, A. V. (2023). Managerialism with Soviet Characteristics and Global Higher Education: Legacies and Paradoxes of University Transformations. In L. Leišytė, R. J. Dee and B. J. R. van der Maulen (Eds.), *Research Handbook on the Transformation of Higher Education*, Cheltenham, Camberley and Northampton, MA: Edward Elgar Publishing (pp. 82–94).

Pustovit, S. V. (2006). Some methodological aspects of ethics committees' expertise: The Ukrainian example. *Science and Engineering Ethics*, 12(1), 85–94.

Shchepetylnykova, L. and Oleksiyenko, A. V. (2024). What comes after post-Soviet? Towards a new concept of de-Sovietization in higher education and research. *International Journal of Educational Development*, 106, article 103014, 1–12.

Shykhnenko, K. and Sbruieva, A. (2022). The code of conduct for research integrity, governance, and ethics in education in the USA, Europe, and Ukraine: Comparative analysis. *European Journal of Educational Research*, 11(4), 2195–207.

Steiner-Khamsi, G. (2006). The economics of policy borrowing and lending: A study of late adopters. *Oxford Review of Education*, 32(5), 665–78.

Sulaieva, O. N., Artamonova, O., Dudin, O., Semikov, R., Urakov, D., Zakharash, Y., Kacharian, A., Strilka, V., Mykhalchuk, I., Haidamak, O. and Serdyukova, O. (2023). Ethical navigation of biobanking establishment in Ukraine: Learning from the experience of developing countries. *Journal of Medical Ethics*, 0, 1–6. doi:10.1136/jme-2023-109129.

UERA (2023). *Research Ethics Guidelines*. https://uera.org.ua/index.php/en/node/217. Accessed 30 May 2024.

Yukhymenko-Lescroart, M. A. (2014). Ethical beliefs toward academic dishonesty: A cross-cultural comparison of undergraduate students in Ukraine and the United States. *Journal of Academic Ethics*, 12, 29–41.

20

Ethical Research in Multilingual Education Contexts: Working with Non-Professional Interpreters

by *Barbara Skinner, Ronan Kelly and Maria Stewart*

Introduction

Multilingual children and adults have diverse knowledges, abilities and identities; however, they may often be marginalised in societies which are dominated by a monolingual language ideology. This dominance plays out in educational research contexts. Hence it is important that educational researchers consider how to thoughtfully navigate multilingual research contexts. For example, we should ask ourselves, how ethical is it for a monolingual researcher to conduct educational research in a multilingual setting? This situation may mean our research participants are unable to convey accurately what they want to say, due to lack of proficiency in the language the researcher is using. Indeed, to be ethical, it is vital that researchers seek to redress inequalities by authentically engaging and representing the voices of multilingual participants (BERA, 2024). Holmes et al. (2013: 286) propose the term 'researching multilingually' to describe those research activities which require the use of more than one language and propose a three-step framework to support this type of research, that is firstly, 'realising'; secondly, 'considering possibilities and complexities' and thirdly, 'becoming purposeful and making decisions'. So, how might an ethically minded, monolingual researcher use this framework to research multilingually?

This chapter will discuss how 'to do' research ethically with participants from diverse language backgrounds, especially when working in a society which is dominated by a monolingual language ideology, in this case, in Northern Ireland. It explores how to 'cross' that linguistic boundary by focusing on the use of non-professional interpreters in educational research.

The content of the chapter is drawn from two doctoral studies which took alternative approaches to using non-professional interpreters to conduct research in multilingual environments. Indeed, the British Educational Research Association (BERA)'s *Ethical Guidelines for Educational Research* stipulates that few ethical dilemmas have straightforward responses or 'have obvious or singular solutions' (BERA, 2024: 7). One of the doctoral studies recruited volunteer adults, whilst the second study engaged multilingual pupils to perform the role of non-professional interpreters.

The following reflections are guided by Holmes et al.'s (2013, 2016) researching multilingually framework. The first step, realisation, involves the researcher becoming aware of the potential for multilingual research practices. After this, they can move to the second step by considering the possibilities and practicalities of multilingual research practices more deeply. Such possibilities must be considered in tandem with complexities, including how to decide which language(s) will be used during various research activities, engaging in reflexive practice to surface how decisions are made. The third, and final, step involves the researcher actively making informed decisions about how they will research multilingually. Researcher intentionality, where a researcher is 'able to articulate the rationale for their researching multilingually choices, rather than simply stating what they did' (Holmes et al., 2013: 297), underpins the entire framework. The following two vignettes discuss the intersection of ethics and researcher intentionality when researching multilingually.

Vignette One: Using non-professional interpreters to bridge the language gap

This vignette is drawn from a doctoral project which examines home-school partnership for migrant pupils. The research was conducted across four primary schools in Northern Ireland and followed a Mixed Methods design. Migrant pupils and their parents participated in questionnaires and focus group interviews. Data was collected from 100 migrant pupils and 63 parents.

At an early stage in the project, I (Maria) came to the *realisation* that the study ought to foreground the hitherto unheard voices of migrant pupils and their parents. This was considered essential given that previous studies in Northern Ireland had only done so to a limited extent (e.g. Jones et al., 2018). However, a multilingual approach was a challenge for several reasons. Firstly, I am monolingual, thus necessitating the use of interpreters. Furthermore, there is little guidance in research literature on how to conduct multilingual research (Holmes et al., 2013). Reliance on another to literally convey my words and those of participants presented the risk that meaning may be lost.

As a recipient of a Department for the Economy Doctoral studentship, I utilised my annual Research Training and Support Grant, which was supplemented by a sum of additional funding from the Vice Dean at Ulster University, to cover the cost of some professional translation of written documentation. However, this was insufficient to cover full costs and necessitated *consideration of* the use of non-professional interpreters. In recent decades, there has been much debate surrounding the use of professional as opposed to non-professional interpreters in interactions with multilingual families across public services (Antonini, 2015). Rimmer (2020) discusses the impartiality of professional interpreters and the accuracy of their translations, suggesting that non-professionals may be less impartial. In contrast, Martinez-Gómez (2015) asserts that non-professionals possess a degree of competency in both languages involved, and are available immediately, often without the need for economic compensation. Having considered the balance of argument in the literature and the practical financial realities of my research context, a *decision* was made to recruit a network of volunteer interpreters.

Ethical considerations are a central issue in any research and should be deliberated on throughout the course of the project (Govil, 2013). BERA's (2024) ethical guidelines advise that 'when researching in more than one language or culture, researchers should consider the effects of translation and/or interpretation on participants' understandings of what is involved' (BERA, 2018, paragraph 11).[1] As a result, consent/assent forms and information sheets were translated into participants' home languages. Interpreters were also made available to answer any queries from potential participants. Further considerations related to how to ensure that volunteers acted ethically within their interpreting role. For example, meaning could be affected if interpreters came from the same cultural background as the participant for whom they were interpreting and were tempted to present the message in a way which would make that culture 'look good', so to speak. To mitigate this, I made the *decision* to hold briefing sessions with interpreters prior to the commencement of focus groups to familiarise them with the aims of the research and questions to be asked (Plumridge et al., 2012) and to highlight ethical issues in doing this type of research. It was essential that they held an understanding of, and 'bought into', the research focus, its ethical issues and applied this to their conduct. Although not mentioned in the latest BERA 2024 guidelines, it is worthwhile considering whether non-professional interpreters, or indeed any other participants from different roles who collaborate in the research process, should have the opportunity to read an information sheet about the project and to formally consent to and withdraw from the process. This more formal level of involvement could better emphasise the importance of their role.

Additionally, as part of getting them to invest in the study, interpreters were also required to complete Child Protection and Safeguarding training and clearance, in addition to signing a confidentiality agreement. The researcher also went to great lengths to build rapport with interpreters, as by building trusting relationships with them they felt more comfortable, hence were able to have participants feel at ease. Guidance was sought from colleagues in the linguistics department at Ulster University on how to interpret competently and in an ethical manner. Recommendations were made that interpreters must fully interpret what is being said as close as English allows, demonstrate no bias, not offer any personal comments and spell out any unusual words to ensure understanding. Interpreters acted as 'conduits of information' (Plumridge et al., 2012: 190) and translated participants verbatim. A further decision was made to involve interpreters in transcribing focus groups so that they could affirm what was being said. This gave them the opportunity to identify any words or phrases they may have omitted in literal translation. In keeping with guidelines (BERA, 2018), I acted with a duty of care towards volunteer interpreters by providing rest breaks and ensuring travel costs were reimbursed.

Nonetheless, some limitations were evident. Due to a dearth of volunteer interpreters, it was not possible to include every language group in each research site. This may be considered both methodologically and ethically problematic. However, efforts were made to include those language groups which constituted the majority multilingual pupils in each site. Seven language groups were engaged in questionnaire data and six in focus groups which still provided considerable depth. Volunteer interpreters were secured for five language groups and professional interpreters were employed for Somali and Tetum. The rationale behind this decision was that Somali-speaking pupils were present in two of the four research sites and Tetum was the majority language group in one research site.

Given that a primary objective of this study was to engage the voice of multilingual pupils and their parents, the use of interpreters was imperative. While misunderstandings may occur, interpreters can and do support access and promote inclusion for research participants across all levels of English-language proficiency. Debate remains surrounding the appropriateness of using non-professionals in this regard. Nonetheless, one cannot overlook the propensity with which they are utilised to assist in translation in educational research. In the absence of clear guidelines specifically related to interpreting, this researcher would suggest adherence to broader ethical principles as recommended by the 2024 BERA fifth edition of its ethical guidelines. Partnered with relationship building and methodologically informed decision-making, such engagement may serve to ensure inclusive research practice for multilingual populations.

Vignette Two: Translanguaging spaces: Secondary school students as non-professional peer interpreters

In this second vignette, I (Ronan) problematise the ethical dynamics of multilingual secondary school students acting as peer interpreters during a series of group interviews. The data was gathered as part of my doctoral study investigating the relationship between language development, identity and social integration for multilingual secondary school students in Northern Ireland. Across five schools, twenty-eight multilingual adolescents participated in a series of group interviews during a school year. The approach to peer interpreting was informed by translanguaging theory which recognises the reality of how multilinguals fluidly draw on all the linguistic and semiotic resources available to them to make meaning and communicate (Li, 2018; Li and García, 2022).

A principle which underpinned my research plan was to engage with multilingual students across all levels of English proficiency. Given the diverse linguistic backgrounds of students participating in group interviews, and English being the shared language among all, the group interviews would be conducted in English. Therefore, one argument might be that for students to communicate effectively, a minimum of intermediate English-language proficiency would be required for participation. I believed that it would be unethical to exclude students from having a voice in the research due to their emerging English-language proficiency. Yet I was unsure of how to create a group interview environment which supported meaningful participation for students with emerging English proficiency.

At this point in my doctoral candidature, I was reading about translanguaging theory, which states that multilingual students draw on a single integrated semiotic repertoire to make meaning and communicate (Li, 2018). This means that they do not isolate and separate languages; thus, having group interviews as English-only zones would not fully engage with how multilingual students make meaning and communicate. Recent research by Polo-Pérez and Holmes (2023) states that applying translanguaging in research methodology challenges the structural inequities of monolingual ideologies in research and produces more trustworthy data by engaging participants' full multilingual resources and identities. I came to the realisation that constructing group interviews as a translanguaging space would better support meaningfully participation. The main approach that I adopted to create a translanguaging space was to collaboratively draw on all the language resources in the group through peer interpreting.

Peer interpreting among multilingual students required consideration of many possibilities and complexities. I first had to consider and justify why peer interpreters would be more appropriate than adult interpreters. Given that a principle in the research was to engage with multilingual students of all language backgrounds, group interviews would involve students who spoke a combined total of thirteen languages. I did not feel that it was appropriate to separate students into language groups for group interviews as this did not reflect the reality of how they experienced schooling. Having group interviews where participants brought a range of languages would have meant that several adult interpreters would have been required at most group interviews. I believed that this would have created a more formal dynamic, making it less comfortable for adolescent students to share their experiences. Peer interpreting represented a more appropriate approach as students were more likely to be comfortable with a peer and would have a deeper shared understanding of the school context. Moreover, translanguaging does not equate to direct translation from language A to language B; it is a fluid practice where students draw on their semiotic repertoire which may encompass features of various languages.

The next consideration was multilingual students' willingness and autonomy in peer interpretation. I could not assume that all multilingual students would be willing to have another student interpret for them or be willing to interpret for another student. The group interviews did not exist in a vacuum. The students participating in them would have existing relationships which would influence their willingness to interpret for each other. Another factor was student autonomy; I considered that it would be most appropriate for multilingual students themselves to identify whether they required support through peer interpreting. If I was to explicitly request that certain students interpret for others, this may have created a power differential in the group.

I made the decision to construct group interviews as a translanguaging space where students were empowered to self-nominate and collaboratively agree on peer interpretation on their own terms. As students were likely to perceive me as an authority figure to some extent, my intention was to legitimise translanguaging as a social practice within the group interview setting. At the beginning of each group interview, I *became purposeful* and explained to all students that they could use any language they preferred and could take as much time as they needed to discuss something in a language other than English. I further explained that because I did not understand all the languages they used, I would be grateful if they could help me to understand in English after they had discussed something in another language.

Across the twenty-two group interviews, some students frequently engaged in peer interpreting while in other group interviews students mainly used English. When there were instances of translanguaging through peer interpreting, it was collaboratively generated by students. This collaborative act involved students engaging in translanguaging to co-construct meaning with contributions in English once they had agreed on shared meaning, taking ownership of the situation. Quotes exemplifying multilingual students' autonomy in translanguaging with peer interpreting included '*we try to sort it out because I think she knows more English words than me*' and '*if I want to translate for my friend I speak Arabic*'. These quotes from students indicate that they felt able to use their linguistic resources and autonomously collaborate with peers to communicate in group interviews.

Multilingual students face structural inequalities where their full multilingual identities and knowledges are marginalised due to monolingual ideologies in society and schooling. Taking a translanguaging informed and student-led approach to peer interpreting in group interviews can contribute towards challenging these structural inequities and, as a result, support more ethical research practices.

Conclusion

This chapter has explored the ethical issues, and how they might be overcome, of using non-professional interpreters by examining two vignettes, one using adult volunteer interpreters and the other using adolescent peer interpreters. Holmes et al.'s (2016) framework underpins the process the researchers took by illustrating what the researchers 'realised', 'considered' and 'decided' upon during the process of using non-professional interpreters. The biggest challenge is ensuring interpreters act ethically by being impartial in the reporting of participants' contributions. For adult volunteer interpreters, this meant making sure the interpreters 'bought into' the research project. This was achieved by organising a briefing session, gaining child protection and safeguarding guarantees and confidentiality statements, as well as building a rapport with them. Also, inviting them to stay with the research process after interpretation had finished by contributing to the transcription of data helped mitigate against lack of accuracy of interpretation. BERA's 2024 guidelines recommend other ways in which rapport and trust may be established, for example, by crediting collaborators. In the two vignettes above, interpreters can be considered as making a 'less substantive contribution' which can be acknowledged at the end of a written publication or a conference presentation, rather than recognising their contribution as 'substantive' and crediting them as 'co-authors'. Also, regarding dissemination, BERA 2024 guidelines suggest that where research is conducted in a setting in which 'English is not the prevalent (or only) language, researchers should make the fruits of their research available in languages that make it locally accessible' (BERA, 2024, paragraph 71). Explaining that this will happen, up front at the start of the project, may encourage non-professional interpreters to see the importance of their role throughout the research process, therefore leading to better investment in the project and in turn more reliable data.

For the adolescent peer interpreters, impartiality was underpinned by building trust with them, by allowing them to take ownership of the group interview space and use it as a place where they could translanguage freely to support each other. The lack of an authoritative figure carrying out the interpretation may also have led to participants being more relaxed and 'real', leading in turn, to more reliable and valid data being collected. However, taking ownership has its limitations too – there may be instances where the peer interpreter did not have enough time to tell the monolingual researcher what was being said or did not want to interpret accurately for fear of offending the researcher. Indeed, the validity and reliability of data gained in the peer interpretation/translanguaging vignette are wholly reliant on the trust and rapport the researcher builds with the multilingual participants.

The main driver for using non-professional interpreters is financial – it often costs nothing in comparison with professional interpretation services. Another is ease of access; often, volunteer interpreters are readily available, especially for language groups which have large populations in the geographical area wherein the research is being carried out. Conversely, this can limit the research. For those language groups which are not common in the research context, it may be hard to find a volunteer interpreter, and as in vignette one, this can mean the voices of some potential participants are excluded. Similarly, in vignette two, if there is a participant who cannot avail of peer interpretation, their voice may be left unheard. In this case, researchers may consider expanding a translanguaging approach to engage students' full semiotic repertoires across creative modes such as drama, music or arts.

There are other limitations in using a non-professional interpreter approach. In vignette two, while the group interviews were audio recorded and transcribed, students' uses of languages beyond English were not translated in the written documents, and this may have left some data unrealised. This decision was taken based on a translanguaging approach where students fluidly constructed meaning during interactions with peers, and precedence was given to how the students themselves represented their understandings in English.

The ethical starting point for use of non-professional interpreters in these two vignettes was the BERA 2018 guidelines[1] which highlight a researcher's responsibilities to participants who are affected by structural inequalities. Updated BERA Guidelines state, 'sensitivity and attentiveness towards such structural issues are important aspects of researchers' responsibilities to participants at all stages of research' (BERA, 2024, paragraph 2) and these were implemented through 'realising' the ethical issue, 'considering' possible solutions and 'deciding' what to do (Holmes et al., 2016), sometimes in advance and sometimes in the moment. At all stages, decisions were taken with the primary objective of capturing the voices of multilingual populations. The aim was to attempt to overcome the inequalities these participants can face due to monolingual, English-only, language ideologies in society and schooling, by allowing their full multilingual identities and knowledges to be given voice.

Reflective questions

1 How can we mitigate against any lack of accuracy and lack of impartiality of non-professional interpreters?
2 In what ways are non-professional interpreters an ethical alternative to the use of professional interpreters in educational research?
3 What would applying translanguaging in research methodology look like in your context?
4 To what extent is it appropriate for multilingual pupils to peer interpret for others?
5 How and to what extent can the diverse language data being produced in a translanguaging group interview be captured, transcribed and analysed in an ethical meaningful manner?

Further reading

1. Holmes, P., Fay, R., Andrews, J. and Attia, M. (2016). How to Research Multilingually: Possibilities and Complexities. In Z. Hua, (Ed.), *Research Methods in Intercultural Communication: A Practical Guide* (1st ed.), Oxford: Wiley-Blackwell (pp. 88–102).

   This book chapter by Holmes and colleagues presents the researching multilingually framework which has been applied in this current chapter. Readers will find a detailed discussion on the possibilities and complexities of enacting the framework across a range of contexts.

2. Rolland, L., King, H. M. and Lorette, P. (2023). Methodological implications of participant and researcher multilingualism: Making language dynamics visible. *Journal of Multilingual and Multicultural Development*, 44(8), 645–56. https://doi.org/10.1080/01434632.2023.2224774.

This journal's special edition directly addresses the methodological implications of language dynamics in research contexts where participants and/or researchers are multilingual.

3. Temple, B. and Moran, R. (Eds.) (2011). *Doing Research with Refugees: Issues and Guidelines*. Bristol: The Policy Press.

    This book explores methodological issues relating to the involvement of refugees in both service evaluation and development and research more generally. It presents a set of good practice guidelines for academics doing research with refugees.

4. **Meier, G., Van der Voet, P. B. and Yan, T. (2024). Research ethics in a multilingual world: A guide to reflecting on language decisions in all disciplines.** *Diametros: An Online Journal of Philosophy*, 80, 38–58. https://doi:10.33392/diam.1926.

    This article addresses the ethical implications of language decisions at all stages of the research process. It highlights that language-related ethical dilemmas are not just organisational but can be social and ideological. It also offers a reflective framework to complement regulatory guidelines.

Note

1   The fourth edition of the BERA *Ethical Guidelines for Educational Research* BERA (2018) was that available and therefore used by researchers at the time of the research generating the reported vignettes.
2   Paragraph 71 (BERA, 2024) 'Where research is conducted in a setting in which English is not the prevalent (or only) language, researchers should make the fruits of their research available in languages that make it locally accessible'.
3   Paragraph 2 (BERA, 2024).

References

Antonini, R. (2015). Unseen forms of interpreting: Child language brokering in Italy. *CULTUS: The Journal of Intercultural Mediation and Communication*, 8, 96–112. https://hdl.handle.net/11585/572467.

British Educational Research Association (BERA) (2018). *Ethical Guidelines for Educational Research* (4th ed.). London: BERA. https://www.bera.ac.uk/publication/ethical-guidelines-for-educational-research-2018-online.

British Educational Research Association (BERA) (2024). *Ethical Guidelines for Educational Research* (5th ed.). London: BERA. www.bera.ac.uk/publication/ethicalguidelines-for-educational-research-2024.

Govil, P. (2013). Ethical considerations in educational research. *International Journal of Advancement in Education and Social Sciences*, 1(2), 17–22. https://citeseerx.ist.psu.edu/document?doi=c0c0efc1c8d4c5b2721694098a831cb00aaf887a&repid=rep1&type=pdf.

Holmes, P., Fay, R., Andrews, J. and Attia, M. (2013). Researching multilingually: New theoretical and methodological directions. *International Journal of Applied Linguistics*, 23(3), 285–99. https://doi.org/10.1111/ijal.12038.

Holmes, P., Fay, R., Andrews, J. and Attia, M. (2016). How to Research Multilingually: Possibilities and Complexities. In Z. Hua (Ed.), *Research Methods in Intercultural Communication: A Practical Guide* (1st ed.), Oxford: Wiley-Blackwell (pp. 88–102).

Jones, S., McMullen, J., Campbell, R., McLaughlin, J., McDade, B., O' Lynn, P. and Glen, C. (2018). *Multilingual Minds: The Mental Health and Wellbeing of Newcomer Children and Young People in Northern Ireland and the Role of the Education Authority Youth Service*. Belfast: EANI. https://www.stran.ac.uk/wp-content/uploads/2019/11/EA-Youth-Service-Newcomer-Research-Report.pdf.

Li, W. (2018). Translanguaging as a practical theory of language. *Applied Linguistics*, 39(1), 9–30. https://doi.org/10.1093/applin/amx039.

Li, W. and García, O. (2022). Not a first language but one repertoire: Translanguaging as a decolonizing project. *RELC Journal*, 53(2), 313–24. https://doi.org/10.1177/00336882221092841.

Martínez-Gómez, A. (2015). Invisible, visible or everywhere in between? Perceptions and actual behaviors of non-professional interpreters and interpreting users. *The Interpreters' Newsletter*, 175–94. https://www.openstarts.units.it/server/api/core/bitstreams/66402c5d-614d-45c5-8622-f0dde59209e2/content.

Plumridge, G., Redwood, S., Akhter, N., Chowdhury, R., Khalade, A. and Gill, P. (2012). Involving interpreters in research studies. *Journal of Health Services Research and Policy*, 17(3), 190–2. https://doi.org/10.1258/JHSRP.2012.01200.

Polo-Pérez, N. and Holmes, P. (2023). Translanguaging as methodology to study language cafés: Implications for managing multilingual data. *Journal of Multilingual and Multicultural Development*, 44(8), 737–50. https://doi.org/10.1080/01434632.2023.2197882.

Rimmer, A. (2020). Can patients use family members as non-professional interpreters in consultations? *British Medical Journal*, 368, m447. https://doi.org/10.1136/bmj.m447.

Section 4

Takeaways

21

Conclusions for the Ecological Web of Educational Research

by *Alison Fox and Nicole Brown*

Towards alignment of British with global research ethical guidance

This edited book illustrating the BERA ethical guidelines in practice would not be complete if we were not revisiting the book's contents and aims in their entirety. As we have seen throughout the book, researchers apply and embed ethical guidelines continually and in principled ways, but do so through interpretation, contextualisation and reconfiguration. In this final chapter, we suggest that these interpretations, contextualisations and reconfigurations are necessary because educational research is not a linear, static, uniform, independent event but a dynamic ecological web. To account for the complexity of the educational research ecosystem, we return to the global code of conduct for equitable research partnerships, introduced in Chapter 1 of this book (TRUST, 2018). We demonstrate how the BERA ethical guidelines align with the four key principles of the TRUST code and how it sits within wider ethical codes of conduct, formed with knowledge not driven by the privileged and particular ways of knowing and being of the Global North towards epistemic justice. Identifying the differences in emphasis and priority, or silences, means we can offer recommendations that might guide future revisions of British and Global North ethical guidance for educational research.

Building on arguments presented in Chapter 1, in particular Table 1.4, we offer the potential for thinking about values and virtues as a cross-cultural opportunity for exploring common principles and expectations of researchers. The cross-cultural approach illuminates a fuller range of potential responsibilities than we might have considered otherwise, including responsibilities to the non-human, wherever our research is conducted. It also helps prioritise other ways of knowing and being, and to challenge our assumptions and biases towards more equitable research decisions and relationship-building.

This book advocates an ecological view of research, attending to the interconnectedness of humans with humans, humans with the non-human and inanimate, and the associated responsibilities we have to one another and our environment. We return to the questions asked in Chapter 1 to avoid sustaining epistemic injustice (Fricker, 2007) and aspiring to counter power imbalances: Whose voices and therefore values are we hearing, or ignoring? Whose ways of being and knowing are we recognising and valuing? As well as the more common focus on gatekeepers and participants, this chapter offers a reminder that our duty of care includes duty to ourselves as researchers, care of ourselves personally and to one another, towards a community of supportive researchers. This should include paying attention to the institutions within which we work, the partners with whom we research and those who fund our work, and hence evaluating the ways the agendas of others place pressures on us as researchers. Researchers need to feel empowered to retain a sense of agency and integrity, whilst also looking to others for sources of support. The authors of this book have illustrated some of the deficits and excesses to be avoided in taking a virtuous approach (see Table 1.4 in Chapter 1).

Fairness

The first area of focus within the Global TRUST Code of research ethics relates to fairness, which encompasses seven articles, and avoids inequitability and partiality (Table 1.3). Research needs to be fair regarding collaborations and localised specificities, researchers must be fair in how they treat contextualised support systems as well as in how they recognise material and immaterial assets (Articles 1 to 7). These foundational principles also underpin many of the individual guidelines of the 2024 fifth edition of the British Educational Research Association's ethical guidelines for educational research, for example, where the guidelines highlight how researchers need to treat their participants with respect (paragraph 1) irrespective of any protected characteristics (paragraph 2), how participants must be prevented from any harm (paragraphs 34–8) or how researchers are accountable to the global community (paragraph 54), to the community of educational researchers (paragraphs 58–69) and to local communities when dissemination specifically is concerned (paragraph 70).

Yet, there is a significant difference: the Global TRUST Code of research ethics lays out a code of conduct, an ethical framework for thinking and working in research settings and contexts across the globe, whereas the British Educational Research Association's ethical guidelines for educational research outline the researchers' responsibilities, which are often seen to be a rulebook (see Chapter 17). Rather than outlining best ethical conduct in specific contexts and settings, the Global TRUST Code of research ethics suggests broader principles of fairness, which are easily transferrable to educational settings. For example, the emphasis on acknowledging the local relevance of research and involving local communities in research within Articles 1 to 4 aligns seamlessly with the principles of participatory research, where the responsibility and control over the research process from agenda-setting through to dissemination are handed over to participants (Tandon, 1988). In this edited collection, the ethical dilemmas mentioned within the context of Syria and Myanmar (Chapter 3) and the Polish community in the UK (Chapter 17) speak to exactly this issue of carrying out research that is sensitive to and inclusive of contextualised experiences. Similarly, the case studies in 'fragile contexts' (Chapter 14) as well as the focus on decolonalisation (Chapter 4) emphasise the researchers' social justice endeavours of making a difference to asylum seekers, and refugees, and otherwise oppressed communities, respectively. Within the British Educational Research Association's ethical guidelines for educational research, these social justice agendas are somewhat sidelined due to what could be argued to be a deficiency model of responsibility, where the researcher is responsible or accountable. The guidelines are not meant to be prohibitive, but as we have seen in the chapters of this book, researchers can perceive them as rigid and directive, which results in individual researchers feeling unsure about how to deal with ethical issues once they are in the middle of their projects. By contrast, the concept of fairness allows for a more flexible and more open approach to doing research ethically. This is particularly evident when considering international dimensions of research, where language barriers may need to be overcome (Chapters 5 and 20). The authors of both chapters highlight the necessity to include interpreters and translators and demonstrate the complexity of working with such research support agents, without whom certain research may not be possible at all. For such circumstances, it is the Global TRUST Code of research ethics that opens the space for meaningful collaborations, in that the researchers are asked to compensate their supporters appropriately as part of the endeavour to undertake fair research.

Respect

The TRUST code (TRUST, 2018) presents four articles under the principle of respect which cover that researchers need to attune themselves to potential cultural sensitivities in advance of their research (Article 8) and endeavour to make those being invited aware that their participation is voluntary, rather than being involved in research imposed as a 'mission-driven exercise' (Article 8) which 'dumps' ethical values onto local ways of being (Schroeder et al., 2018). Researchers should strive to obtain community assent as a way of being invited into a research setting to show respect for its ways of being (Article 9) and identify any local requirements to fulfil (Article 9). This might involve local ethics review, in whatever guise (Article 10), calling that researchers show respect for any such committees and protocols (Article 11).

By avoiding disrespect or dependence (Table 1.3), respect has always been a key tenet of the BERA ethical guidelines (BERA, 2024). The BERA call for an 'ethic of respect' (paragraph 1) includes responsibilities to one another (paragraphs 58–69 and 82–3). Chapter 12 reminds of how early career experiences of disrespect by, for example, 'harmful (and hurtful) criticism' can lead researchers to feeling 'paralysed by self-doubt' (add final book page number). Paragraph 61 specifically calls out defamatory criticism, and paragraphs 76-9 of the guidelines advise on respectful authorship practices (BERA, 2024) affecting all those who have been involved in generating knowledge. This is where the Contributor Role Taxonomy (CRediT – https://credit.niso.org/), which recognises fourteen roles in the research process, is useful to consult and guide research recognition and acknowledgement.

Respect is explored further in the BERA ethical guidelines (BERA, 2024): Paragraphs 56-7 highlight the researchers' responsibilities to respect knowledge and diverse ways of knowing in their research design. Researchers are challenged to extend their responsibilities to non-humans and the environment by consciously assessing the effects their research might have and by taking environmentally sustainable decisions (paragraph 24). The importance of being attentive to power differentials to empower and build capacity, rather than inadvertently contribute to marginalisations (e.g. paragraph 2). Chapters 5 and 20 in this book also highlight attention to gender and preferred language(s) of researchers, gatekeepers and participants. These approaches can be seen to make a turn from deficit to hope, avoiding seeing people and situations as vulnerable and instead looking for research to support resilience of communities and places (Davis and Aldieri, 2021).

Showing cultural sensitivity (Article 8) through a commitment to inclusion is threaded throughout this book. Attending to the preferred languages of individuals is highlighted, which might involve including co-researchers for in-country data gathering (e.g. Chapter 3). A collective of European Early Career Researchers is leading the way in explaining how multilingualism should be considered to benefit a project from design to dissemination (Meier et al., 2024). Chapter 17 authors discuss the role of names, which should affect researcher approaches to culturally acceptable generation of appropriate pseudonyms (see also Chapters 3 and 7). Making researchers aware of historical, political and ethnic considerations could help avoid naïve assumptions and clumsy, or even disrespectful, actions. Whilst involving those from the research context offers the chance to gain close-to-the-ground perspectives, the dangers of blurring boundaries and exposing others to risks were raised in Chapter 9, echoing further exemplification of these risks to translators in research in Africa by Barbara Mercer-Moser (in Fox et al., 2020). Sensitisation to the context and possible expectations of a researcher should be included in pre-research training to avoid imposing research (Article 8).

Whilst institutional ethics committees offer researchers in many Higher Education Institutions checks and balances through ethical review which should include guiding a researcher to gain local approvals for their research, this is not universally available. Colleagues from Ukraine remind us to review researcher awareness of access to ethics review (Chapter 19) which, from their empirical research in Ukraine, was found to be limited. Increasingly, non-institutional ethical review boards are being developed, which offer closer-to-context ethical review of projects. You can read how the Chartered College of Teaching in the UK has developed a research ethics review board populated by close-to-practice researchers (Chapter 18). Independent research ethics committees have been set up since 2012 in Aotearoa New Zealand (https://aotearoaresearchethics.org) to cover anyone without access to institutional review boards wanting to conduct research in Aotearoa New Zealand, and since 2016, a similar board has been established in the UK (http://irec.org.uk). Attention needs to be paid in collaborative research to avoiding assumptions on where power lies simply because of access to ethical review (Article 9). The views of non-HEI partners will be vital to maximising the local applicability and acceptability of research plans being submitted to institutional ethics committees (e.g. Chapter 15) and avoiding the dominance of UK partner's processes in international collaborative research (e.g. Chapters 3 and 5). There should be nothing procedural about procedural aspects of ethics, that is, when needing to go through ethics review processes. Authors point us to the work of Gray et al. (2017), in calling for cultural competence in applying ethical frameworks (also referred to in the BERA guidelines paragraph 53) and the use of multilingual dialogue to avoid blind spots in what is seen, heard and accounted for in applications for research approval.

Avoiding imposition (Article 8) extends to dissemination, as highlighted in the BERA guidelines (e.g. paragraphs 70 and 81). Chapter 15 calls for researchers to agree with those in the setting as to what is worthwhile to report, whose time, and how resources should be involved. In the spirit of open science (Klebel et al., 2024) and in a world where datasets are being used to train Artificial Intelligence tools (SOA Policy Team, 2024), we are reminded by authors in Chapters 8 and 9 that today's researchers have a responsibility to prepare participants to think about whether they consent for future use of their data beyond their immediate involvement as a resource for tomorrow's researchers. For thinking about this, the 'FAIR Guiding Principles for scientific data management and stewardship'

(Go Fair, 2016) provide guidelines to improve the Findability, Accessibility, Interoperability and Reuse of digital assets. Researchers therefore have responsibilities to be upskilled through training in data anonymisation, de-identification and understanding the requirements of metadata needed to responsibly archive data in open repositories (e.g. Nelson, 2015).

Care

To enact a duty of care, avoiding carelessness or 'smothering' (Table 1.4), the TRUST code headlines the importance of tailoring informed consent to local requirements (Article 12), towards 'genuine and appropriate access to all research participants and local partners to express any concerns they may have' (Article 13). This links to notions of assent as well as consent (paragraphs 23 and 25, BERA, 2024) and of 'voluntary informed and ongoing consent ... without any duress' (paragraph 8, BERA, 2024). The TRUST code demands that researchers do not undertake high-risk research in settings just because this is possible. If it would not be acceptable in the researcher's home setting, this should not be allowed elsewhere just because it is possible due to an absence of local ethical review or a lack of awareness of the potential sensitivity of issues to be covered. Local stakeholders should be made aware of the perceived risks and make the final call on what is acceptable research in their context (Article 14). Safety and wellbeing measures for all those in danger of 'stigmatisation ... incrimination ... discrimination or indeterminate personal risk' should also be agreed as sufficient and appropriate by local partners (Article 15). The minimisation of harm (paragraph 34) and avoidance of compounding structural inequalities (e.g. paragraph 2) appear explicitly in the BERA ethical guidelines. Both the BERA guidelines (paragraph 82) and TRUST code (Article 19) refer to remembering to conduct risk management for themselves, including addressing conflicts of conscience (Article 19), disclosures (paragraph 27) and positioning with relation to sponsors (paragraph 53). Chapter 14 of this book focuses on the notion of self-care, as introduced in the fifth edition of the BERA ethical guidelines (BERA, 2024, paragraph 82).

There are many examples in this book as to how consent and assent protocols can be tailored to particular groups and communities. Examples are given of planning alternative protocols (e.g. Chapter 3) and also when researchers became alert to the need to review consent protocols. This could be when appreciating that the research was not being perceived as the researcher expected and additional offers of consent/assent/dissent were important for the research not to be imposed (Chapter 17) or when planned protocols were not followed leading to participants feeling uncomfortable and a researcher needing to support them in withdrawing from certain activities (Chapter 15). Authors flag up the importance of keeping parent/guardian behaviours in view (Chapter 15) and paying attention to the gatekeeper expectations, which may see their role extending beyond permitting access to a setting to being involved in the way the research is mediated to participants (Chapter 6).

Time investment towards trusting researcher-gatekeeper relationships can help researchers gain an understanding of how research should best proceed such that a researcher enacts their duty of care not only to the direct participants but also to the community more broadly. This might need researchers to adapt research method protocols, such as including observers during interviews (Chapter 6). In some cultures where lives are lived collectively and communally, this might be anticipated. Researcher-gatekeeper relationships can help gain a deeper appreciation of how to progress research, even if it is challenging to pursue in a setting politically without alienating stakeholders (Chapters 3 and 9) or when needing to make participants feel safe and avoid further discrimination when discussing sensitive issues related to inequality and bias (Chapter 6).

Researcher responsibilities to demonstrate their care by evaluating the impact of their research on animal and environmental, as well as human, welfare (Articles 16–18) and any depletion of resources (Articles 16) are in the TRUST code as matters to be addressed in advance of starting research, in ways future BERA ethical guidelines might draw upon. Looking to other cultures, for example those built on notions of ubuntu across Africa, highlights societal approaches to embracing community and environment. Coming to a rich appreciation of a community's ways of living and being will help researchers appreciate the connection of people with their environment and anticipate the impact of a project, and hence how to mitigate this. Chapter 11 offers a framework for researchers and institutions wanting to enact principles of environmental sustainability in research. This call to action is being promoted through the development of a voluntary cross-sector Concordat for Environmental Sustainability in Research and

Innovation (https://wellcome.org/who-we-are/positions-and-statements/environmental-sustainability-concordat) to which UK research-active institutions are being invited to sign.

Honesty

The section honesty of the Global TRUST Code of research ethics encompasses four articles that outline in which ways a researcher may demonstrate honesty and avoid deception, dishonesty and bluntness (Table 1.4). The main principles here are that researchers should not be taking advantage of localised specificities if their research work takes place in areas where educational, administrative, policy or legal standards are lower than in their own countries (Articles 21 to 23). Instead, researchers should continue to uphold their countries' high standards in how they adjust their relationships in the field, which relates not only to their conduct but also to the division of labour and definitions or roles and responsibilities (Article 20). Where the British Educational Research Association's ethical guidelines for educational research are concerned, honesty is not a separate category per se but is built into the notion of transparency within the responsibilities to participants or the responsibilities for publication and dissemination, for example. Researchers are required 'to be open and honest' (paragraph 27) in relation to the research aims, objectives, context and methodology, although 'covert research can be defensible' (paragraph 3). Therefore, the guidelines around transparency (paragraphs 27–30), for example, are not completely on par with the conceptualisation of honesty in the Global TRUST Code of research ethics. Honesty is not a measure of compliance or accountability in the way that transparency is. Honesty is about human behaviours that are characterised by empathy and empowerment, behaviours that demonstrate that the researcher's knowledge about their own privilege and their subsequent attempt to minimise that privilege. This interpretation of honesty is recognisable within the British Educational Research Association's ethical guidelines for educational research, where there is an emphasis on conflicts of interest (paragraphs 30 and 53) or where the researcher is tasked to reflect on whether they are capable of and the right person to undertake the planned research (paragraph 7). This edited collection highlights how a focus on transparency, in the sense of compliance and accountability, may be problematic for researchers in the field. For example, authors explain the difficult decisions that had to be taken in the context of collaborations (Chapter 12), when publishing jointly with local communities (Chapter 15), and in settings where the research work involves other professionals or research support systems, like interpreters (Chapter 20). The ethical issues at play and how these researchers have dealt with them demonstrate that humanity may be at the heart of decision-taking in the field. Similarly, there are case studies that highlight the discrepancy of standards between the researchers' own settings and the contexts of their research and how a privileged view should not mean taking advantage of individuals but need to incorporate relationship- and capacity-building activities. Chapter 6, for example, showcases the process of consent in difficult circumstances, where the participants have auditory processing difficulties and/or are migrant children. The case studies from Syria and Myanmar (Chapter 3), by contrast, evidence the benefits of relationship-building activities as an opportunity to protect participants.

Concluding insights

As argued in Chapter 1, looking globally to a code created through international cooperation and connecting that locally to British association guidance is helpful in identifying areas of universal views on virtuous research as well as new insights to take into future research. As editors of this book, we are aware that any guidelines which are not wholly prescriptive are open to interpretation. We were therefore not surprised when the contributors to this book showed a range of responses to the BERA ethical guidelines (BERA, 2024), both in the anticipation and design of their studies and in their reflections post-study. The result is a wide range of personalised approaches to ethics in practice. Therefore, the book offers concrete illustrations of what it may mean to be culturally appropriate when it comes to ethical approaches to research design and conduct. The contributions reveal how the decisions researchers make are rooted in their world views of what constitutes knowledge (ontology), how knowledge can be generated (epistemology), and the values underpinning their approach to ethical knowledge generation (axiology). As we learn from other cultures across the globe, we come to appreciate how these positions are culturally and socially influenced, and we do not act as isolated individuals. We advocate:

- Avoiding the dangers of excess and deficit (Chapter 1).
- Not rushing research proposals, however well intentioned, but to slow down entry to research settings: to come to know them and those who inhabit the setting.
- Stepping back from research settings which are familiar to a researcher, placing a fresh metaphorical researcher 'hat' on, to see the normative behaviours, interactions and expectations afresh.
- Linking educational research with the slow movement. There already exists a slow-science movement, calling for a healthier and better science culture (Alleva, 2006), on the basis that fast science is 'bad for both science and scientists' (Frith, 2019). This has already been proposed to be needed within education to generate slow knowledge (Biesta, 2013).
- Prioritising the relationship building needed to reimagine the role of a researcher as a guest – to be invited in by a host – reversing traditional assumptions of approaching a research setting.

Slow, ethical educational research needs critical and careful thought about researcher positionality and what this means for building/keeping/not losing trust, as well as thought about the decisions needed to enact a duty of care to the ecological web associated with a project. It also needs the open-mindedness of researchers to seek out other ways of being, to listen to what is being said – including to the silences – and to act even when difficult decisions are the best way forward. To avoid being accused of conducting helicopter research (Haelewaters et al., 2021), attention is needed from the start to how the research might end, including a relational legacy. For these complex and ongoing considerations ethical reflexivity (Gewirtz and Cribb, 2006) is needed. This will exercise our moral responsibilities to design and enact equitable, inclusive and worthwhile research, not only judged by our own values but also by others, thus demonstrating our commitment to decoloniality We offer the Think-Listen-Act framework (Table 21.1) for ongoing ethical reflexivity positions.

This framework connects the BERA ethical guidelines and TRUST code to situate a researcher in the web of ecological relationships to show how each relationship affects and should support one another. We hope that working through the table will help researchers think through actions they can take to practice ethical conduct and decision-making.

Table 21.1 A Think-Listen-Act framework for supporting ethical reflexivity.

	Think	Listen	Act
Open-mindedness	Map who and what could be affecting and affected by your research idea; Read and identify your assumptions and biases.	Find out about the political, ethical, social, language and environment context of your research setting.	Be prepared to adjust any aspect of your research topic, design or setting; Commit to maximising the benefits of the study to all involved or affected.
Attention to the local	Identify all those in the selected setting whether directly or indirectly involved.	Meet representatives from those in different societal positions to your research and ask their advice; Listen to the subtext and look for power imbalances.	Identify ways of working and relationship building that include the required and the courtesy; Offer access to research knowledge generation through the preferred languages of those involved; Carry out your commitments to benefiting the setting.
Care for one another	Identify who also could benefit from your research journey.	Make time to hear about other researchers' experiences.	Include capacity building in all aspects of academic life.
Care of self	Reflect on the opportunities and risks of your research; Identify your values and motivations.	Be attentive to the embodied experience of researching and your needs.	Do not ignore your own needs but seek support; Be proactive in having this this support in place.

Future directions

With the continued technological advances, sociological developments and societal understanding, the world, and therefore educational research, continue to evolve. Where once educational research was relatively clearly defined as the research into learning and teaching matters in schools and universities, educational research nowadays comes in many forms and formats. Depending on the conceptualisation of learning as facilitation or coaching and depending on the researchers' understanding of learning settings as formal or informal, learning and teaching research is now explored in cross-, trans-, and inter-disciplinary settings of medical education and legal scholarship as well as in the conventional school settings. As a result, ethical guidelines will also continue to be subject to revaluations and redefinitions. The preface to the latest edition of the British Educational Research Association's ethical guidelines for educational research begins with a statement that the 'intended audience for these guidelines is anyone undertaking educational research' (p. 7), that the guidelines are 'intended to inform and support researchers as they develop their ethical thinking and practice' (p. 8), but that ultimately, these guidelines 'are likely to require situated judgments' (p. 7). As we have seen throughout the entire edited collection, but specifically in this final chapter, the '*spirit* of the guidelines' (p. 8) is still open for debate, misinterpretation and controversy. Introducing the more generic framework of the Global TRUST Code of research ethics in this final chapter enabled us to demonstrate potential future developments for ethical guidelines within the education sector. Future-proofing good ethical research therefore is not the reiteration of lengthy manuals but capacity-building activities and training sessions. Rather than specifying individual cases or developing responses to 'what if ...' questions, an attitudinal shift within education is required, a shift away from approval, accountability and monitoring to enabling and empowering researchers by trusting that they are inherently ethical in their work, and that they are undertaking educational research for the greater good.

Reflective questions

1 If you were to undertake research following the Global TRUST Code of research ethics and the British Educational Research Association's ethical guidelines for educational research, what do you think would be the challenges in adhering to both?
2 What do you think are your fundamental ethics principles?
3 In your experience, what are the limitations and risks of ethics codes of conducts like the Global TRUST Code of research ethics that may be offering a broad framework rather than detailed specific guidelines?

4 From your perspective, why do you think the British Educational Research Association's ethical guidelines for educational research are outlined as detailed specific guidelines rather than a broad framework?
5 What do you imagine would happen if there were no ethical guidelines or codes of conduct and no ethics approvals systems in place?

Further reading

- The TRUST code is introduced by those who have been involved in developing it through two short videos (2.53 minutes), which allow the voices and identities of the creators to be heard and seen. An introduction to the background of the code can be found at: https://youtu.be/3nRFWNmx1Y4 (2.53 minutes). A presentation of the articles for each dimension can be viewed at: https://youtu.be/zQu7njpSmmk (4.25 minutes)
- The following two-page summary offers a clear presentation of what is involved in enacting the FAIR principles for responsible data management. GoFair (2016). 'FAIR Guiding Principles for scientific data management and stewardship.' https://www.go-fair.org/wp-content/uploads/2022/01/FAIRPrinciples_overview.pdf.
- The Committee of Publication Ethics (COPE)'s discussion document about academic authorship would be worth all researchers reading before becoming involved in publishing, whether as a lead author or a contributor. It covers expectations, resources and guidance on what to do if you want to dispute your rights. https://doi.org/10.24318/cope.2019.3.3.
- The following article recommends tailored training for research in particular contexts, a community of ethical enquiry, and planned debriefing which accounts for the layering of responsibilities revealed from the collective biography it presents. Baker, S., Bellemore, P. & Morgan, S. (2023). Researching in fragile contexts: Exploring and responding to layered responsibility for researcher care. *Women's Studies International Forum*, 98(May–June), article 102700, 1–12. https://doi.org/10.1016/j.wsif.2023.102700.

References

Alleva, L. (2006). Taking time to savour the rewards of slow science. *Nature*, 443(7109), 271. https://doi.org/10.1038/443271e (last accessed 19 October 2024).

Baker, S., Bellemore, P. and Morgan, S. (2023). Researching in fragile contexts: Exploring and responding to layered responsibility for researcher care. *Women's Studies International Forum*, 98(May–June), article 102700, 1–12. https://doi.org/10.1016/j.wsif.2023.102700.

BERA (2024). *Ethical Guidelines for Educational Research* (5th ed.). London: BERA. https://www.bera.ac.uk/publication/ethical-guidelines-for-educational-research-fifth-edition-2024.

Biesta, G. (2013). *The Beautiful Risk of Education*. Boulder, CO: Paradigm Publishing.

Committee On Publication Ethics (COPE) (2015). *Case 15–07: Ethics Committee Approval*. https://publicationethics.org/case/ethics-committee-approval (last accessed 19 October 2024).

COPE (n.d.). *Guidance for Editors: Research Audit and Service Evaluations v2_0*. https://publicationethics.org/sites/default/files/Guidance_for_Editors_Research_Audit_and_Service_Evaluations_v2_0.pdf (last accessed 19 October 2024).

Davis, B. P. and Aldieri, E. (2021). Precarity and resistance: A critique of Martha Fineman's vulnerability theory. *Hypatia*, 36(2), 321–37.

Fricker, M. (2007). *Epistemic Injustice: Power and the Ethics of Knowing*. Oxford: Oxford University Press.

Frith, U. (2019). Fast lane to slow science. *Trends in Cognitive Sciences*, 24(1), 1–2. https://www.cell.com/trends/cognitive-sciences/abstract/S1364-6613(19)30242-6 (last accessed 19 October 2024).

Fox, A., Baker, S., Charitonos, K., Jack, V. and Moser-Mercer, B. (2020). Ethics-in-practice in fragile contexts: Research in education for displaced persons, refugees and asylum seekers. *British Educational Research Journal*, 46(4), 829–47.

Gewirtz, S. and Cribb, A. (2006). What to do about values in social research: The case for ethical reflexivity in the sociology of education. *British Journal of Sociology of Education*, 27(02), 141–55.

GoFair (2016). *FAIR Guiding Principles for scientific data management and stewardship*. https://www.go-fair.org/wp-content/uploads/2022/01/FAIRPrinciples_overview.pdf (last accessed 19 October 2024).

Gray, B., Hilder, J., Macdonald, L., Tester, R., Dowell, A. and Stubbe, M. (2017) Are research ethics guidelines culturally competent? *Research Ethics*, 13(1), 23–41. https://doi.org/10.1177/1747016116650235.

Haelewaters, D., Hofmann, T. A. and Romero-Olivares, A. L. (2021). Ten simple rules for Global North researchers to stop perpetuating helicopter research in the Global South. *PLoS Computational Biology*, 17(8), e1009277. https://doi.org/10.1371/journal.pcbi.1009277.

Klebel, T., Traag, V., Grypari, I., Stoy, L. and Ross-Hellauer, T. (2024). The academic impact of Open Science: A scoping review. *SocArcXiv papers*. https://royalsocietypublishing.org/doi/full/10.1098/rsos.240286.

Meier, G. S., Van der Voet, P. B. and Yan, T. (2024). Research ethics in a multilingual world: A guide to reflecting on language decisions in all disciplines. *Diametros: An Online Journal of Philosophy*, 80, 38–58. http://dx.dio.org/10.33392/diam.1926.

Nelson, G. S. (2015). April. Practical implications of sharing data: A primer on data privacy, anonymization, and de-identification. *SAS Global Forum Proceedings*, pp. 1–23. https://www.lexjansen.com/pharmasug/2016/IB/PharmaSUG-2016-IB06.pdf.

Schroeder, D., Cook, J., Hirsch, F., Fenet, S. and Muthuswamy, V. (2018). *Ethics Dumping: Case Studies from North-South Research Collaborations*. Chamonix: Springer Nature.

Society of Authors (SOA) Policy Team (2024). *The SoA responds to Taylor & Francis Group's sale of data to develop AI*. 22 July. https://societyofauthors.org/2024/07/22/the-soa-responds-to-taylor-francis-groups-sale-of-data-to-develop-ai/ (last accessed 20 October 2024).

Tandon, R. (1988). Social transformation and participatory research. *Convergence*, 21(2), 5.

TRUST (2018). *The TRUST Code – A Global Code of Conduct for Equitable Research Partnerships*. https://doi.org/10.48508/GCC/2018.05.

Index

Page numbers in italics refer to figures and tables; page numbers followed by n denote footnotes.

academia writing 274–5
Academic Integrity and Transparency in AI-assisted Research and Specification (aiTARAS) Framework 203
academic publishing 375–6
academic writing 272
Academy of Social Sciences (AoSS) 7–8
accessibility 54–5
accountability 66
activism 83, 255, 256
adolescent(s) 395, 397–406, 441–2, 444, 445
advisory committee 60
advisory panel 58
agency
    funding agency 342
    human agency 7, 19
    researchers 360, 452
    research participants 144, 149, 158, 206, 403, 404
    teacher agency 193
alertness 18, 82
American Educational Research Association, *Code of Ethics* (2011) 29
anonymisation/pseudonymisation 63, 85, 171, 173, 205, 355, 360, 372 n.22, 399–402, 457
anonymous/anonymity 52, 63, 64, 83, 85, 168, 170–6, 181, 183, 185, 186 n.2, 236 n.3
    breach of anonymity 174
Anscombe, Elizabeth 13

anti-migrant hostility 397
Aotearoa New Zealand 456
aretological dimension, ethics 12
Aristotle
    Nicomachean Ethics 16
    Virtues and Vices 7
Arizpe, Evelyn 121
artefacts 32, 72, 283, 360, 364, 366
artificial intelligence (AI) 30, 38 n.1, 144, 165, 168, 193. *See also* GenAI tools
    alternative approaches 205–8
    balancing risk and potential benefit 196–7
    collecting and managing evidence 197
    consent 198
    effectiveness of 193
    epistemic tensions 195–201
    evidence types 193–4
    participatory approaches 206
    personalised learning 195
    positionality 198–201
    research integrity 196
    research plan 201–5
    sensitive data 197
    stakeholder perspectives 198
assessment 50, 56, 167, 191, 193, 315, 316, 412
    in education 192, 224, 231, 301, 309
    of research 201, 202, 209, 213 n.4, 348
    risk 61, 66, 136 n.29, 238 n.10, 359, 393 n.7
assent 116, 133 n.2, 399

Association of Internet Researchers
  Internet Research: Ethical Guidelines (Version 2.0) 30
  Internet Research: Ethical Guidelines (Version 3.0) 144
attribution 38 n.2
audience 113, 117
audience-friendly format 90 n.6
Australian Broadcasting Corporation (ABC) 333
authoring/authored/authorship 7, 13, 17, 187 n.10, 258, 262, 277, 286, 308, 309, 316, 320 n.6, 347, 455, 464
autoethnography/autoethnographic 72, 199, 370 n.8, 383
autonomy 34, 168, 181, 183, 316, 359, 363, 365, 401, 413, 418, 430, 443
awareness claims 78

Baby, Grace Anna 270
Baker, Sally 270, 326–7, 329, 400
Barclay, K. 328
Baumfield, Vivienne 243
beneficence 168, 414, 418
benefits 35, 82, 157, 179, 197, 316, 352
benevolence 8
Berman, R. C. 97
bias 12, 83, 165, 166, 196, 197, 199, 200, 201, 206, 208, 224, 228–34, 310, 315, 378, 440, 452, 458
Bickmore, K. 221
Bielska, B. 145, 148
bioethics 427
Bird, D. 117
British Educational Research Association (BERA) 1, 3, 6, 85, 89 n.1, 90 n.5, 234, 323–4, 399, 463
  applicability of 45
  attribution 38 n.2
  contradictions with local practices 425, 428, 430
  digital/online research 38 n.1
  Ethical Guidelines for Educational Research (2011)(3rd edition) 398–401, 404
  Ethical Guidelines for Educational Research (2018)(4th edition) 401, 445–6, 447 n.1
  Ethical Guidelines for Educational Research (2024)(5th edition) 42, 97, 99, 106, 108, 144, 156, 168–9, 185, 186–7 n.3–14, 186 n.1, 243–7, 251, 270, 289–90 n.1–8, 320–1 n.1–12, 369–70 n.1–10, 400–2, 404, 418–19, 439, 444
British Petroleum (BP) 250
British Psychological Society, *Code of Human Research Ethics* (2021) 32, 35
Buddhist traditions 8
budget cuts 59–60
Burke, R. 327

calibration 231
Cambridge Teacher Research Exchange (Camtree) 350–8
  online open-access digital library 355–6
  quality criteria 355
Capewell, Carmel 42, 43, 114, 130
care 15, 42, 457–9. *See also* duty of care
  collaborative scholarly writing 272
  for self 323–4 (*see also* self-care)
Carpenter, David 7–8
Caton, Lucy 270
Centre for Climate Change and Social Transformations (CAST) 252
Chartered College of Teaching 409–10, 418
  Chartered College of Teaching Research Ethics Panel 395, 409–18
ChatGPT 193, 202
check-box approach 273
Child Protection and Safeguarding training 440
children, ethical decision-making
  active participation, children 117
  adult-child power differentials 115–18, 133 n.1
  child's cognitive skills 118

Index

migrant children, primary schools 119–25
  picturebooks and photography 120, 131, 304, 333
  power-related issue 128, 129
  race and discrimination 122–4
  rapport-building stage 116
  rights 113–31, 397–406
  school gatekeepers 125–30
  silence, children 121–3, 131
  taking time, knowing the children 118–19
  working with Children and Young People 114, 248, 395, 397–406, 441, 442, 444, 445
Chong, Sin Wang 270, 348, 377–9
Christians, C. G. 95, 96
Classroom Assessment Scoring System (CLASS) 222
classroom observation 221–3
  ethics 223
  observer judgements 222
  privacy and confidentiality 223
  teacher behaviours 221, 222
classroom(s) 34, 121, 151, 153, 166, 169, 193, 204, 209, 221–34, 364, 410
climate
  activism 256
  anxiety 248, 257–9, 261
  change 14, 214 n.12, 243, 247–8, 250–2, 262, 264 n.3
  education 257–62
  socio-political 62
collaborative approach 78
collaborative review 378
college(s) 42, 71–3, 76, 77, 82–4, 86, 409–19
colonisation 75
communal caring space 329, 338
communication 32, 55, 56, 60–2, 66, 67, 98, 100, 105, 108, 114, 130, 149, 155, 166, 183, 205, 211, 226–8, 277, 279, 280, 284, 303, 325, 329, 360, 364, 365, 410

community groups
  culture 64
  dissemination 358–66
  diverse 47
  inclusion 351
community of educational researchers 123, 135 n.26, 142 n.48, 253–4, 320 n.2
Concordat for Environmental Sustainability in Research and Innovation (2024) 14–15
Conference of Parties (COP) 14
confidentiality 30, 64, 85, 89 n.2, 114, 126, 130, 165, 168, 170–6, 183, 185, 197, 202, 206, 214 n.14, 223, 225, 236 n.1, 237 n.9, 262, 355, 369 n.3, 372 n.28, 401, 428, 440, 444
confirmation bias 233
conflict 53, 54, 278–9
Conflict Impact Assessment (CIA) tool 61
conflict-specific training 50
Confucius traditions 8
Connor-Bones, Una 42
consent 64, 121, 127, 133 n.2, 135 n.24, 136 n.30, 177, 183, 187 n.9, 198, 371 n.15, 372 n.29, 399, 440
contextual barriers 62–3
contextual familiarity 50
contingency plans 66
Contributor Role Taxonomy (CRediT) 308, 316, 455
Cooke, Carolyn 270
courage 9, 17, 210
Courtney, Matthew 166
Covid-19 pandemic 58, 59, 65, 324–31
Creative Commons (CC) 38 n.2
creativity 230, 232, 281–4
critical friend 81
critical reflexivity 76–7
Culley, L. 117
cultural broker 81, 325, 342 n.2
cultural code-switching 80
cultural sensitivities 454

cultural sensitivity 54, 455
curriculum 13, 34, 47, 73, 193, 253

data analysis 56, 63, 78, 134 n.4, 148, 174, 187 n.12, 197, 200, 201, 203, 209, 300, 306, 320 n.6, 371 n.15. *See also* interpretation
  thematic analysis 300, 359
data collection 51, 53, 56, 108, 205, 333, 455
data protection 176, 177, 187 n.11, 223, 356, 413, 428, 429
Data Protection Act, UK (2018) 413
data security 63
data storage 63
Day, N. A. 250
The Day War Came 123
debriefing 327–30
decolonalisation/decolonisation 387–9, 453
decolonising research ethics 42, 87–8
  critical reflexivity 76–7
  definition and principles 71–2, 74–5
  other(ed) ways of knowing 80–2
  positionality, author 73–4
  reciprocity 77–80
  self-determination 77–80
  transformative praxis 82–7
Dennis, Azumah 42
deontological dimension, duty 12
design 42, 49, 50, 56, 97, 204
  educational/course design 138 n.38, 195
  ethics 147, 148
  research design 51, 60, 66, 102, 133 n.3, 136 n.32, 138 n.38, 148, 150–4, 158, 159, 196, 216 n.19, 236 n.5, 251, 333, 350, 359, 397, 400, 403, 404, 425, 455, 460
  tool design 202, 208
diary/ies 114, 116–18, 404
digital ethnography 328
digital/online research 27, 30, 38 n.1

digital platforms 277–81
disclosure 84–5, 87
disembodiment 279
dishonesty 17, 427, 459
disrespect/disrespectful 8, 17, 101, 454, 455, 454
disruptive behaviour 225–4
dissemination 3, 6, 13, 27, 78, 103, 347–50, 356, 358–6
dissent 362, 399
distance learning 410
distress 32, 61, 133 n.3, 145, 148, 150, 151, 154–5, 158, 225, 226, 236 n.5, 258
DiverseEd 417
Dockett, S. 399, 400
doctoral candidates/researchers/students 30, 48, 49, 71, 128, 177, 270, 272, 298, 307–9, 316, 323–40, 381, 382, 384, 385, 426, 442
  research in, fragile contexts 324
  transition from novice to expert 332–4
doctoral supervisors 181, 270
double-blind review 378–9
Dowdeswell, Emily 270
draw-and-write technique 125, 128, 129, 131
Dunlop, Lynda 166
duty of care 133 n.3, 149, 236 n.5, 330, 419, 457–9

early career researchers (ECRs) 375–6
  access and capacity issues 381–2
  maximising participation 382
  peer review 380–1
  platform development 383–91
  workshopping 388–9
Eaton, S. E. 96, 250
'eco-anxiety' 248
ecology/ecological 34, 46, 243, 248, 256, 285, 377, 451–62
  humans with the non-human 452

educational research ethics 23
  digital/online research 27, 30
  ethics of publication 27, 30–1
  human rights 23, 27, 31, 32, 39 n.3, 56, 60, 125, 193, 205, 209, 216 n.22, 333
  inclusivity for neurodiversity 27–8, 31–2
  independent research 23, 28–9, 33–4, 135 n.26, 136 n.29, 146, 238 n.10, 357, 393, 456
  intercultural research 23, 28, 33, 42, 45–67, 95
  international research 2, 28, 33, 42, 46, 63, 95–109
  inter-university collaborative research 28, 32–3
  practitioner research 28–9, 33–4
  sensitive issues 23, 29, 34–5, 123, 125, 126, 136 n.29, 180, 206, 393 n.7, 458
  sustainability 29, 35–6
  vulnerable groups 29, 34–5
Education and Training Foundation 72
Ellefson, Michelle 165
empathy 329–30
English as a Foreign Language (EFL) 101, 102
English for Academic Purposes (EAP) 101
English language 97–100, 103–8. *See also* language
environmental justice 243
environmental sustainability 243
  climate change education 257–62
  community of educational researchers responsibilities 253–4
  educational researchers, responsibilities to 255–7
  education, vision for 244
  environmentally conscious research 260
  environment responsibilities 251–3
  international collaborations and conferences 255
  negative emotions 248
  participants responsibilities 247–9
  participatory workshops 258
  potential co-benefits 260–2
  researchers, responsibilities *245*, 245–7, 264 n.2
  stakeholders responsibilities 249–51
epistemic 75, 77, 81
  epistemicide/epistemic violence 13, 19, 20, 88, 254
  freedom 19
  injustice 452
  justice 197
  tensions 195–201
epistemology/ies/ical 75, 76, 81, 82, 85, 99, 194–7, 199, 200, 201, 204, 205, 207, 254, 460
  onto-axio-epistemology 76, 85
Equality Act (2010) 135 n.20, 171, 176, 177, 277, 415–6, 419
ethical approval 49
ethical code 90 n.5
ethical decision-making 85–7
ethical dilemmas 2, 3, 43, 45, 79, 108, 114, 156, 158, 168, 169, 184, 185, 284, 285, 313, 324, 411, 418, 430, 438, 453
  AI in education 194–5
  autonomous administration 49–52
  climate anxiety 258–9
  co-working and supervisory experience 312–14
  educational policies 49–52
  evidence synthesis 300–3
  exploitative risk 79
  journal peer review 378–9
  large-scale data 169
  maternal health 58–64
  migrant children, primary schools 120–1
  multilingual contexts 100–3

multilingual research teams 105–7
non-verbal cues, dissent 364–6
observational research 225–6, 233
observer bias 229–30, 233–4
online interviews 146–9
practitioner research 352–3
research ethics panel 410–11
school gatekeepers 126–7
sensitive data, anonymity 177–9, 182
sharing participant data openly 171–3
uncomfortable disclosure 84–5
young-researchers 361–2
ethical guidelines 5, 14, *24–6*, 27–9, 32, 45, 65, 144, 210, 277, 397, 457–9. *See also individual entries*
ethical relation-building/relationships 82
ethical review 3, 34, 54, 127, 158, 209, 262, 352, 366, 456, 457
ethical tensions 270
ethical thinking 2, 6
ethical traditions 5
ethic of care 145–6. *See also* duty of care
ethic of respect 181, 185, 411. *See also* respect
ethics commissions 427
ethics committee 426. *See also* ethics review board; ethics review panel; institutional review board
ethics dumping 33
ethics of language. *See also* language
multilingual contexts 99–103
multilingual research teams 103–7
ethics of publication 27, 30–1
ethics review board 33, 127, 146, 171, 456. *See also* institutional review board
ethics review committee(s) 33, 34, 46, 78, 96, 98, 99, 100, 116, 146, 150, 153, 155, 158, 159, 201, 202, 207, 330, 339, 352, 356, 359, 363, 366, 412, 413, 425, 426, 427, 429, 454, 456. *See also* ethics committee; ethics review panel; institutional review board

ethics review panel 3, 410–19. *See also Chartered College of Teaching Research Ethics Panel*
ethnic federalism 56
Ethnic Health Organisations (EHOs) 60, 63
ethnography/ic 73, 78, 89 n.3, 206, 328, 415
fieldwork, during Covid-19 324–31
Eudaemian ethics 7
The European Commission Directorate-General for Research and Innovation 80
European 49, 71, 74, 80, 82
Early Career Researchers 455
European Union (EU) 398
evidence-based practices 34
evidence-informed practice 409
evidence synthesis 297
advice and feedback 301
anticipatory approach 313
appraising the quality 298
contributor taxonomy 316
co-working and supervisory experience 311–17
data-extraction phase 315
fairness, assessment 309
power imbalance 301–2, 309, 310
project log 315–16
question-answer format based document 307–8
reflexivity 306–8, 310–11, 317
reliability 298, 310, 317
researcher logbook 303–5, *306, 307*
research questions and search strategy 314
and supervision 298–300, 317
supervisor-supervisee/student-student partnership 307
expectation bias 234

face-to-face meeting 104
fairness 15, 45, 309, 452–4
Farrow, Robert 166

feedback 106, 383
fee waivers 390-1
Fensham-Smith, Amber 348
Flanders Interaction Analysis Categories (FIAC) 222
Flynn, A. 256
focus groups 48, 51, 57, 72, 78, 100, 101, 418, 440. *See also* interviews
Foot, Philippa 13
Foreign, Commonwealth & Development Office (FCDO) 61
fragility/fragile contexts, research in 323
  altering research methods 328-9
  community of educational researchers, responsibility 338
  conference presentation 332-5
  doctoral students 324
  emotional and mental challenges 325-7, 330
  empathy 329-30
  ethnographic fieldwork, during Covid-19 324-31
  imposter syndrome 331-2
  researchers' wellbeing 339
  supervisor reflections 330-1
  supervisor, reflections of 336-7
  support systems 329-30
The Framework for Responsible Research, UKRI 246
Fricker, M. 13

Garcia, S. G. 328
Gardner, C. J. 256
gatekeeper(s) 18, 46, 51, 53, 97, 114, 125-31, 136 n.30, 138 n.41, 225, 325, 399, 404, 452, 455, 458
GenAI tools 192
General Certificate in Secondary Education (GCSE) 398
General Data Protection Regulation (2018) 176-8
geography/ies/graphically 24-6, 86, 144, 145, 169, 172, 174, 175, 252-4, 259, 388, 445

geopolitical
  context 51
  fragmentation 47
global code of conduct 15
globalisation 15, 45
Global North 3, 29, 75, 253, 451-2. *See also* Aotearoa New Zealand; UK
global research, ethical guidance 451-2
Global South 36, 75, 125, 253. *See also* Myanmar; Pakistan; South Africa; Syria; Thailand
Global Sustainable Goals (2030) 14
Global TRUST Code 452-4, 456, 459, 463
global virtues 14-15
Glocalism 15
Gonzalez, M. C. 85
Govaerts, Fadoua 348
Gray, B. 456
greenhouse gas emissions/emitters 166, 259, 261
group interviews 442-3; *See also* interviews
guardian 32, 126, 137 n.34, 138 n.38, 138 n.41, 150, 223, 229, 238 n.9, 371 n.16, 372 n.28, 399, 458
Guenther, K. M. 401

Hanna, Helen 42, 114
harm 5, 33-5, 41, 56, 247-8, 453
Hasson, Felicity 42
Hawkins, Carly 270
Hickmann 248
higher education 1, 192, 193, 195, 199, 200, 271-3, 277, 287, 312, 377, 383, 423, 432
Higher Education institution (HEI) 49, 58, 166, 171, 191, 196-8, 289 n.7, 354, 393 n.2, 394 n.8, 396, 456
Higher Education Research and Development Society of Australasia (HERDSA) 383
Hindu traditions 8
Holmes, P. 95, 97-8, 437, 438, 442, 444
Holmes, Wayne 166

honesty 15, 45, 66, 459–60. *See also* dishonesty
humanist commitment 45
human rights 27, 31
humility 10, 17, 131
hurriedness 274–5
Hursthouse, Rosalind 13
hydrofeminist scholarship 285

identity politics 125
   author 378, 379
   cultural 69, 89 n.1, 215 n.18
   peer reviewer 378
   researcher 122, 131, 336
   research participants 86, 398, 441
Ilie, Sonia 165
imposter syndrome 324, 331–2
inclusion 3, 13, 101, 105, 107, 415–18
inclusivity for neurodiversity 27–8, 31–2
independent research 28–9, 33–4
indigenous groups 67, 74
individualism 12
inequality 13, 67, 86, 206, 271, 310, 458
influence 113–14, 117
informed consent 96, 107, 236 n.2. *See also* consent
in-session seminars 101
insider/outsider status 46, 54, 84, 86
institutional conflict of interest 33
institutional responsibility 389–90
institutional review board 48, 456. *See also* ethics committee; ethics review board
integrity 34, 65, 67, 90 n.5, 118, 134 n.4, 136 n.28, 137 n.37, 139 n.44, 193, 195–7, 200, 208, 209, 210, 230, 231, 238 n.15, 239 n.16, 253, 335, 336, 362, 366, 414, 427, 429, 432, 452
inter-coder reliability 299, 304
Intergovernmental Panel on Climate Change (IPCC) 256, 258, 266
internal accountability 223

international advisory panel 58
international and/or intercultural research 28, 33, 42, 45–6, 67
   accessibility 54–5
   budget cuts 59–60
   communication 62
   confidentiality 64
   conflict 54
   Conflict Impact Assessment (CIA) tool 61
   consent 64
   contextual barriers 62–3
   contextual challenges 52–3
   Covid-19 pandemic 58, 65
   cultural sensitivity 54
   data security 63
   location, politics of 73–4
   methodological challenges 53
   permissions processes 64
   political shifts 60–1
   positionality, researcher 46
   project partners 62
   social media restriction 61–2
interpretation 123, 174, 199, 200, 201, 207, 231, 306, 320 n.6, 356, 387, 444, 451. *See also* data analysis
interpreters 97, 396, 437–46, 454, 460
   autonomy 443
   bridging the language gap 438–41, 444
   limitations 445
   secondary school students 441–5
   willingness 443
interview 50, 52, 72, 76, 100, 102, 108, 114, 126–9, 182, 200, 201, 204, 208, 224, 225, 229, 230, 232, 260, 328, 331, 333, 359, 398
   focus groups 48, 51, 57, 72, 78, 100, 101, 418, 440
   group interviews 442–3
   interviewees 51, 52, 145, 328, 418, 431
   interviewers 97, 145
   online 30, 43, 51, 143–60, 328

inter-university collaborative research
  28, 32–3
Irgil, E. 326
IRIS-Connect 223

Jowett, A. 152
justice 168, 414–15, 418

Kalinowska, K. 145, 148
Kara, Helen 121
Kinsella, E. A. 75
Kitchener, K. S. 6
Kitchener, R. F. 6
knowledge
  local 51
  production 74 (*see also* epistemic)
  as property 79
Kohn, T. 412
K 12 educational settings 192
Kurdish autonomous administration
  46–9
Kushnir, Iryna 424

Lahman, M. K. 401
Lakhanpaul, M. 117
language. *See also* ethics of language
  medium of communication 108
  role of 95–7
large-scale quantitative data 165–7. *See also* quantitative
  addressing issues 173–4, 179–81
  administrative data 176–7, 184
  alternative methods, sharing 175
  education research 168, 170, 184
  ethical issues 171–3, 178–9
  participatory approaches 182
  safe data access protocols 179–80
  sensitive data, anonymity 176–82
  sharing data publicly 168, 170–6
learning management system (LMS), AI-enabled 166, 191
  alternative approaches 205–8
  balancing risk and potential benefit
    196–7
  collecting and managing evidence
    197
  consent 198
  effectiveness of 193
  epistemic tensions 195–201
  evidence types 193–4
  participatory approaches 206
  personalised learning 195
  positionality 198–201
  research integrity 196
  research plan 201–5
  sensitive data 197
  stakeholder perspectives 198
linguistic hegemonies 13–14
literature review 104, 208, 297, 314, 320
  n.6
  systematic review(s) 270, 298,
    311–14, 316, 317
Liu, Qi 270
local communities 14, 56, 63, 64, 67, 196,
  453, 460
low- and middle-income countries
  (LMICs) scholars 390
Lowe, R. 115
literacy 32, 96, 176, 178
  feedback 383–4, 389–90
  low literacy levels 64
'Lundy model' 113–14, 116, 130

Macfarlane, Bruce 8, 16
  Virtues and Vices of Research 17
MacLeod, J. 78
Madison, D. S. 87
Manifesto for Education for Environmental Sustainability
  243–4
Martinez-Gómez, A. 439
maternal health 55–8
maternal mortality 55
Mazzei, L. A. 122
McGranahan, C. 79
mean path, negotiating 16–17
Measures of Effective Teaching project
  221

Meier, G. 98, 107
methods 117, 118, 125, 143, 152, 153, 166, 195, 199, 205, 225, 228, 229, 231, 232, 416, 458
  diaries 114, 116–18, 404
  interviews/focus groups 48, 51, 57, 72, 78, 100, 101, 418, 440
  observation 221–3, 225–6, 229, 233
  surveys/questionnaire 90 n.4, 104, 108, 148, 167, 169–70, 200, 215 n.18, 221, 237 n.7, 415, 417, 419, 423, 425, 428, 432, 439, 441
methodology 43, 77–8, 81, 85–7, 124, 201, 204, 206, 222, 297, 300, 303, 318, 404, 442, 459. *See also* Mixed Methods research
  of friendship 85–7
migrant children, primary schools 119–25
migrant pupils 439
mind/body separation 83
'mission-driven exercise' 454
mitigation of risk 61, 138 n.38, 207. *See also* risk
Mixed Methods research 199, 200, 205, 207, 315, 438
monolingual language ideology 437–8
Montreal Statement on Research Integrity in Cross-Boundary Research Collaborations (2020) 28, 29, 32
Muijs, Daniel 166
multicultural/multiculturalism 3
  children's literature 121
multilingualism/multilingual education 3, 14, 47, 49, 396, 455, 456
  autonomy 443
  education 437–46
  limitations, non-professional interpreter 445
  non-professional interpreters, bridging the language gap 438–41, 444
  research 95–107, 437–8

secondary school students, non-professional peer interpreters 441–5
  willingness 443
multimodality 282, 283
Myanmar 55–64
My Two Blankets 123

National Agency for HE Quality Assurance 429
National Institute for Health and Care Research (NIHR) 311
neurodiversity 28
Neves, J. 390
Non-governmental Organisation (NGO) 50, 258, 260, 261
non-humans 214 n.12, 251, 264 n.3, 455
non-maleficence 169, 414
non-reciprocal relations 79
Nygaard, L. P. 272

observational research 221
  accountability 224–8
  additional observer training 231, 234
  children's behaviour 226–7
  feedback, improve children's writing 224–5
  observer bias 228–32
  reassigning 231–2
  triangulation 232
observer bias 229–30, 233–4
Office for Standards in Education, Children's Services and Skills (OfSTED) 72, 76–7, 80, 84, 86
'one-size-fits-all' approach 56
online conferencing tools 144
online interviews 143–4, 328
  data collection methods 145
  data security 145
  ethical preparation 147–8
  face-to-face *vs.* online interviews 152–5, 159
  follow-up communications 149–51

making changes to projects 158
mutual trust 145
participant wellbeing 148–9, 154–5, 157–8
positive aspects 144
research ethics mentors 157
support structures 156–7, 159–60
online research/internet-based research 27
online survey platform 170, 172, 173
ontology/gical/gically 5, 99, 460
  onto-axio-epistemology 76, 85
open access publishing 82–3
open meetings 78
Open Researcher and Contributor ID (ORCID) 376
open science principles 172, 174, 181, 183

Pakistan 257–61
paradigm(s) 45, 99, 143, 197, 311
Paraskeva, J. M. 254
Parker, C. 221
participants
  access to 51–2
  anonymity 397, 399–402
  consent 399
  multilingual contexts 99–103
  responsibilities 41–3, 247–9
  safety 52
  shared data 170–6
  withdrawal 117, 140 n.40
partners 15, 32, 33, 56, 58–60, 62, 63, 65, 104, 108, 193, 202, 260, 261, 273, 276, 285, 286, 452, 456, 457
  project partners 58, 62
partnership(s) 28, 56, 58, 60–3, 65, 66, 80, 135 n.20, 307, 366, 367, 380, 387, 415, 438, 451
Peace Circles 221
  pedagogy(ies)/ pedagogic/ pedagogical 47, 73, 76, 103, 193, 195, 253, 351, 353
peer interpreting 441–4

peer review 31, 314, 347, 352, 375–7
  ECRs 380–2
  maintaining the blindness 378–9
  open-minded and inclusive approach 387–9
  open peer review 382
  platform development, supporting ECR 383–91
  suitable peer reviewers 379–80
  sustainability 376
  transparency 388
permissions 64, 73, 86, 90 n.5, 126, 137 n.37, 278, 352, 399
personalised learning 195
philosophy 12–13
PICO (Population, Intervention, Comparison and Outcome) 313
Pihlainen, Kaisa 42
Pinter, A. 403–4
plagiarism 424, 427, 430, 431
Plato, The '*Republic*' 7
Plows, V. 400
pluralism 45
Polish-born adolescents, UK 397, 398
  anonymisation/pseudonymisation 399–402
  children as agency 403–4
  participant consent 399
  positioning in research projects 403
politics/political 13, 42, 46, 48, 51–5, 63–6, 86, 89 n.2, 137 n.37, 215 n.18, 250, 259, 455
  dissemination 347
  identity 125
  instability 47
  of location 73–4
  shifts 60–1
Polo-Pérez, N. 442
Pongpajon, Chawin 42, 114
positionality 73–4
postdoctoral researcher 298
Posthumanist Collective 272, 273, 275–7, 283
post-publication review 378

Index

power
  differentials 233
  imbalances 452
  relationships 89 n.2, 235–6 n.1
practitioner 28–9, 33–4
praxis 42, 75, 82–7
procedural ethics 98
professional research ethics 98
programme 34, 56–8, 135 n.26, 167, 200, 298–302, 308, 311, 312, 314, 320 n.2, 363, 377, 381, 382
protection
  child protection 440, 444 (*see also* safeguarding)
  data protection 176, 177, 187 n.11, 223, 356, 413, 428, 429
  environment protection 29
  legal protection 96, 178, 182
  for participants 323, 328, 398, 405
  password protection 214
  for researchers 133 n.3, 237 n.5, 272
  of rights 31, 207, 209, 399
publication 3, 6, 27, 30–1, 83, 84, 103, 106, 108, 170, 171, 181, 260, 275, 307, 433. *See also* ethics of publication
publishing
  alternative approach 356–8
  collaborative peer process 354, 366
  development group 354
  digital footprint 360
  power dynamics 267
  publish or perish culture 274, 348–50, 375
  publishing practitioner research 350–8, 369–70 n.6
  training workshops 359
  young-researchers 358–66
Publons work 380
Puntil, Donata 270
Pustovit, S. V. 427

qualitative
  data 198, 200–1, 206, 208, 300, 333, 426
  evidence 197
  interviews 47, 182, 359
  observation 221, 222
  research 155, 221, 260, 300, 416
quality 8, 42, 78, 80, 86, 192, 317, 347, 351–7, 366, 376–7, 388
  data 52–3, 118
  in Further Education college 71–2
  moral 210
  publications 348
  research 169, 411, 427
  supervised evidence syntheses 297–318
  teaching and learning 226, 409
quantitative
  data 99, 100, 165, 166, 171, 200, 201, 206 (*see also* large-scale quantitative data)
  evidence 197
  observation 222
  research 100, 169, 300, 416, 425, 426
questionnaires 104, 108, 169, 221, 417, 419, 439, 441. *See also* survey
Quickfall, Aimee 42, 43

Raffoul, A. W. 247
Rahman, Abdul 328
Rajab, T. 97–8
Ratnam, C. 326–7, 329
Ravitch, S. 199
reciprocity 9, 20, 42, 75, 77–80, 262, 283, 285, 325
reflexivity 199–200, 298, 299, 306–8, 310–11, 330–1, 461, *462*
refugee community 325
regional stakeholders 60
re-identification 178, 180

reliability 192, 201, 208, 222, 234, 298–9, 301, 304, 309, 310, 313, 315, 317, 445
reliance 439
reproducible 173, 175, 297. *See also* quality, research; reliability
research
　ethics 98
　integrity 196
　multilingually 437
　partnerships 66–7
Research Accreditation process 178
researchers 1–2, 5, 237 n.6–8, 238–9 n.13–18
　care 323–6
　confidential data and information 30
　dual roles 228
　positionality 46
　reflective research 89 n.2
　resilience-building 389–90
　responsibilities 90 n.6, *245*, 245–7, 270
　rights and interests 90 n.4
　safety 50, 61–2, 66
　self-care 226
　share knowledge 256–7
　situational and positional status 65–6
　time and effort 89–90 n.3
　wellbeing 336, 339, 393 n.7
research ethics panel 410. *See also* ethics committee
　applications submitted 412–13
　autonomy 413
　beneficence 414
　establishment 410–12
　inclusion 415–17
　informing participants, research outcomes 418
　justice 414–15
　non-maleficence 414
　validity 412, 418
　workload 415
respect 15, 31, 42, 64, 66, 67, 74, 77–80, 454–7. *See also* ethic of respect

responsibilities 2–3, 12, 23, 30–3, 41–3, 48, 59, 90 n.6, *245*, 245–57, 264 n.2, 270, 338
review committees 33
Riggan, M. 199
rigour 53, 200, 232, 300, 301, 309, 313, 314, 317, 333, 336, 351–4, 366, 381, 412, 418. *See also* quality, research
Rimmer, A. 439
risk 30, 34, 46, 51, 52, 59, 61, 63, 66, 79, 82, 87, 96, 129, 136 n.29, 144–5, 159, 178, 179, 182, 184, 192, 196–8, 200, 203–9, 227, 248, 250, 252, 261, 262, 282, 315, 323, 327, 329, 360, 361, 365, 414, 457
Rizvi, U. Z. 79
rules-based approach 103
rules of engagement 337
Rushton, Elizabeth 166

safeguarding 31, 34, 85, 136 n.29, 147, 150, 156, 160, 227, 233, 238 n.10, 271, 286, 289 n.5, 350, 360, 393 n.7, 430, 440, 444
safety 46, 48, 50–3, 61–2, 64, 66, 136 n.29, 156, 192, 203, 238 n.10, 272, 286, 393 n.7, 428, 457
Sandoval, C. 78
Scholarly Peers 378, 383–5
scholarly writing 272
school 34, 47, 120, 124–9, 147, 150, 172, 223, 225–8, 248, 253, 260, 299, 353, 398, 410, 415, 441, 463
　gatekeepers 125–30
　primary school 114, 119, 120, 131, 224, 250, 438
　secondary school 114, 131, 228, 250, 257–8, 398, 399, 441–4
Schroeder, Doris 15
Scottish Educational Research Association, *Ethical Guidelines for Educational Research* (2005) 28, 31

security
  assessment/measures 51
  concerns/risks 48, 51–3, 55, 144
  cybersecurity 55
  data/information security 63, 145, 187 n.11, 360
  environment 49
  of participants 64
self-care 150, 270, 323–4, 339
self-determination 77–80
self-reflection 128
self-reflexivity 46
semi-structured interviews 125–6, 423–5
sensitivity 45, 51, 52, 62, 69 n.2, 78, 90 n.5, 135 n.20, 137 n.37, 178, 183, 187, 324, 338, 363, 457
  cultural 54, 455
  political 63
sensitive issues 29, 34–5
Shaun Tan, *The Arrival* 120
Shore, C. 412
silence 121–3, 131
single-blind review 378
situational complexity 96
situational familiarity 50
Slote, M. 8
Smith, H. J. 96–7
social isolation 326
social justice 87, 184, 318, 319, 350, 351, 453
social media 54–5
sociology/ogies/gical 462
South Africa 114, 119, 120, 122–4, 130
space 113, 116, 121, 126, 127, 129, 130
sponsorship 250
Springgay, S. 283, 285
Spyrou, S. 122
stakeholders 2, 7, 15, 18, 31, 48, *48*, 57, 60, 64, 165–6, 184, 195, 198, 205, 216 n.19, 249–51, 264 n.4, 366, 428, 458
  regional stakeholders 60, 64
STEMinus 191–4, 202, 204, 206–7, 209

Stephenson, R. 390
storage of data 30, 63, 144, 186 n.2, 187 n.11, 247, 413
structural inequalities 444
structured observation approach 229
student behaviours 230–1
student-centred teaching method 228–9, 231, 232
supervision 56
supervisor 330–1
supervisor-supervisee/student-student partnership 307
support systems 329–30
Surmiak, A. 145, 148
survey 90 n.4, 148, 167, 169–70, 200, 215 n.18, 221, 237 n.7, 415, 417, 423, 425, 428, 432
sustainability 29, 35–6. *See also* environmental sustainability
Syria 46–9
Systematic Review 298, 311–17
Szulc, J. M. 145

Tannock, Stuart 250
teacher behaviours 221, 222, 233
teacher-led approach 229
Teacher Tapp 80
Teaching English to Speakers of Other Languages (TESOL) programme 298, 299, 302
technology lag 144
Tegama, Natalie 270, 348
teleological dimension 12
Thailand 114, 125–9
Thambinathan, V. 75
thingification 81
Think-Listen-Act framework 462
Thornton, Eleanor 192–3
traditional examination processes 192
transformative praxis 82–4
  friendship 85–7
  uncomfortable disclosure 84–5
translanguaging theory 442–3

translation 13–14, 96–8, 106, 107, 424, 431, 439–41
translators 97, 108, 424, 454, 455
transparency/transparent 62, 168, 169, 170, 173, 175, 187 n.7, 192, 200, 201, 203, 208, 210, 211, 212, 231, 247, 313, 314, 353, 354, 360, 375, 388, 459, 460
Tri-Council Policy Statement: Ethical Conduct for Research Involving Humans (2018) 33
TRUST code 15, 17, 18. *See also* global code of conduct
truthfulness 8, 9–11, 85. *See also* honesty
Twiner, Alison 348
Tyyska, V. 97

UK 90 n.5, 168, 176, 187 n.9, 255, 297, 310, 456
  England 71, 104, 258, 259, 409
  Northern Ireland 298, 438, 439
  Scotland 25, 26, 27, 28
  Wales 406 n.1
Ukrainian Educational Research Association (UERA) 424–6
Ukrainian higher education (HE) community 432
  awareness-raising work 431–2
  BERA research ethical guidelines 424
  culture of respect, research participants 428–31
  establishment, challenges 425–7
  ethical research, education 423–4
  path-dependency mindset 430, 432
underrepresented groups 417
United Kingdom Research and Innovation (UKRI) Global Challenges Research Fund 58
United Nations (UN) 14, 50
  Convention on the Rights of the Child (UNCRC) 31, 113, 130, 133 n.2, 134 n.10, 137 n.34, 359, 371 n.12, 398, 400, 403
  Department of Safety and Security (UNDSS) 50
UNICEF 359
Universal Declaration of Human Rights 31
Universal Declaration on Bioethics and Human Rights 31
university 27, 32–4, 49, 56, 63, 72, 73, 78, 96, 101, 103, 126, 135 n.26, 146, 147, 153, 158, 271, 272, 275, 298, 313, 380, 381, 430, 463. *See also* Higher Education institution (HEI)
university-based research 352, 366

Vackova, Petra 270
values 452
van der Voet, P. 98
verbal communication 108, 226, 227. *See also* communication
Verlie, B. 256
virtues/virtuous 452
  behaviours 7–8, 16
  cultural traditions *9–11*
  ethics 5, 8, 210
  human agency, role of 7
voice 13, 31, 36, 55, 72, 75–9, 95, 108, 113, 116–17, 119–21, 130, 195, 254, 270, 281, 287, 302, 357, 360, 363, 416, 437, 442, 445, 452
vulnerable 74, 76, 116, 124, 133 n.3, 135 n.20, 160, 223, 236 n.5, 237 n.7, 259, 260, 274, 284, 302, 309, 330, 333, 400, 404, 455
  groups 23, 29, 34–5
  vulnerability 34–5, 146, 258, 323, 324, 331, 364

wellbeing 323–5
  arts-based research approaches 284
  becoming-wit(h)ness, concept of 285
  collaborative writing 276–7, 286, 287
  creative writing 281–4, 287
  and development 3

digital/online writing 277–81
institutionalised ethical guidelines 272–3
isolation 275
national guidance 271–2
participant 148–9
professional counselling 327
research 103
of researcher(s) 136 n.29, 238 n.10, 326, 327, 336, 339, 393 n.7, 428
sharing of responsibility 276
writing as experiment 283–4
writing as material 280–1
writing as production 274–7
Williams, Gareth 424
willingness 443
Wood, Phil 42, 43
workload 415, 418
workplace support 34

Xavier, Anna 270

Yau, T. 98
Young People's Advisory Group (YPAG) 114, 117, 118, 130